# PROFESSIONAL COUNSELING EXCELLENCE THROUGH LEADERSHIP AND ADVOCACY

# PROFESSIONAL COUNSELING EXCELLENCE THROUGH LEADERSHIP AND ADVOCACY

Edited by

Catherine Y. Chang, Casey A. Barrio Minton,
Andrea L. Dixon, Jane E. Myers, and Thomas J. Sweeney

Routledge
Taylor & Francis Group
New York   London

Routledge  
Taylor & Francis Group  
711 Third Avenue  
New York, NY 10017

Routledge  
Taylor & Francis Group  
27 Church Road  
Hove, East Sussex BN3 2FA

International Standard Book Number: 978-0-415-89072-4 (Hardback)

---

**Library of Congress Cataloging-in-Publication Data**

---

Professional counseling excellence through leadership and advocacy / [edited by]  
    Catherine Y. Chang ... [et al.].  
        p. cm.  
    Includes bibliographical references and index.  
    ISBN 978-0-415-89072-4 (hardback)  
    1. Educational counseling. 2. Student counselors--Professional relationships.  
3. Educational leadership. I. Chang, Catherine.

LB1027.5.P658 2011  
371.4'22--dc22                                                                    2011015455

---

Visit the Taylor & Francis Web site at  
http://www.taylorandfrancis.com

and the Routledge Web site at  
http://www.routledgementalhealth.com

# Contents

# *Foreword*

CAROL L. BOBBY

Charles Dickens' 1843 novella, *A Christmas Carol*, is a classic that has stood the test of time. The story of Ebenezer Scrooge and his visitations from the Ghosts of Christmas Past, Present, and Future are well known around the world regardless of where one lives or what one's religious beliefs may be. It is a story of a mean, miserly fellow who said "Bah, humbug" whenever he was confronted with an opportunity to be kind or generous to others.

Although the story was written in criticism of the industrial revolution's effects on society, the story can also provide the careful reader with a layman's understanding of how to foster the development of leaders and advocates in the counseling profession. Consider the following:

- Scrooge is visited by the Ghosts of Christmas Past, Present, and Future so that he may see how his past and present actions will impact his future. An understanding of the counseling profession's past and present can serve as a guide to where the profession wants to see itself in the future. Who were the past leaders, who are the current leaders, and who are the future leaders that will serve as guides?
- The Ghosts forced Scrooge to look at his behaviors and the effects he has had on others' lives. As a result, Scrooge had an opportunity to redeem himself and change his behaviors before it was too late. Looking at oneself is not always easy. Self-reflection takes courage. Effective leadership often requires the courage to look at situations and oneself with a critical eye and to make changes.
- Scrooge is transformed by his "theoretical" evening with the Ghosts. He is given an opportunity to change and he embraces it. His "bah, humbug" attitude is replaced with compassion, generosity, and service to others. Leaders realize that there comes a time when theory must be put into practice. Advocates realize that the counseling profession is built upon service to all.

Like Dickens' novella, *Professional Counseling Excellence through Leadership and Advocacy* is destined to be a classic in counselor education. It is the first counselor education textbook to devote itself solely to examining how the development of leadership and advocacy skills in professional counselors enhances the profession's work on behalf of clients, communities, and society at large.

Acknowledging that the counseling profession is still relatively young, the editors have wisely included chapters that look to the past and the present. But they also give glimpses into the future world of counseling, looking at issues such as accountability, future training needs, and social justice as the fifth force in counseling.

Bound to be a favorite chapter for all who read the book is Chapter 4, "On Becoming a Leader: A Journey." In this chapter, the book's editors share their personal experiences with becoming leaders. What becomes immediately apparent is that each became a leader based on different life experiences and by following different paths. The chapter is fascinating, providing insight into the importance of self-reflection, taking risks, and an attitude of service, while simultaneously recognizing that there is no one personality or life experience that is required to become a leader.

Counselor educators will also appreciate the practical and useful exercises and questions provided in the chapters. The book practically teaches itself, but there can be no doubt that its use with a group of students will foster rich and rewarding discussions.

Professional counselors who read this text may not start out with a "bah humbug" attitude, but the book will provide them the opportunity to confront and reflect upon their past actions, look at how they are behaving in the present, and give them the knowledge and skills they need to make a difference in the future. Everyone will benefit from the "servant leaders" that this book aims to develop.

# Introduction

## OUR PHILOSOPHY: LEADERSHIP AND ADVOCACY ARE CRITICAL, RELATED, INSEPARABLE, AND FOCUSED ON WELLNESS

The Council for Accreditation of Counseling and Related Educational Programs (CACREP) national preparation standards (2009) now require leadership and advocacy knowledge and skills for counselor training that did not exist in previous standards. While doctoral programs have courses and experiences that address some aspects of the standards, few if any do so comprehensively. Equally important, entry-level (master's degree) programs have not traditionally addressed leadership and advocacy competencies in their curricula. Addressing these standards is an important new dimension to counselor training; however, it is not only the standards but the reality of professional training and practice that require attention.

Relatively speaking, counseling is a young profession. Only in the last 30 years have we had widespread accreditation of training programs, certification for professional counselors nationally, and the possibility of state licensure for those trained in our field. It is only recently that every state has required credentialing for professional counselors, yet licensure laws change and we face a continual need to ensure that trained counselors are assured the right to practice within the scope of our competencies. The need for leadership is particularly critical since every dimension of what it means to be a profession is finally in place, yet threatened by the capricious nature of the political process relative to reauthorization of our licensure laws, turfism from other professions, and a host of other factors. In this context, advocacy becomes a critical focus of our leadership efforts.

We view advocacy as a two-pronged concept, including both advocacy for the profession and advocacy for those we serve. It is difficult if not impossible to determine which comes first. If we do not have a strong profession that is recognized, respected, and empowered, trained professional counselors will lack the right to practice what we have been trained to do. At the same time, if we fail to advocate for our clients, we risk losing the fundamental reason for entry into this profession—to help others achieve their optimum potential for human development and wellness.

Embedded within and throughout this text is a call for social justice and social advocacy as a part of counselor competencies. The disparity between those who are privileged and those who are not results in far too many individuals that would benefit from counseling services not getting them. They are being deprived in no small part because of the lack of counselor positions or third-party payment. This is most apparent in rural areas, inner cities, among those less economically advantaged, in third world nations, and among those on the fringes of society because of physical, mental, or emotional challenges, or those who are disenfranchised because of racism, sexism, ageism, disabilities, or other forms of prejudice and oppression. Advocacy for those that need counseling services is an imperative, and one that is addressed most successfully among counselors skilled in leadership and advocacy for the counseling profession as well as client development and change.

The counseling profession is founded on a philosophical position of contributing to the prevention of obstacles and more importantly the enhancement of human development over the life span through comprehensive counseling services. This position has found a voice in the wellness movement now apparent in our society. Research findings across disciplines support the basis for this philosophical stance, including wellness research in counseling over the past 20 years. As a profession, we continue to develop a broad base of empirical support for counselors to bring their knowledge and skills to bear on wellness for individuals in schools, colleges, businesses, and industries, and throughout local communities in this country and globally.

Counselors-in-training must develop the skills to be effective leaders in the profession and in the settings and communities where they serve. Clearly, such leaders will be advocates for groups and individual clients as well. Both our profession and the clients we serve require that counselors be trained as advocates and leaders for professional, social, and personal change. Leadership and advocacy are critical skills, closely related, sometimes inseparable, and jointly focused on positive, wellness-enhancing action for clients, communities, and our profession. Figure 1 demonstrates this connection, and underscores the need for a mission that drives training and practice in leadership and advocacy.

## OUR RATIONALE: TRAINING EXEMPLARY COUNSELORS AND COUNSELOR EDUCATORS FOR LEADERSHIP AND ADVOCACY

A series of qualitative interviews conducted by Chi Sigma Iota (CSI) with leaders and scholars in counselor education ($N = 8$) resulted in a consensus that while both professional and client advocacy are essential competencies for future counselors,

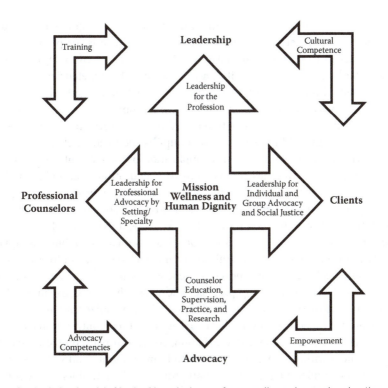

**Figure 1**    A relational model of leadership and advocacy for counseling and counselor education.

there is a lack of adequate attention to these concepts in current counselor preparation programs. The need to address the distinction between professional and client advocacy and to prepare counselors to be leaders and advocates in both arenas is largely missing in counselor education today. Contributing to this condition is the absence of comprehensive texts addressing these important areas.

As a consequence, this book was developed for counselor educators and supervisors, master's- and doctoral-level counseling students, and practicing professional counselors working in all settings. We believe it will be suitable principally as a text for doctoral courses in leadership and advocacy, and as a practice-oriented book, it also will be suitable for practicum/internship courses at both the master's and doctoral levels. By addressing specialty-specific settings with activities and exercises for use in practicum and internships, it also may serve as a culminating professionalization text. Our hope is that the book will be used in doctoral seminars to help students achieve a broad scope and vision of leadership and advocacy that includes client advocacy, advocacy for the counseling profession, and social justice. In addition, it will be a resource for students and practicing counselors to use as templates for leadership and advocacy interventions in their specialty areas.

The 2009 CACREP standards emphasized the need for outcome measures of counselor competencies throughout all aspects of counselor preparation. It is not sufficient to simply write syllabus objectives using terminology found in the standards. Evidence of activities and measures of competencies need to be documented. This book addresses the special competencies needed by culturally competent advocates and leaders by work setting. Competencies promulgated by the American Counseling Association (ACA) and other organizations as well as the CSI Principles and Practices of Leadership Excellence are included.

Each chapter includes a section on application of the concepts presented for individuals, groups and classrooms, counselor education, and global applications. Concrete examples based on the authors' experiences where leadership and advocacy competencies were required are integrated throughout the chapters.

Careful reading of the 2009 standards makes it clear that counselor education programs *may* emphasize one or more of the areas mentioned, but it is equally clear that for *all* graduates, doctoral program objectives must address *all* of the professional leadership roles and competencies needed within counselor education, supervision, counseling practice, and research. As a consequence, this book addresses these topical areas and more. We also realize that master's-level counselors are called upon every day to account for their contributions to better schools, agencies, and communities. Helping create a climate conducive to client empowerment within a society dedicated to human dignity and wellness for all is a core value underlying the work of all professional counselors. Every professional counselor has opportunities to promote these values through leadership in whatever setting or with whatever population they find themselves working. Helping those entering the profession to understand this as a responsibility and to prepare them for the obstacles that will inevitably confront their efforts is essential to their future success.

## SUMMING UP: COUNSELOR LEADERSHIP AND ADVOCACY

Professional advocacy is a means to an end that benefits professional counselees, the betterment of society, and raises the role of counselors to a level of servant leader. The servant leader has personal qualities, knowledge, skills, and habits that exemplify the best in leadership capacity. Through this servant leader role, professional counselors will win a position of respect and appropriate recognition as partners in promoting a healthy and just society where respect for human dignity and wellness are its highest aspirations.

## OVERVIEW OF SECTIONS AND CHAPTERS

The first section of this book addresses the foundations of leadership in counseling. Chapter 1 provides a description of key events and processes in the historical evolution of the counseling profession. In Chapter 2, the theory and philosophy of leadership are presented, including research in support of exemplary leadership practices. The leadership competencies promulgated by the CSI Principles and Practices of Leadership Excellence are presented in the third chapter, along with examples from experienced and successful leaders. The fourth chapter provides exercises and guidelines to help readers reflect and learn about themselves as they engage in roles as servant leaders.

The second section of the book is focused on the dual prongs of professional and client advocacy. Chapter 5 addresses how to become an effective professional advocate, while Chapter 6 reviews the principles and standards that make advocacy roles integral to the competencies of professional counselors. In Chapter 7, advocacy is presented in terms of social justice, leading to the description in the following chapter of a new theoretical model for client advocacy. Examples of advocacy in action comprise the content of the final chapter in this section.

Part III brings together the dual roles of leader and advocate from various perspectives, with chapters on counselor education, clinical supervision, counseling practice, and research. The emphasis in each chapter is on making the theory and practice of leadership and advocacy concrete, and demonstrating how both concepts are integral to excellence in professional training and practice.

The chapters in Part IV encourage readers to look to the future as leadership and advocacy become increasingly integrated, inseparable, and infused into counselor training and practice in this country and beyond. Chapter 14 provides concrete curricular examples of how to integrate leadership into entry-level and doctoral training curricula, while Chapter 15 does the same for professional and client advocacy in both master's and doctoral programs. Chapter 16 addresses issues of accountability in professional preparation and practice.

The appendices to this book will be especially helpful to counselor educators. These include specific attention to the CACREP standards related to leadership and advocacy and the manner in which each chapter contributes to and addresses the specifics of counselor preparation. Rubrics are included to provide examples of how the standards may be assessed and met.

It is our hope that this book will serve its intended uses and contribute to excellence in counselor preparation, supervision, and practice. We welcome feedback and suggestions for creating even better learning experiences for counseling students and professionals.

**Catherine Y. Chang**
**Casey A. Barrio Minton**
**Andrea L. Dixon**
**Jane E. Myers**
**Thomas J. Sweeney**

# *About the Editors*

**Catherine Y. Chang**, PhD, LPC, NCC, is an associate professor at Georgia State University and program coordinator for the Counselor Education and Practice doctoral program. She has published and presented in the areas of social justice and advocacy, multicultural counseling competence, privilege and oppression issues, and supervision. She has held several leadership positions, including president of Chi Sigma Iota (2009–2010) and vice president for the Asian and Pacific Islander American concerns of the Association for Multicultural Counseling and Development (2010–2013). She is the recipient of the American Counseling Association (ACA) Research Award, the ACA Counselor Educator Advocacy Award, the Association for Assessment in Counseling and Education (AACE) MECD Research Award, and the Alumni Excellence Award from the Department of Counseling and Educational Development at UNCG. She serves on the editorial boards for *Counselor Education and Supervision*, the *Measurement and Evaluation in Counseling and Development*, and *Counseling Outcome Research and Evaluation* journals.

**Casey A. Barrio Minton**, PhD, NCC, is an associate professor and counseling program coordinator for the University of North Texas Counseling Program. She specializes in crisis intervention and evidence-based counselor education and was recognized in *Counseling Today* as "on the cutting edge" in counseling research. Dr. Barrio Minton serves as president of Chi Sigma Iota (CSI) International (2011–2012), secretary for the Association for Assessment in Counseling and Education (AACE) (2010–2012), and co-chair of the AACE Task Force regarding CACREP Assessment and Evaluation Guidelines (2009–current). A former CSI leadership fellow, she is the recipient of the ACES Outstanding Publication in Counselor Education Award, SACES Pre-Tenure Counselor Educator Award, ACES Outstanding Dissertation Award, and CSI Outstanding Research Award. Dr. Barrio Minton serves on editorial boards for *Counseling Outcome Research and Evaluation* and the *Journal of Professional Counseling*; she is an ad hoc reviewer for *Counselor Education and Supervision*.

**Andrea L. Dixon**, PhD, NCC, is an associate professor in the Department of Counseling and Psychological Services at Georgia State University. Dr. Dixon worked as an elementary and high school counselor and has also worked as a counselor in the private practice and university counseling center settings. She has published and presented in the areas of mattering to others, ethnic minority identity development, the adolescent period of the life span, cross-cultural competence and multicultural counseling, competent school counseling, students' academic persistence and achievement, and wellness across the life span. She has held several leadership positions, including secretary of Chi Sigma Iota (2008–2010). She received the 2008 Association for Multicultural Counseling and Development's Emerging Leader Award. She serves on the editorial boards for *Professional School Counseling*, the *Journal of Multicultural Counseling and Development*, and the *Journal for Specialists in Group Work*.

**Jane E. Myers**, PhD, LPC, NCC, is a professor of counselor education at the University of North Carolina at Greensboro. A fellow of the American Counseling Association and the Chi Sigma Iota Academy of Leaders for Excellence, she is a past president of the American Counseling Association, the Association for Assessment in Counseling, the Association for Adult Development and Aging, and Chi Sigma Iota International, and past chair of the Council for Accreditation of Counseling and Related Educational Programs (CACREP). She was selected for inclusion in *Leaders and Legacies in Counseling*, and identified as one of 25 individuals viewed as among the most significant leaders in the counseling profession over the last century. She has written and edited numerous publications, including 16 books and monographs, over 150 refereed journal articles, and was noted twice, most recently in 2010, as being in the top 1% of contributors to the *Journal of Counseling and Development*, ACA's flagship journal.

**Thomas J. Sweeney**, PhD, founding president and executive director of Chi Sigma Iota Counseling Academic and Professional Honor Society International, is also professor emeritus of counselor education at Ohio University in Athens. He was both a public school teacher and school counselor before earning his doctorate. His publications include books, monographs, chapters, and over 80 articles in nationally referred journals. He was listed among the top 5% of contributors to the American Counseling Association (ACA) *Journal of Counseling and Development* over a span of 15 years. His book *Adlerian Counseling* (Routledge, 2009) is in its fifth edition. He is a past president of the American Counseling Association (ACA) and two of its divisions, and for six years was the founding chair of the Council for Accreditation of Counseling and Related Educational Programs (CACREP). He is the recipient of numerous awards and has had two awards named in his honor for distinguished leadership and service.

# About the Contributors

**Michael D. Brubaker**, PhD, LCDCII, NCC, is an assistant professor and academic coordinator of the Addictions Studies Program in the School of Human Services in the College of Education, Criminal Justice, and Human Services at the University of Cincinnati. His clinical and research interests have focused on underserved and socially marginalized populations, including the homeless, those who identify as lesbian, gay, bisexual, transgender (LGBT), and Native Americans. He has been recognized for excellence through the Dr. Daya and Mrs. Usha K. Sandhu Multicultural Counseling and Diversity Student Research Award. Furthermore, he was a CSI fellow and intern, serving on the CSI Strategic Planning Committee, and later leading the task force to create the CSI Community Engagement Committee, which he currently chairs. In addition, he is a trustee of the Association for Lesbian, Gay, Bisexual, and Transgender Issues in Counseling.

**Craig S. Cashwell**, PhD, LPC, NCC, ACS, is a professor in the Department of Counseling and Educational Development at the University of North Carolina at Greensboro. He has authored over 90 publications, primarily in the area of spirituality in counseling. He has held multiple leadership positions, including chair of the CACREP board of directors, president of ASERVIC, and the ACES representative to the ACA governing council. Additionally, he serves on the editorial boards for the *Journal of Counseling and Development* and *Counseling and Values*. He has received numerous awards for his work, including the ACES Outstanding Counselor Education and Supervision Article Award, the ASERVIC Lifetime Service Award, and the UNCG School of Education Teaching Excellence Award.

**Brian J. Dew**, PhD, LPC, is an associate professor in the Department of Counseling and Psychological Services at Georgia State University and currently serves as the department chairperson. Dr. Dew has served as president of the Association for Lesbian, Gay, Bisexual, and Transgender Issues in Counseling (2006–2007) and currently serves on the executive council of the Association for Counselor Education and Supervision. Dr. Dew has been awarded the 2007 Outstanding Faculty Research Award from Georgia State University's Department of

Education, 2007 Outstanding Addictions and Offender Professional Award by the Association of Addictions and Offender Counseling, and was the recipient of the 2009 SACES Courtland Lee Social Justice Award.

**Elizabeth A. Doughty Horn**, PhD, LCPC, is an assistant professor at Idaho State University. Her professional areas of interest include issues of grief and loss and professional identity. She has taught and presented on various issues related to advocacy and is currently part of an interdisciplinary team of professionals and students providing health screenings to the underserved in Idaho. She is active in professional counseling organizations, serving in leadership positions, has published on issues relating to grief and loss, and has trained to become a CACREP site team member.

**Judith C. Durham**, APRN, PhD, NCC, LPC, is an associate professor and clinical mental health internship coordinator at Saint Joseph College (Connecticut) in its Department of Counseling and Family Therapy. She has published and presented in the areas of multicultural counseling, supervision, multicultural supervision, advocacy, social justice advocacy, and using supervision to prepare social justice counseling advocates. She has held numerous leadership positions on national and regional levels, including serving as NARACES president (2004–2005) and ACES president (2007–2008). During her term as ACES president she focused the 2007 ACES national conference on advocacy: Vanguards for Change: Aces and Social Justice.

**Harriet L. Glosoff**, PhD, LPC, NCC, ACS, is a professor of counseling at Montclair State University. She has published and presented in the areas of ethics, spirituality and cultural issues, advocacy, preparing counselors as social justice advocates, and clinical supervision. She has held numerous leadership positions on the national, regional, and state levels. Recent examples include serving as a board member of the Association for Ethical, Spiritual and Religious Values in Counseling (2009–present), president (2006–2007) and secretary (2003–2004) of the Association for Counselor Education and Supervision (ACES), co-chair of the American Counseling Association (ACA) Ethics Committee (2004–June 2006), and member of the ACA Code of Ethics (2002–2005) Revision Task Force. She is the recipient of the Southern Association for Counselor Education and Supervision (SACES) Tenured Counselor Educator Award (October 2009).

**Rachael D. Goodman**, PhD, LPC, NCC, is an assistant professor in the Counseling and Development Program at George Mason University. Dr. Goodman's research and clinical interests focus on social justice counseling and outreach, traumatic stress and disaster response, and counselor training and advocacy. She has served as the clinical coordinator of counseling outreach trips to post-Katrina New Orleans and southern Africa, under the auspices of the Association for

Multicultural Counseling and Development (AMCD). While serving as president of the Florida Association for Multicultural Counseling and Development (FAMCD), she led an outreach to the Haitian and Haitian American community in Florida following the 2010 earthquake in Haiti. Dr. Goodman is the recipient of the Outstanding Research Award from Chi Sigma Iota and the Daya Sandhu Multicultural Counseling Student Research Award from AMCD.

**Laura K. Harrawood**, PhD, LCPC, LMFT, NCC, is an assistant professor at Idaho State University. Her areas of professional interest include individual supervision, supervision in couples and family counseling, group theory and practice, innovative teaching methods, counselor identity development, and issues related to grief and loss. Dr. Harrawood has published in the area of death education, ethics, and the training of couple and family counselors. She has served as a manuscript reviewer for *Omega: Journal of Death and Dying* and currently serves on the editorial review board for *The Family Journal: Counseling and Therapy for Couples and Family*. Dr. Harrawood has been active in state professional organizations, serving as the president of the Idaho Association of Counselor Educator and Supervision (2008–2009) and secretary (2008–2009). She has also served as a CACREP site team member.

**Danica G. Hays**, PhD, LPC, NCC, is an associate professor and department chair of the Department of Counseling and Human Services at Old Dominion University. She has published over 60 refereed journal articles, book chapters, and books in the areas of research methodology, assessment and diagnosis, trauma and gender issues, and multicultural and social justice concerns in counselor preparation and community mental health. Dr. Hays has been a faculty member at Old Dominion University since 2006, and her primary teaching responsibilities are master's- and doctoral-level research methods courses, assessment, and doctoral supervision. Dr. Hays has received several national awards, including the ACA Research Award, ACA Counselor Educator Advocacy Award, Association for Assessment in Counseling and Education AACE/MECD Patricia B. Elmore Award for Excellence in Measurement and Evaluation Research, Association for Counselor Education and Supervision (ACES) Outstanding Graduate Student Leadership Award, and Chi Sigma Iota International fellow.

**Nicole R. Hill**, PhD, LPC, is a professor at Idaho State University. Her professional areas of interest include multicultural counseling, counselor development, advocacy, triadic supervision, and play therapy. She has published and presented on various topics, such as advocacy, multicultural counseling, supervision, professional wellness, and counselor development. Dr. Hill serves on the editorial review boards for *Counselor Education and Supervision* and *Journal of Counseling and Development*. Her leadership experience includes serving as secretary of Chi

Sigma Iota (2010–2012), president of Rocky Mountain Association for Counselor Education and Supervision (2010–2011), president of the Idaho Counseling Association (2004–2005), communications officer for Counselors for Social Justice (2008–2010), and co-chair of the American Counseling Association Human Rights Committee (2004–2007). Since 2003, she has served as a CACREP site team member for various accreditation teams. In 2009, she received the Publication in Counselor Education and Supervision Award.

**Victoria E. Kress**, PhD, is a professor, counseling clinic director, and the director of the clinical mental health, addictions, and college counseling programs at Youngstown State University. She has a long history of serving CSI as chapter faculty advisor for the Eta chapter, Counselor Educator Task Force chair, Faculty Advisor Committee chair, CEU Committee chair, and as a National Advocacy Committee member. Most recently, she was elected president-elect-elect of Chi Sigma Iota. She has published over 45 refereed articles, numerous book chapters, and has co-authored a book on client advocacy and ethics issues that relate to the DSM. She was the 2008 recipient of the ACES Distinguished Mentor Award. She started the ACES advocacy interest network and chaired this network for many years. She specializes in child sexual abuse and trauma, and is a court-appointed guardian *ad litem* who advocates for abused/neglected children.

**Courtland C. Lee**, PhD, is a professor and director of the Counselor Education Program at the University of Maryland, College Park. He is the author, editor, or co-editor of ten books on the following topics: multicultural counseling, counseling for social justice, and counseling African American males. Additionally, he has published numerous book chapters and journal articles on counseling across cultures. Dr. Lee is a past president and fellow of the American Counseling Association. He is also a past president of the Association for Multicultural Counseling and Development, Chi Sigma Iota, and the International Association for Counseling. He is a charter member of Chi Sigma Iota's Academy of Leaders for Excellence and recipient of the CSI Thomas J. Sweeney Professional Leadership Award. He is the first and only U.S. citizen named as a fellow of the British Association for Counseling and Psychotherapy. Dr. Lee is the former editor of the *Journal of Multicultural Counseling and Development* and the *Journal of African American Men*. He currently serves on the editorial board of the *International Journal for the Advancement of Counselling.*

**Todd F. Lewis**, PhD, is an associate professor of counselor education in the Counseling and Educational Development Department at the University of North Carolina at Greensboro. Dr. Lewis earned his doctorate in counselor education and supervision from Kent State University and is a licensed professional counselor and a national certified counselor. Dr. Lewis has held previous leadership positions as IAAOC president, IAAOC treasurer, and president of two chapters of Chi Sigma Iota. His professional publications have primarily been in the areas of adolescent and collegiate substance use, motivational interviewing and its application, and Adlerian models applied to drinking. Dr. Lewis teaches in the areas of substance abuse counseling, advanced clinical assessment, motivational interviewing, and counseling adolescents. He counsels part-time at the Presbyterian Counseling Center in Greensboro, North Carolina, where he is conducting clinical trial research on the effectiveness of counseling in combination with medication for clients struggling with opiate addiction.

**Larry C. Loesch**, PhD, NCC is professor emeritus, University of Florida, Department of Counselor Education. He served as president of CSI, AMEG (now AACE), FAMEG, FCA, and SACES, a CACREP board member, and in many other professional positions. He has been an evaluation consultant for the NBCC since 1980. He was a co-recipient of the ACA's 1983 Research Award and of its 1992 Hitchcock Distinguished Professional Service Award. He received a 1998 Professorial Excellence Award from the University of Florida. He was a Fulbright Scholar in Slovakia in 2001. He is a fellow of the American Counseling Association. He received the 1998 CSI Thomas J. Sweeney Professional Leadership Award and is a member of CSI's Academy of Leaders.

**Matthew John Paylo**, PhD, is an assistant professor and interim director of the student affairs program at Youngstown State University. He has published and presented in the areas of social justice and advocacy, multicultural counseling, and the assessment of multicultural and advocacy competencies. Matthew engages and challenges his students to advocate for the counseling profession as well as for marginalized and discriminated populations.

**Jayne E. Smith**, MA, NCC, is a doctoral student in counselor education and supervision at Old Dominion University. Ms. Smith was an adjunct professor and university supervisor at the University of San Diego. She directed a training clinic within John Muir Charter School serving former high school dropouts and international refugees in San Diego County. During that time, Ms. Smith developed and implemented programs geared toward empowerment and leadership for young adults. Additionally, she trained and supervised clinical mental health counseling students with an emphasis on developing advocacy and multicultural competence. Ms. Smith has published in the forthcoming *Experiential Activities for Teaching Career Counseling and for Facilitating Career Groups* (Volume III).

**Linwood G. Vereen**, PhD, LPC, NCC, is an associate professor in the Department of Counseling at Idaho State University. Professional interests include multicultural foundations, supervision, group work, supervisor development, advocacy competencies, and student-athlete development. Dr. Vereen has served on the review boards for *Counselor Education and Supervision*, the *Journal of College Counseling*, and the *Journal of Negro Education*. Professional leadership includes serving as the ACA Western Region chair, president of the Idaho Counseling Association, and leadership development chair and membership chair for the Idaho Counseling Association. Since 2001, Dr. Vereen has served as a CACREP site team member.

**Carrie A. Wachter Morris**, PhD, NCC, ACS, is an assistant professor at Purdue University in the school counseling program. She has published and presented in the areas of crisis intervention and innovation in counselor education. Her development of a serious game for suicide assessment training was featured in *Counseling Today*. Dr. Wachter Morris serves as president-elect-elect of the Indiana School Counselor Association (2012–2013). A former CSI leadership fellow, she is the recipient of the Indiana School Counselor Association Outstanding Counselor Educator Award, a Purdue University Teaching for Tomorrow Fellowship Award, and the Early Career Award from the University of North Carolina at Greensboro School of Education. She serves on the editorial board for *Professional School Counseling*, is a founding advisory board member for the Ganley Foundation, and advocates for Indiana school counselors through testifying at the statehouse and serving on an advisory board to the state superintendent of public instruction.

**Jill E. Whittaker**, MA, is a counselor education doctoral student and fellow at Montclair State University, and an adjunct instructor and supervisor at The College of New Jersey (TCNJ). She received her master's degree in school counseling and bachelor's degree in elementary education and psychology from The College of New Jersey. She worked as a school counselor for a number of years, where she acted as a practicum/internship site supervisor. Her research interests include gender issues in counseling, faith/spirituality, supervision, and meaning-based counseling in the schools.

**Chris Wood**, PhD, NCC, NCSC, is an associate professor in the Department of Counseling and Human Services at Old Dominion University. He is incoming associate editor of the *Professional School Counseling* journal. He has previous experience as a high school counselor, a guidance department chair, a counselor/group leader at a residential youth facility for troubled teens, and a career counselor at an alternative school serving grades 7–12. Dr. Wood was a research assistant on a $1.3 million Community Employment Education Center grant from the Office of Adult and Vocational Education and a faculty research associate on a grant from the National Research Center for Career and Technical Education. He is co-editor of the forthcoming sixth edition of the National Career Development Association's (NCDA) *A Counselor's Guide to Career Assessment Instruments*.

# I

---

## *FOUNDATIONS OF LEADERSHIP IN COUNSELING*

---

# 1

# *Leadership for the Counseling Profession*

## Thomas J. Sweeney

Exemplary leaders respect and build upon the history of their organization.

—Principle 3, Principles and Practices of Leadership Excellence, CSI Academy of Leaders, 2009

## INTRODUCTION

The counseling profession has evolved over several decades. When I spoke with the editors about their thoughts on our first chapter, I asked: Do you think anyone will care about what came before our present development as a profession? I was surprised by how enthusiastically they recounted the importance for them to have learned of the events that both preceded and were integral to the evolution of counseling as a profession. These events have been described in a variety of sources, including the *Handbook of Counseling* (Sweeney, 2001). Indeed, the editors agreed that this book is written to address the unfinished business of our earlier history. Not only is it important, but it is essential for emerging leaders to have a context for understanding the complexities and challenges facing all professional counselors. The counseling profession seeks a new cadre of leaders formed from among those now entering the profession. Whatever is to be done must fundamentally build upon that which preceded it. Leaders do not start with a blank paper to form a new plan. Wise leaders know this intuitively and act upon it.

## From Whence We Came

Throughout our history, many individuals have emerged as leaders and advocates to move the counseling profession forward. Some were quiet but unwavering in their purpose to help create a profession dedicated to promoting wellness and human dignity through counseling services. Then there were those in the foreground of leading the charge in public forums or legislative hearings. Some did so through elected positions or as volunteer leaders of membership organizations. Still others did so through their positions as professional counselors, counselor educators, supervisors, or administrators. Though too many to mention here, their collective efforts are recorded throughout the literature of our profession in works such as the American Counseling Association (ACA) *Encyclopedia of Counseling* (ACA, 2009). For those interested in the contributions and stories of several of those individuals who have stood out because of their leadership in counseling, West, Osborn, and Bubenzer's (2003b) work is now a classic. The focus of this chapter is on events and not individuals; however, it is the collective efforts of these individual leaders and advocates that has created the vital profession of counseling as we know it today.

Some of our challenges are from within, which has resulted in the counseling profession developing not as "one voice" but with strands, with some specialty areas defining themselves as separate professions while most others emphasize the core values of counseling with specialties as a secondary emphasis. Much of this debate, and the rich histories of the counseling specialty areas, was chronicled in a 1995 special issue of the *Journal of Counseling and Development* (Myers, 1995). The continued evolution of the specialties is reflected in the current debate over the role of school counselors as defined by counseling associations (e.g., the ACA and the American School Counseling Association) and organizations such as the Education Trust (see Education Trust, 2003 and Dixon & Dew, Chapter 12, for more information on school counselor role definitions).

The origins and influence of specialty issues on a unified voice for counseling will be illustrated with a view to school and rehabilitation counseling later in this chapter.

> Who is holding back more rapid movement to the better society that is reasonably possible with available resources? In short, the enemy is servants who have the potential to lead but do not lead. (Greenleaf, in Beazley, Spears, & Beggs, 2003, pp. 39–40)

One of the most revealing aspects of preparing this chapter was the breadth and depth of what is written about leadership and leaders in general. As a consequence, definitions and illustrations abound, but they tend to be global in nature. In Chapter 2, Lewis reviews the literature on leadership and leadership theory, and in Chapter 3, Myers addresses characteristics and research on leadership among professional counselors and counselor educators. As a consequence, I chose to adapt the more global concepts to counseling leadership without exploring the many variations on these concepts. In addition, I use the adopted statements of Chi Sigma Iota (CSI) for definitions specifically related to the profession.

Professional leadership milestones in client advocacy that are a rich part of our history are found in Section II, Chapters 8 and 9.

Key Terms

*Leadership.* For the purposes of this chapter, leadership is defined to be those actions by individuals in professional counseling that contribute to the realization of our individual and collective capacity to serve others competently, ethically, and justly as helping professionals. This leadership can be found in all settings and at all levels from local through international service to others needing and desiring our assistance.

*Leader.* The editors of the book particularly identify with Greenleaf's (2003) characterization of "servant leader." Such persons aspire to a vision of service that reflects well upon the profession; those who serve within in it strive to convey a message of service and empowerment to all whom we serve as professionals. Some do so through their positions within schools, colleges, agencies, and commerce, while others also act as ambassadors and representatives of the profession through appointed or elected positions within its organizations. In all cases, they do so out of a spirit of service and selflessness.

*Counseling profession.* For purposes of clarity among helping professionals who use counseling as a method or its techniques, the graduate education of members of the profession of counseling is defined by the national standards of the Council for Accreditation of Counseling and Related Educational Programs (CACREP, 2009). Individuals whose programs of study in counselor education were accredited by the Council of Rehabilitation Education (CORE) also are a part of this definition (CSI, 2010b).

*Professional counselors.* Professional counselors are persons who hold their highest graduate degree in counselor education, preferably from a nationally accredited preparation program, are credentialed by authorized state or national agencies, and adhere to competency standards on matters of ethics, diversity, and behavior in order to contribute to the realization of a healthy society by fostering wellness and human dignity. As a consequence, counseling is a professional relationship that empowers diverse individuals, families, and groups to accomplish mental health, wellness, education, and career goals (CSI, *20/20 Vision for the Future of Counseling definition,* 2010a).

Further, the ACA in its Code of Ethics defines *counselor* as "a professional (or a student who is a counselor in-training) engaged in a counseling practice or other counseling-related services. Counselors fulfill many roles and responsibilities such as counselor educators, researchers, and supervisors" (2005, p. 20).

*Wellness.* Is "a way of life oriented toward optimal health and well-being, in which body, mind, and spirit are integrated by the individual to live life more fully within the human and natural community" (Myers, Sweeney, & Witmer, 2000, p. 252).

## ANTECEDENTS TO COUNSELING AS A PROFESSION

The roots of counseling as a profession intersect to form our uniqueness. Several key areas combine to create a foundation both for understanding past leadership and advocacy efforts and for defining future leadership needs. These include the philosophical foundations of our profession, our educational roots, our identity roots, and the impact of national and global events.

### Philosophical Roots of Counseling as a Profession

Philosophy speaks to core values of why we do what we do and toward what ends. The philosophical foundation for the counseling profession in this country is established within the Bill of Rights and fortified by the Constitution and system of government of the United States. As will be noted in the sections of this book on advocacy, our desire to continue to promote the services of the counseling profession is driven by the inherent promise of all citizens having the inalienable rights of life, liberty, and the *pursuit of happiness.*

Counseling also has its earliest roots in a holistic value for human development. Arthur Jones (1934) published what became a classic text: *Principles of Guidance.* In his first chapter, he articulated what became the common view of what we now call the case for counseling:

> Guidance is based upon the fact that human beings need help. To a greater or lesser degree we all need the assistance of others. The possibility of education, as well as the necessity for it, is founded upon the essential dependence of people upon one another. Young people, especially, are not capable of solving life's problems successfully without aid. Many critical situations occur in our lives, situations in which important and far-reaching decisions must be made, and it is very necessary that some adequate help be provided in order that decisions may be made wisely. (p. 3)

Here we note the pragmatic nature of all human existence: that is, we need one another as social beings. Each person must make decisions about life. With help, we hope to make them more wisely. Implicit within Jones's statements is the need that we all have for help throughout our lives. Human development, therefore, facilitated throughout the life span by *deliberate, positive assistance is needed and normal* in the course of the human condition. Today, we speak of the need for wellness as the paradigm for helping achieve optimum well-being as our goal for all counseling interventions (Myers & Sweeney, 2005). Research on wellness counseling dates back to the 1980s and has expanded to include studies in dozens of countries around the globe and across the life span (Myers & Sweeney, 2008). Leadership and advocacy for these values is a part of our history and inevitably an essential part of our future.

### Educational Roots of Counseling as a Profession

Counseling has had closer ties with education perhaps more so than any other profession. As was true of Jones's definition above, the early education literature referred to counseling as a part of good education. For example, Brewer (1932) espoused a position that guidance be infused into the total school curriculum and that every teacher share the responsibility for its implementation. There are still educators today who would support that position or a variation on it by saying that every teacher or administrator "counsels." A few years later, others proposed that guidance be a part of, but not synonymous with, education. For example, Hamrin and Erickson (1939) stated:

> *Guidance* is a term appearing with increasing frequency in education literature and as a topic of discussion at meetings of professional organizations. Some writers and speakers use the term *guidance* synonymously with the term *education*; others identify and characterize as guidance only those activities that are concerned with the vocational aspects of life. (p. v)

Subsequently, the term *guidance* went through its own acceptance as suitable for what "guidance counselors" did in school. Guidance became no longer suitable for the professional preparation, practice, and identity desired by those who earned advanced degrees in *counselor* education. In fact, the work of professional counselors both inside and outside of educational settings became too complex to be subsumed under rubrics like guidance or personnel.

Changing terminology related to the definition of counseling as a profession is reflected in the history of our primary professional association. The groups of professionals who came together in 1952 called themselves the American Personnel and Guidance Association (APGA). In 1983, APGA changed its name to the American Association for Counseling and Development (AACD), signifying the profession's commitment to the core meaning and values of promoting wellness and development across the life span. Expansion of professional counselors' roles into community mental health settings was a major impetus behind a final name change, in 1992, to the American Counseling Association. Philosophical and emotional attachments to the terms *guidance, personnel,* and *development* were underscored by the discussions that led to this name change, and significant if not dramatic changes in our profession that accompanied the last three decades of the twentieth century. I was part of the AACD Governing Council at the time, and witnessed a strong move among members of counseling specialty groups to be identified with one, strong, unified profession of counseling; hence the name change to ACA signified a recognition of commonalities across categories of members. Clearly, such significant changes did not occur in the absence of strong leadership, with a number of persons stepping forward to speak in a unified voice that helped others in the profession embrace a vision that moved us closer to professional unity than at any time in our collective past.

One of the founding organizations of what was APGA, the American College Personnel Association (ACPA), was composed largely of deans of students and other related administrative personnel. Not surprisingly, the name change process from APGA to AACD, and finally to ACA, was a difficult one for many ACPA members. While college counselors had been affiliated with ACPA, their interests were more like those of the majority of ACA members. Therefore, when ACPA disaffiliated from what became ACA in 1992, the college counselors created a new organization, the American College Counselors Association (ACCA). This was a bold step for those who chose to keep their identity with counseling. The issues of professional identity that led to this organizational change within this specialty area of counseling are still evident within the literature and other organizations of other specialties (Smith, 2001).

### Profession or Professions of Counseling?

School and rehabilitation counselors, for example, are pulled in different directions by competing organizations (e.g., ACA, ASCA, the National Education Association, the National Rehabilitation Association, and their affiliated organizations for counselors) (Myers & Sweeney, 2001). The result of this competition is some who believe that specialties are separate professions unto themselves (i.e., we are not a unified profession with specialties but rather a profession of specialties). There is some history to suggest, however, that all specialties have far more in common than differences (ACA, 2009; Myers, 1995).

School counselors historically were associated with teacher education. In fact, the National Council for the Accreditation of Teacher Education (NCATE) was reviewing and accrediting school counseling programs within colleges of education years before the Council for the Accreditation of Counseling and Related Educational Programs (CACREP) was established in 1981. It is also notable that NCATE did not require the use of counselor education standards in their program reviews or require members of our profession to participate on their site visitation teams. As a consequence, school counselor education programs were accredited under review procedures not satisfactory to most counselor educators or school counselors. National needs and federal legislation discussed in the next section, however, intersected to create the tools and means to transform counselor education beginning as early as the 1940s and 1950s. These situations contributed to new leadership in the Association for Counselor Education and Supervision (ACES) directed toward the development of professional preparation standards for all counselors, which later led to the creation of CACREP (Myers, 1995; Myers & Sweeney, 2001; Sweeney, 2001). Therefore the earliest standards for the preparation of counselors were those based first in school counseling.

While the nature of school counseling has changed dramatically with changes in society and increases in major mental health problems in schools, many school counselors still find a comfortable fit within education as their primary identity and school counseling as their profession. Other school counselors, however, have been influenced by the development of counseling as a unified profession (i.e., core preparation with specialties). While the school culture and setting are still an essential part of their identity, they perceive themselves as professional counselors with specialized knowledge and competencies working in schools. Rehabilitation counselors have a similar situation with respect to professional identity.

Rehabilitation counseling has the unique distinction of being the only counseling specialty established by congressional legislation in Public Law 565 of the 83rd Congress in 1954. When federal legislation provided for the preparation of vocational rehabilitation counselors in 1955, those responsible decided it was more appropriate to train rehabilitation counselors at the same level and in ways analogous to school counselor training. As a result, vocational rehabilitation programs tended to be in colleges of education where the master's degree was considered an appropriate entry-level degree, but with notable exceptions when, for example, they are located in medicine or psychology departments. Professional orientation for some of those trained in these programs may be less distinctly professional counseling and more rehabilitation, with vocational assessment, case management, and placement included in the core of preparation. The result of this orientation leads some to view rehabilitation as a separate profession.

Rehabilitation counseling preparation programs, however, include the core curricula common to all counselor preparation programs as defined by CACREP. This came about in no small part because of the deliberate and persistent efforts of some leaders in rehabilitation counseling to have all accreditation of counseling programs under one joint agency versus having two (i.e., CACREP and CORE). In fact, during CACREP's first six years as chair, I helped to hold meetings between the two agencies' leaders to discuss the possibility of creating a new coalition to reduce the cost and hassle of accreditation. Many counselor education programs were being expected to meet two similar but separate sets of counselor education accreditation requirements. We made some progress, and one of CORE's former chairs subsequently became the chair of CACREP. Unfortunately, more recent efforts to merge the two agencies failed once again in spite of efforts by leaders within CACREP and rehabilitation counseling (CACREP, 2007).

Further evidence that many rehabilitation counselors identify with the profession can be found in those who have lobbied to be eligible for licensing in the various states as licensed professional counselors. Among their spokespersons, Maki and Tarvydas (in press) describe rehabilitation counselors as counselors first, with rehabilitation as their specialty, in contrast to earlier leaders who sought to define this specialty as a separate profession. These developments are integral parts of our history, and both current and future leadership and advocacy efforts are directly affected by this history. As a consequence, we will continue to need new leaders and advocates who understand the scope of the counseling profession, the core areas that are common across specialties and settings, and the unique contributions of specialties that allow us to serve the spectrum of persons in need of help. In every setting and at every level, leaders are needed who will step up to the challenges to advocate for both professional counselors and clients. Without these actions, the progress earned by earlier generations will inevitably be lost.

So as we attempt to understand issues in counseling such as why some school counselors do not affiliate with ACA or why CACREP and CORE are separate agencies that accredit counselor preparation programs in the same department or university, the historical antecedents should prove helpful. Also noteworthy, the strong emotional attachments to these various positions tend to defy simple solutions or explanations. Many professional counselors believe that if we are to be a more influential, positive force in shaping public policy in matters of well-being and dignity for all, that we must find a way to do so with one voice for the profession (see CSI, 2010a). We urgently need leaders who help us to create and implement a vision and advocates who promote that vision on a daily basis. Changes in politics, funding, priorities, and legislation make continued vigilance, leadership, and advocacy necessary to solidify professional gains and effectively address new and emerging challenges at local, state, national, and global levels.

## HISTORICAL TURNING POINTS: NATIONAL AND GLOBAL EVENTS

As we face the challenges of the first decades of the twenty-first century, the old saying that history repeats itself seems to be true. At the turn of the twentieth century, industrialization, immigration, unemployment, youth seeking excitement in the cities, and social injustices were rampant. Those with wealth and power were growing in number and influence while the majority of the population struggled to make a living. The need for reform grew out of these circumstances. With some editing, the description of the challenges before us could be adapted to this century. What follows are a few illustrations of how leadership and advocacy helped to shape our profession in these similarly turbulent times.

### Vocational Needs and National Interests

Frank Parsons is often cited as an early twentieth century social reformer. He saw the need for assisting youth in their search for suitable work. His Vocational Bureau in the Civic Service House in Boston was the first such effort to institutionalize vocational guidance. His book, *Choosing a Vocation* (1909), was published posthumously and his methods became the foundation of what many called vocational guidance. His efforts were further advanced when in 1910 the first conference of what became the National Vocational Guidance Association (NVGA) met in Boston. Descendant members in 1952 helped to establish ACA. NVGA has since been renamed the National Career Development Association (NCDA), illustrating again the shift from guidance as well as vocation to a more inclusive career and development emphasis (Gladding, 2008).

The same vocational needs that Parsons identified exist today. Many professional counselors miss the fact that they have career development as a core component of their preparation, which is unique to the counseling profession. Too few professional counselors capitalize upon this distinction, and as a consequence, we now see "coaches" filling a need for career assistance. Once again, unstable economies and globalization have clearly called attention to the need for greater career planning and development over the life span.

### The Impact of War and Social Change

In addition, the last century had a number of events impact not only counseling but closely related professions as well. Two world wars increased the need for better measurements to assess the capabilities of service persons for the armed services. As a consequence, the postwar years in the 1920s saw increased research and development of measurement techniques. In addition, the adequacy of placement within the school curricula and an evaluation of the end results brought educational guidance into greater prominence. No Child Left Behind legislation and policy of recent years seem quite similar in this regard. The Depression years of the 1930s also contributed to the perception that vocational guidance was an important need for our citizenry. A number of local, state, and federal programs, sponsored by efforts such as President Roosevelt's New Deal legislation, resulted in what we now call counseling services as adjuncts to health, social, employment, and educational concerns.

Utilizing personnel in the most efficient manner possible in World War II again brought into sharp focus the need for effective assessment and placement of personnel. Postwar business and industry in the late 1940s continued this interest by investing in testing programs to identify and place personnel within their growing corporate structures. As was true following World War I, returning soldiers were a major impetus for change. With disabilities in both physical and emotional functioning, new services and programs were needed to help young persons reenter the labor market and resume productive lives. In response to societal needs, leadership emerged in the postwar decades that lay the foundation for what became the counseling profession.

One of first defining moments for counseling came following the passage of the George-Barden Act of 1946. This piece of legislation provided funds through the U.S. Office of Education to encourage support of state supervisors of guidance and counselor educators. Vocational education funds were provided to reimburse for counselor training programs, and states were encouraged to create certification for school counselors. As a consequence, state school counselor certification preceded other forms of state counselor credentialing even though national standards needed to create uniformity were lacking. Variance in state-to-state requirements for school counselor certification continues to exist today.

There were approximately 80 colleges and universities purportedly training school counselors in the late 1940s. Half of the programs were at the undergraduate level. Undergraduate programs in counselor education, however, were discouraged by the federal leadership's decision in the early 1950s not to fund them under the George Barden Act (Hoyt, 1974). This decision no doubt had a profound effect on the university programs that had undergraduate emphases at that time, and many, if not most, were discontinued. Counseling since that time has been defined as a graduate-only profession. The graduate degree was instrumental in helping to establish state regulations of the title and practice of counseling in all states and to increase the profession's leverage in seeking other benefits for clients through state and federally funded programs.

Obviously, these events did not just happen. Professional counselors saw the need for change, and some stepped forward to ensure that change occurred. In each of the chapters in this section of the book, the question of whether leaders are born or made is often considered, both implicitly and explicitly. Leadership also has a situational component. Our profession has evolved through critical time periods when individuals have stepped forward to advocate and provide leadership for needed change. The most effective leaders have exemplified the values of our profession and worked together creatively and cooperatively to promote professional development. Though it is tempting to single out a few, the scope of writing in our professional textbooks and literature suggests the futility of such efforts. Leaders have emerged from our specialties and our core, and will continue to do so as we move through the current century (Sweeney, 2001; West et al., 2003b).

Other major societal events and congressional actions helped create even greater urgency for such leadership. Counselor educators and state supervisors of guidance from all over the country stepped up to the challenge. In the following sections, I will provide several examples for such turning points.

### National Defense Education Act of 1958

Undoubtedly one of the most important pieces of legislation to affect the counseling profession's ascendancy on university campuses came with the passage of Public Law 85-864, the National Defense Education Act (NDEA) of 1958. This act provided funds for guidance and counseling graduate institutes, fellowships in counselor preparation, and expanded guidance and testing programs in schools. Many of the leaders who wrote textbooks; developed preparation standards; helped create and develop specialties in counseling; advocated for wider employment of counselors in schools, colleges, and community settings; and volunteered as spokespersons for counseling were from this and subsequent generations of counselors. The origin of the legislation and its intended purposes are important as well.

In 1957 the Soviet Union launched a successful space capsule. U.S. leadership in rocket and space technology was in serious question. Our national pride was injured. In addition, national defense against Soviet communism was uppermost in the minds of Congress. This act was to identify, prepare, and guide the most gifted and talented youngsters into engineering and other technical careers important to our space race with the Soviets. School testing programs were quickly assembled throughout the country. Teachers were identified by their principals as promising guidance counselors and sent off to summer or academic-year institutes, all expenses paid.

Within a matter of a few short years, the number of counselors in schools quadrupled. Not surprisingly, the number of universities training counselors and the number of counselor educators also increased dramatically. However, the shift from school to community (mental health) counseling was about to begin, and a new, young cadre of leaders and advocates emerged to help create new areas of emphasis and specialties within the profession.

The Great Society

President Lyndon Johnson may be best known for his pursuit of the war in Vietnam, but it was his war on poverty that propelled a significant shift in the destiny of counseling practitioners. During President Kennedy's administration, the Community Mental Health Services Act of 1963 established community mental health centers throughout the country. This act provided funds for a variety of mental health workers, including counselors, to deliver services to those in need at the grassroots level. Since Johnson had long been a staunch advocate for what he considered to be the underdogs in our society, he lobbied Congress successfully to pass the Economic Opportunity Act of 1964 (PL88-452). This was his major effort to create a war to eliminate poverty. How different our social consciousness could have been had there not been the Vietnam War and Johnson's social agenda had been allowed to grow to fruition.

The Economic Opportunity Act was intended to expand opportunities for youth, stimulate communities to attack the roots of poverty, help destitute rural families, expand small business activities in poor areas, improve adult education, encourage states to use public assistance programs to help the poor lift themselves out of poverty, and recruit and train volunteers to help staff programs. At the very time school counseling programs and school counselor education were experiencing the full impact of NDEA funding, new legislation shifted the focus from schools to communities and from the gifted and talented to the disadvantaged and poor. This was the beginning of what became a refocusing of counselor education in many universities from principally school counselor preparation to a community or mental health counseling emphasis.

The call to address the needs of those who were destitute and in crises came into clear focus. This call was a major impetus for the formation in 1976 of the American Mental Health Counselors Association (AMHCA), which subsequently affiliated with APGA in 1978. Shortly after joining APGA, AMHCA ambitiously instituted a national certification for mental health counselors. In the early 1990s, AMHCA leaders sought to support professional unity (AACD, 1991), and as a consequence, this certification is now administered by the National Board of Certified Counselors, Inc. (NBCC).

It is noteworthy that although this new group of members responded to the same urgent message for serving the needs of persons in mental health crises, they chose to define the essence of mental health counseling as that of promoting healthy lifestyles, eliminating stressors that detract from such lifestyles, and preserving or restoring positive health (Seiler & Messina, 1979). Adherence to this philosophical position is one of the defining distinctions that mental health counselors bring to any community or interdisciplinary team. Professional counselors are not alone in this position now, though, as others came to embrace the value of prevention and enhancement of optimum health.

National Accreditation and Credentialing

The origins of the first core areas of counselor education can be traced back to the U.S. Office of Education (USOE), which published a series of eight reports on counselor preparation, six on course content and two on in-service education (Hoyt, 1974). These expectations are much revised and expanded in present standards but continue as a requirement for all counselor education. Although the USOE initiated the reports, it is notable that they were prepared by state counseling supervisors and university counselor educators who were no doubt among the key leaders of that time. These reports set the pattern for school counselor education and influenced the design of the master's degree in counselor education in general, similar to events reported earlier for rehabilitation counseling. The initiative for advancement of the profession was about to shift, however, from government to the professionals themselves. By the late 1950s, the stage was set for counselor educators, state supervisors, and practitioners to take the leadership for national preparation standards for school counselors.

The first effort to establish counselor preparation standards outside of government influence was by leaders of the Association for Counselor Education and Supervision (ACES) and the American School Counselor Association (ASCA). ACES adopted standards for the preparation of secondary school counselors in 1964, but they were not broadly accepted or used until the late 1970s. Master's degrees required one year of preparation, and there was great resistance to the vision of some leaders who advocated for two years of graduate study with an internship. ACES later developed and adopted doctoral preparation standards in 1978. Both sets of these early standards were subsequently revised to incorporate core requirements plus specialties into the newly formed CACREP in 1981. The foundation was set for defining what it meant to be prepared as a professional counselor.

Also notable about the development of the preparation standards is the context of the 1970s and 1980s. There were concurrent efforts by counseling leaders to establish our credibility with national accrediting agencies and university administrators as well as state legislators for the purposes of counselor licensure. Without national standards neither was possible; both initiatives required sustained and effective leadership often by a few individuals and groups totally dedicated to a vision that carried them forward year after year. Implementation of the standards to advance both accreditation and credentialing could not have occurred without such individuals.

The years before the establishment of CACREP, NBCC, and state licensing boards was a time when there were other alternatives to a clear, direct identity as a professional counselor. Many counselor educators who could do so sought state or national credentialing from allied fields such as marriage and family therapy and psychology. In some cases, it was a necessity since psychology laws defined everything a professional counselor did as the practice of psychology. For some, however, it was truly a change in professional identity. Some counselor educators identified with the credentials administered by other helping professions and embraced their ethics, organizations, and issues. This left many students to wonder what their professional identity should be upon graduation. For other professional counselors, it was a wake-up call to advocate for our "field" to become a profession (Sweeney & Sturdevant, 1974).

In Virginia as a result of a counselor being charged by the state psychology board to stop his practice, a court made a ruling that "the profession of personnel and guidance counseling is a separate profession (from psychology) and should be so recognized" (*Weldon v. Virginia State Board of Psychologist Examiners*; Seiler & Messina, 1979, p. 4). This assisted in getting the first state license for professional counselors passed in 1976. It would be another 30-plus years before every state provided such an opportunity for professional counselors. In the meantime, many professional counselors experienced and continue to experience difficulty regarding parity with other practitioners who in some cases were less qualified. The fact that this situation continues today underscores the continued need for effective professional leadership, and professional advocacy.

One case in which I was involved is particularly illustrative. Dr. Culbreath Cook was arrested and booked for a felony by the City of Cleveland prosecutor on behalf of the Ohio State Board of Psychology (*City of Cleveland, Ohio v. Cook*, 1975). His private practice stopped immediately. His neighbors and church members withdrew, unable to know what to think about an otherwise responsible citizen and friend. His charge was practicing psychology without a license. He did not claim to be a psychologist, although earlier he had made attempts to contact the board to learn of its implications for him, as the law had only recently been enacted in 1972.

APGA/ACA's newly formed Committee on Licensure decided to come to Cook's aid as an advocate on his behalf as he was a member of ACA. The fact that he was African American seemed particularly troubling since he was in every respect well educated and a competent practitioner providing needed services to the community. The possibility of racism being a factor made ACA's advocacy all the more important in his defense. After hearing the arguments, the judge decided that the prosecution had not presented a case warranting further deliberation. In short, the judge agreed with the defense that the Board of Psychology had overstepped its authority by trying to regulate another equally competent practitioner and dismissed the charges. Because the judge offered no opinion, however, professional counselors could take little comfort in such victories as Dr. Cook's. Likewise, Dr. Cook's reputation and practice had already been damaged.

As will be discussed in Chapters 5–9 on advocacy, counselors' consciousness to advocacy not just for professional counselors but all who are denied their "inalienable" rights is no less important today nor needed than in the past. For these and related reasons, the APGA's Governing Council adopted a position in favor of vigorously pursuing licensure in every state on behalf of professional counselors (APGA, 1974). By doing so, these leaders created the opportunity for future professional counselors to be advocates on behalf of those they seek to serve.

APGA leaders also realized by the early 1980s that state credentialing was going to take a long time even with concerted effort, especially since in the way of all legislation, credentials would be defined by the legislators. They saw a need for a profession-driven credential for professional counselors. As a consequence, NBCC was incorporated in 1982 independent of ACA in order to avoid Federal Trade Commission (FTC) antitrade scrutiny prevalent at that time. The NBCC has grown in the number of certified counselors (NCC), types of certifications, and outreach and advocacy efforts in this country and abroad (see www.NBCC.org).

There is still much that remains to be done (see CSI, Counselor Advocacy Leadership Themes, 2011). It is clear that historical, sociopolitical, and cultural events over the last century have greatly influenced counseling as we know it today. In addition, through the evolution of accreditation agencies, legal guidelines, and professional organizations, we have come to a more cohesive, professional, and recognizable identity as counselors. The foundation of our professional identity begins in counselor education and preprofessional preparation. Therefore, it is vital to the future of professional counseling that the counselor educators and supervisors who are mentoring the new leaders and advocates are themselves well grounded in the philosophy, history, and aspirations of the profession.

## MOVING FORWARD: COUNSELOR EDUCATION AND COUNSELOR EDUCATORS

The preponderance of counselor educators includes graduates of colleges of education and departments of counselor education. Unlike other professions, however, until recently national preparation standards permitted counselor education programs to employ members of other professions to prepare their students. Beginning in 2013, CACREP requires that new counseling faculty hired after this time will be expected to have their highest graduate degree in counseling/counselor education. This is an affirmation that specific preparation to teach, supervise, and conduct research in counselor education is essential. An unintended consequence of this practice of employing those from other professions to teach in counselor education has been that entire programs have been made up of faculty from other professions either full time or as adjunct faculty. In some cases, doctoral programs in psychology are housed in the same department as master's programs in counseling. Not infrequently the counseling programs help to support the doctoral program. Although these counseling programs help support the doctoral programs, these doctoral programs are discouraged from hiring counselor educators due to their accreditation standards.

Historically, holding membership in both APGA/ACA and the American Psychological Association (APA) was not uncommon, as many counselor educators were affiliated with APA Division 17, Counseling Psychology and state psychology associations. Nevertheless, many counselor educators were completely unaware in 1967 that APA adopted an initiative to aggressively establish state legislation that would limit the practice of counseling to doctoral trained psychologists or those under their supervision (Sweeney & Sturdevant, 1974). By the early 1970s, these efforts were being established in both legislative and administrative actions within the states. A fundamental difference between psychology and counseling emerged in both legislation and member organizations.

The tension between psychologists and professional counselors became even more pointed when employment opportunities became an issue. Psychologists lobbied state agencies to require only trained psychologists be hired to provide mental health services, and they worked to establish requirements for other mental health service providers to work under the supervision of psychologists. They lobbied then, as many state psychologists' organizations still do, to limit professional counselors' scope of practice and ability to hold administrative and supervisory positions. Of course, in the business of legislative lobbying today, professional counselors find social workers, marriage and family therapists, and psychologists as both allies and adversaries, depending upon the issues.

What sometimes confuses those new to our profession is the apparent overlap among various mental health professions in terms of knowledge base and skills, yet marketplace conflict is clearly a reality. What often defines our uniqueness begins with the philosophy of practice discussed earlier. An example of seeming overlap yet significant differences in practice may be found when looking at what has come to be defined as positive psychology compared to counseling for wellness. Positive psychology has come into prominence during the past decade and is focused on emotional (psychological) health. Wellness in counseling theory and research can be traced to the late 1980s (Sweeney & Witmer, 1991), and in both theory and practice comprises a holistic approach to promoting optimum development that incorporates all aspects of body, mind, and spirit. Counseling practitioners will no doubt find value in both the positive psychology and wellness literature when seeking ways to promote greater well-being among their clients. In practice, however, I have found wellness perspectives more useful, as they are practice based. Professional articles in counseling journals place a priority on implications for practice, while others also suggest future research that is clearly needed (Barrio Minton, Fernando, & Ray, 2008).

Research on counseling for wellness is still in the growth phase with opportunities for both academic and practitioner-based studies emerging regularly. Professional counselors have a leadership opportunity to identify populations, settings, and best practices interventions to study as an ongoing research agenda. Insurance companies, business, and governments are now advertising and promoting healthier lifestyles (Secretary of Health and Human Services, 2010). Those leaders with a best practices and outcomes wellness research agenda should find more favorable opportunities for funding from both government and nongovernment sources.

## Counseling Leadership and Advocacy Needs and Resources for the Future

In virtually every counseling setting and specialty there is a story of leadership and advocacy. Some of these will be shared in subsequent chapters. In every practice there is a need for individuals with vision, commitment, and passion to meet the counseling needs of special populations. It is beyond the scope of this chapter to attempt a summary of the significant developments in specialties, but for those who have the interest, they are worth pursuing (see ACA, 2009; Myers, 1995).

There is a clear mandate in the CACREP (2009) standards for counselor education programs to prepare graduates for leadership roles in supervision, teaching, research, counseling, and leadership and advocacy (particularly Doctoral Standards, Sections II and IV). When interviewing a select group of doctoral program counselor educators about their views on the need for a book such as this one, it became clear that they perceive leadership and advocacy competencies as essential to all professional counselors, not just those in doctoral programs. Perhaps no organization has done more to contribute to these expectations through counselor education than CSI, the counseling honor society, with its 270-plus chapters spanning more than 25 years of mentoring leaders at both the master's and doctoral level ($N = 72,000$). These chapters involve both experienced and new members to the profession, particularly in roles as officers, committee chairs, and participants in a variety of leadership roles under the mentorship of over 500 CSI faculty members. Through its funds to chapters each year, CSI supports co-curricular activities of its chapters in counselor education that accreditation site teams have cited for helping to meet CACREP standards in both leadership and advocacy. In addition, the society supports leader fellowships and internships for members each year. Other counseling organizations, notably ACA and ACES, also provide leadership training for emerging leaders; however, CSI is the primary organization promoting leadership among students in counseling (Luke & Goodrich, 2010).

## CONCLUSION

Counseling has attained the status of a profession through sustained and effective leadership resulting in national preparation standards, accreditation of preparation programs, credentialing of practitioners through both state legislative means and national certification, ethical standards for its membership, advancement of its knowledge base through research and scholarly publications, professional development of its membership through continuing education and competency standards related to settings, clientele, diversity, and cultural plurality, and through its organizations that structurally support these endeavors. We also are experiencing a sense of urgency for advocacy of not only the profession but also those we seek to serve. Advocacy is a function of effective leadership and will be explored in more depth in Section II of this book.

Competency standards and resources designed to ensure professional counselors are advocates for those less or never served express the hope for a just society where human dignity and wellness are a reality for all. While much can be said about our progress as a profession, even more needs to be said about what remains to be done and the requirement for new leaders as we move into the future. This book speaks to both the history and the promise of counseling to promote a better future for all, notably through professional counselors' roles as leaders and advocates.

## ACTIVITIES

Where are the Jeffersons and Lincolns today? The answer, I am convinced, is that they are among us. Out there in the settings with which we are all familiar are the unawakened leaders, feeling no overpowering call to lead and hardly aware of the potential within. (Gardner, 1990, p. 181)

1. Volunteering works best if you do something with others and for others. It is also wise to start out small. After considering the reasons that you chose to become a counselor, list them related to reasons for service

(concern for those less advantaged) versus personal benefit (you like the work setting, kids, enjoy listening/helping). It is fine to have more items on one list versus another list. Of those you listed, which two seem most compelling for you to stay in counseling as a career? What is it about them that made you choose them? How might you use them to volunteer to become a leader of a project that could further others' interest in these ideas? Who might you talk with about your ideas (e.g., faculty advisor, friend, supervisor, CSI chapter officer)? Give it a chance and see what happens! (Doctoral Standards II C 1)

2. Identify and interview faculty members you know, school counselors, private practitioner counselors, etc., who are leaders at some level within their roles as counselors. Develop a short list of questions about how they emerged from graduate student to professional counselor to a leader. Approach one or more of them about investing 20–30 minutes talking with you about their career story. Hint: Just use a few open-ended questions. They will do the talking (office, coffee shop, skype, or telephone). (Doctoral Standards II C 1–3)

3. Imagine what it would be like today if you were entering an occupation that had no accepted standards for preparation, no state or national credentials, no ethical standards for practice, no foundation for serving a pluralistic and culturally rich and diverse population, and as a consequence, no defined areas of competence or scope of practice. What might that mean for career opportunities, career advancement, credibility with those you seek to serve, or freedom from arrest or cease and desist orders from state credentialing boards of an allied profession? What populations served by counselors today might not be getting the assistance that they deserve had some counselors not stepped forward to lead and advocate for professional counseling? (Doctoral Standards II C 1–4, 7)

## DISCUSSION QUESTIONS

1. As you reflect on the history of our profession, what themes stand out? What were the qualities of effective leaders?
2. How are leaders in counseling different from leaders in other professions?
3. What do you see as the major issues facing the counseling profession today? What kinds of leaders are needed to help address these challenges?

# 2

# Foundations of Leadership
## Theory, Philosophy, and Research

Todd F. Lewis

## INTRODUCTION

The study and analysis of leadership by academic researchers spans many decades and has produced a number of theoretical propositions for what leadership is, what qualities make effective and ineffective leaders, and how contextual factors play a role in leadership success or failure. Many of these theories emanated from fields outside the counseling profession, such as organizational behavior; however, they are applicable across many disciplines, including nursing, engineering, military, academia, and as I will demonstrate, counseling and counselor education.

The application of leadership theory to the profession of counseling has received scant attention in the literature. Paradise, Ceballos, and Hall (2010) were blunter in their assessment: "These issues [leadership and leader behavior] have been neglected throughout the entire short history of counseling" (p. 46). This is unfortunate considering that professional counselors and counselor educators are, by their very nature, leaders. They are not leaders in the sense that a corporate CEO is a leader, but leaders of clients, students, members, colleagues, associations, honor societies, and perhaps most importantly, leaders of service to others. To this end, leadership theory can help emerging leaders in counseling broaden their leadership goals and visions and provide a foundation of knowledge from which to develop their own leadership styles. At the same time, the prevailing theories of leadership can benefit from what the counseling profession has to offer; that is, professional counselors and counselor educators have a unique perspective based on knowledge of human motivation and behavior that can inform and enhance leadership. Paradise et al. (2010) supported this contention, stating that counselors, because of their unique training and skills, can be effective leaders across a wide variety of settings.

In the 2009 Council for Accreditation of Counseling and Related Educational Programs (CACREP) standards, leadership and advocacy are expected learning outcomes of counselor training programs. Specifically, counselor education doctoral students are expected to understand leadership theory and demonstrate leadership skills in professional counseling organizations or counseling programs. They are expected to understand advocacy models and demonstrate leadership for important social justice and political issues that impact professional counselors and those whom they serve. School counselors are expected to know the qualities, principles, skills, and styles of effective leadership so they can enhance the student learning environment in our schools. They are expected to design, implement, manage, and evaluate a comprehensive school counseling program, a task that requires considerable knowledge and skills in leadership and advocacy. As Paradise et al. (2010) pointed out, professional counseling's increased focus on social justice, advocacy, equity issues of race, culture, gender, and religion, and disaster relief services demands that leadership and leader behavior are not only needed but expected in these areas.

What makes someone a leader? Is it inborn traits such as intelligence? Drive and motivation? Luck? A certain leadership style? A certain leadership style that matches a particular context? And, how does professional counseling fit or not fit with prevailing leadership theory? What are the unique contributions that professional counselors can make to leadership? In the next several pages, I hope to address these questions. This chapter is about foundations of leadership from the broad perspective of leadership theory. I first invite the reader to journey with me through the various theories of leadership that began to emerge in the early 1900s through more contemporary models of today. Because many of these theories do not emanate from the counseling profession, I attempt, where possible, to provide examples of how a concept might apply in a counseling setting. Following this journey through leadership theory, I discuss perspectives in leadership from professional counseling; the reader will find that counseling's developing philosophy of leadership is consistent with many theoretical leadership concepts that have been found to play a large role in effective, successful leadership. I also give due attention to the unique ways that professional counseling expands leadership theory and how professional counselors are natural leaders. Special focus will be on Chi Sigma Iota International and its strong commitment to the service leadership model. I conclude the chapter with some ideas for emerging leaders in professional counseling and how they can use theory to expand the pursuit of leadership excellence.

## What Is Leadership?

The attention given to general leadership across several disciplines is staggering. As Paradise et al. (2010) pointed out, scholars, theologians, philosophers, and others have been fixated on leadership and leaders for millennia. Anyone perusing through the self-help or business sections of any large bookstore would be amazed at the range of "how to" leadership books. Gladding (2007, as cited in Paradise et al., 2010) stated that leadership is the most researched topic in the world. Yet, with all this research and theory behind leadership, its application is still not fully comprehended (Paradise et al.).

According to Robbins and Judge (2010), leadership is about dealing with change. By way of establishing a vision for the future, leaders provide direction for themselves and their followers. Leaders also bring others together by communicating their vision and inspiring others to move through obstacles on their way to accomplishing important organizational or professional goals. Robbins and Judge defined leadership as "the ability to influence a group toward the achievement of a vision or set of goals" (p. 376). This influence can either be formal or informal and direct or indirect; either way, the ability to influence is the key behavioral element according to this definition (we'll see how this definition can expand later in the chapter). The bottom line is that the counseling profession, as in any profession or organization, needs strong leaders for optimal effectiveness. Leaders are needed to shake things up, propose new and innovative ideas, create visions, and serve students, clients, and the public with counselors' many talents and skills. Let's take a look at some of the more popular theories of leadership that have emerged across the past several decades.

## THEORIES OF LEADERSHIP

### Trait Theories

A survey of human history is replete with strong leaders such as Socrates, Napoleon, Churchill, FDR, Mother Teresa, and John F. Kennedy, to name a few. What made these individuals and so many others great leaders? Some would say that each had strong traits that allowed him or her to lead with confidence and purpose. Indeed, the search for identifying personality, intellectual, and physical attributes or traits in leaders dates back to when leadership research began (Robbins & Judge, 2010). However, research efforts into identifying key traits in leadership have been disappointing, as traits found in effective leadership were many and varied (Zaccaro, Foti, & Kenny, 1991). What was missing was a taxonomic structure for organizing and classifying traits. One such structure is the Big Five personality framework (i.e., OCEAN, standing for openness, conscientiousness, extroversion, agreeableness, and neuroticism; Judge, Bono, Ilies, & Gerhardt, 2002). Many of the personality traits found to be associated with effective leadership fit under one of the Big Five personality components (Robbins & Judge).

Connecting key leadership traits with the Big Five personality constructs allows trait theory greater theoretical grounding and thus greater relevance to leadership endeavors. In general, researchers have found extraversion to be the most important trait in leader emergence, but not necessarily leader effectiveness

(Judge et al., 2002). Conscientiousness and openness to experience also have shown to be connected to effective leadership (Robbins & Judge, 2010). According to Robbins and Judge, leaders who like being around others (extroversion), who are disciplined and able to keep to their word (conscientious), and who are creative and flexible (open) appear to have advantages when leading others.

Another important trait found in effective leaders is emotional intelligence (George, 2000). A cornerstone of emotional intelligence is empathy. Empathetic leaders are adept at sensing others' concerns, listening to what others say, and correctly identifying the reactions of others (Robbins & Judge, 2010). In essence, leaders with high emotional intelligence care about their members or followers. Although the link between leadership and emotional intelligence has not been well established from an empirical perspective, expert opinion, anecdotal evidence, and case studies appear to support the notion that it is essential for good leadership (Zeidner, Matthews, & Roberts, 2004).

Summarizing the current status of trait theories of leadership, Robbins and Judge (2010) stated that (1) traits can and do predict leadership, especially by couching leadership traits under the umbrella of the Big Five personality construct, and (2) trait theories say more about who will emerge as a leader rather than predicting leader effectiveness.

Behavioral Theories

One of the most famous series of scientific investigations on leadership was the Ohio State studies conducted in the 1940s. These studies were in partial response to the disappointments resulting from then prevalent trait theories (the trait–Big Five connection had not been made until the early 1990s, and until then, trait theory was seen largely as failing). In essence, the Ohio State researchers were interested in what behaviors effective leaders engaged in, and could these behaviors be taught to others? From a list of more than a thousand dimensions of behavior, two emerged that accounted for the vast majority of leader behaviors as described by employees: initiating structure and consideration (Robbins & Judge, 2010).

*Initiating Structure*

Initiating structure includes behaviors such as organizing and assigning tasks, setting goals and overseeing their completion, and holding high standards of performance. Tasks associated with initiating structure include those that are traditionally associated with leadership behavior, such as organizing, defining, and directing the work activities of others (Schultz & Schultz, 2010). Leaders high in initiating structure tend to worry more about the bottom-line results rather than getting along with others.

*Consideration*

Consideration includes an awareness and sensitivity to the feelings and emotions of employees, colleagues, students, and clients (Schultz & Schultz, 2010). Leaders high on consideration place relationships at a premium; they demonstrate caring, attention, and empathy toward others' feelings about work, goals, and tasks. In consideration, a person's employment relationships are described by mutual trust, respect for others' ideas, and consideration for feelings (Robbins & Judge, 2010). Followers describe leaders high in consideration as approachable, treating all as equals, and expressing appreciation and support (Robbins & Judge).

Researchers have demonstrated that consideration leads to greater trustworthiness among employees, who in turn tend to work harder for the organization. Korsgaard, Brodt, and Whitener (2002) found that employees of a credit union tended to trust managers who communicated openly and showed greater concern about employee welfare. In other words, consideration type behaviors, at least in this sample, led to greater trust between manager and employee. Employees who held greater trust for their managers also tended to engage in activities beyond their job description compared to employees who held a lesser amount of trust in their managers (Korsgaard et al.).

Elements of consideration have been used to describe counseling leaders. West, Osborn, and Bubenzer (2003a) suggested that to be effective, the vision conveyed by counselor leaders to "students, colleagues, university administrators, legislators, and other constituents needs to be a product of 'riding the circuit,' reflecting the leader's familiarity with and appreciation of the needs and hopes of the persons he or she serves" (p. 10). Clearly, West et al.'s point is that leaders in the counseling profession need to have high consideration to be effective and suggest that counselors indeed prefer this style of leadership.

Taken together, initiating structure and consideration provide a valid description of leadership, although early studies on the two dimensions were equivocal about the two-factor conceptualization of leadership (Robbins & Judge, 2010). However, in a large meta-analysis, Judge, Piccolo, and Ilies (2004) found that initiating structure correlated positively with leader satisfaction and group or organizational performance. Consideration had stronger correlations with follower satisfaction, motivation, and leader effectiveness. Initiating structure had a slightly higher correlation with leader job performance and group organization performance. These findings suggest that both initiating structure and consideration can lead to positive outcomes for both leaders and their groups. It may be that both are needed for effective leadership, although there is limited research to support this hypothesis. Sometimes, however, the situation may dictate what style of leadership one adopts. That is, leader behavior is contingent upon the situational context.

Contingency Theories

A review of the leadership literature across many disciplines reveals that predicting leadership success is complex; a few traits and behaviors help, but often are insufficient to account for the full range of leader impact and success. Major corporations hire CEOs to come in and pull organizations out of the doldrums. They are hailed as saviors of the organization during these difficult times, but when times are good their style is no longer useful. The inconsistent findings about what styles and traits lead to effective leadership led researchers to consider contextual or situational factors (Robbins & Judge, 2010). Contingency theories of leadership grew from this gap in the literature and stated that for condition *a*, style *x* would be most appropriate, but for condition *b*, style *y* would be the best fit. Condition *c* was then best addressed by style *z* (Robbins & Judge). This line of reasoning led to several contingency theories, two of which will be discussed here: Fiedler's contingency model and the path-goal theory.

### Fiedler's Contingency Model

The Fiedler contingency model, proposed by Fred Fiedler (1967), holds that correspondence between leader style and the amount of situational control a leader has plays a large role in the effectiveness of a leader. Fiedler posited two leadership styles, task oriented and relationship oriented (similar to initiating structure and consideration proposed in the Ohio State studies), and assumed that they were fixed styles. Thus, if a situation calls for a relationship style focus and the leader is task oriented, either the situation must change or a new leader who matches the situation must be considered (Robbins & Judge, 2010).

Situational control plays a large role in Fielder's model. Factors that impact situational control include leader-member relations, the amount of structure that a task requires, and how much power the leader holds (i.e., power over salary, promotion, rewards, and punishments). According to Robbins and Judge (2010), Fiedler proposed three control situations: low, moderate, and high. For example, a situation in which a leader has high control would be an American Counseling Association (ACA) division president who has good relationships with her members, engages in structured tasks and activities, and holds sufficient power over the direction of the organization. The opposite also can serve as an example; An ACA committee leader who has poor relations with the members, who is charged with activities that are highly unstructured, and who holds no power over the members would be predicted to have low situational control and poor leadership effectiveness (Robbins & Judge, 2010).

According to Fiedler's model, there are two ways to improve leader effectiveness: change leaders to match the situation (i.e., secure a new leader; remember that according to Fiedler, leadership style does not change) or change the situation to match the leader (Robbins & Judge, 2010). The ACA committee leader in the previous paragraph may wish to enhance his leadership effectiveness by increasing situational control. For example, he might attend leadership training workshops, explore how he can better structure committee activities and meetings, brainstorm with other ACA leaders and organizations, and request more control and power over the committee and organization. Although all of these might not be possible, even changing one or two situational variables can increase leader effectiveness.

*Path-Goal Theory*

Path-goal theory proposes that effective leaders help followers reach organizational goals by illuminating the paths they should follow to reach goals and providing them with the energy, resources, and other means to do so (Schultz & Schultz, 2010). Leaders who adopt a path-goal strategy may outline the general direction of the agency, committee, or organization and then make sure the members, staff, or colleagues have the resources in place to make it happen. Path-goal theory predicts that followers will report higher satisfaction, motivation, and performance if they receive sufficient direction from their leader, accomplish organizational goals, and are rewarded for their achievements (Schultz & Schultz).

According to House (1996), leaders can adopt four styles to facilitate employee goal accomplishment:

1. *Directive leadership.* Provides psychological structure for employees; employees are told what to do, how to do it, and clarifications are provided if needed.
2. *Supportive leadership.* The leader displays concern for welfare of employees and creates a supportive, noncontentious work environment; the leader shows concern for feelings and respect for ideas; followers feel supported.
3. *Participative leadership.* The leader encourages employee input on making decisions, asking employees about their thoughts, opinions, and suggestions for improving organizational functioning and tasks; employees have opportunity to participate in decisions and offer insights into the direction of the organization.
4. *Achievement-oriented leadership.* The leader encourages excellent performance and creates challenging goals for employees in an effort to "set a tone" of high job performance.

Unlike Fiedler's contingency model, path-goal theory allows for flexibility in leadership style depending on the situation and employee characteristics (Schultz & Schultz, 2010). In other words, leaders must choose which style is best suited given the situation at hand. For example, a department chair of a counselor education program would probably perform best using a combination of supportive and participative leadership styles, as the directive style is likely to be perceived as redundant for colleagues who have much experience and high ability, such as departmental faculty (House, 1971). However, path-goal theory allows for flexibility in style, as a department chair may need to be more directive for pretenured faculty who perhaps need more specific direction at the start of their careers.

### Leader-Member Exchange (LMX) Theory

A criticism of the aforementioned leadership theories is that there is too much focus on average leadership styles and situations that most likely lead to organizational success. A key variable that is missing in these theories is individual differences among followers and how these differences shape leader abilities and success (Schultz & Schultz, 2010). That is, each leader-member relationship (dyad) must be considered separately because leaders interact with followers differently (Schultz & Schultz) based on motivation, personality, commitment to goals, and so forth.

The leader-member exchange theory holds that improving the quality of the leader-member relationship can improve employee performance and satisfaction. Research has shown that LMX predicts individual empowerment (Chen, Kirkman, Kanfer, Allen, & Rosen, 2007). It seems that the higher the LMX, the more likely employees will seek out negative (or constructive) feedback (Chen, Lam, & Zhong, 2007), communicate with their leaders more frequently and in turn receive higher performance ratings (Kacmar, Witt, Ziunuska, & Gully, 2003), and engage in "pay back" behavior in which employees go beyond the typical duties of the organization to benefit the leader and other members (Ilies, Nahrgang, & Morgeson, 2007). Overall, the quality of relationships between leaders and members appears to have a significant impact on organizational and employee performance.

Leader-member relationships, of course, do not develop in a vacuum. There are several contextual and organizational factors that can impact the quality of the LMX (Schultz & Schultz, 2010). For example, a concept called *perceived organizational support* (POS) was found to impact the quality of LMX (Erdogan & Enders, 2007). A leader who feels supported by his organization, academic unit, dean, or director of a counseling agency will in turn feel and express more support for his followers, thus positively impacting the LMX. Personality, motivation levels, and personal histories also can impact the quality of the LMX. Based on this theory, professional counselors and counselor educators who are leaders would do well to nurture all relationships with their members and attend to those that are not as strong. Doing so would appear to impact the productivity level and leadership effectiveness, as predicted by LMX theory.

### Charismatic, Transactional, and Transformational Leadership

Two contemporary theories of leadership include charismatic leadership and transformational leadership. A common element in both of these theories is *inspiration*. Charismatic and transformational leaders inspire their followers through words, actions, and deeds. Leaders who are charismatic and transformational generally have good relations with their employees and serve to inspire them to accomplish their goals and reach their full potential.

Indeed, history is replete with charismatic leaders, such as John Adams, Abraham Lincoln, and Martin Luther King Jr., and many have emerged in the current business arena, such as Richard Branson (chair of Virgin Group), Steve Jobs (co-founder of Apple), and Carol Bartz (CEO of Yahoo). Counselor education has a strong history of charismatic leadership from the likes of Courtland C. Lee, Jane E. Myers, Thomas J. Sweeney, and Samuel T. Gladding (West et al., 2003b). What is it that charismatic leaders have in common? According to Conger and Kanungo (1998), charismatic leaders share the following characteristics:

1. *Vision and communication to others.* Not only do charismatic leaders create a vision that will improve the status quo, but they find ways to articulate this vision to followers in a clear and understandable way.
2. *Healthy risk taking.* Charismatic leaders are willing to take risks to see their vision to fruition, including personal risks, financial risks, and self-sacrifice.
3. *Responsive and sensitive to follower needs.* Charismatic leaders are perceptive to the needs, emotions, and wants of others. They know others' abilities and are responsive in how to best maximize them.
4. *Outside-the-box thinking and behavior.* Charismatic leaders thrive on novelty. Followers will most likely view decisions and ideas as fresh and running against how things have always been.

A perusal of these four key characteristics as outlined by Conger and Kanungo (1998) reveals that charismatic leaders demonstrate many of the positive elements from the leadership theories discussed thus far. For example, sensitivity to follower needs (number 3) appears to correspond to leadership that is high in consideration, supportive, and engenders a strong LMX. The vision and personal risk components are the unique aspects that charismatic leadership offers.

Charismatic leaders demonstrate hard work and certain behaviors that are professionally attractive to others. Indeed, charismatic leadership theory suggests that some followers attribute extraordinary leadership skills and abilities when they observe certain leader behaviors. In the counseling profession, the extraordinary work of Dr. Tom Sweeney, founding president and executive director of Chi Sigma Iota Counseling Academic and Professional Honor Society International (CSI), is an example of charismatic leadership. Dr. Sweeney first had a vision of an honor society dedicated solely to the profession of counseling. Under Dr. Sweeney's hard work and perseverance, CSI has grown to over 72,000 members worldwide and is an authority in leadership training among counselors in training, professional counselors, and counselor educators.

Researchers have suggested that charismatic leaders influence followers through a series of processes that take into account the leader behaviors, the role of followers' values, and conditions that favor the emergence of charismatic qualities (Shamir, House, & Arthur, 1993). Robbins and Judge (2010) articulated Shamir et al.'s theory into a four-step process for how charismatic leaders influence and motivate followers.

1. The first step is creating a vision. A vision can be thought of as a long-term strategy and hope for the future of the company, organization, or academic unit that situates it in a better position than what is currently the case. In the example of Dr. Sweeney above, his vision for a counseling honorary was designed to serve counseling professionals and as an avenue to help them (students, faculty, and clinicians) acquire sound leadership skills. Chi Sigma Iota also has established a strong awards program to honor outstanding leaders in the profession of counseling.

2. The second step is a vision statement, which is a formal articulation of the organizations' mission (Robbins & Judge, 2010). CSI's mission statement is prominently displayed on its website (www.csi-net.org), clearly conveying Sweeney's vision for CSI.

3. The third step in the process of how charismatic leaders influence their followers is through words and actions (Shamir et al., 1993). The leader conveys new values and goals based on the new vision and vision statement and then acts in a way consistent with these goals and values. Charismatic leaders set a tone of cooperation and mutual support. Followers might observe their leader in "the trenches" with them, helping to solve problems and implement the organization's vision. Dr. Sweeney has lived the purpose and mission of CSI through clinical work, teaching, research, and service to the counseling profession.

4. The fourth step in the process is that charismatic leaders attempt to mobilize followers by using emotion, energy, and conviction (Robbins & Judge). Dr. Sweeney's passion for counseling and leader development is reflected in his numerous professional accomplishments. The importance and conviction he has placed on promoting excellence in counseling through CSI has been a cornerstone for leader development in the field.

Charismatic leaders may even engage in unconventional behaviors to drive home the importance of the new vision. Bill Parcells, former charismatic leader and football coach of the New York Giants, New England Patriots, New York Jets, and Dallas Cowboys, was known to hang slices of cheese in mousetraps in the players' locker room when the team demonstrated some success. The message to the team was clear: Don't bite the cheese! In other words, don't take the bait: Parcells' point was that the players better not "take the bait" and get caught up in the media and fan hoopla about how they were great. If the players got caught up in this message and became overconfident (and thus bit the cheese), the trap would spring, meaning that the players would lose focus and perhaps even games. Parcells' consistent vision for the teams he has coached was for players to remain humble and constantly work hard to improve. Hanging mousetraps with cheese in the locker room is certainly an unconventional way to get this message across!

In general, researchers have demonstrated positive correlations between charismatic leadership qualities (e.g., vision, communication) and self-set goals, self-efficacy, and performance (Kirkpatrick & Locke, 1996). Individuals working for charismatic leaders exert more effort, go above and beyond the call of duty, and ultimately experience greater happiness with their jobs (Robbins & Judge, 2010). However, situational components may impact the effectiveness of charisma. For example, the level of employment or activity may have an impact on how charisma influences followers. That is, senior-level employees are in a position to create a vision and implement it with some success. For lower- or mid-level leaders, it may be more of a challenge to utilize one's charisma, to lead others, or to create a vision that aligns with the goals of the organization (Robbins & Judge, 2010).

*Transactional and Transformational Leadership*

Many researchers have made the distinction between transactional leaders and transformational leaders. In general, transactional leaders behave in ways consistent with initiating structure (from the Ohio State studies), the directive leadership style from path-goal theory, and the task-oriented style from Fiedler's model. Transformational leaders, on the other hand, behave in ways consistent with consideration, the supportive and participative styles from the path-goal theory, and the relationship-oriented style from Fiedler's model. The differing characteristics of transactional and transformational leaders are presented in Table 2.1.

**Table 2.1**   Comparison and Contrast between Transactional and Transformational Leader Characteristics

| Transactional Leader | Transformational Leader |
|---|---|
| *Contingent reward*: Contracts with employees to receive rewards for good effort; recognizes accomplishments. | *Idealized influence*: Provides vision and creates vision statement; instills pride in organization; gains respect and trust from followers. |
| *Management by exception (active)*: On the lookout for any deviations from the established rules or guidelines; calls employees out; takes corrective action. | *Inspirational motivation*: Sets and articulates high expectations; expresses key organizational objectives in easy-to-understand manner; helps subordinates focus their efforts. |
| *Management by exception (passive)*: If standards for performance are not met, then intervention takes place. | *Intellectual stimulation*: Promotes and encourages intelligent discourse; places premium on rational thought; solves problems carefully. |
| *Laissez-faire*: Gives up taking responsibilities; avoids making tough decisions; overdelegates to subordinates. | *Individualized consideration*: Provides personalized attention to employees; treats followers equally and with respect; coaches/advises. |

*Source:* Adapted from B. M. Bass (1990), as cited in Robbins, S. P., and Judge, T. A., *Organizational Behavior*, 14th ed., Prentice Hall, Upper Saddle River, NJ, 2010.

It is important to note that leaders do not have to be exclusively transactional or transformational in their leadership approach. Robbins and Judge (2010) suggested that transformational leadership builds on transactional leadership. That is, transformational leadership can help take an organization or department beyond required tasks, roles, and goals. If one is a good transactional leader, but is limited in transformational abilities, then the leader will most likely have modest success. The ideal leader, according to Robbins and Judge (2010), is one who is transactional and transformational.

## LEADERSHIP IN COUNSELING

The counseling literature appears to offer little discussion of leadership in the field (West et al., 2003a). However, the various leadership theories surveyed above, although from diverse professions, provide a foundation from which to explore the development and growth of leadership in counseling. Many of the concepts from these theories have considerable application to counseling. For example, take consideration as outlined from the Ohio State studies several decades ago. Consideration has been found to be an effective and important component of leadership across many disciplines. It entails getting along with others, holding concern about others' needs, and respecting follower thoughts, ideas, and feelings. Professional counselors and counselor educators are by their very nature considerate individuals, focusing on relationships, respecting emotions, and treating individuals fairly and equally. Indeed, Kelly (1995), in a survey of 479 counselors, reported that concern for the welfare of others was rated the highest value among ACA members. Thus, a predominant value system among professional counselors includes care and concern for the interpersonal and intrapersonal functioning of those they serve and work with on a day-to-day basis. Counseling students often enter the profession because of an interest in others and a strong desire to lend a helping hand (West et al., 2003a). These findings suggest that professional counselors possess a critical foundation for effective leadership: consideration.

Another example is LMX theory. In LMX theory, good relationships equate to greater productivity, enhanced motivation, and greater employee satisfaction. Professional counselors and counselor educators are trained in the art and science of building good relationships. They are taught skills to help others communicate better, appreciate the work and effort of others, and teach others how to show respect. The training in essential helping skills solidifies one's ability to forge strong relationships. As predicted by LMX theory, professional counselors and counselor educators are effective leaders because of their ability to improve relationships.

The transformational leadership style is a consistent theme that runs through the literature on leadership and professional counseling (e.g., West et al., 2003a). As noted, transformational leaders broaden and elevate the interests of followers, generate awareness and adherence to the mission and purposes of the group or organization, and motivate followers to go beyond self-interests for the benefit of the group (Yammarino & Bass, 1990). Along with motivating followers, transformational leaders also have been found to recognize differences and honor unique strengths among followers (Yammarino & Bass). Preliminary research in counseling has confirmed that the transformational style is prominent, while no other "pure" leadership styles, such as transactional or passive, were found (Lewis & Wester, 2004).

## A Leadership Model for Professional Counselors

West et al. (2003a) conceptualized leadership in professional counseling as consisting of a set of behaviors and attitudes that can be learned. In their model of leadership, they outline three dimensions, context, vision, and action, which serve as the foundation for leadership development and growth in professional counseling. Let's explore these dimensions below.

### Context

West et al. (2003a) argued that leadership begins with an appreciation of professional context, both present and historical. Appreciation of context ensures that leaders remember and show respect for the hard work and sacrifices others made to make counseling the profession it is today. Indeed, the Chi Sigma Iota Principles and Practices of Leadership Excellence (CSI, 2009) stated that leaders in the counseling profession should know and value the pioneers, advocates, and contributors that shaped the profession and allowed for professional counseling practice to continue (e.g., pioneering counselor licensure laws). Context also means holding a solid understanding of the current issues that face the counseling profession today, something West et al. called peripheral vision. For example, professional identity, professional advocacy and recognition, and enhancing/promoting multicultural competence are all current issues that counseling leaders must understand and embrace to be effective. West et al. further proposed their belief that leaders need to constantly be in touch with whom they serve, demonstrate an ability to relate well with others, and engage in dialogue about goals and work. Doing so ensures leaders stay current with what is on the minds of their followers. In other words, West et al. suggest that counseling leaders need to be high in consideration.

### Vision

West et al.'s next dimension of leadership for counselors, vision, appears remarkably similar to the transformational style. The authors remarked,

> We see leadership as an action, or actions, taken by a person in a defined context at a particular moment of time to stir imagination in ways that move people to create or realize a vision. But, leadership is not a solitary act. Rather it is a part of

an ongoing conversation among people that enables people to establish and move toward their goals. (p. 12)

Effective counseling leaders inspire others by communicating a vision in ways that engender creativity and innovation and by acting in collaboration with others to accomplish goals.

*Action*

The third dimension of West et al.'s counseling leadership model is action. The authors call for reflexivity when carrying out actions based on a grand vision. The reflective process, familiar to many counselors from clinical work, allows for one to evaluate if an action is preferred or if another action would be better. It is a necessary skill when leaders are thinking about how to communicate and articulate their vision to others (West et al.). Many times, a vision might be a hint of an idea but not well fleshed out. A reflective process invites others into the conversation; through this dialogue, a leader's vision becomes clearer and more intelligible.

West et al.'s model of counseling leadership can serve as a foundation from which current and emerging leaders can draw inspiration. The authors pointed out that counseling professionals hold unique talents, abilities, and skills that define effective leadership. These abilities manifest as high consideration, the theoretical concept that appears to bind the three dimensions, context, vision, and action, together.

## Service: The "Missing Component" in Leadership Theory and Research

A survey of leadership theories offers many perspectives on what constitutes effective and ineffective leadership. A consistent theme throughout these theories is the idea that caring and concern for others and forming good relationships engender greater productivity, satisfaction, and performance. Professional counselors would seem to be natural leaders because they value helping others and interpersonal growth. Leadership can manifest as helping a family communicate better, being an ACA division president, or advocating for legislation to provide greater access to counselors. Regardless of the leadership venue, the foundation for many professional counselors is a desire to help and to fulfill their value of benevolence.

### Chi Sigma Iota—A Model of Service Leadership

What is missing across theories of leadership is an emphasis on *service*. CSI promotes leadership development among counseling professionals and has built a philosophy of leadership based on service (Herr, 2010). In fact, the first principle of CSI's 10 Principles and Practices of Leadership Excellence is "service to others, the profession, and the associations are the preeminent reasons for involvement in leadership positions." Chi Sigma Iota stipulates that to realize this form of leadership, one must accept leadership positions primarily for the purpose of service rather than personal gain or reward. Chi Sigma Iota's incorporation of a service component of leadership is critically important for the counseling profession because it is aligned with the value of wanting to make the world a better place. Servant leadership is inherent in CSI's many successes (Herr, 2010) and is one way professional counseling can *build upon existing leadership theories.*

Chi Sigma Iota's commitment to service leadership stems from the work of Greenleaf (1970a, b). "Servant as Leader" was an essay that Greenleaf published in 1970. According to Greenleaf, the servant leader is a servant first; that is, one begins with a natural motivation to assist others. Greenleaf contrasts a leader who wants to serve first with a leader who wants to lead first. In the former instance, the leader is motivated by a desire to help others improve their lives, whereas the in the latter instance the leader is motivated by personal gain, such as power or acquiring wealth. The leader first and servant first are two extreme positions. Indeed, some individuals may have elements of both motivations within their leadership style. As Greenleaf suggested, there are an infinite variety of leadership styles within these two extreme positions.

Servant leadership encompasses a distinct philosophy based on reflection of how one's leadership impacts those served (Greenleaf, 1970a, b). Greenleaf argued that caring for others, the strong and the weak, is how a good society is built. Greenleaf's hope was to promote this caring vision through leadership in small and large institutions. Institutions and organizations that are built upon service to others expand possibilities for creativity, innovation, and growth (both personal and institutional). Chi Sigma Iota has embraced and promoted the "servant as leader" philosophy. As Herr (2010) noted, CSI respects and values scholarship and clinical practice, and is dedicated to finding avenues in which chapter members can serve the larger community.

A review of the 10 Principles and Practices of Leadership Excellence (see Appendix B) illuminates that service is at the heart of leadership in the counseling profession. In addition to service, counselors are encouraged to focus on respecting membership, recognizing others, empowering and encouraging others, and seeking feedback for self-reflection (CSI, 2009). These principles are consistent with high consideration and promoting healthy LMX, both of which engender inspiration, satisfaction, and growth among members.

Given the comprehensive mission that CSI carries out, effective leadership is an essential component to its continued success (Herr, 2010). Chi Sigma Iota provides opportunities for leadership at the chapter and national levels through positions on committees, task forces, and elective offices. Opportunities for leadership training are offered every year for promising master's and doctoral students. These experiences are invaluable for emerging leaders who want to serve their profession and society as a whole.

It is important to note that many other professional counseling associations offer emerging leader and mentorship programs. For example, the ACA provides a leadership handbook designed for all new ACA division presidents, president-elects, and region leaders. Two leadership training workshops are held every year in Alexandria, Virginia, near Washington, DC (ACA headquarters). As the past president of the International Association of Addictions and Offender Counselors (IAAOC), I participated in these training workshops and recall learning valuable information on leadership knowledge, skills, and tasks. An underlying philosophy behind these workshops was helping emerging leaders think about how best they can serve and advocate for their members, constituents, clients, and society.

### Mentoring as a Form of Leadership

Mentoring is an important component of leadership in professional counseling. The CSI Academy of Leaders for Excellence (2009) outlined in principle 8 that counseling leaders prioritize "mentoring, encouraging, and empowering." Mentoring, by definition, is when a senior member or employee sponsors and supports a less experienced member (Robbins & Judge, 2010). Of course, mentoring is not unique to professional counseling, yet it is taken seriously by counselor educators and supervisors. Successful mentors are good teachers, and they derive benefit by passing down what they have learned and leaving a legacy (Robbins & Judge). The connection between mentoring and leadership was articulated by Black and Magnuson (2005), who concluded in their study that counseling leaders not only focused on their leadership responsibilities and activities, but also emphasized empowering and mentoring as a form of leadership.

### Areas for Leadership Growth in Professional Counseling

A review of the literature on leadership theory and leadership in counseling leads one to conclude that professional counselors and counselor educators are high in consideration, transformational skills, and positive LMX. Counseling by nature is a relationship-enhancing endeavor, and so it is not surprising that counselor qualities would translate into effective leadership. In addition, CSI, a beacon of leadership in the counseling field, emphasizes leadership as service, and this service component has been a glaring omission in traditional leadership theory. Servant as leader is what professional counseling brings to the leadership table!

Despite being high on traits, abilities, and actions that generally lead to positive outcomes, Gibson, Dollarhide, and McCallum (2010) reminded professional counselors that in the process of becoming leaders, they must take into account several factors, including contingencies of the situation, cultural orientation, and individual differences, such as personality and general mental ability. All of these factors, and more, determine if someone will emerge as an effective leader. Many universal traits, beyond transformational qualities, are associated with effective leadership. Examples include drive, leadership motivation, honesty and integrity, self-confidence, cognitive ability, and knowledge of the profession (Kirkpatrick & Locke, 1991). As Robbins and Judge (2010) noted, perhaps the best leadership style is an integrative one, combining elements of transactional, transformation, and contingency theories. Gibson et al. suggested that an integrative approach to leadership is useful because it points to many possible factors that can contribute to effective leadership.

Indeed, one leadership approach or style may not fit every counseling organization (Herr, 2010). Although counseling leaders are most likely high in consideration and transformational qualities, these may not be the best leadership styles given the situation. The link between transformational leadership and positive effects on organization performance has not been established for larger, more complicated organizational structures (Ling, Simsek, Lubatkin, & Veiga, 2008). For example, assume that an ACA organization (e.g., committee, division) has become quite complex and leaders are required to report to an executive board. Leaders of such an organization may find greater success with a transactional style in which they set goals, articulate expectations to members, focus on efficiency of established routines, and clarify how rewards might be disseminated for outstanding effort. Transformational leadership has been found to be effective for smaller organizations when the leaders have easy access to members' work and can utilize their relationship skills effectively (Ling et al., 2008). Flexibility in leadership style also is important when working with individuals outside of the counseling profession, such as legislators, educational systems, and community leaders.

Herr (2010) noted that whereas CSI provides leadership development, proposes strategic objectives, and emphasizes professional excellence among professional counselors and their leaders, it has not reviewed the type of leadership that most effectively fits its purpose and goals as it moves forward. Given that the counseling profession appears to promote leadership, it is surprising that little research has been done to examine the actual leadership styles or characteristics associated with these styles. Furthermore, it is unclear if the theoretical concepts as outlined in this chapter, which have been studied immensely in other professions (e.g., business, military, and government sectors), can be generalized to counseling. Thus, it is imperative that professional counselors and counselor educators engage in research to maximize leadership behaviors in an effort to move the profession forward.

Paradise et al. (2010) stated that despite the fact that many counseling professionals earn leadership positions, little focus has been given to training for leadership. Thus, many questions remain regarding what aspects of leadership fit best the purpose and goals of professional counseling and what is the best way to train counselors as leaders. Paradise et al. proposed several questions that could generate interesting research:

To what degree do their unique skill-sets and attributes facilitate leadership success? How did these counselors become leaders? How do counseling/therapy skills—for example, problem solving, active listening, conflict resolution, anger management, managing a private practice, to name a few—transfer to leadership settings? How do they assist or mentor others in developing leadership skills? (p. 48)

Many counseling scholars have identified a need for greater focus on leadership and associated skills. Niles, Engels, and Lenz (2009) proposed the need for leadership in the development and advocacy of the career development field. They contended that vocational counseling could benefit from effective leadership and advocacy models used in other countries. Greater leadership also has been called for in clinical mental health counseling settings (Mellin, 2009) and school settings (Amatea & West-Olantunji, 2007), particularly leadership related to advocacy for troubled and disadvantaged children and social justice for students who live in poverty. Overall, the need for leadership and advocacy in professional counseling and across the many areas of counseling is greater than ever.

Finally, professional counselors wanting to expand their leadership experiences are encouraged to think broadly in terms of leadership style and use theory as a guide. There has been much written about leadership theory outside of the profession that can be of value as professional counseling forges ahead. It is my contention, however, that professional counseling also can be a model of effective leadership for other professions by continuing to refine theory and engaging in quality leadership research.

## CONCLUDING REMARKS

In this chapter, I reviewed several leadership theories. Several of the concepts, abilities, and activities are remarkably similar to the vision, goals, and training of professional counselors. Professional counselors are naturally high in many traits that correspond with effective leadership. Chi Sigma Iota has been an advocate for professional counseling since its inception in 1985 and is a strong proponent and advocate of service leadership. Professional counselors are encouraged to explore the many considerations when taking on a leadership role and to draw inspiration from professional organizations, like CSI, for how to best utilize their considerable talents in the role of leader.

## EXERCISES FOR APPLICATION

Exercise 1: Stand by your quote (associated with standard I.1 in CACREP doctoral standards and O.1 in School Counseling Standards).

**Objective:** To introduce leadership discussion and awareness and to help students, groups, or individuals tie concepts to leadership theory.

**How to use this exercise:** The counselor, instructor, or group facilitator introduces the topic of leadership and encourages each participant to make a personal statement about his or her understanding of what makes a good leader in counseling (for students) or in life (for clients).

**Activity description:** Have students or clients place thoughtful leadership quotes on the walls—leave plenty of room between the quotes and make certain the print is large. It works best if the quotes touch on different aspects of leadership; in short, have a variety of different quotes.

Ask the participants to leave their chairs and walk around the room reading each of the quotes (there is no particular order). Then have them stand by one quote that resonates well with their personal views on what makes a good leader. In a one-on-one counseling situation, you might have the client list as many thoughts about leadership as possible. When all participants have selected a quote (you can have more than one person by a quote), have each explain to the group why his or her chosen quote is important to him or her—share a leadership insight (again, for one-on-one counseling, the client could simply go through all of his or her quotes about leadership).

The facilitator can write key ideas or words on the white board. In a classroom setting, the instructor can help students connect key words/ ideas to concepts of leadership theory and what is applicable to counseling leadership. In one-on-one counseling, the counselor can help the client narrow down his or her list to one or two central thoughts about leadership and then explore how to develop these concepts in life.

Source: Adapted from Tom Siebold, *Stand by Your Quote*, 2010, retrieved from www. workshopexercises.com.

Exercise 2: Your Leadership Calendar (associated with standard I.1 in CACREP doctoral standards and O.1 in School Counseling Standards)

**Objective:** To extend learning of leadership concepts outside of the classroom or client setting.

**How to use this exercise:** This exercise is a good homework activity.

**Activity description:** Ask the participant(s) to mark 12 different days on their calendar spread out over 4 or 6 weeks. At the end of each marked day, participants should write down some leadership behavior (either positive or negative) that they exercised during that day. Each behavior should be followed by a reaction statement that answers two questions: "How did I feel about my action or behavior?" and "How is this action or behavior consistent with what I know about effective leadership?" The exercise can help students, clients, or group members reflect on their behavior and perhaps identify ways to improve their leadership behavior. Also, encouraging students to tie their actions to leadership theory can enhance their comprehension.

**Options:** On each marked day, the participant can send his or her personal leadership comments to a selected partner from the class or group. This is a good method for accountability and feedback.

Source: Adapted from Tom Siebold, *Stand by Your Quote,* 2010, retrieved from www.workshopexercises.com.

## DISCUSSION QUESTIONS

1. Compare and contrast the various leadership theories as outlined in this chapter. Which theory or set of theories do you believe is most applicable to professional counseling? Why?

2. An ACA division of which you are a member has been struggling lately. Reports include financial problems, membership retention issues, and communication breakdowns. Because of your visibility within this division, assume you have been asked to take a leadership position (president) and get it back on track. You are confident that you have the skills, but a little unsure of how to proceed. Based on the leadership theories discussed in this chapter, what leadership qualities would you bring to the table? What aspects of leadership theory would be most important to you? Why?

3. Assume that you have been asked by your immediate supervisor to take on a leadership task relevant to your counseling setting (e.g., school, community, etc.). Specifically, the supervisor has asked that you develop a program to enhance advocacy for clients or students whom you serve. This task requires considerable leadership, and you decide to acquaint yourself with leadership theory within and outside of counseling. Construct the advocacy program, and discuss what leadership skills and concepts you will apply.

# 3

## Professional Leadership, Leading Well

### Characteristics, Principles, and Ethics of Effective Counseling Leaders

JANE E. MYERS

## INTRODUCTION

A quick search of Amazon.com reveals over 62,000 available books on leadership. Surely anyone wanting to understand more about this topic has many places to search and learn. While there are both similarities and differences in approaches to the topic, whether you read about the intentional leader (Shaw, 2005), the transformational leader (Burns, 1978), or the heroic leader (Cohen, 2010), whether the focus is on creating leaders at every level (Townsend & Gebhardt, 1997) or training leaders for the next generation (Penney & Neilson, 2010), several aspects of leadership are commonly discussed: whether leaders are born or made, the characteristics of leaders who are effective, and leadership ethics. Knowledge of the growing body of leadership literature is important for professional counselors, and we also need to be familiar with the emerging literature on leadership in our profession.

The purpose of this chapter is to help you understand and develop competencies of effective leaders. To begin, I discuss common aspects of leadership found in the literature in the context of leadership in counseling. I then consider leadership ethics with a focus on Chi Sigma Iota's Principles and Practices of Leadership Excellence (CSI, 2009), the only existing statement of leadership ethics in our professional literature. Characteristics of effective leaders are discussed in relation to the Principles and Practices. Examples of leadership dilemmas and effective leadership are included throughout the chapter. I provide exercises and discussion questions to help you explore your own potential for leading well.

Key Terms

**Leadership ethics:** Leadership ethics are statements that guide leaders in resolving the ethical and practical dilemmas that arise during leadership experiences.

**Leadership principles:** Leadership principles are statements of ethics intended to guide leaders in the pursuit of excellence in leadership.

**Leadership practices:** Leadership practices are best practices for being ethical and effective leaders.

## On Becoming a Leader and a Counseling Leader

In Chapter 1, the contributions of many leaders to the evolution of counseling as a profession were explored, and in Chapter 2 leadership theories were considered. In the fifth chapter of this book, you will read about the personal journeys of the editors in becoming professional counseling leaders. A central question for reflection as you read these chapters is: Are leaders born or made? Take a moment to reflect on this question before reading on. There is a general consensus in the literature on the answer, which leads to a discussion of characteristics of effective leaders and effective counseling leaders.

## Are Leaders Born or Made?

John Gardner was president of the Carnegie Corporation and secretary of Health Education and Welfare under the Johnson administration. In the latter capacity, he oversaw the launch of Medicare and, subsequently, a vast improvement nationally in health care to older adults. He led the creation of the Corporation for Public Broadcasting, received the Presidential Medal of Freedom, and is well known for both his experience and his influence as a leader. In his seminal book *On Leadership* (1990), Gardner observed that some leaders are born; however, most leaders are made. From his perspective, leadership potential lies dormant in most people, lacking only a reason to be brought forth. Perhaps many people really are leaders, but they fail to define who they are and what they do in a manner that reflects their leadership characteristics.

Gardner (1990) defined leadership as "a process of persuasion and example, by which others are motivated to take action" (p. 5). Hall and Janman (2010) observed that what constitutes leadership is hard to define but easy to observe. They stated: "Leadership is like beauty; it's hard to define but you know it once you've seen it" (p. 7). Apparently, leadership acts are often easier to observe in others than to see in ourselves. Though we may criticize leadership that is ineffective, knowing the characteristics of leaders who facilitate positive change can give us role models in our journeys toward leadership excellence.

Characteristics of Effective Leaders

Many authors have written about characteristics of effective leaders. For example, Herr, Heitzman, and Rayman (2006) provided an extended discussion of the differences between leaders and managers, noting that there are fundamental processes of leadership, such as strategic planning and visioning that are universally recognized as hallmarks of good leaders. Townsend and Gebhardt (1997) described nine commandments of leadership, the first and most important of which was: "Thou shalt develop a personal philosophy of leadership, share it . . . , and live by it" (p. 215). Much of the literature on leadership is based on the dynamics of military, government, or business settings. Effective leadership in organizational and professional settings is both similar to and different from leadership in these more traditional settings (Gardner, 1990), and gender differences become important when looking specifically at leadership in counseling.

Cohen (1998, 2010) provided an example of traditional leadership perspectives in his definition of eight characteristics of effective leaders, based on his experiences as an officer in the armed forces and a consultant to Fortune 500 companies throughout the United States and abroad. Presented as "universal laws of leadership," these included the following:

1. Maintain absolute integrity by choosing right over wrong, adhering to core beliefs and values in spite of changing circumstances, and being someone others can depend upon.
2. Know your stuff, including people and their strengths and your organization and its mission.
3. Declare your expectations, so that others are clear about your vision and can choose to support that vision through their actions.
4. Show uncommon commitment, setting an example for others to emulate.
5. Expect positive results as your continued enthusiasm will increase morale for everyone.
6. Take care of your people, ensuring that they receive training for their positions, resources to do their job well, and recognition for their accomplishments.
7. Put duty before self, sharing credit when things go well and taking blame when they go badly, and acknowledging that while authority for tasks can be delegated, the responsibility for organizational success rests with the leader.
8. Get out in front, be visible, and serve as a role model for others in all that you do.

Cohen's work clearly reflects desirable qualities of traditional male leaders. The composition of professional counselors is over three-fourths female (American

Counseling Association, 2009) and raises the question of whether these qualities are equally applicable to leaders in our profession. A recent study by the Girl Scouts of America (2008) provides some insight to this question. Titled *Change It Up: What Girls Say About Redefining Leadership*, the report of this mixed methods study of boys and girls in middle school provides important insights about gender differences in leadership. One implication that stands out in the Girl Scout Study is that girls, beginning in middle school, are avoiding leadership opportunities because they do not want to be ridiculed, made fun of, or thought of as bossy. Girls are not rejecting all leadership roles, but prefer leadership styles such as listening, supporting, consulting, and collaborating that they consider both more appropriate and increasingly necessary in today's rapidly changing, technologically sophisticated workplaces. In short, many females evaluate leadership based on the traditional male-dominant model, and they do not want to be in leadership positions as a consequence. Young women are emerging as strong leaders, but in positions where they can choose their leadership styles and outcomes. What we know of leadership in counseling suggests that this is true of men in our profession as well.

## PROFESSIONAL COUNSELING LEADERSHIP

Penney and Neilson (2010) observed that "if we are to have effective leaders [for the counseling profession] in the future, we must find those potential leaders now and provide them with leadership training and development" (p. 1). If you are reading this book, we want to find *you*. It might help to know that, at the time this book was written, there had been few studies of leadership in our profession and little was known about leadership in counseling. What we do know is reviewed in this section.

West, Osborn, and Bubenzer (2003b) identified dimensions of leadership in the counseling profession, including context, vision, and action, within which leaders express their leadership potential. These dimensions were exemplified in the personal narratives of 25 individuals identified through a Delphi process as being among the most influential leaders in our profession over the last century. All leaders' stories were written by someone who knew them well and could speak both to their development as leaders and to their influence on the counseling profession. West et al. used the Chi Sigma Iota Principles and Practices of Leadership Excellence (2009), described below, to demonstrate how these leaders exemplified excellence in the counseling profession.

In a more recent study, West, Bubenzer, Osborn, Paez, and Desmond (2006) examined the literature on leadership in an effort to better understand leadership in counseling. They observed that both master's- and doctoral-level counselors in training could "benefit from preparation for positions of leadership" (p. 46). These authors believe that leaders are made, not born, and attempted to determine how to train leaders by defining what current leaders actually do. It is noteworthy that developing a vision and a sense of community were identified as initial aspects of leadership, while reflective thinking was identified as the final phase of leadership.

Magnuson, Wilcoxen, and Norem (2003) conducted a qualitative study of career paths of leaders in professional counseling. Their initial observation was that the theory of planned happenstance provided a good explanation for their findings. According to this theory (Krumboltz, 1998), unexpected events constitute opportunities, and the role of professional counselors is to help clients prepare to learn from and embrace unexpected happenings. In short, leaders in counseling were offered opportunities that, once accepted, started a trajectory that allowed them to contribute to the profession based on their fundamental values, professional identity, and commitment.

Magnuson et al. (2003) observed five important themes common to the development of counseling leaders. The first was personal attributes and values, including the strong influence of family and professional models. Other key elements in the choice to become leaders were professional passion, professional identity, and professional affiliation. Their model of career paths of professional leaders demonstrated the influence of family support and professional role models, serendipity, and seized opportunities as critical influences on the development of leaders.

Similar findings were presented by Black and Magnuson (2005) following a qualitative study of women leaders in the counseling profession. These authors interviewed 10 leaders and 2 mentees of each leader. They developed an extensive description of the leaders' attributes and behaviors grouped according to personal (e.g., authentic, passionate/tenacious), interpersonal (e.g., compassionate, empowering), and professional (e.g., visionary, intentional). They noted that "leaders passionately described a deep sense of intrinsic motivation, investment, persistence, and commitment to task completion…the majority of protégés related that the benefits of leadership seemed intangible" (p. 340). Most of the leaders expressed a commitment to social justice and the provision of strength-based services to underserved populations. "Their influence was exercised *with* people and situations rather than *over* people in order to command another person or situation…[they preferred] win-win outcomes…[they] recognized the responsibility that came with influence" (p. 340). Finally, the leaders in this study each expressed doubt about their capacities to lead effectively; rather, they emphasized their commitment to empowerment of clients and the promotion of human dignity and wellness as overarching goals (p. 341).

Gibson, Dollarhide, and McCallum (2010) observed that a new generation of leaders is emerging in our field, and that passion and a strong sense of professional identity are driving factors in the choice to serve. These findings are consistent with the findings from the Girl Scouts of America (2008) study as well. These authors conducted qualitative interviews with six nontenured assistant professors who were serving or had recently served as presidents or president-elects of divisions of the American Counseling Association. A major finding of this study was that the role models of these leaders "were actively involved in demonstrating traits of leadership and professionalization... [and]... encouraging their students... to be leaders in professional organizations" (p. 290). Consequently, the participants developed an identity that included the personal expectation of service to and professional responsibility for the counseling profession.

Wester and Lewis's (2005) study was conducted to answer two primary research questions: (1) Are CSI members significantly different in the amount of research and service they engage in than non-CSI members? (2) Is membership to a professional organization, such as CSI, related to the amount of research and service an individual engages in? From their sample of 232 members of ACES, these authors determined that CSI membership was significantly related to professional research and service. CSI, uniquely among professional associations in counseling, places a strong emphasis on the development of effective and ethical leadership skills beginning during professional preparation programs.

Luke and Goodrich (2010) reported the results of a qualitative study of 15 early career counselors who had been active as leaders in Chi Sigma Iota chapters during their professional preparation programs. They noted that these leadership experiences provided unique, real-world involvement beyond the classroom and curriculum. CSI leadership positions allowed student leaders to develop cognitive, affective, and behavioral skills for dealing with interpersonal conflict. They developed leadership skills that helped them foster creativity, set boundaries, and promote inclusion with other leaders at the chapter level. "All participants alluded to their CSI leadership experience as being a formative and integral part of their professional identity as counselors" (p. 71). The results of this study "supported the findings of Wester and Lewis (2005) indicating that their CSI chapter leadership was a significant component of their educational experiences, as opposed to being an ancillary component within counselor training... involvement with CSI filled a void within the counseling educational curriculum" (p. 73).

## LEADERSHIP ETHICS

The CSI mission and strategic plan specify training of leaders for the counseling profession as a primary goal of this organization. Such training occurs at both the chapter and international levels. CSI produces training and leadership development materials to support this goal. A noteworthy statement is CSI's Principles and Practices of Leadership Excellence (CSI, 2009), a statement of leadership ethics and best practices developed by CSI's Academy of Leaders for Excellence. At the time the principles were developed, this group had a combined total of more than 500 years of leadership experiences at all levels of the counseling profession.

Before examining these principles, it is helpful to know how other professional associations in counseling address leadership ethics.

A search of the American Counseling Association Code of Ethics and standards of practice (2005) using the word *leadership* revealed that this document does not include attention to leadership issues. However, the ACA code does define a leader in terms of a professional counselor's involvement in support networks of clients: "Counselors recognize that support networks hold various meanings in the lives of clients and consider enlisting the support, understanding, and involvement of others (e.g., religious/spiritual/community leaders, family members, friends) as positive resources, when appropriate, with client consent" (A.1.d.).

The National Board for Certified Counselors (NBCC) Code of Ethics (1998) states: "Certified counselors who assume an executive leadership role in a private practice organization do not permit their names to be used in professional notices during periods of time when they are not actively engaged in the private practice of counseling unless their executive roles are clearly stated" (Section G, Private Practice). No other statements about leadership appear in the NBCC code, which is to be expected as the purpose of credentialing relates to counseling practice, not professional leadership.

It is noteworthy that the Council for Accreditation of Counseling and Related Educational Programs (CACREP) incorporated leadership training for professional counselors in the standards for both entry-level and doctoral preparation (2009). These standards are explained more fully in Chapters 11 and 15. They reflect a profession-wide commitment to leadership knowledge and skills as competencies for all professional counselors.

## The CSI Principles and Practices of Leadership Excellence

The CSI Principles and Practices of Leadership Excellence include 10 statements or principles, each with an accompanying statement of practice, intended to demonstrate the meaning of exemplary practice for exemplary leaders. In this section, the CSI Principles and Practices are presented, and examples of leadership excellence in counseling are explored. Case examples are provided to demonstrate the application of the principles in leadership settings. Reflection questions and discussion questions are included at the end of the chapter to encourage additional exploration of these principles. These principles and practices are repeated verbatim with permission from Chi Sigma Iota International. Quotation marks reflect the original CSI wording.

### Principle 1: Philosophy of Leadership

Exemplary leaders recognize that service to others, the profession, and the associations are the preeminent reasons for involvement in leadership positions.

**Practice.** Leaders recognize that service to others is a hallmark for effective leadership that requires: careful consideration of the magnitude of their commitment prior to accepting a nomination for a leadership role; acceptance of leadership positions primarily for the purpose of service rather than personal reward; and willingness to seek counsel prior to decision making that affects others.

The servant leader philosophy espoused by Greenleaf (1970a, b) emphasizes the role of leaders as first being those who want to serve. The choice to be a leader is made because one wants to be of service to others, not because of a desire to influence or change others. The latter motivation reflects a desire for power and control, while the former reflects a desire to place the needs of others foremost in one's decision-making processes.

Ed Herr, in a position paper on leadership written for Chi Sigma Iota (2010), observed that a single leadership style does not fit all organizations. However, given the mission of CSI, its vision, strategic plan, and strategic goals, the servant leader philosophy fits this organization well. As a consequence, those who aspire to leadership in CSI are encouraged to study the servant leader paradigm.

Greenleaf suggested questions for reflection in regard to one's choice to be a leader: Herr (2010) selected several of these questions as relevant for counseling leaders: "Do those served grow as persons? Do they, while being served, become healthier, wiser, freer, more autonomous, more likely themselves to become servants: and, what is the effect on the least privileged in society? Will they benefit or at least not be further deprived?" (www.csi-net.org/leadership).

### Case Example

In 2010, a leadership development workshop was sponsored by Chi Sigma Iota International, for which several past presidents were recruited as speakers. Each was asked to speak to the nature of leadership in some way. All spoke to the unique mission of the organization and how adherence to the mission provided them freedom to explore and create services for others through various leadership roles. A commitment to both professional advocacy and social justice was evident in the remarks of each speaker. Many organizations in counseling incorporate the servant leader philosophy. Take a moment before reading on to consider what this philosophy means to you. Are there times you have seen leaders who clearly ascribe to this perspective?

### Case Example

Dr. Othmer, a university counselor educator, was contacted by staff at a local hospital where her students were frequent interns. The hospital staff had noticed a difference in the counseling students that distinguished them from students in other mental health professions. The staff were impressed with the strength-based, wellness philosophy of the counseling students and asked for help developing a wellness-oriented psychoeducational support group for cancer survivors. The group was developed over the course of a semester and continued for four years, with counseling students each semester being the group facilitators. The hospital staff continued to be impressed with the counseling students and approached the university again to participate in a cooperative grant project to evaluate the program, with a goal of convincing hospital administrators to provide additional funding.

Dr. Othmer and her students worked together to develop a community-based grant project, which eventually was funded, to support and study the cancer survivor program. Working together, they were able to provide support for the effectiveness of the group and establish it as a working model for other health care settings. In this real-life example, the blending of missions from two different organizations, each comprised of individuals who sought to help, support, and empower others, resulted in successful outcomes for everyone involved. Joint leadership emerged from an identified need, and professional counselor students played a vital role in creating sustained, positive change.

### PRINCIPLE 2: COMMITMENT TO MISSION

Exemplary leaders show evidence of a continuing awareness of and commitment to furthering the mission of their organization.

**Practice.** Leaders maintain a continuing awareness of and dedication to enhancing the mission, strategic plan, bylaws, and policies of the organization throughout all leadership functions. They work individually and in teams to fulfill the objectives of the organization in service to others.

The mission of an organization is a succinct and clear statement of the organization's purpose. The mission identifies the uniqueness of the organization and its niche in relation to other organizations. It is a guide for those involved in the organization that reflects an implicit and often explicit set of values shared by those in the organization. There are literally hundreds of thousands of organizations in the world with differing missions designed to achieve various organizational goals. When we join an organization or participate in its programs, we make a statement that we are supporting the mission and programs of that specific organization. We join different organizations to support different purposes. From an ethical perspective, to join an organization and work contrary to its purposes constitutes unethical practice.

The vision of an organization is a statement of what the organization aspires to be. It helps members feel a sense of pride and excitement about being a part of the group, and a part of something much bigger than themselves. A vision helps the organization to stretch and grow. Both the mission and vision drive the development of a strategic plan. The plan describes how the organization will actualize its mission and vision through strategic goals and action strategies. Many plans are lengthy and complex; others are succinct and easily communicated.

*Case Example*

If you attend a meeting of the executive council of Chi Sigma Iota International, you will observe that each meeting begins with a review of the CSI strategic plan (www.csi-org/whatiscsi), which is presented in one page. The officers, who are all active in multiple counseling associations, discuss the unique mission and vision of Chi Sigma Iota, and raise consciousness to the importance of the mission as they begin deliberations, discussions, and decisions. Many good ideas surface during council meetings, and the discussions at some point often sound like this: This is a great idea. Is it something that CSI can and should do, or is it something that is best done by another organization? Is this within the scope of our strategic plan?

The vision also guides CSI executive council discussions in important ways. Decisions about the future, in terms of goals and resource allocations, are necessary to achieve the organizational vision. Officers take time before each meeting to do their homework, and to become aware of current policies and procedures, and organizational history and goals. Prior preparation allows leaders to be both responsible and responsive, aware of factors that will affect their decision making and able to consider those factors in depth as they make decisions concerning effective use of the organization's resources. They are able to discriminate between a really good idea and a really good idea for this particular organization. They take notes, and they follow up with other organizations to be sure that really good ideas are never lost.

### Principle 3: Preservation of History

Exemplary leaders respect and build upon the history of their organization.

**Practice.** Leaders study the history of their organization through review of archival documents (e.g., minutes of meetings, policies) and other resources, and discussions with current and former leaders, and they act to build upon that history through informed decision making.

Although innovation and change is often something leaders are challenged to help construct and implement, their ability to be effective in helping others support needed change depends to a great extent on their understanding of an organization's history. As counselors, we know that clients are most likely to feel safe to explore their issues and commit to change when they feel both understood and accepted. In organizations, which are comprised of people, similar principles apply. People in organizations are willing to change when they know the history of the organization is understood and important aspects of values and mission will be preserved in any process of change. Hence, helping provide a sense of stability and continuity is a hallmark of effective leaders.

At the same time, commitment to a mission, vision, and strategic plan, combined with an understanding of history, may help leaders understand that organizations really do not need to change. What they need to do is to do better what they were created to do. Discussions with current and former leaders often help clarify organizational goals and promote movement in this direction. Rather than thinking we can learn all we need to learn from documents and websites, exemplary leaders seek consultation with others, especially former leaders, to ensure that continuity of organizational goals and services to members is a reality.

*Case Example*

The author was faculty advisor to two student counseling organizations housed in the same counselor education program: the Counselor Education Student Association (CESA) and a chapter of Chi Sigma Iota. Over time the two organizations began to work on common projects and share common goals. Committees appointed in one organization had a counterpart in the other, and eventually a co-chair from each organization was appointed annually to work with the other to achieve common goals. The organization presidents began one year with a serious discussion surrounding the organizational missions, and asked difficult questions of one another: Are both organizations needed? If not, which one is necessary and which is not necessary?

Over the course of the next nine months, the students sought input from their members through focus groups, open forums, and surveys. They also interviewed the faculty as a whole and individually and consulted with former leaders of both organizations. Near the end of the year, they presented a ballot to all members of the department explaining the rationale for merging the two organizations and received a unanimous vote to endorse the merger. They had one caveat—that the history of the organization to be discontinued would be preserved. The officers strongly supported a newly created, single organization, as being the structure that would best serve the students, faculty, and alumni of the program. At the same time, they wanted the values and contributions of the former organization to be remembered and to be an integral component of services to members in the future. These young professionals exemplified the servant leader philosophy. Throughout their decision-making process and implementation phase, the student leaders demonstrated firm commitment to the needs of both organizations and central to their actions were the needs of others. The actions of these student leaders were not determined by a desire to maintain their roles and positions, but rather their actions were guided by a desire to best serve their membership and the greater community.

### Principle 4: Vision of the Future

Exemplary leaders use their knowledge of the organization's history, mission, and commitment to excellence to encourage and create change appropriate to meeting future needs.

**Practice.** Leaders draw upon the wisdom of the past and challenges of the future to articulate a vision of what can be accomplished through imagination, collaboration, cooperation, and creative use of resources.

Change is inevitable. In fact, one of the most exciting aspects of being involved in organizations with a servant leader philosophy is the potential for leaders to help create positive change. In such organizations, both the history of the organization and the talents of members and new leaders are continually considered. Rather than starting each new year with a blank slate and allowing new leaders to create new programs, exemplary leaders start each new year with training, asking how things have been done before, what resources have been used, what challenges have been met and unmet, and how prior programs have contributed to the organization's mission. Exemplary leaders build on what has been done before, knowing that time is often misspent recreating structures, timelines, and programs, while even better member services can be provided when previous strategies are the starting point for creating better programs.

According to Dictionary.com, creativity does not mean ignoring or negating the past; rather, it means having the power to innovate, to contribute something new of value. Creative professional counseling leaders seek ways to build organizations through understanding of resources, including people, and the dynamic process of group interaction through which the whole, or Gestalt, becomes something far greater than the sum of its parts.

### Case Example

Susan was an active member of a counseling organization and was continually frustrated that discussions were interesting, even exciting, but nothing ever happened. She sought consultation from several experienced leaders, telling them that great and creative ideas were always being presented, but she felt that meetings lacked focus and she was often frustrated as good ideas kept getting "lost." She was advised to develop a written plan for her favorite project, including a rationale that explained the need for the project and the relationship of the project to the organization's mission, vision, and strategic plan; the purpose of the project; resources needed; and two or three possible strategies for accomplishing an important goal. She wrote up her proposal and included three options for implementing the project over time.

When the group met, the focus of the discussion was centered on her proposal. Agreement with the rationale and importance of the project was immediate, and several new ideas were contributed to support the need for the project.

The purpose was slightly revised and expanded to include both short- and long-range objectives, and the majority of the meeting time was spent deciding on an action plan and committing resources to implement that plan. Susan began to help other leaders develop proposals for projects in which they had an interest. As a consequence, the organization was able to develop, and sustain, a number of new services for its members.

*Case Example*

Alberto was a school counselor practicing in a rural school. The economy of the surrounding area had been devastated by the loss of manufacturing companies, unemployment was high, and most families lived at or below the federal poverty level. Resources for school counseling programs were extremely limited. The one school counselor was challenged to meet the needs of more than 600 students, as well as teachers and families. He chose to implement a wellness approach to help children, especially, learn to identify and use their strengths to create positive life changes.

Alberto began by conducting a series of workshops for teachers and school personnel to orient them to the wellness philosophy and goals. He then began conducting psychoeducational workshops for students and their families, teaching them about wellness, strategies for assessing their wellness, and strategies for creating wellness lifestyles. As he began to receive support from school administrators and the local community, he was able to apply for community and state grants to support the wellness initiatives. Importantly, he was able to show improvements in school attendance and eventually academic performance among students who participated in the wellness activities, thus providing visibility for the role of school counselors and ensuring the continued support of the administration and community for his work.

### PRINCIPLE 5: LONG-RANGE PERSPECTIVE

Exemplary leaders recognize that service includes both short- and long-range perspectives.

**Practice.** Leaders act to impact the organization before the year of their primary office, during the year of their primary office, and beyond that year, as appropriate, to assure the ongoing success of the organization.

When I was elected to my first elected professional association office as president-elect of a division of ACA, one of the past presidents took me aside and asked me about my plans and goals as a leader. I had just been told I won the election, and I would be serving for three years, first as president-elect, then as president, and finally as past president. I was not sure how to respond and was surprised when he looked me squarely in the eye and said: "You know, your year as president-elect is the most important one of all." I did not immediately understand what he was saying, but after finishing my year as president, I looked back and said to myself, "If I could do this over again, I would be a *really* good president, because now I know how to do it."

The president-elect year really is the most important one. That is the time the new leader learns about the organization; its history, values, and traditions; its niche in relation to other organizations and society; the expectations of its members; and the activities expected of its elected officers and presidents. This is the year when the leader sets goals for the following year, important goals for how to make a difference in the organization and how to improve services to its members. The year as president is terribly busy—planning, coordinating, and chairing meetings; delegating activities to officers and committee chairs; responding to requests from outside entities and from members; and more. Sometimes there is just not the luxury of time to think creatively, as the president is responsible for seeing that all officers implement the mission, vision, and goals for the year.

Past presidents are also important organizational resources. They are a repository of information about issues, projects, programs, memos, people, and more. Many past presidents think that their work is done and discontinue active involvement, failing to attend meetings or respond to organizational mailings. Such disengagement may be a disservice to the incoming president and officers, as the past presidents' understandings and advice may help create continuity for the organization. On the other hand, past presidents more than any other officers need to appreciate the dynamics of their role. They are no longer president, but can be wonderful advisors, supporters, and encouragers to the president. When past presidents try to continue to act as the president, problems may be expected, and consultation with experienced leaders is important to avoid frustration for all concerned.

*Case Example*

Phil was an active president of his organization and had three pet projects he sought to promote during his year in office. Two of the three became institutionalized with a continued commitment for organizational resources and support. The third was not supported. Rather than accepting the decision of his colleagues as a normal organizational practice, Phil decided to continue to champion his cause. He attended every meeting and asked that his project be on the agenda for discussion. He continually presented motions to devote organizational resources to the project, though none were ever approved.

His successor as president, frustrated with the amount of time being devoted to Phil's issue, sought consultation from two experienced leaders. She learned that Phil's actions were not uncommon, and that some leaders have trouble letting go. She was advised to meet with Phil individually and discuss her concerns. She was also advised that she needed to have agenda control and structure her meeting using parliamentary procedure. She could include Phil's concerns on her agenda as "old business," while also including new business items. By a vote of her officers at the start of each meeting, she could place a priority on discussion of reports and new business items only. These discussions typically filled the available meeting hour, and eventually the old business item promoted by Phil was dropped from further consideration.

An important piece of advice from former leaders was to help Phil transition to new projects by asking for his active involvement in achieving specific goals. In addition, Phil was asked to coordinate one of the other two projects he had developed the prior year. Hence, he felt validated and understood he still had important roles to play in the organization.

### PRINCIPLE 6: PRESERVATION OF RESOURCES

Exemplary leaders act to preserve the human and material resources of the organization.

**Practice.** Leaders assure that policies and practices are in effect to assure financial responsibility and continuing respectful treatment of human and other material resources of the organization.

Resources of organizations may be both tangible and intangible, material and financial. All organizations need a written plan or policy statement that specifies how resources are to be maintained and used. If resources include money, policies for how the money can be spent, who authorizes expenditures, and how records on income and expenses are maintained are essential. An annual budget is a requirement to ensure that spending occurs according to a plan preapproved by elected officers. Policies should include forms for requesting and recording expenditures and reimbursements and a policy to guide decisions when projected expenses may exceed the amount budgeted.

It is important for leaders to recognize that the money an organization has belongs to the members, not the leaders. Leaders are stewards of organizational resources, not owners of resources. In developing policies about money, consultation with financial experts (e.g., accountants, bank managers) is desirable. Annual audits of resources should include both financial and material assets. A good policy to consider is that of developing an annual budget for the year based on income from the prior year, a number that is known, rather than projecting possible income for the current year and budgeting on numbers that may or may not be realized.

### Case Example

The newly elected officers of an organization learned that they had a bank account but no annual budget and no financial policies. Rather, the prior officers simply spent money "when needed" and failed to keep records. In terms of principle 6, the new officers quickly learned that they could not act to preserve their resources as they really did not know what they had. They did learn that there was a large cabinet in a closet full of an assortment of things: cups, plates, soda bottles, napkins, name tags, and so on.

The officers decided they needed financial and resource policies to guide effective and ethical decision making relative to the resources of their members. They consulted with an accountant who offered pro bono assistance to help them set up financial request and reimbursement forms and an Excel file for recording an annual budget and income and expenses. They asked a local bank president to meet with them to discuss the components of a sound financial policy and to review their policy once it had been developed. They also contacted similar organizations for examples of financial policies. Once in place, they presented the new policies to their membership with an assurance that members' dues and contributions would be maintained in a respectful and ethical manner, and that future financial decisions would be made in accordance with the policies.

An interesting component of the financial policies had to do with decision making on major purchases. A caveat in the policy statement was that a major purchase or deviation from the annual budget could not be approved during the same meeting when it was proposed. The officers wanted to be sure that adequate "think time" was provided to ensure thoughtful decision making at all times.

### Principle 7: Respect for Membership

Exemplary leaders respect the needs, resources, and goals of their constituencies in all leadership decisions.

**Practice.** Leaders are deliberate in making decisions that are respectful of the memberships' interests and enhance the benefits to them as active members in the organization.

As noted above, leaders are stewards of organizational resources and committed to lead in relation to a specific organizational mission and purpose. Members join an organization to support that mission. Hence, leaders have a responsibility to understand members' needs and priorities and take actions consistent with those needs.

*Case Example*

A small group of leaders of an organization became very excited about a new project to support a community agency. This agency was struggling to provide services to an underserved population and clearly could benefit from support. So, the leaders decided to make a donation to the agency from existing organizational resources. Before the check was written, the leaders stopped to ask if such a donation of their members' assets was consistent with the mission and goals of the organizational and ethical principles of leadership. Although everyone supported the agency and the idea, the leaders eventually decided on another course of action. Why?

In their discussions, the leaders affirmed that members' dues were collected for a specific purpose stated in their mission and goals. Fund-raising projects had been conducted to expand their financial resources, and the advertised reason for the fund-raising had been to support students' professional development and attendance at conferences. To use their existing funds for another purpose created an ethical dilemma. How would members and others feel who had donated funds for one purpose, if the funds were used for another purpose? Would they be supportive even if the expenditure was for a purpose that was "noble"?

The officers sought consultation with members and former leaders, especially leaders who had been active in prior fund-raising. What they learned was that each member had a different organization they thought was worthy of support; however, the funds for *this* organization needed to be spent for the purpose for which they had been raised. If the leaders really wanted to support another organization, a new fund-raising effort was needed. They learned through consultation with leaders and fund-raisers that donations to worthy causes, whatever those causes may be, were specific to that cause and could not be spent otherwise, if the leaders wanted to be successful fund-raisers in the future.

### PRINCIPLE 8: MENTORING, ENCOURAGEMENT, AND EMPOWERMENT

Exemplary leaders place a priority on mentoring, encouraging, and empowering others.

**Practice.** Leaders assure that members are provided with opportunities to develop and apply their unique talents in service to others, the profession, and association.

All organizations have members, and some members obviously want to be leaders. Others may be great leaders but do not recognize their leadership potential. Perhaps they see leadership as something negative rather than a way to help achieve important personal and professional goals. One way to help members decide if they want to be leaders is to help them understand the organization's mission and goals. Those who do not want to lead but want to be sure that certain services are provided to others may readily be recruited to help—and subsequently find themselves in a position of leadership. Reflections by the authors in Chapter 4 provide examples of the powerful influence of mentoring.

### Case Example

Fernando was frustrated because no one came to meetings advertised for those who wanted to be leaders in his association. After consulting with former leaders and some leaders he saw who were being effective, he changed his strategy. He scheduled and invited members to a meeting to learn more about the organization. At the meeting, he explained the mission, vision, and goals of the organization. He asked officers, committee chairs, and former chairs to attend and talk about their roles. Finally, he passed around a sign-up sheet so members could volunteer to participate in various activities. He was pleasantly surprised when a large number of names appeared. When he asked for feedback on what had happened, several members volunteered that they liked to help others in specific ways, but they did not want to be a "leader." They just wanted to do what they wanted to do!

### PRINCIPLE 9: RECOGNITION OF OTHERS

Exemplary leaders assure that all who devote their time and talents in service to the mission of the organization receive appropriate recognition for their contributions.

**Practice.** Leaders maintain records of service to the organization and provide for public recognition of service on an annual basis, minimally (e.g., letters of appreciation, certificates of appreciation).

Everyone has unique talents and skills, and not everyone wants to be involved in an organization as a leader. Those who do commit time and effort on behalf of others are worthy of recognition. Recognition need not be formal and part of annual ceremonies, though such recognition is appropriate for any organization. Brief e-mails, cards, and notes of appreciation throughout the year are also appreciated and help motivate leaders to continue during especially difficult or busy times. Taking time for a brief chat over coffee or tea is a good way to stay connected with other leaders and help them feel noticed and appreciated for their work.

While public recognition can be nice and is often appreciated, many people prefer to contribute behind the scenes, and those persons should be recognized in a manner that matches their work preferences. For example, note cards with a short thank you let people know their contributions were noticed, on a personal level, without cause for fanfare but with an expression of appreciation. For such individuals, it is nice to know that someone noticed, but not at all necessary. In a large organization, presidents need to depend on committee chairs and other officers to keep them informed of member contributions. Asking and letting others know that this is a priority is essential if accurate information is to be gathered and maintained. After various functions, getting a list of who participated and their contributions is one way to keep track of such involvement.

### Case Example

Catherine was the president of an organization that included 4 elected officers, 10 committee chairs, and as many as 40 committee members at any given time. She wanted to encourage each person, but she did not have time for individual meetings with so many people. She asked each committee chair for a list of committee members' names and e-mail addresses. She then found a free online e-card provider and sent thank you notes to all committee members letting them know their work was appreciated. At another time, she put an inexpensive piece of candy in each member's mailbox with a postcard saying "thank you from the members and leaders of XXX organization." Over the year, when volunteers were needed, Catherine found that many people were willing to be involved.

### Principle 10: Feedback and Self-Reflection

Exemplary leaders engage in self-reflection, obtain feedback on their performance in leadership roles from multiple sources, and take appropriate action to better serve the organization.

**Practice.** Leaders seek feedback, for example, from members of their leadership team, personal and leadership mentors, and past leaders of the organization. Exemplary leaders experiencing significant life transitions or crises actively and regularly seek consultation from such mentors regarding their capacity to continue the work of the organization during such duress. Leaders take action congruent with that feedback, which reflects their commitment to these Principles and Practices of Leadership Excellence.

We all experience life events, situations, and crises that challenge our coping resources. We all mean to do well when we commit to an organization, project, or purpose. Yet, life happens. When we find ourselves making excuses, not following through, and not doing what we agreed to do, we may feel guilty. Because our motivations are good, we seek to continue in roles that sometimes we simply are not prepared to fill, and when our efforts are less than our best, we do a disservice to ourselves as well as others. From the perspective of servant leadership, we have lost our focus on others and have begun to serve for some other reason.

Sometimes it is difficult or impossible to see our predicament, and others need to help us find our way gently. Consultation with those we admire and trust is important; however, being open to feedback can be hard. It is precisely when we most need this type of feedback that we are least apt to be open to receiving it. We may realize after the fact that we were ineffective in leadership roles because of personal challenges. The purpose of this leadership principle is to help prevent such 20/20 hindsight and help us take action in the moment to ensure that the needs of others and of organizations take precedence.

**Reflections.** Has there been a time in your life when you felt overwhelmed due to circumstances or events and unable to complete things you had committed to do? How did you feel? Did you seek feedback? Were any other persons or organizations affected by your decisions? Based on this principle, what steps could you have taken to resolve your concerns while helping others?

Can you think of a time when you have observed someone in a leadership position become immobilized by personal concerns that kept them from following through on a commitment? Using this principle, what steps could be taken to help them make an ethical and effective leadership decision.

## SUMMARY

Leadership is a competency of professional counselors. Professional preparation standards, ethical codes of professional associations and credentialing bodies, and CSI's Principles and Practices of Leadership Excellence provide a foundation for developing leadership knowledge and skills. Readers are encouraged to reflect on the personal meaning of each of the 10 leadership principles as part of the process of developing effective leadership skills.

## EXERCISES FOR APPLICATION

Individual Exercises

1. Review the CSI Principles and Practices of Leadership Excellence. Select one or two that are most meaningful to you. Write a brief statement about the principle that explains why it is important to you. What experiences have you had that relate to this principle? What events or actions have you observed in other leaders in response to this principle? (CACREP Doctoral Standards, Section I:1, 2)

2. Review each of the 10 leadership principles and practices. What are some examples of each principle that you have seen in practice in meetings, classes, professional or community organizations, and so on? Write these up as case examples to accompany each principle and practice. (CACREP Doctoral Standards, Section I:1, 2)

3. Think about a time you served in a leadership role. This could be any time you assumed an official role in an organization or simply helped other people make decisions. As you look back, what principles of leadership affected your decision making? Write these up as case examples to accompany each principle and practice. (CACREP Doctoral Standards, Section I:1, 2; J:1)

4. Draw your leadership lifeline. When have you been in positions of leadership and what were your roles? These could be activities, such as leadership of younger siblings as an oldest child, leadership of classmates in getting to school safely, or leadership of student organizations or student government. Perhaps you took a lead role in a sports group or community or church team, or on a group class project. Describe one or two leadership activities, then reflect on the 10 Principles and Practices of Leadership Excellence. Which principles were evident as you engaged in your leadership roles? (CACREP Doctoral Standards, Section I:1, 2; J:1)

Group Exercises

1. Have each person in the group select one of the principles that is meaningful to them. Divide into dyads and discuss the principle you selected

and why you selected that one. In the large group, share and summarize your small group discussions. (CACREP Doctoral Standards, Section I:1, 2; J:1)

2. Have each person in the group select an organization to observe. Ask permission to attend a business meeting of that group. It could be a professional association, student organization, faculty senate or council, city or county council meeting, and so on. Take a copy of the CSI Principles and Practices of Leadership Excellence to the meeting. Make notes on examples of exemplary leadership (or lack thereof) in relation to the principles. Summarize your observations and report them when your class next meets. (CACREP Doctoral Standards, Section I:1, 2, 4, 5; J:1)

3. Discuss your leadership lifelines in dyads or triads. What does this tell you about your characteristics as a leader? How do those match characteristics of effective leaders described earlier? (CACREP Doctoral Standards, Section I:1, 2; J:1)

## COUNSELOR EDUCATION LEADERSHIP DEVELOPMENT ACTIVITIES

1. Read Dr. Ed Herr's CSI position paper on leadership (csi-net.org/leadership). Attend a meeting of your local CSI chapter and reflect on the qualities of leaders relative to this paper. What does servant leadership mean in this context? (CACREP Doctoral Standards, Section I:1, 2; J:1)

2. Review one or more of the papers and articles on counseling in other countries that are provided through the CSI Global Network (csi-net.org/international). What examples of leadership excellence are evident in the country you have studied? (CACREP Doctoral Standards, Section I:1, 2; J:1)

## DISCUSSION QUESTIONS

1. Servant leadership is explicitly mentioned in principle 1 in the CSI Principles and Practices of Leadership Excellence. How is this philosophy related to each of the other principles?

2. What is the importance of an organizational mission, vision, and strategic plan?

3. How do your ethical practices as a professional counselor affect your work as an ethical and effective leader?

# 4

# *On Becoming a Leader*
## A Journey

Jane E. Myers, Catherine Y. Chang,
Andrea L. Dixon, Casey A. Barrio Minton,
and Thomas J. Sweeney

## INTRODUCTION

The authors in this section have each addressed different aspects of leadership; however, all have been focused on the dynamics of leadership in the counseling profession. The book editors are all experienced professional counselors and counselor educators, and leaders who have served within universities while students, in universities as faculty members, and in voluntary professional association and leadership positions at the university, community, state, regional, national, and international levels. In this chapter, we each reflect on our personal experiences with and philosophy of leadership, and share salient aspects of our developmental journeys as leaders. We emphasize the key role of professional identity in helping others discern and develop their leadership potential.

Covey (1990) explained the importance of being intentional in determining our personal mission or purpose in life. In his widely read book *The Seven Habits of Highly Effective People,* Covey suggested that a powerful way to develop a personal philosophy is through the writing of a personal mission statement, a narrative that describes who you are and what you believe to be your core purpose in life. As noted in Chapter 3, Townsend and Gebhardt's (1997) first commandment of leadership, "thou shalt develop a personal philosophy of leadership, share it ..., and live by it ..." (p. 215), underscores the importance of developing a philosophy, and engaging in continued reflection and commitment to one's personal philosophy of leadership.

Reflections such as those provided in this chapter are an important means of discerning one's personal mission and hopefully will help you, our readers, to begin or continue the process of reflecting on your own journey toward leadership excellence.

We provide our reflections as a stimulus to you to help you determine your own mission, and how being a professional counselor is part of that mission. Consistent with the overall philosophy of this book, our stories speak to how each of us has recognized the importance of being true to our personal and professional mission. For each of us, that mission revolves around the pursuit of personal and professional excellence. We seek to actualize our mission on a daily basis by promoting wellness and human dignity in spheres of influence ranging from our homes and communities to our schools, students, and peers, and to the national and international arenas. We work with colleagues around the world who share our vision of excellence in counseling leadership and advocacy.

As you read the editors' personal journeys, we invite you to consider how what we know about leadership and about leadership in counseling are reflected in our stories. We suspect the same factors will be evident in your stories as well. Consistent with the recommendations of Chang, Hays, and Milliken (2009), we encourage you to seek supervision on your leadership journey, through reflective activities, the development of mission statements, participation in leadership training, and other activities that help you explore the meaning of your desire to help others through a career in professional counseling. You will find that leadership involves you in both client and professional advocacy, and that self-awareness, knowledge of client issues, and community collaboration will be critical tools that help you become the counselor, advocate, and leader you truly want to be.

In this chapter, each editor provides reflections on how he or she came to be a leader and the personal meaning of leadership. We provide exercises and activities for self-reflection that will be helpful to anyone contemplating becoming more of a leader and advocate for professional counselors and clients. These include exercises that can be completed individually, group values clarification activities designed to help small and large groups increase awareness of and discover their unique leadership styles and gifts, and activities helpful to Chi Sigma Iota chapters to foster leadership development among chapter members.

## DEFINITIONS OF KEY TERMS AND CONCEPTS

**Reflection:** "Mental concentration" (American Heritage online dictionary, n.d.).

**Self-reflection,** synonyms: "self-contemplation, self-examination, self-observation, self-questioning, self-scrutiny, soul-searching" (Merriam-Webster's online dictionary, n.d.).

**Personal mission statement:** "A statement that focuses on what you want to be in terms of character and what you want to do in reference to contribution or achievements. Writing a mission statement can be the most important activity an individual can take to truly lead one's life" (Covey, 1990).

## IN PURSUIT OF EXCELLENCE BY WAY OF SERVICE—CATHERINE Y. CHANG

Good leaders must first become good servants.

—Robert Greenleaf

There are many theories of leadership in the literature, and over the years, I have searched for the leadership theory that is most congruent with my professional identity as a counselor educator and professional counselor. This search process has led me to the concept of servant leadership. Essentially, I believe that I am, or at least am aspiring to be, a servant leader, and that this concept is consistent with what inspires me both personally and professionally.

The term *servant leadership* was first coined by Robert Greenleaf (1970a) in his essay "The Servant as Leader." Servant leadership is characterized by a desire to serve and a belief that leadership development is an ongoing process. The servant leader is mindful of those she serves, and her effectiveness is determined not by what she has accomplished, but by considering what effect that leadership has on those who have been served (Greenleaf, 1970a, 1998). According to Greenleaf (1998), the best test for the servant leader is to ask, "Do those served grow as persons? Do they, while being served, become healthier, wiser, freer, more autonomous, more likely themselves to become servants? And, what is the effect on the least privileged in society? Will they benefit or at least not be further deprived?" (p. 27). These core questions are consistent with my professional identity as a counselor and my personal belief in the dignity of all persons and the importance of supporting one's community, locally and globally.

The importance of finding the right fit with an organization cannot be stressed enough. As I reflect on my leadership development, I realize I was and am drawn to organizations where I feel connected to both the leadership/membership and the organization's mission. For me, both conditions have to be present to foster individual leadership growth. Chi Sigma Iota and the Association for Assessment in Counseling and Education (AACE) are two such organizations; however, they are not the only ones.

As with many first steps, the genesis of my involvement with both organizations was a simple invitation by servant leaders. With CSI, the chapter president invited me to join, and then as my involvement increased, I was asked to be a member-at-large of the chapter. I was later invited to be nominated and eventually elected president of our chapter. The initial catalyst for my journey with AACE began when my faculty mentor invited me to the reception at the ACA conference and introduced me to the leadership of AACE. These individuals saw potential in me and mentored me to develop both professionally and personally. They embody what it means to be servant leaders.

In addition to these personal connections, I believe in the importance of promoting excellence in counseling (CSI) and the importance of assessment and evaluation (AACE) in the work that we do as professional counselors. I believe and support the mission of CSI: "We promote a strong professional identity through members who contribute to the realization of a healthy society by fostering wellness and human dignity" (www.csi-net.org). I believe that assessment is fundamental to the work we do as professional counselors. All counselors must have a working understanding of assessment and evaluation in order to provide effective and ethical treatment to their clients and community.

Because of my mentors and vital organizations, I have been entrusted with the privilege and obligation to serve the next generation of professional counselors and counselor educators through my service. It is my hope that as I progress through this journey, I can also embody some of the characteristics of servant leadership identified by Greenleaf (2004): listening, awareness, empathy, stewardship, growth, and building community.

## REFLECTIONS FROM A "FOUND" LEADER—ANDREA L. DIXON

For a true leader, the danger is not to take the risk.

—Henry Miller

I took the risk required of leaders. However, it was only after being a leader found me. I have always believed that leadership came to me in my life, versus seeking it out for myself. However, once I took that initial risk, my journey has never been complete and has continued to evolve. From a very early age I was "found" as a leader by my family and through my desire to work with others in capacities that highlighted my innate leadership qualities. In my own family, I was the oldest child with a younger brother who was diagnosed as autistic when I was six years of age; thus, the helper and a leader within me emerged. Being a leader felt natural for me. It is from that early age that I continually found myself drawn to organizations and groups that allowed my leadership potential to develop and to emerge. I also found myself actively seeking mentorship from various individuals who rolemodeled ethical and competent leadership in a variety of manners. Needless to say, leadership came to me, called to me; for me, leadership is not simply another activity in which we as professional counselors are required to participate.

Today, my personal philosophy of leadership entails an unspoken expectation of us to act as advocates for the principles and values that we believe in on both personal and professional levels. It involves calling upon my inner voice to act in a manner that others will respect and identify with, and to be an advocate and leader for social change on behalf of others who may not have a voice, and for groups and causes around our world. I now realize that not all define leadership in the same manner as do I; however, I have found that to be refreshing throughout my life and career. It allows many of us to be leaders in our own ways, staying true to who we are as individuals and professionals, and thus affecting future generations of leaders in personal and professional manners. I have been able to be a leader in both vocal and silent manners—always reminding myself of the risk taking that leaders before me welcomed.

I have welcomed the opportunity of leadership from elementary school and beyond and have acted as a leader in various forms. I am a professional counselor, an educator, a researcher, a writer, a volunteer, a reviewer, a board member, a colleague, a friend, and so many more roles that allow me to live my leadership and advocacy philosophy daily. I have held leadership positions in schools, private practice, universities, and in numerous professional and personal ventures on a volunteer basis. I have worked on behalf of others and alongside others who have inspired me and the work I do. I have observed and watched my mentors lead and have been in awe of the changes they have facilitated in our world. And, I have found motivation through them and others to continue my leadership development and journey: professional, personal, social, spiritual, and charitable motivation. I challenge each of you to find your motivation and to offer your leadership to others in order to affect change in our world.

I have a fond memory of an important mentor to me asking: "And now what are your plans?" I remember pausing, thinking, and feeling about this question because I knew what she was asking. I responded in the way my very first mentor in life (my mother) would have hoped that I would: "I intend to be the best that I can be and offer myself and my energy to others and to causes in order to point the way for others. I will be a leader; it's all I have ever known." I am proud and honored to have been found as a leader. It can be a trying journey at times, but one that is well worth the effort when you are able to stand beside others that inspire you and motivate you. I am grateful every day and every single time I take the risk. I can only hope that you will risk and become, and continue to be, the leader you find within yourselves. On behalf of your beliefs, stay open to that risk.

## REFLECTIONS ON MY LEADERSHIP EXPERIENCES AND CHALLENGES—CASEY BARRIO MINTON

When work, commitment, and pleasure all become one and you reach that deep well where passion lives, nothing is impossible.

—Nancy Coey

As I reflect upon my leadership experiences and challenges, I realize it is time to share a secret. I am not a leader. I am a citizen, a professional counselor, and an educator who is firm in her ideals, has a strong sense of justice, believes in our profession, and is willing to work for the things in which she believes. I have been *doing* leadership for most of my life, but I am not *a* leader.

The distinction between *leadership* as a verb and *leader* as a noun is subtle yet critical. When we focus on the verb, leadership is simply a method for advancing our professional mission: fostering wellness and human dignity for our clients individually and society at large. When we focus on the noun, we risk shifting attention to individual personalities, agendas, and egos. With this distinction in mind, I would like to reflect upon two elements that have been central to my own leadership development: passion and mentorship.

A shy, awkward, and serious child, I began my journey toward leadership in my early teens. At the time, I knew nothing of leadership, wellness, social justice, or the counseling profession. I simply had a sense that not everyone had the same opportunities as everyone else, and I wanted to be connected to my community in a meaningful way. Searching for a place to belong, I began volunteering for service activities coordinated through our family's faith community. As I helped children in an after-school program, raked leaves, and served food, I listened to others' stories of pain and resilience. I was inspired by the hope I heard from those who had been horribly marginalized or abused, and I became angry about the systems that allowed such injustices to keep happening. In those encounters, I found my meaning, purpose, and passion. Although my life goals and leadership focus have emerged more clearly throughout each season of my personal and professional journey, it is this same passion that undergirds and fuels my leadership activities today.

Fueled by passion, I continued engaging in my service activities and inviting others to do the same. During each season of my development, I was surprised, inspired, and humbled as (I assumed) confident, natural leaders around me began taking an interest in me and inviting me to leadership. During each step of the process, I resisted, arguing that I had neither the skills nor the inclination to be a leader. I would much rather take a picture than be in a picture; I am much more comfortable ensuring a speaker has the setup he or she needs rather than making speeches. Rather, I simply do what is needed to be done.

Over time, my mentors helped me experience leadership as a verb rather than be distracted by my visions of leaders as nouns. They helped me articulate my passions and goals, modeled servant leadership skills, found ways to affirm those things most important to me, connected me with opportunities, and shared their own triumphs and disappointments when I needed them most. It was through relationships with these mentors that I developed the confidence and skills for following my passion in our common professional mission—first as a student and new professional, and now as an established counselor educator and elected representative for professional associations such as Chi Sigma Iota and the

Association for Assessment in Counseling and Education (AACE). Over time, I have come to accept leadership as simply a vehicle for using my passion in fulfillment of our professional mission.

Whether or not you are interested in leadership in your personal and professional life, I urge you to stop for a moment. What is it about fostering wellness and human dignity that stirs something in you? What will you do with the well-earned gift of membership in our profession?

## I NEVER GAVE LEADERSHIP OR ADVOCACY A PASSING THOUGHT—JANE E. MYERS

You must be the change you wish to see in the world.

—Mahatma Gandhi

Growing up, I never once thought about becoming a leader or an advocate. I was not a member of any club, let alone an officer. I was never active in student government. In college, I did not join clubs. I did not participate in student government. I was the last person anyone would think of as leader. No one, including me, thought of me that way. I grew up poor, in a family that was socially isolated and defined by conflict. As I reflect on how I wound up active in leadership and advocacy in the counseling profession, I can think of three factors that influenced my thoughts, feelings, and behaviors.

First, I watched my mother. She made sure I went with her and helped with her job and volunteer activities. As a special education teacher in inner city schools, she was not expected to do much more with her students than try to teach them basic living skills. Yet repeatedly her students "tested out" of special education into mainstream classes. She empowered her students to view themselves as capable rather than hopeless. She helped them imagine and seek a better future. She advocated for them with school administrators, other teachers, social service personnel, and parents. She helped create environments in which they had the support they needed to succeed. I could not help but admire and respect her as I watched her help each student create a new vision of themselves and their future.

My profoundly "retarded" deaf-mute older brother lived at home until he was 17. At that time, the neighbors signed a petition and the local court ordered him placed in a state hospital. My mother did more than simply visit him. She organized parent groups to raise money for needed items, like a television for the ward. She organized social events to bring families together and integrate the hospital residents into family and social relationships. She advocated with administrators and health care personnel for better living circumstances for my brother and his peers. She made a difference in the lives of many people she never met, but cared about nonetheless.

Second, as I pursued my passion to become a rehabilitation counselor and work with persons with disabilities, I learned in my course work that being an advocate was an integral part of my role. I learned to advocate with employers, health care providers, groups, and families to ensure that disabilities did not become handicaps that prevented individuals from living their lives to the fullest. I learned that being nationally certified and graduating from an accredited program would both make me better prepared to do my job well and provide an assurance to potential employers that indeed I could do the job well. Professional credentials, and professional recognition, meant people would listen to me when I spoke, I could follow my passion with some degree of success, and I could make a positive and lasting difference in the lives of individuals and their families and communities.

When I transitioned from being a rehabilitation counselor to being a program director of services for older adults in Florida, I quickly found myself working with individuals and groups of older adults to advocate for needed services. I went with them and on their behalf to meet with government officials and county and city commissioners to lobby for funding. I learned to write grants to obtain funds so people in need could have those needs met. My third lesson was that working with community groups and policy makers could create lasting and positive change in communities, and that would contribute to greater wellness for individuals and families.

I returned to school to pursue a doctorate in the hopes of learning more about how to better serve older adults, and to gain the needed credentials to ensure that those in positions of power would see me as knowledgeable and listen when I spoke on behalf of those in need, especially older persons. I was encouraged to become involved in professional association work as a means to network with other counselors who shared my interests, and to work with them to fill unmet needs relative to gerontological counselor training. I found that through service I could be an effective advocate, and through training professional counselors I could share my own passion with those who would help others throughout their careers. Chang et al. (2009) would say I became aware, I acquired knowledge, and I networked in community. As I reflect, I would say I found my passion. I learned somewhat later that some called me a leader. All I thought I was doing was captured by Gardner (1990): "living by example to motivate others to take action for the greater good of all" (p. 1).

## ON BECOMING A LEADER: MY JOURNEY—THOMAS J. SWEENEY

Courage is the one sure foundation of character. Without courage there can be no morality, no religion, no love. One cannot follow truth or love so long as one is subject to fear.

—Mahatma Gandhi

My earliest recollections of leadership are of my mother, who volunteered to help with our elementary school Parent Teachers Association (PTA). She came to this country at the age of 12 and was a tenth grade dropout expected to care for her younger siblings and to do the housekeeping and cooking while her parents worked. Once married with children, she had every reason to be a content stay-at-home mom, as was the custom in her day. However, she apparently thought otherwise. I remember overhearing teachers who had no idea of her educational background speaking of her in positive terms and of watching in wonder as she presided over a meeting in what to me was a large auditorium. She later became the municipal PTA president and representative in the state capital for our city. So family was my earliest exposure to what I came to learn was leadership.

My older brother was so active in high school that he had to decline the presidency of one organization in his senior year to accept the presidency of the school student council. It was another big deal to me. I was in awe of my big brother.

So as true is with many others who become involved in professional leadership (Luke & Goodrich, 2010), I volunteered to be class Red Cross representative, student council member, and so forth, throughout my elementary and secondary school years. As I now know, it did not come as easy for me as my brother, since I am a dedicated introvert and must exert considerable energy to step out and "externalize" myself to others. I was fortunate to have some talent as a singer and performed before audiences in that capacity, as well as doing some drama and musical acting. My drama and history teachers were my heroes then, so becoming a teacher seemed like a good idea.

My next formative experiences with leadership happened during my undergraduate years in a social fraternity. Being an introvert, they recruited me to sing in their fraternity choir; otherwise, I suspect I likely would not have been "rushed." I worked my way through college, so social time was scarce, but I felt drawn to be active in the chapter. I watched as the more effective leaders conducted meetings (much like my mother had), made motions at strategic times, spoke eloquently to their points, listened well, and generally won the cooperation of the members. So I proceeded through the positions of pledge master, treasurer, and president until I graduated and became an inner city junior high school teacher.

I loved middle school and high school teaching but felt frustrated in not reaching many of the inner city students I had in my classes. I had grown up in a culturally and racially diverse neighborhood where I attended the city school also equipped for children with disabilities. We were the partners of other such children during special occasions, including fire drills. They were our "buddies." These formative experiences contributed to my concern and respect for others who were "different" but otherwise every bit my peer and neighbor.

Since my secondary school "guidance" experience was less than satisfactory, I went to graduate school in counseling in an effort to correct what I found lacking in my own school experience: encouragement, understanding, and guidance in my career planning. These lacks became my passion for helping others. My experience as a high school counselor in an outstanding pupil personnel program helped me to see the benefits of effective counseling services on a citywide scale. In my mind, completing my doctorate became a means to helping further systemic change for even greater good than I could effect in a single school.

My graduate advisors were not the type of mentors we speak of today, but they did model active leadership as a means to bringing about change. When I entered counseling, none of the hallmarks of a profession were apparent. When I realized this fact, I was motivated to seek change. Professional leadership positions came as a consequence of wanting to see my chosen career as a legitimate profession and not just an occupation. I remain committed to this goal as a part of my professional vision and passion, but I found it not enough to sustain my efforts.

I believe, however, that my aspirations for bringing about change on a more socially conscious scale came about as a result of my maturation as a counselor educator. As said by de Saint-Exupéry in *The Little Prince* (1943), "It is only with the heart that one can see rightly; what is essential is invisible to the eye" (p. 87). Once I could look beyond achieving my career goals. I sought to be of greater service to others and society at large in a more holistic way.

During my early years as a counselor educator, I rediscovered Alfred Adler's theory involving encouragement for developing "social interest" in self, others, and community. Adler's writings and those of Rudolf Dreikurs, whom I got to hear lecture, demonstrated and helped me to articulate my personal and professional values into a coherent philosophy and psychology for living and working with others. Cooperation earned through genuine respect for the qualities, ideas, and efforts of others has been the fruits of their legacy. It is in a community spirit of mutual respect and social equality that Dreikurs believed social problems must be solved. I could not agree more. Today we speak of social justice in just such terms.

Especially in Dreikurs's later years he worked tirelessly and vigorously for these values and the democratic methods that he taught as essential tools of those who would be leaders in homes, schools, communities, and society at large. I hope as he did that my efforts will result in a profession that contributes to a life of dignity and wellness for all. This overarching goal makes all the time and effort worthwhile, especially as I see the new leaders embracing their own visions of service with a high level of social interest toward others.

## EXERCISES FOR APPLICATION

Individual Leadership Values Clarification and Personal Growth Exercises

1. **Personal reflections on leadership.** Write a 3- to 5-page reflection on your personal definition and philosophy of leadership. This reflection

must include a brief review of the current literature on leadership and advocacy. (CACREP Doctoral Level Standards, Section IV, I:1, 2)

2. **Personal definition of leadership.** Leadership roles can take on a variety of forms. Prepare a written statement of how you define leadership and what it means to you (3–5 pp.). This can include your personal and professional journey to date as well as your goals for your future leadership development. (CACREP Doctoral Level Standards, Section IV, I:1, 2)

3. **Lessons from great leaders.** The greatest leaders come from around our world and have various personal and professional stories that helped them to become great leaders. Investigate websites and memoirs from who you believe to be three of our great leaders in the twenty-first century from around the world. These may include business, spiritual, or counseling leaders. Prepare a bulleted list of their most poignant quotations for you that will help to motivate you in your continual leadership development. (CACREP Doctoral Level Standards, Section IV, I:1, 3–5)

4. **Defining leadership and advocacy.** How do you explain the difference between leadership and advocacy? What are some times in your life that you have functioned in each role? How did you feel? (CACREP Doctoral Level Standards, Section IV, I:1, 2)

5. **Reading books on leadership.** Read a book about leadership. Write a review and share it with other counselors through the CSI Counselor's Bookshelf (csi-net.org/bookshelf). (CACREP Doctoral Level Standards, Section IV, I:5)

6. **Reflecting on leadership memories.** Think back to the first opportunity that you had to observe someone leading others; this may even be a childhood recollection, for example, your teacher, a fellow schoolmate, another adult on an outing with others. Think of it as a moment in time captured on a digital camera. See those around you, what are they doing? What are you doing? What are the sounds you hear? Are there voices, conversation, "orders" to follow? How are you feeling at this moment? Do these feelings have a physical location in your body?

   Have you had similar feelings and sensations again since that time? Specifically what went on during that experience? What are the similarities between these two experiences? What are you saying to yourself about those who lead versus those who follow leaders? Do you have a preference for one position over the other, for example, prefer to be helping another in authority or leadership versus prefer to be the one overseeing plans being implemented to action, and so forth?

   What might these preferences say about your future involvement in organizations? Might you be limiting yourself by assumptions that are not valid for you today? What assets do you bring to others through organizations? With whom might you talk about your insights and how to explore or act upon them?

7. **Finding your passion.** View Randy Komisar's brief lecture "How Do You Find Your Passion and How Do You Pursue It?" by visiting http:// ecorner.stanford.edu/. After viewing, discuss the following with a partner: (1) In what ways have you experienced the "two questions that will drive you crazy and paralyze you?" (2) Komisar advises, "Rather than thinking about *the* passion, free yourself up to think about a portfolio of passions." What is in your portfolio of passions? How does contributing to wellness and human dignity unite your portfolio?

## PERSONAL ACTION PLAN FOR LEADERSHIP

1. **Developing my action plan.** Develop your own personal action plan for leadership. This can include current as well as future leadership endeavors. In your action plan, include action steps for accomplishing those leadership goals as well as the skills that you have that will make you an effective leader. (CACREP Doctoral Level Standards, Section IV, J:1)

2. **Developing my mission statement.** Develop a mission statement for yourself as a professional counselor. How can leadership roles help you actualize your mission? (CACREP Doctoral Level Standards, Section IV, J:1)

Servant Leadership Projects

1. **Read and reflect.** Read Greenleaf's essay on servant leadership and Herr's position paper on leadership in Chi Sigma Iota and write a personal reflection related to your thoughts on servant leadership.

2. **Volunteer in your community.** Volunteering is a large part of becoming and remaining a leader at the university, community, state, regional, national, and international levels. Be an active leader by volunteering your time and energy to at least two professional organizations each year. This can include organizations focused on your own personal and professional interests, and can include being a committee chairperson, committee member, mentor to other developing professionals, or editorial review board member.

3. **Volunteer in your professional association.** Volunteer to be an ad hoc reviewer of one of the counseling profession's refereed journals' editorial boards. Request mentoring from the editor, associate editor, or editorial assistant in providing written reviews of manuscripts and the manners in which leaders in our field offer constructive feedback to one another on research and writing endeavors. (CACREP Doctoral Level Standards, Section IV, J:1)

Engagement with Leaders

1. **Interview a leader.** Interview someone who you consider to be a leader in the counseling profession. Write a 3- to 5-page summary of the interview as well as your personal reaction to that interview. How did the interview support or challenge your definition of leadership and also your understanding of the skills necessary to be a good leader? What did you learn from this interview that will make you a better leader? (CACREP Doctoral Level Standards, Section IV, I:1)

2. **Spend time with leaders.** Interview and spend time with various individuals in your professional life that you view as leaders in your field. These can include individuals from university, community, state, regional, national, and international levels. Reflect on the qualities that these individuals present and role model for you as you continue your developing leadership style and foci. (CACREP Doctoral Level Standards, Section IV, I:1)

3. **Attend professional association conferences.** Each year, leaders in development should try to attend at least two professional counseling organizations' annual conference meetings and plan to observe leaders in action. While at the meeting, attend at least two board or editorial meetings that allow you to observe our profession's leaders in action. Document a few of the qualities that you observe these leaders exhibiting in their verbal presentations and in their interactions with others. Reflect on these qualities, the ones that you admire most, and set goals for yourself that will allow you to develop these qualities in your own developing professional leadership style. (CACREP Doctoral Level Standards, Section IV, I: 1, 5)

Group/Classroom/Professional Conference Leadership Development Activities

1. **Enhancing leadership through social justice.** The group project is designed to develop and enhance your leadership skills while bringing awareness and social change related to a social justice issue. Therefore, the project is to be grounded in counseling and psychological theories that require a thorough review of the relevant literature. The project should take approximately 10–15 hours to complete outside of class time. You will present your group project to the class with details of the knowledge gained and a reflection of your experience. (CACREP Doctoral Level Standards, Sections IV, I:1, 2; I:4; J:1, 2)

2. **Group sharing of leadership reflections.** In small groups in classes or workshops, discuss your personal reflections on leadership. Then, identify themes that emerged from your discussion. Are there common themes in your leadership journeys? What differences did you observe within the group? (CACREP Doctoral Level Standards, Section IV, I: 1,4, 5)

3. **Observing group member roles.** This activity will require six to eight individuals as a minimum but can be accommodated for a class or workshop. Two observers will be asked to note the interaction and behavior of the other group members. They should be positioned outside of the group so that all members are easily observed. They are to note the roles of members during the interactions, including frequency and multiple roles: initiator, idea contributor, question raiser, clarifier, resource contributor, observer, encourager, summarizer, follow-up role taker, other (observer designate). Observers can create a form with roles down the left margin and names across the top of the page.

The group is asked to plan a professional development workshop for professional counselors in their area. The workshop is to be scheduled to maximize the number of participants who can attend and with a topic that has sufficient appeal to merit them investing both time and funds to attend. There is a modest budget ($100) to help with start-up costs, but the hope is that success with this effort will result in funds sufficient for sustaining future start-up costs for a workshop series and provide some revenue to support other good works of the organization.

The group has 20 to 30 minutes to address the above topic. When the group reaches the agreed upon time to finish, they are briefly to write down their impressions of how the group process worked to achieve their goal, that is, how successful were they in planning a professional development workshop. The process observers summarize their notes from the group interaction orally. These should be objective and nonjudgmental. Group members are free to ask questions of the observers while also offering their own impressions that were recorded upon completion of the exercise.

The group can revisit the exercise in terms of, for example: Who among the members had prior experience with planning such an event? How did this experience or lack thereof affect those who participated and when? How did the different roles affect the outcome of the activity? Is it possible to learn new roles that could affect the process and outcome? If the outside observers had been able to intervene and make suggestions, when and how might they have done so (if at all)? Overall, how has this exercise clarified each member's perceptions of membership and leadership roles in an organization? (CACREP Doctoral Level Standards, Section IV, I: 1–5; J:1, 2)

## DISCUSSION QUESTIONS

1. As you reflect on the leadership journeys of the authors of this chapter, which one most resonates with you and why?
2. Discuss your reaction to the servant leader theory.

3. Based upon the group exercise to develop a professional counselors' workshop to help organizations raise funds, none of the roles were characterized as "negative" or "blocking" in this activity. Yet, *in vivo*, there are those who tend toward the negative in any activity of which they are a part in some organizations. If you agree with this position, how do you neutralize such negativity so that a group does not get sidetracked into irrelevant discussions or hard feelings among its members? What specifically can anyone do to help facilitate a group with such members? Can you offer specific illustrations from your own observations and experience? What seem to be the qualities and behaviors of those who successfully lead a group with a negative participant? Are these learned characteristics? If so, where and how can you learn them?

# II

## FOUNDATIONS OF
## ADVOCACY IN COUNSELING

# 5

## *Professional Advocacy*
### Being Allowed to Do Good

THOMAS J. SWEENEY

### INTRODUCTION

All professional counselors enter the counseling profession with a desire to help others. More recently, this has been reflected in broad-based concerns for social justice for all people, but especially for those less able to advocate for themselves or who are marginalized as groups within societies (see Lee, Chapter 7). Client advocacy inherently feels right to all of us in counseling, but especially to those who first enter the field. Advocating for professional counselors and the services they provide may seem self-serving. However, a professional counselor does not need to be in the field long before realizing that in the absence of advocacy for the profession, the right to be a professional counselor serving any particular population can be severely limited by regulations or practices of other professions (Myers, Sweeney, & White, 2002; Myers & Sweeney, 2004; Sweeney, 2003).

In this chapter, I will provide a brief overview of the broad scope of professional advocacy compared to that of client advocacy. I will review the historical events and advocacy efforts within the counseling profession, highlighting the major organizations that provide support and leadership for professional advocacy, noting recent achievements and some of the challenges that we face in our efforts. Finally, I will discuss what every professional counselor can do to help contribute to these efforts.

Key Terms

> **Professional advocacy** involves knowledge, skills, and competencies that advance the profession through deliberate, thoughtful actions that inform

and influence others to support professional counselors because of the benefits their services bring to individuals, groups, and institutions.

**Counselor professional identity** is comprised of five components, including (1) an understanding of the profession's history and philosophical foundations of the profession, (2) knowledge of the roles and functions of counselors and how they are similar to and different from other mental health professions, (3) a sense of pride in the profession, (4) involvement in professional organizations and advocacy, and (5) knowledge of professional codes of ethics and law as it pertains to the counseling profession (Remley & Herlihy, 2007).

## BEING ALLOWED TO DO GOOD

Every occupational group must be proactive in the marketplace or they will become extinct over time. Professional advocacy often can be done most effectively while addressing client advocacy as well, and our history reflects an essential concern for clients' issues even when we ourselves were discriminated against as service providers (see *City of Cleveland v. Cook*, 1975, discussed in Chapter 1). While it is uncommon to speak of professional counselors being discriminated against, there are many examples in the marketplace where practicing professional counselors have not been accorded respect and privilege equal to their training and credentials. As the first chair of the ACA Committee on Licensure in 1975, I was there when professional counselors in private practice reported having received cease and desist orders from psychology boards mandating them to discontinue providing psychological services to clients, and experienced professionals were demoted or not advanced in careers while others no more qualified were shown preference. State legislators have been lobbied by other professional groups to prevent professional counselors from using assessment instruments common to our practice (Fair Access Coalition on Testing, May 17, 2007). In my position with the honor society headquarters, I have learned of practitioners who have been denied third-party reimbursement as preferred providers. When applying for mental health positions, professional counselors have not been hired when equally qualified with individuals trained in other mental health professions. Researchers have received feedback from national grant review boards that our research areas are not well defined or supported by empirical studies (J. E. Myers, personal communication, December 12, 2010). These are only a few examples of how inadequate professional advocacy is affecting professional counselors in the marketplace of human services. I want to begin, however, with a few illustrations of how professional counselors have readily embraced client advocacy during the same period when professional advocacy was evolving.

## CLIENT ADVOCACY: HISTORICAL MILESTONES
## AND MARKERS OF PROGRESS

In 1971, the *Personnel and Guidance Journal* (currently the *Journal of Counseling and Development*) published a special issue on counseling and the social revolution, in which there was a call for counselors to engage in social change processes and address issues related to racism, sexism, destruction of the environment, and ending warfare (Chang & Gnilka, 2010). The Association for Non-White Concerns (ANWC) was established as a division of the American Counseling Association (ACA) the following year. With the emerging multicultural nature of our society, ANWC changed its name to the Association for Multicultural Counseling and Development (AMCD) in 1985, a change that some individuals thought might limit the scope of influence of this division (Parker & Myers, 1991).

The movement toward multiculturalism brought with it a broader perspective to include cultural variables, such as gender, sexual orientation, social class, and religion (Ratts, Toporek, & Lewis, 2010b). The American Association for Counseling and Development (AACD; currently ACA) published a position paper on human rights in 1987 imploring counselors to advocate for social change through personal, professional, and political activities (Chang & Gnilka, 2010). In keeping with the growing emphasis on multiculturalism of the 1980s, Sue, Arredondo, and McDavis (1992) published "Multicultural Counseling Competencies and Standards."

After many years of operating informally, the Association for Gay, Lesbian, and Bisexual Issues in Counseling (AGLBIC), now the Association for Lesbian, Gay, Bisexual, and Transgender Issues in Counseling (ALGBTIC), became a division of ACA in 1997 (Rhode, 2010). About this same time there was an increased focus on social justice issues as a component of multicultural counseling competencies, and an increased call for professional counselors to engage in social action. Lee and Walz's (1998a) book, *Social Action: A Mandate for Counselors*, called upon professional counselors to step out of their offices and engage the systems that created negative circumstances that brought counselees into counseling. In 1999, the *Journal of Counseling and Development* (Robinson and Ginter, editors) published a special issue on racism.

Counselors for Social Justice became a division of ACA in 2002, and the ACA governing council adopted the advocacy competencies (Lewis, Arnold, House, & Toporek, 2002). The increased emphasis on multiculturalism and social justice issues within counseling was also reflected in the revised ACA Code of Ethics (ACA, 2005). Particularly, the new Standard E.5.c directs counselors to "recognize historical and social prejudices in the misdiagnosis and pathologizing of certain individuals and groups and the role of mental health professionals in perpetuating these prejudices through diagnosis and treatment" (p. 12). Lee and Walz's (1998a) *Social Action: A Mandate for Counselors* and the second edition of the book, *Counseling for Social Justice* (Lee, 2007a), provided counselors a sound rationale and tools for being client advocates for social systemic change.

More recently the Association for Counselor Education and Supervision (ACES) adopted the theme "Vanguards for Change: ACES and Social Justice" and sponsored a Social Justice Summit as a part of its national conference (Chang & Gnilka, 2010). In addition, over half of the summer 2009 issue of the *Journal of Counseling and Development* (Goodman, editor) was devoted to the client advocacy competencies. So counseling has embraced client advocacy, social justice, and social equality as core beliefs and behaviors of ethical, competent practice for all counselors. The profession also has created organizations, activities, and literature readily available to advance these values. As noted elsewhere throughout this text, this is all very good. Notably to the matter of "being allowed to do good," we have done far less to advance professional advocacy in a similar fashion.

### Professional Advocacy: Historical Milestones and Challenges

Professional counselors in the field learn that in order to be allowed to do good in their work with clients, they must be able to educate others about our profession's philosophical emphasis upon promoting wellness and human dignity for all, our graduate-level preparation standards, excellence in accreditation and specific credentialing requirements, ethical values and enforcement provisions, behavioral competencies for a multicultural and diverse society, and scopes of practice, including those unique to our profession. It is a part of our professional responsibility to educate, inform, and promote these qualities to legislators, employers, third-party payers, and the public at large (Smith, 2001). Counselor educators seeking to impart this orientation to the profession must depend in large part upon textbooks that necessarily tend to be general in nature with respect to professional advocacy. Unfortunately, unlike our professional position statements on client advocacy, no statements of competencies for professional advocacy exist. Eriksen's (1997) lone work on professional advocacy, which included numerous specific strategies for counselors acting as professional advocates (though not competencies), is no longer in print, and copies of the initial edition are difficult to obtain (though not impossible, as periodically used copies are available online). There have been substantial efforts to correct this imbalance of initiatives, but unlike client advocacy, we are not nearly as far along in our professional advocacy efforts as needed given the evolution of our profession with accredited training programs, national and state certifications, and state licensure in all 50 states.

A premise of this book is that advocacy for both clients and the profession is essential for the future of professional counseling. While 30-plus years of efforts have resulted in all states now credentialing professional counselors, advocacy for the profession has evolved without the benefit of consensus or collaboration on such basic matters as a common definition for what it means to be a professional counselor. Over two decades ago, ACA endorsed a plan for professionalization that included a substantial emphasis on professional advocacy (ACA, 1991). This and other calls for collaboration and coalitions to advance the profession (Myers et al., 2002; Myers & Sweeney, 2004, Smith, 2001) have emphasized the need for a strong statement of professional identity and a strong unified profession. The absence of consensus on essential issues such as a definition of *professional counselor* remains a challenge to other efforts to promote counselors and counseling outside of the profession.

This by no means suggests that ACA and its divisions have not made significant advances on behalf of professional counselors. Most notably, the American School Counselors Association (ASCA) and the American Mental Health Counselors Association (AMHCA), as well ACA's branches, have been critical in the efforts to promote counseling services and to gain state licensing for professional counselors. These and other efforts are chronicled in association documents and websites. The National Board for Certified Counselors (NBCC) also has reported substantial success in professional advocacy efforts (see NBCC.org). Some notable examples of successful advocacy efforts are as follows.

The U.S. Department of Veterans Affairs (VA) has created occupational standards for Licensed Professional Mental Health Counselor (LPMHC) positions within VA health care facilities. While professional counselors have worked within the VA previously, they have not been considered full-fledged mental health service providers on par with other master's-level professionals. Both pay grade and level of supervisory responsibility are now on par in 2011 as a result. More advocacy work remains, however, as other agencies have yet to adopt the grandparenting provisions of the VA and to have similar occupational standards for counselors adopted for use in all federal agencies and programs (www.counseling.org).

Support for the establishment of universal access to health insurance coverage with the enactment of the Patient Protection and Affordable Care Act includes provisions that help professional counselors as health care providers as well as health care consumers. Beginning in 2014, health plans will be prohibited from discriminating against providers on the basis of their type of license. In addition, health plans will be required to cover mental and behavioral health services as part of their benefit package. Combined with the recently enacted federal mental health parity law, these provisions should broaden insurance coverage for mental health services provided by counselors (www.counseling.org).

A Congress-commissioned Institute of Medicine (IOM) TRICARE study recommended independent practice authority for professional counselors. The study was commissioned to provide guidance on whether to remove the physician referral and supervision requirement for counselors' services within TRICARE, the health care program serving members of the armed forces and their dependents. Congress subsequently passed legislation to this effect (www.counseling.org).

In addition, the NBCC has been advocating for professional counselors in various states regarding their scope of practice, especially with respect to testing (Fair Access Coalition on Testing (FACT)) and promoting professional identity among providers of mental health services not only in this country but also abroad. NBCC International has nine field and regional offices in other countries and works with the World Health Organization (WHO), the United Nations Educational, Scientific, and Cultural Organization (UNESCO), and the Organization for Economic Cooperation and Development (OECD) to help bring counseling to those populations under and never served through counseling services.

The Council for Accreditation of Counseling and Related Educational Programs (CACREP) standards revisions (2009) also represents a significant step forward for counseling. As noted in Chapter 1, the standards help to define what it means to be a professional counselor. Now they also define what it will mean to be a counselor educator. Beginning in 2013, new faculty hired in counselor education will be required to have their doctoral degree in counselor education. As basic as this may sound to anyone in another profession or new to counseling, our national standards for counselor preparation only now express support for those who were prepared to be counselor educators and supervisors as well as clinicians. In addition, the standards also reflect the importance of counselor multicultural competencies in an ever-increasingly diverse society and global community.

### Professional Advocacy: Current Status

The results of a survey by Myers and Sweeney (2004) of 71 leaders in state, regional, and national professional and credentialing associations in counseling concerning professional advocacy efforts, resources, and obstacles is relevant to the current discussion, especially since this is the only national study of advocacy efforts in our profession to date. The participants in the study indicated that while there were a variety of ongoing advocacy initiatives, there were also specific needs for resources and interprofessional collaboration, and agreement on the importance of professional advocacy for the future of the profession.

The respondents to the survey were identified based on their leadership positions in the counseling field. Thus, it was not surprising that the average numbers of years in the profession was high (i.e., 21). Most of the respondents had degrees and credentials in counseling and identified themselves as professional counselors. It is probable that those who responded were more interested and involved in advocacy than the leaders who did not respond. The large number of nonrespondents (61%) was troubling to me because the data may reflect only the thoughts of those who were most committed, rather than being definitive for the leadership as a whole. In fact, the nonrespondents may be indicative of a part of the problem we experience in gaining traction on matters of professional advocacy compared to client advocacy. *Could it be that too few leaders have a clear vision of the need for professional advocacy, and that this contributes to a root cause for our lack of more progress?*

Possibly corroborating this conjecture was the lack of success of an effort to replicate the professional advocacy survey for trends over time that was sent to over 100 leaders of counseling organizations in 2010. The number of respondents was too few to conduct data analysis (K. Mobley & J. E. Myers, personal communication, December 15, 2010). The lack of respondents to the 2010 survey may be the most significant finding of any regarding the absence of urgency for professional advocacy among current leadership.

The respondents to the 2004 survey believed that the public image of counseling and professional counselors was the area of greatest need, surpassing or perhaps serving as a precursor to advocacy for jobs. It is clear that respondents to this survey believed that the public lacks awareness of who professional counselors are, as well as the services that we provide. The need to enhance our public image is not a new idea. Nor is the idea that greater access to jobs is a direct by-product of greater public awareness of professional counseling. We need a bold plan to enhance our public image.

## PROFESSIONAL ADVOCACY: THE NEED FOR A PLAN

The first major proposals for a professional advocacy plan began in the 1990s and included the work of the AACD Professionalization Directorate (1991) and the Chi Sigma Iota (CSI) Counselor Advocacy Leadership Conferences Proceedings (1998). The ACA Professionalization Directorate organized a meeting and brought together representatives of counseling credentialing bodies, ACA and its divisions, and related organizations. It was surprising to all present at that meeting that this was the first time in the history of our profession that all of these groups were invited to the same table to discuss how to advocate for and advance our profession. Three subgroups—accreditation, credentialing, and ethics—developed strategic plans with specific goals for a 5- to 10-year period. Included among the goals were advocacy for a professional member category in ACA's membership and a name change from the American Association for Counseling and Development to the American Counseling Association. These goals were accomplished within the first year. Longer-term goals included the development of a unified statement of counselor professional identity and a strong plan for professional advocacy.

The Counselor Advocacy and Leadership Conferences were sponsored by CSI in an effort to bring together the same groups to further the advocacy agenda for the profession. ACA leaders willingly participated but chose not to co-sponsor the conference. A critical outcome of the conferences was agreement that advocacy was indeed a two-pronged effort, with client as well as professional advocacy both needing sustained attention. Each of the organizations present has pursued advocacy to a greater or lesser degree. CSI has continued to promote and support advocacy among its chapters and members, providing space on its website to showcase local, state, and national advocacy projects and contributions (see csi-net. org/advocacy). NBCC has invested substantial effort and resources in advocacy at all levels, including state, national, and international levels, and ACA, as described below, has recently implemented its 20/20 Vision for the Future of Counseling (ACA, 2010). These efforts require sustained leadership and a clear vision, and above all the collaboration of all invested in the future of our profession.

I offer one caveat: Wishing will not make it so that the profession realizes these aspirations of public respect and opportunity to serve. I participated in meetings during the early 1990s of the executive officers of CACREP, NBCC, ACA, and CSI in which an ambitious blueprint was proposed to raise public conscious-ness to the education, role, and value of professional counselors' services. We titled it Public Awareness of Counselor Excellence (PACE), and we envisioned it to be a joint project of these organizations over a 10-year-plus period of time. We formulated a draft blueprint to meet both short- and long-term objectives, including needed resources, funds, and activities. We were proposing to engage marketing experts to help with implementation, including a public personality who could do public service announcements for radio and television. Much like the respondents to our survey (Myers & Sweeney, 2004), these representatives were among the most knowledgeable and committed leaders of our profession, and they were prepared to advocate on the national level with an unprecedented visibility for professional counselors. After the meeting it was agreed that each would return to their respective governing bodies with this blueprint for input and hopefully endorsement.

Open dialogue sessions for regular members were planned and conducted at the ACA annual conference. Members attending conference programs were enthusiastically supportive of the plan. Few members had ever heard of it again, however, because it died in a committee of the ACA governing board, never to be presented again. As a consequence, the other participants withdrew as well. To paraphrase a cartoon character's remark, "We have met the enemy and they are us!"

I am hopeful for the future of professional advocacy, however, as I am wit-nessing a new generation of leaders who share the passion and the conviction that "if it's to be, it's up to me!" Studies of present and aspiring young leaders, though modest in size, corroborate my impressions that those who practice lead-ership in their counselor education honor society chapters benefit from a strong professional identity and a motivation to be servant leaders (Herr, 2010; Luke & Goodrich, 2010). As graduates in counselor education, they also tend to publish scholarly works, present peer-reviewed programs at conferences, and serve in professional leadership positions to a greater extent than those who do not have these experiences (Wester & Lewis, 2005). Such leaders offer hope for greater progress for professional advocacy in the future.

## PROFESSIONAL ADVOCACY: THE NEED FOR A VISION

The formation of a viable, long-term, national plan that is periodically revised will increase the likelihood of success in professional advocacy efforts. The effectiveness of such a plan depends on the achievement of consensus concerning a number of matters. These include a common statement of professional identity, promotion of a positive public image, effective intraprofessional collaboration, and participation by each counselor in professional advocacy behaviors. Inherent within these observations is the need for leadership at all levels and by all specialties.

Often those outside of the profession do not discern the differences between professional counselors and other professionals who use counseling as a method of intervention. While the public and media have adopted *counseling* and *counselor* as an alternative to *therapy* and *treatment*, they are just as likely as not to be interviewing a social worker, psychologist, or nurse without so much as a mention of a mental health counselor or other professional counselor. As a consequence, learning how to advocate for the counseling profession is an essential leadership competence that all counselors need to master (CACREP, 2009). We have a history of professional advocacy tied principally to state counselor credential legislation, to state and federal legislation and regulations to include counselors as providers of services in schools and agencies, to accreditation of counselor education in higher education, and increasingly through overseas efforts of NBCC-I and CACREP that reflect progress in professional advocacy.

Beginning in 2005, over 30 organizations were invited to determine where the counseling profession should be in the year 2020 and to identify the best means of arriving at that point. The initiative, 20/20: A Vision for the Future of Counseling, was co-sponsored by the American Counseling Association and the American Association of State Counseling Boards and all ACA divisions and regions, as well as the NBCC, CACREP, the Council on Rehabilitation Education (CORE), the Commission on Rehabilitation Counselor Certification (CRCC), Chi Sigma Iota (CSI), and the National Rehabilitation Counseling Association (NRCA).

At that time the delegates identified seven principles as critical to the mission of continuing to move the counseling profession forward:

- Sharing a common professional identity is critical for counselors.
- Presenting ourselves as a unified profession has multiple benefits.
- Working together to improve the public perception of counseling and to advocate for professional issues will strengthen the profession.
- Creating a portability system for licensure will benefit counselors and strengthen the counseling profession.
- Expanding and promoting our research base is essential to the efficacy of professional counselors and to the public perception of the profession.

- Focusing on students and prospective students is necessary to ensure the continuing health of the counseling profession.
- Promoting client welfare and advocating for the populations we serve is a primary focus of the counseling profession (ACA, 2010).

The work of this initiative is still ongoing, and the internal political issues of the profession are much like those of the past and not at all unlike those of other professions. With new leadership and the initiative of each member, however, the value of professional advocacy is still very much a part of the future of counseling.

What Every Professional Counselor Can Do: Tangible Strategies for Advocacy

Eriksen (1997, 1999) and Milsom (2009) provided a number of practical guidelines and actions that counselors in training as well as experienced professional counselors can use to help advocate for the profession. Among their recommendations are the following:

1. Identify the problem: This may be the most critical step since everything else will depend upon its clarity and emotional valence, that is, how strongly it motivates self and others to action. When I first visited Dr. Cook in his attorney's office after he was arrested and booked for practicing psychology without a license (*City of Cleveland v. Cook*, 1975), the plight of all such counselors became very immediate and urgent to me. Often it is the plight of one or more counselees that helps us to understand why it is the ratio of counselors to students in schools is entirely too high to be as effective as you are educated to be in graduate school.

2. Assess the available resources: There are the matters of time, funds, and support from others that must be considered. Any successful advocate will be a "possibility" thinker, but that optimism must be put into action after a careful inventory of resources. I look for what I call "spark plug" individuals, who with the right motivation make positive things happen. We find in the honor society chapters that students networking with practicing counselors or a faculty member results in a synergism that draws on enthusiasm and experience that is beneficial to any project. In addition, it is best to build support in increments, that is, for volunteers, to invite them to do a specific job, for a specific time period, and provide enough direction to ensure they can do so successfully. Funding is another consideration, and this is one of the reasons for membership in professional organizations. Through organizations it is possible to raise funds for deserving causes and enjoy the extra influence of their name being associated with the cause.

3. Engage in strategic planning: Eriksen (1997) proposed that a small group of the most concerned members deliberate on the short- and long-term goals of the group. Among the questions to ask:
   a. What is our main concern? (e.g., too few counselors to meet the needs of the students)
   b. Who is our target audience? (e.g., parents, school board members)
   c. What do we want the audience to know? (e.g., how the ratio of counselors to students affects absenteeism, behavior problems, school achievement)
   d. What is a realistic timeframe for addressing our concerns? (weeks vs. months)
   e. How can we best go about addressing our concerns? (e.g., collect data, develop message materials (PowerPoint, handouts), earning parent-teacher organization and administration building support)
4. Train others to be advocates: This is the preparatory step to action. Eriksen (1997) makes the point that counselors are prepared to be skilled in human relations, and using these skills as advocates is among their greatest assets. Having started with an important cause for which to advocate, using our skills to listen, respond, and present alternatives should come easily. Practice, however, will be beneficial to even the seasoned professional. Anticipating questions, objections, and emotional issues can facilitate what might otherwise be unproductive if not counterproductive efforts.
5. Implement a plan of action: As simple as this sounds, the implementation phase is not likely to be linear. In some cases, as with counselor licensure legislation, it took years of advocating and regrouping after setbacks. The planning group will want to monitor and assess progress and potentially revise their plan accordingly.
6. Celebrate accomplishments: I want to underscore Eriksen's (1997) attention to this stage. All of those who have invested time, money, and effort to any cause, large or small, deserve an opportunity to periodically celebrate progress as well as closure on any initiative. This can be as simple as time and resources permit, but it is essential that everyone's efforts are acknowledged and progress and accomplishments enjoyed.

Finally, every professional counselor can be an advocate for the profession by making a point to identify with it. When asked, what do you do? Simply say, for example, I am a professional counselor, a licensed professional counselor, a professional counselor in training. Having a clear, simple statement of what that entails also helps as needed. Also, when preparing business cards or signing a professional letter, list your credentials and degrees. You worked hard and earned them. You have a right and deserve to be proud of them as well.

## CLOSING THOUGHTS

Professional advocacy is vital to the health of the counseling profession and its place among helping professionals. Contrary to our motivations for entering the profession, our desire "to do good" is in jeopardy without greater attention to this effort. Significant strides have been made in the recent past, and ongoing efforts by counseling organizations have the potential for creating more in the future. Leadership emerging from among those new to the profession is one of our greatest assets for the future. With increased attention to leadership and professional advocacy in graduate counselor education programs, mentoring leaders while they are still students will be all the more important to our success.

## DISCUSSION QUESTIONS

1. Specialties in counseling include setting specific identities (e.g., school, college, agencies), populations (e.g., addictions, children, persons with disabilities, older persons), and methods (e.g., group, marriage, and family), but all begin with essentially the same core preparation. List and discuss two or three of the key benefits as well as disadvantages for public advocacy to identifying primarily with a specialty compared to benefits of identifying with professional counseling as a primary identity.

2. In this chapter professional advocacy has been presented as a responsibility of all counselors. Do you agree? If so, why? If not, why not? What are the possible consequences of each position with respect to counselors and those we serve or could serve in the future?

## ACTIVITIES

1. Using your graduate program of studies as your "credentials" to submit for licensing or certification as a professional counselor (if you like, also school counselor, rehabilitation, mental health), assume that you wish to apply to three different states for consideration of employment. Visit one of the websites with such requirements posted (e.g., ACA, NBCC, ASCA). How well does your preparation meet the expectations of the various states' requirements? Are there courses or experience requirements that you do not meet? How might this affect your mobility and availability to apply for employment after graduation or at some point in the future? "Portability" or reciprocity of credentials (being able to earn a credential in one state and move to another state where it is accepted as well) is among the unresolved issues in professional advocacy. Could this be an important issue for you and your peers to become advocates?

Speak with your faculty about how you might become an organizer for such an effort in your program. (Doctoral Standards, II, B 2, 3)

2. One of the simplest ways for professionals to advocate for their profession is by using their titles and degrees on their business cards, letterhead, signature block, and related professional correspondence. It also can be done incorrectly. For example, some individuals will be so proud as to sign: Dr. James Doe, PhD LPC, NCC. *Dr.* and *PhD* are redundant. Also, a business card is different than a résumé since the résumé affords the opportunity to include the identification of the degrees or credentials, for example, master of science, counseling, CACREP nationally accredited program, or certified mental health counselor. You might ask some counselors that you know to share copies of their letterhead or business cards. Take some time to design a business card and prepare a draft résumé as though you were preparing for a job application submission. Invite your faculty instructor to offer you feedback and suggestions. (Doctoral Standards, II, B 2, 3)

# 6

## *Professional Advocacy*
### A Professional Responsibility

Catherine Y. Chang

## INTRODUCTION

Advocacy, the act of arguing on behalf of an individual, group, idea, or issue in the pursuit of influencing outcomes, has been and will continue to be fundamental to the practice of counseling (Chang & Gnilka, 2010). Core to this book and others is the belief that advocacy is a two-pronged concept that includes both client/social advocacy and professional advocacy (see introduction; Chang, Hays, & Milliken 2009; Eriksen, 1997, 1999b; Hof, Dinsmore, Barber, Suhr, & Scofield, 2009; Myers, Sweeney, & White, 2002); therefore, the purpose of this chapter is to build on the ideas presented in Chapter 5, "Professional Advocacy: Being Allowed to Do Good," and to operationalize the concept of professional advocacy.

In this chapter, I will provide a discussion of the existing models/structures of professional advocacy that highlight the importance of the relationship between professional advocacy and competencies of professional counselors. Central to these advocacy models/structures is the importance of professional identity as a counselor; therefore, I will discuss the importance of professional identity as it relates to professional advocacy. Additionally, I will provide practical examples of how to address Section II ("Professional Identity") of the 2009 common core entry-level standards and Sections I and J ("Leadership and Advocacy") doctoral-level standards by the Council for Accreditation of Counseling and Related Educational Programs (CACREP, 2009).

Key Terms

> **Professional advocacy.** For the purpose of this chapter, I will be using the CACREP definition of *advocacy* interchangeably with *professional advocacy*, with the caveat that professional advocacy has the direct intention

of benefiting the counseling profession and also may benefit the client and society. According to CACREP (2009),

> advocacy—action taken on behalf of clients or the counseling profession to support appropriate policies and standards for the profession; promote individual human worth, dignity, and potential; and oppose or work to change policies and procedures, systemic barriers, long-standing traditions, and preconceived notions that stifle human development. (p. 59)

**Professional identity.** According to Solomon (2007), professional identity is both a cognitive process and psychological resource that helps motivate individuals and helps individuals make meaning of their work. As it applies to professional counselors, professional identity relates to one's understanding of the definition of counseling and the counselor role. Furthermore, professional identity includes an understanding of the historical foundation of counseling and ethical standards of practice.

## PROFESSIONAL ADVOCACY MODELS

Every occupational group must be proactive in the marketplace or they will become extinct over time. Counselors must not only believe in their profession's preparation standards, graduate programs, credentialing requirements, and scope of services, but they must educate, inform, and promote them to legislators, employers, third-party payers, and the public at large (Chi Sigma Iota, 1998, 2011, p. 1).

### CSI Advocacy Themes

During the May 1998 Counselor Advocacy Leadership Conference I sponsored by Chi Sigma Iota (CSI), representatives from the conference identified six essential common themes on advocacy. Representatives revisited the six themes during the December meeting (Counselor Advocacy Leadership Conference II). Although the purpose of the resulting publication was not to present a model, I believe the ideas provide not only a foundation for considering one's advocacy efforts, but also concrete goals, activities, and obstacles; therefore, these themes are included in this section. The six themes are counselor education, intraprofessional relations, marketplace recognition, interprofessional issues, research, and prevention/wellness (CSI, 1998, 2011).

### Counselor Education

This theme consists of the goal of ensuring that all counselor education students graduate with a clear identity and pride as professional counselors. Objectives and activities to accomplish this goal include that all counselor education faculty will identify as counselor educators for their primary professional identification and, as such, maintain membership in professional organizations, including the Association for Counselor Education and Supervision, and maintain certification as professional counselors (CSI, 1998, 2011).

### Intrapersonal Relations

This theme calls for a "unified, collaborative advocacy plan for the advancement of counselors and those whom they serve" (CSI, 1998, 2011, p. 5). Activities to promote this concept include determining a common identity to articulate publicly and collaborating on advocacy projects. Additionally, this theme calls for a comprehensive, collaborative advocacy plan for the counseling profession.

### Marketplace Recognition

The goal in marketplace recognition is to ensure that all professional counselors in all settings receive compensation for their services, and that all professional counselors are able to practice within their scope of competencies. Actions to promote market recognition include (1) counseling organizations will advocate both at the state and national legislative levels so that professional counselors will be recognized as service providers in the areas for which they have competence, (2) professional counselors will be trained in developing advocacy skills, and (3) professional counselors will be recognized by the media as providing valuable services to individuals, couples, families, organizations, and society at large (CSI, 1998, 2011).

### Interprofessional Issues

Professional counselors will work collaboratively with other agencies, groups, and disciplines on matters that impact the counselors and our clients. Activities in this theme include identification of groups and organizations for potential collaboration and development of a strategy to address other organizations or groups who may negatively affect the employment or scope of practice of professional counselors (CSI, 1998, 2011).

### Research

Governing agencies (e.g., CACREP, CSI) urge professional counselors to base their advocacy activities on sound scientific research. In order to accomplish this goal, CSI (1998, 2011) promotes conducting outcome research, assessing the outcomes of counselor preparation, determining the state of counselor employability, and assessing the public awareness of counseling.

### Prevention/Wellness

The final theme identified is the promotion of "optimal human development across the life span through prevention and wellness" (CSI, 1998, 2011, p. 11). This theme includes promotion of client wellness as well as promotion of counselor wellness. Actions that foster prevention and wellness include (1) identifying client and counselor needs, (2) engaging in social action activities, (3) implementing strategies that encourage clients to be self-advocates, and (4) training and retaining counselors who are dedicated to personal wellness.

Although this chapter presents these six themes as discrete categories, CSI cautions that they are not discrete and cannot be separated (CSI, 1998, 2011). Additionally, it is stressed that advocacy by its very nature must address both client (i.e., client/social advocacy) and counselor (i.e., professional advocacy) needs. Eriksen's (1997) advocacy model and Chang et al.'s (2009) supervision model, discussed below, are equally applicable for and incorporate this dual focus on professional and client advocacy.

## Eriksen Model

Based on participant observation and key informant interviewing, Eriksen (1997) identified seven advocacy steps counselors must progress through in order to advocate for the profession: (1) develop your professional identity, (2) identify the problem, (3) assess the availability of resources, (4) engage in strategic planning activities, (5) train professional counselors to advocate, (6) implement a plan of action, and (7) celebrate accomplishments.

### Professional Identity

Eriksen (1997, 1999) argued that a clear sense of professional identity is essential to any advocacy activity. As counselors, we need to know who we are and what we are promoting before we can successfully engage in advocacy. The importance of having a solid professional identity is not new to the profession of counseling (see Hanna & Bemak, 1997; Myers et al., 2002; Ritchie, 1990); more details will follow later in this chapter.

### Problem Identification

An important first step in advocacy is deciding what is worthy of advocacy efforts. Quoting from one of her participants, Eriksen wrote: "I think that may be the most challenging part of advocacy... coming to some agreement among ourselves as to what problems should receive priority attention" (1997, p. 23). Once problem identification occurs, Eriksen further suggested that counselors need to frame the concern so that decision makers and the wider public will be motivated to take action.

### Resource Assessment

An assessment of your resources includes both internal and external sources. The internal resources include availability of your time, money, personnel, expertise, and motivation. External resources consist of individuals outside of the counseling profession who may also support the advocacy efforts, including former members, partner agencies, influential community members, and any other stakeholders the counselor can identify (Eriksen, 1997, 1999).

## Strategic Planning

Eriksen (1997, 1999) proposed the creation of a small core group of counselors who are committed to solving the problem. This core would determine both long-term and short-term goals that reflect the concerns of the larger group. This small group would also develop a list of activities for the larger group as well as develop documentation to disseminate to the stakeholders.

## Training Advocates

In order for advocacy efforts to be successful, they must involve more than one individual and multiple advocacy strategies. Eriksen (1997, 1999) asserted that by training members of an organization you motivate and encourage them to be more involved. She suggested that advocacy training could be conducted in the form of workshops, conferences, or legislative days. Trainings could include the following topics: methods of approaching your legislators, what kinds of information to share, public speaking, assertiveness, and communication skills.

## Implementation of Plan

The implementation plan phase not only encompasses taking action but also includes ensuring that you have a solid plan and that the group members are aware of and competent to perform their assigned tasks. Additionally, this phase involves assessment of one's efforts both during and following the activity. The formative assessment can provide the core group with information that they can use either to modify or to reallocate their resources. The final evaluation can help determine future steps (Eriksen, 1997, 1999).

## Celebration

Finally, an important aspect of the advocacy process is to celebrate both the small and big accomplishments. This time of celebration consists not only of reflecting but also sharing your successes with others, which could be helpful toward future advocacy efforts. Eriksen (1997) has noted that advocacy is a continuous process and a part of this phase "involves celebrating the successes, grieving the losses, and regrouping for the next effort. Whether counselors have won or lost, there is always more to do" (p. 72).

## Three-Tier Model of Advocacy

Chang et al. (2009) developed a three-tier model of advocacy using a social constructivist framework based on the belief that social advocacy (Lee & Walz, 1998a) and professional advocacy (Myers et al., 2002) are necessary to promote advocacy and optimal psychosocial health and wellness in the clients we serve. Fundamental to this model is the belief that client/social advocacy and professional advocacy are intricately related. According to Myers et al., counselors can more effectively advocate for their clients if other mental health professionals, legislators, and policy makers recognize the profession. Reality, from a social constructivist perspective, is a social construct; human interactions construct and reflect reality (D'Andrea, 2000). Thus, our sense of reality is based on social, cultural, and historical contexts and is flexible and changeable. Knowledge is constructed based on one's understanding of the importance of culture and context (D'Andrea, 2000; Vygotsky, 1978). Chang et al. encourage professional counselors and counselor educators to consider social justice issues relative to two fronts (i.e., client advocacy and professional advocacy) and across three tiers (i.e., self-awareness, client services, and community collaboration). Although Chang et al. developed this model for use with supervisees, it can easily be adapted and applied to all counselors and counselor educators.

Tier 1 includes an awareness of our own biases so that we can be sensitive to the cultural and social context of our clients. This tier includes an awareness and understanding of what advocacy means to us as professional counselors. Additionally, it includes the development of a strong professional identity and professional pride in being a counselor (professional advocacy).

Tier 2 encompasses activities that directly impact client issues and client welfare. On the client advocacy front, professional counselors are encouraged to understand the interrelatedness and interactions of various social, political, and educational systems that affect their clients. On the professional advocacy front, professional counselors are encouraged further to develop their professional identity and professional pride through licensure and certification efforts, with the understanding that a clearer professional identity leads to greater competence in client work (Chang et al., 2009).

Tier 3 involves community collaboration. On the client front, this includes educating the community about the relationship between oppression and mental health issues. On the professional advocacy front, professional counselors can learn about the importance of advocating for our profession through collaborating with various mental health agencies as well as working with policy makers (Chang et al., 2009).

One limitation of this model is its lack of empirical support. However, the current literature related to social and professional advocacy informs its principles. The authors do recommend that researchers test this model in future studies.

### The TRAINER Model

Hof et al. (2009) developed the TRAINER model to demonstrate how social and professional advocacy can integrate into training of advocates. Hof et al. also proposed a formal set of professional advocacy competencies that consist of four categories of advocacy interventions (i.e., promoting professional identity, increasing the public image of counseling, developing interprofessional/intraprofessional collaboration, and promoting legislative/policy initiatives). The design of this model fosters professional development and education of training advocates that focuses on providing concrete ways for the training of advocates to address the needs of their clients while simultaneously raising awareness of the counseling profession through the professional advocacy competencies. This model includes a seven-step collaborative process: (1) target, (2) respond, (3) articulate, (4) implement, (5) network, (6) evaluate, and (7) retarget (p. 18).

In the first step, *targeting*, the training advocate conducts a needs assessment and identifies a client population that social and professional advocacy efforts could serve. Following the needs assessment, the training advocate works together with the client group and the client ally groups to identify conditions that require professional advocacy using the professional advocacy competencies previously identified as a guide (*responding stage*). After the responding stage, the training advocate moves to the *articulation stage*, in which the training advocate works on planning the content and the logistics of the event. As a part of this stage the training advocate again acts alongside the client group, client ally groups, professional colleagues, and others who are invested in promoting the identified needs of the targeted group. The articulation stage is followed by the *implementation stage*, which includes not only implementing the event created during the articulation stage, but also the process of formatively evaluating and adapting to the needs of the group during the training event (Hof et al., 2009).

The next stage is *networking*, in which the advocate groups attendees of the event together and asks them to collaborate in order to generate a personal or collaborative advocacy plan that includes individual, institutional, community/social-level social and professional advocacy initiatives related to the training topic. One outcome of this stage is to foster partnership initiatives among the members of the attendees of the event. During the *evaluating stage*, the advocates ask participants to provide feedback on the value of the training event. Hof et al. (2009) suggested conducting follow-up surveys to determine if there have been any changes in the community based on the training event. Finally, the model ends with the *retargeting stage*. In this stage, the trainer advocate reevaluates all the steps taken and uses data from the evaluation stage to determine how well the interventions met professional advocacy competency goals and also how to determine the next steps.

Hof, Scofield, and Dinsmore (2006) reported that the TRAINER model leads to effective outcomes based on implementation of the model in three settings: (1) a national training on social advocacy, (2) a student-led conference, and (3) the American Counseling Association (ACA) conference. These training sessions generated 52 plans of action to implement social and professional advocacy, and longitudinal follow-up studies indicate positive impacts based on the action plans. This model provides support and resources for those wanting to engage in social and professional advocacy. More specifically, by identifying professional advocacy competencies, this model helps to operationalize professional advocacy and provide counselors with concrete directions regarding how to engage in professional advocacy activities (Hof et al., 2009).

## PROFESSIONAL IDENTITY

All the models presented in the previous section highlight the importance of professional identity across counseling specialty (e.g., mental health counseling, school counseling, student affairs, and college counseling). The topic of professional identity is not new to the counseling profession. Interestingly, although many view professional identity as central to professional advocacy (see Myers et al., 2002), the term *professional advocacy* is not in the 2009 CACREP standards; however, the term *professional identity* is in the standards. The term *advocacy* is also included in the standards, but in this context it relates more closely to client advocacy (CACREP, 2009). CACREP does present a definition of advocacy in the glossary that encompasses action taken on behalf of both the client and the counseling profession. In this section, I discuss the importance of maintaining a solid professional identity and then discuss how counselor educators can train counselors who have a solid professional identity and who meet the standards set forth by CACREP in 2009.

### Professional Identity: Essential for Advocacy

Based on an extensive review of the literature, Calley and Hawley (2008) identified the following factors as related to professional identity in counseling: (1) values of the profession, (2) scope of professional activities, (3) emphasis of scholarship, (4) theoretical orientation, (5) historic knowledge of the counseling profession, and (6) counselor credentialing and training.

Despite the strides that counseling has made over the years to meet the criteria (i.e., professional organization, an ethical code, accrediting body, credentials, and licensing) to be a profession (Feit & Lloyd, 1990; Ritchie, 1990), some argue that professional counseling has not fully matured and developed a professional identity due to the fact that counseling is a diverse profession that is continuing to evolve (Gale & Austin, 2003). Additionally, Gale and Austin point out the challenges to a collective professional identity in counseling, including training, specialization and credentials, and professional counseling associations.

A prerequisite or at least a co-requisite for effective professional advocacy is the development of a solid professional identity as a counselor. Interestingly, Myers and Sweeney (2004) reported that participants in their national survey identified the public image of counseling and counselors as a current advocacy need. The participants did not believe that the public had a clear understanding of who we are as professional counselors and what we do. This is consistent with Eriksen's (1999) findings. Participants in her study identified a lack of a clear sense of professional identity as an obstacle to advocacy. In order for us to educate the public about who we are and what we do, we as a profession need to have a clear and solid professional identity. And, I would argue that by participating in professional advocacy activities, we continue to foster and fortify our professional identity. I believe the following case exemplifies the interrelatedness between client advocacy and professional advocacy and the importance of having a clear professional identity.

### The Case of Ann

Ann is an intern at a community mental health agency in a rural area. She works in the partial hospitalization program. As part of the program, all the clients attend a group co-facilitated by Ann and a man who had worked for the mental health system for years without a degree or certification.

This particular group happened to consist only of women, and many of these women were dealing with recovery from addictions as well as a history of sexual assault. They were discussing safety and the male group leader made the comment that women should at least fight back; he reported that he knew lots of women who were able to avoid being raped by fighting back (this was not the first time the male therapist had made inappropriate and inaccurate comments). Despite the power differential between Ann and this male group leader, she spoke up and shared her perspective in order to educate not only the male group leader but also the group members. Ann informed the male facilitator and the group that it is the perpetrator who is responsible for the attacks, not the survivors, regardless of whether they were able to or attempted to fight back or not (client advocacy). Following the group, Ann approached the male group leader and shared her concerns related to his comments. She also shared with him what it means to be a counselor from her perspective (professional advocacy).

The next day in another group with the same group members, Ann gave the women an opportunity to discuss their group experience. Many of the women thanked Ann for speaking up in group the previous day as well as for giving group members an opportunity to process the experience. She also reported the inappropriate comments made by her co-facilitator to her clinical director and advocated to have him removed from working with the women's group (professional advocacy). In supervision, Ann reported having a clearer sense of what it meant to be a professional counselor after confronting her co-facilitator and advocating for his removal from working with the women's group.

Because Ann had a clear professional identity and understood the importance of maintaining competent counseling professionals, she was able to advocate for the counseling profession. Additionally, she was able to advocate and empower her clients because she understood the role that power played in the counseling relationship. Applying the three-tier model of advocacy (Chang et al., 2009), Ann demonstrated advocacy across the three tiers and at both fronts: client advocacy and professional advocacy. At the self-awareness level, Ann demonstrated an awareness of the importance of understanding cultural context and the role power and privilege have on the counseling relationship. She understood the importance of having professional pride and demonstrated this through her discussion with the male group facilitator. At the client issue level, Ann demonstrated an understanding of how the male facilitator's comments were impacting the group and the importance of addressing this issue the next day. Her actions had a direct impact on the quality of client care. Additionally, at the community collaboration level, she modeled for the group appropriate counselor behavior and worked with her supervisor to ensure that the male facilitator no longer worked with the women's group.

### Promoting Professional Identity

The 2009 CACREP standards address two main areas of professional identity issues, including Section II, "Professional Identity," of the common core entry-level standards and Section II, "Professional Identity," of the counselor education and supervision doctoral standards. There is one additional reference to advocacy in each of the specialty standards (i.e., addictions counseling; career counseling; clinical mental health counseling; marriage, couples, and family counseling; student affairs and college counseling) in the section "Diversity and Advocacy." The counselor education and supervision doctoral standards have an additional section on "Leadership and Advocacy."

Below are several activities and exercises that counselor educators can integrate into their courses that are designed to promote professional identity and address both Section II of the 2009 CACREP common core entry level and the leadership and advocacy section of the doctoral standards.

#### *Professional Organization Fact Sheet*

Students work in small groups (two to three students) to create a fact sheet that compares and contrasts two professional counseling organizations (e.g., American Counseling Association, American School Counseling Association, American College Counseling Association). The fact sheet can be creatively formatted, but it must be typed and of professional quality. The fact sheet must include the following information: (1) Explain the role of the professional organization, member benefits, services to members, and advocacy activities of the organization on behalf of its members; (2) list ways that these organizations collaborate with other mental health organizations; and (3) identify current trends within the professional organizations (adapted from Georgia State University (GSU), 2011). This activity meets the following 2009 CACREP entry-level standards: Standard II, Section G.1.b and f.

#### *Volunteer Service Experience*

This design of this project provides students with an opportunity to observe institutional and social barriers that may impede access, equality, and success as well as to observe effective strategies to support client advocacy. Students will volunteer 12 hours of service over the course of a semester to a community/school agency. As a part of this volunteer experience students will complete reflection journals where they will record their observations and personal feelings related to the experience. Students can structure the journal however they like and at a minimum the following questions need to be addressed: (1) Before volunteering, what assumptions or biases did you have about this client population? (2) What previous experience, if any, have you had with this client population? (3) Describe your volunteer activities. (4) What barriers and obstacles did you observe? (5) What effective strategies did you observe? (6) What did you learn about yourself and the profession of counseling? (7) Identify areas of professional advocacy that need rectification based on your experience. (8) What advocacy steps can you take to address some of the issues you identified? Identify some potential external resources (GSU, 2011). This activity meets the entry common core standard, Section II, Standard G.1.h.

*Advocacy Project (Orr, 2010)*

This is a three-part group project that provides students with the opportunity to explore a particular career counseling topic of interest to you and design a specific advocacy intervention geared toward a specific population in counseling. You will select your group members early in the semester, and the project will be completed in cooperation with several of your peers as a task group. One grade will be assigned for all of you and will be based on the quality of your collective work, adherence to the American Psychological Association's writing guidelines, adherence to the ACA code of ethics regarding research and publication, and working with marginalized/oppressed populations. The overall effectiveness of your group's social action will also be taken into account. The project consists of the following parts:

**Assignment I: Research paper.** Each task group will collaborate to write a research paper (one per group) on a career/vocational (or any other specialty area) topic of their choice related to a particular issue or client population in counseling.

**Assignment II: Take action.** The focus of this step in the assignment is action. Based on the research you conducted for your paper in Assignment I, you are expected to collaborate with your team members to prepare and deliver an advocacy project that will directly benefit a population that is typically identified as marginalized or underserved. This advocacy project assignment gives you the opportunity to address a social concern related to career counseling that has particular importance to you and your fellow task group members. *Once you and your team members have identified a deliverable action for this advocacy* *project, please have it approved by the instructor.* After taking action, each member of the task group is expected to complete a one- to two-page reflection paper. Members should reflect on the process and outcome of the action taken.

**Assignment III: Presentation.** Each team will present a compilation of information gained throughout this advocacy project. These presentations are expected to be brief (five to seven minutes) and should include a summarization of the following information: target population or social justice issue for your project, a rationale for your project, specific goals for your project, outcomes of your project, an example or a detailed account of the advocacy action, and individual and group reflections on the process of the advocacy project. This project meets the following CACREP doctoral-level standards: Section IV, G.2, G.3, G.4; Section II, C.4.

*Leadership and Advocacy Project*

This project is suitable for a doctoral program that follows a cohort model. During the course of your three years, collaborate with your cohort to develop a project related to leadership, and professional and social advocacy. The aim of the project is to develop and enhance your leadership skills while bringing awareness and social change related to a social justice issue. Therefore, students need to ground the project in counseling and psychological theories (e.g., advocacy models, social change theories), which requires a thorough review of the relevant literature as well as an investigation of the current social issues affecting the counseling profession. The project should take approximately 10–15 hours to complete outside of class time. You will present your project to the seminar detailing not only the knowledge gained but also a reflection of your experience. Your cohort will consult with the instructor to develop this project. This assignment fulfills the CACREP doctoral standards I.2, 3, 4, 5, and J.1, 2.

## SUMMARY

In this chapter, I presented several models/structures of professional advocacy for counselors and discussed the importance of professional identity related to professional advocacy. Professional advocacy and professional identity are interrelated and mutually enhancing constructs. Finally, I introduced several activities that counselor educators can integrate into various counseling courses that address the 2009 CACREP standards related to professional identity and professional advocacy.

## DISCUSSION QUESTIONS

1. Review the six CSI advocacy themes (see csi-net.org/advocacy). Which one is most salient for you and why? What steps can you take now to promote one of the advocacy themes?
2. Compare and contrast the various advocacy models presented in this chapter. Taking one of the models, design a research study to test it.
3. Review the case of Ann. What can you do in your practice that promotes client advocacy and professional advocacy?
4. As a profession, what are some of the challenges we face in advocating for ourselves and our clients? How can we reframe or navigate these obstacles?

# 7

# Social Justice as the Fifth Force in Counseling

## Courtland C. Lee

- The recent financial meltdown has brought economic hardship around the country, the likes of which mirror the Great Depression of the last century. While corporations receive generous government handouts, the poorest of the nation's population sees no relief. Significantly, both the number of children in poverty and the child poverty rate increased between 2008 and 2009 (DeNavas-Walt, Proctor, & Smith, 2010).
- Racial, gender, religious, and sexual orientation intolerance are evident in various forms. This narrowness and exclusivism leads to discrimination against people who are "different," often stripping them of their human rights (Human Rights Watch, 2010).
- The gap in academic achievement between students of color and low-income students and their more advantaged White and middle-class peers in the nation's schools remains pervasive (Haycock, Jerald, & Huang, 2001).
- Four children die from maltreatment every day, a number largely under-counted. Neglect, often associated with poverty, leads to slightly more child deaths each year than abuse. A young boy in Maryland dies from a toothache because his mother cannot afford to pay an $86 dentist bill (Department of Health and Human Services, 2004).

These bullet points underscore a major challenge that confronts the United States in the second decade of the twenty-first century. Data suggest that we live in a nation that is often characterized by systemic intolerance and social inequities. To borrow a phrase from the great educator and social activist Jonathan Kozol, we appear to live in a nation of savage inequalities (1991). It seems evident that in many respects the nation is built on inequities of power and privilege. These inequities take their toll on human development and seriously stifle wellness and human dignity.

Given the nature of the issues that have the potential to impact human development negatively, it is crucial that leaders in the counseling profession reflect on the nature of their helping role. My goal in this chapter is to provide direction for this reflective process. I will first explore the nature of social justice as a theoretical construct and its meaning for counselors and those who aspire to be leaders in the profession. I then examine a developmental process for those leaders who commit themselves to becoming agents of social justice in their life and work. I conclude with a concrete example of how counseling leaders can translate this commitment into action for the benefit of clients and society, as well as a set of reflective questions on the nature of social justice and advocacy.

## THE NATURE OF SOCIAL JUSTICE

A review of the literature would suggest that social justice involves promoting access and equity to ensure full participation in the life of a society, particularly for those who have been systematically excluded on the basis of race/ethnicity, gender, age, physical or mental disability, education, sexual orientation, socioeconomic status, or other characteristics of background or group membership. Social justice is based on a belief that all people have a right to equitable treatment, support for their human rights, and a fair allocation of societal resources (Bell, 1997; Lee, 2007a; Miller, 1999; Rawls, 1971).

As a theoretical construct, social justice places a focus on issues of oppression, privilege, and social inequities. Oppression is the process of subjecting a person or group of people to a harsh or cruel form of domination, while privilege is viewed as the rights and advantages enjoyed by a relatively small group of people, usually as a result of some form of perceived social status. The forces of oppression and privilege often converge to perpetuate inequities where groups of people are marginalized in society, often on the basis of the characteristics mentioned previously.

For counselors, social justice implies professional conduct that opposes all forms of discrimination and oppression. Counseling practices that are rooted in social justice seek to challenge inherent inequities in social systems. Significantly, it has been argued that from a theoretical perspective, social justice is the fifth force in the counseling profession, following the paradigms of the psychodynamic approach, the cognitive-behavioral approach, the humanistic approach, and multiculturalism (Ratts, D'Andrea, & Arredondo, 2004). The construct of social justice, therefore, represents an important theoretical foundation of counseling practice.

Social justice counseling is considered the next evolutionary step in the discipline of multicultural counseling—advancing from understanding the experiences of oppressed or marginalized groups toward social action, with the goal of helping to achieve social equity for these groups (Lee, 2007a; Ratts, Toporek, & Lewis, 2010b).

In order to understand fully the construct of social justice and its relationship to the counseling process, the important concept of advocacy must be considered. Advocacy refers to the act or process of advocating or supporting a cause or proposal (*Merriam-Webster Unabridged Dictionary*, 2010). An advocate, therefore, is an individual who pleads for a cause. In addition, an advocate can be a person who argues another individual's cause or proposal (Lee, 1998).

The concept of advocacy helps to frame the context of counseling for social justice. As advocates, counselors are called upon to channel energy and skill into helping clients challenge institutional and social barriers that impede academic, career, or personal-social development. In addition to counseling at an individual level, when necessary, counselors need to be willing to act on behalf of marginalized or disenfranchised clients and actively challenge long-standing traditions, preconceived notions, or regressive policies and procedures that may stifle or prevent wellness and human dignity. Acting as advocates, through efforts both with and for clients, counselors can help people become empowered so that they can challenge systemic barriers and seize new educational, career, or personal-social opportunities (Lee, 2007a; Ratts et al., 2010).

There are three important aspects of the advocate role for professional counselors. First, advocates are counselors who view helping from a systemic perspective. Second, advocates attempt systemic change in partnership with clients who often lack the knowledge or skill base to effect such change alone. Third, advocates must have an understanding of important systems change principles along with the skill to translate them into action (Lee, 2007a; Ratts et al., 2010).

The concept of advocacy provides the basis for the role of counselor as an agent of social justice. A leader in the counseling profession with a belief in the possibility of an equitable and just society should dedicate himself or herself to social justice and develop a voice as an advocate. Counseling for social justice is more than a professional obligation: it is about living one's life in a manner that is dedicated to promoting access and equity. Social justice, therefore, becomes more than a mere abstraction, but rather a commitment to work to make the world around one a better place. The essence of being an agent of social justice is being able to not only "talk the talk," but also "walk the walk."

## THE COUNSELING LEADER AS AGENT OF SOCIAL JUSTICE: THE PROCESS OF BECOMING

Social justice and the professional action that counselors take to promote access and equity must be considered within the context of the awareness that a counselor possesses of himself or herself as both a person and a professional. Therefore, the process of becoming a leader in the counseling profession who is committed to social justice and advocacy begins with self-exploration. Lee (2007b) delineated six steps in a counselor call to action for the personal development of a counselor who is committed to becoming a force for promoting access, equity, and social justice: (1) explore life meaning and commitment, (2) explore personal privilege, (3) explore the nature of oppression, (4) strive for cultural competence, (5) commit to becoming globally literate, and (6) establish a personal social justice compass. I expand on these steps below and provide an important social justice leadership development paradigm:

## 1. Explore Life Meaning and Commitment

Anyone who has aspirations of being a leader and advocate for social justice in the profession of counseling must start the process by reflecting on the following existential questions: What do I do and why do I do it? How do I do it? Who do I do it for? What do I believe about my clients? What do I believe about myself? Am I a leader or a follower? Do I have courage? Do I have the courage of my convictions? What am I passionate about? What makes me angry? What are the results of my efforts? Am I committed to fostering and supporting a society that is more enlightened, just, and humane through my life and work?

## 2. Explore Personal Privilege

Next, it is important to examine the nature and extent of one's personal cultural privilege.

Cultural privilege can be conceived along several dimensions. First, it is generally unearned. In most cases individuals are born with it and their privilege tends to be innate. This is certainly the case with skin color or gender, for example. Second, individuals with privilege generally tend to be unaware of the unearned benefits that accrue from their privileged status. Third, privilege gives the individual who has it distinct cultural, social, and economic advantages. Individuals with privilege are generally seen to be in a position of social dominance when compared with those who lack these advantages (Lee & Diaz, 2009). McIntosh (1989) stated that privilege is like an invisible weightless knapsack of special provisions, maps, passports, codebooks, visas, clothes, tools, and blank checks. Significantly, in the United States, privilege generally comes with race/ethnic background (White), gender (male), religion (Christian), sexual orientation (heterosexual), ability status (able bodied), and socioeconomic status (accumulated wealth) (Lee & Diaz, 2009).

It is important that anyone aspiring to leadership in the counseling profession reflect on the nature of the cultural privilege he or she may possess due to his or her skin color, gender, sexual orientation, age, religious affiliation, socioeconomic status, ability status, or other social or cultural characteristics. One must evaluate the degree of privilege he or she enjoys in society by virtue of such demographic or cultural characteristics. This evaluation must begin with a personal acknowledgment of such privilege and how it may contribute to societal inequities. One must get beyond the guilt that often comes with the realization that privilege often gives one unfair advantages over others in society. A leader must challenge himself or herself to find ways to exploit his or her cultural privilege in any venue that will promote equity, human rights, and a fair allocation of societal resources.

### 3. Explore the Nature of Oppression

Leaders must also consider the impact of oppression on their life and work. It is crucial that one ask of himself or herself: How have I been a victim of oppression in my life or work? How have I contributed to the perpetuation of oppression in my life or work? Have I used personal or professional privilege or power in unjust ways?

### 4. Strive for Cultural Competence

Counseling for social justice and advocacy must be predicated on the development of a set of attitudes and behaviors indicative of the ability to establish, maintain, and successfully conclude a counseling relationship with clients/students from diverse cultural backgrounds (Lee, in press a; Roysircar, Arredondo, Fuertes, Ponterotto, & Toporek, 2003). A counseling leader must ask himself or herself three crucial questions that are basic to the cultivation of the awareness, knowledge, and skill set that are the foundation of culturally competent counseling: Who am I as a cultural being? What do I know about the cultural dynamics of people whose worldviews are different from mine? How do my counseling skills promote wellness and human dignity in a culturally competent manner?

### 5. Commit to Becoming Globally Literate

While cultural competency is important to a social justice orientation, counseling leaders must go further and become truly committed to living cultural diversity as a reality rather than experiencing it as an abstraction. It is important, therefore, that leaders embrace a lifestyle that will help them to become globally literate. Global literacy refers to the breadth of information that extends over the major domains of human diversity. To be globally literate is to possess basic information needed to negotiate the diverse interconnected global society of the twenty-first century (Lee, in press b). Global literacy goes beyond mere competency to embracing a way of life that encourages maximum exposure to and understanding of the many-faceted realities of multiculturalism and diversity. A globally literate person is one who has knowledge of ethnic variations in history, has both domestic and international travel experience, reads at least one major newspaper (in paper form or via the Internet) or watches newscasts on a consistent basis, reads literature from other cultures, and is open to new cultural experiences, actively seeking out diverse cultural activities. In addition, global literacy entails embracing cultural differences and respecting diverse lifestyles and religious/spiritual traditions.

A counseling leader who is globally literate is a person who is committed to making cultural diversity a foundational aspect of his or her life. A broad perspective on systemic challenges to wellness and human dignity and one's sense of social justice and advocacy must rest on a working knowledge of the cultural realities of and current events taking place in the four corners of the globe.

### 6. Establish a Personal Social Justice Compass

Counselors who are leaders must develop a set of personal principles and ideals to direct their commitment to social justice and advocacy. These principles and ideals should provide an ethical and moral compass to guide both their life and work. Five important documents underlie the development of such a compass. The first of these documents is the Universal Declaration of Human Rights adopted by the United Nations in 1948 (United Nations, 1948). This historic and landmark document establishes a set of universal principles that were conceived as the foundation of global freedom, justice, and peace. This declaration, in part, states that all human beings have a basic right to work, an education, and a standard of living adequate for the health and well-being of self and of family, including food, clothing, housing, medical care, and necessary social services. Any counselor committed to social justice should be familiar with this document and its enlightened ideas about the possibility of a better world.

The second major document is the American Counseling Association (ACA) Code of Ethics (2005). All counseling should be predicated on ethical practice. A social justice perspective on counseling, in particular, rests on understanding and adhering to those recently added sections of the code that state that counselors have an ethical responsibility to engage in advocacy initiatives, both with and on behalf of their clients, that challenge systemic barriers to psychosocial development. In particular, Section A.6 of the code specifically calls for counselors to advocate not only at the individual level, but also at the systemic level to explore potential environmental barriers that may negatively impact on client development and well-being.

The ACA advocacy competencies represent the third significant document to consider in establishing a personal compass (Toporek, Lewis, & Ratts, 2010). From the student/client level to the public arena, these competencies provide a social justice framework and prescribe best practice in advancing advocacy on behalf of those individuals with whom counselors work.

The fourth of these suggested documents is the multicultural counseling competencies (Sue, Arredondo, & McDavis, 1992). This seminal document provides a set of counselor dispositions that characterize the awareness level, knowledge base, and skill set that is necessary for competent counseling intervention into the lives of clients from diverse cultural backgrounds.

The final document is the Chi Sigma Iota advocacy themes, particularly Theme 6, which addresses the important issue of client wellness. In addition to advocating for basic human rights for all persons, the CSI advocacy themes, based in the CSI strategic vision and strategic plan, establish an agenda for all counselors to commit themselves to the promotion of human dignity and wellness for all individuals. The themes are supported by CSI's Principles and Practices of Leadership Excellence, described in Chapter 3, that help all counselors understand our role as leaders for the profession and the clients we serve.

Taken together, these documents embody the essence of social justice ideals and principles. While none of them are perfect, they represent a collective attempt to articulate an important vision of best counseling practice in a world of social injustice. Collectively, they provide an ethical, philosophical, and conceptual framework for developing inner direction to advance social justice in one's efforts as both a counselor and a leader.

The process of becoming an agent of social justice is underscored by passion, courage, and commitment. Counseling for social justice is more than a professional obligation; it is about actively living one's life in a manner that is committed to promoting access and equity, and wellness and human dignity for all persons. Counselors, especially those who aspire to be leaders, must have the courage of their convictions and be willing to stand up and articulate social injustices to agents of power who are often unable or unwilling to hear about them. Courage also entails being willing to go beyond the safety of one's theoretical orientation or professional socialization. The process of becoming committed to counseling for social justice must be about not only talking the talk, but also walking the talk.

## THE COUNSELING LEADER AS AGENT OF SOCIAL JUSTICE: FROM TALKING THE TALK TO WALKING THE TALK

The 2009 Council for Accreditation of Counseling and Related Educational Programs (CACREP) entry-level standards call for demonstrated knowledge of "advocacy processes needed to address institutional and social barriers that impede access, equity, and success for clients" (CACREP, 2009, p. 10). They also call for demonstrated knowledge of "counselors' roles in developing cultural self-awareness, promoting cultural social justice, advocacy and conflict resolution, and other culturally supported behaviors that promote optimal wellness and growth of the human spirit, mind, or body" (CACREP, 2009, p. 11). Similarly, the CACREP doctoral standards for counselor education and supervision call for "pedagogy relevant to multicultural issues and competencies, including social change theory and advocacy action planning" (CACREP, 2009, p. 54). This demonstrated knowledge implies a set of counselor competencies that reflect an advocacy and social justice orientation to client interventions. Counselors must be able to work not only at the individual level, but also at the systems level to promote wellness and human dignity. The following case study is an example of counseling leadership for social justice.

## The Case of Ann

Ann (not her real name) is a graduate of an entry-level school counseling program. Her first job was as a counselor at a charter school in an urban, inner city area. The population of the school was predominantly Latino. In addition, the overwhelming majority of the students came from poor families. The school did not have much of a college-going culture, and a large percentage of the students dropped out before graduation. Those who did graduate usually ended up in low-paying jobs or unemployed.

Armed with data that showed that Latinos are approximately 10% less likely than non-Hispanic Whites and 5% less likely than African Americans to attend college (U.S. Department of Education, 2002), Ann decided to take action at her school. She committed herself to motivating and supporting students and their parents in a college access process. In addition to her intervention with students and parents, she used these data to challenge long-standing school and school system policies and procedures that blocked college access for Latino students. Against the advice of her colleagues and despite their skepticism, Ann had every senior fill out a college application. She also provided the students and their families with information about college and the college-going process. In addition, she worked with teachers at a nearby university to provide the students with supplemental academic support. As a result of her action, at the end of the academic year 70% of the senior class was accepted into a two- or four-year college or university.

## Case Discussion

Ann's story is an example of counseling leadership for social justice in action. Ann received her master's training in a school counseling program whose training philosophy is grounded in the principles of access, equity, and social justice in the delivery of counseling services. Further, all students develop skills to promote the academic, career, and personal-social development of students in culturally diverse urban settings. Using the 2009 CACREP standards as a framework, the program curriculum is designed to prepare professional school counselors who will be leaders, advocates, and systemic change agents in urban educational settings. The curriculum emphasizes increasing awareness, knowledge, and skills to work with economically, socially, and culturally diverse urban student populations. The aim of the program is to develop professional school counselors who are committed to closing the achievement gap in urban schools.

Ann entered the program with a deeply ingrained passion for social justice that stemmed from her own childhood experiences with marginalization and poverty. While in the program she had the opportunity to explore her life meaning and assess her commitment to being an advocate for disenfranchised youth and their families. She struggled with her cultural privilege as a young White woman and assessed how it might help or hinder her effectiveness when working with young people whose cultural realities were different from hers.

Through her didactic coursework and experiential activities in the program, Ann explored the nature of oppression in her own life, having been born to an unmarried teenage mother. She often reflected on the painful dynamics associated with the oppression she experienced growing up in a poor single-parent home. Similarly, Ann was constantly exposed to issues of cultural diversity in her classwork as well as her practicum and internship experiences, which helped to her expand her level of awareness, knowledge base, and skills repertoire—the foundation of cultural competence.

Significantly, as Ann progressed through her training within an urban educational environment, she realized that coming from a small desert community in the western part of the country, she had a great deal to learn about the world. She worked hard at expanding her knowledge about the world. She made it a personal goal to become globally literate.

Ann graduated from the school counseling program with a strong personal social justice compass that pointed her toward advocacy for marginalized student groups because, from her perspective as both a professional school counselor and a person, it was both the ethical and moral course to pursue. She arrived at the charter school in Los Angeles, therefore, with both the commitment and the courage to take a leadership role in addressing the lack of college attendance on the part of Latino students. Ann proved to be a committed and courageous leader and advocate for social justice. She would not accept the status quo of educational failure at her school and set about to change the system in a manner that would promote wellness and human dignity for scores of Latino students and their families. She walked the talk.

## APPLICATION EXERCISE

The following case is presented for the reader to reflect on his or her own awareness and understanding of issues of social justice and advocacy in counseling practice.

### Case Study: The Baptiste Family

André and Willette Baptiste (not real names) are an African American married couple who live in New Orleans. They have two children, a son age 10 and a daughter age 8. André has worked as a mechanic at an auto repair shop and Willette has been employed as a maid in hotels in the French Quarter and the Central Business District. They were the owners of a small "shotgun" house in the Lower Ninth Ward of the city. The house was so named because it was narrow, about 12 feet wide, with doors at each end. It is said that if one fired a shotgun at such a house, the bullet would enter the front door and travel straight through and exit via the back door.

On August 29, 2005, the Baptiste family's life was profoundly impacted when Hurricane Katrina struck New Orleans. While the family was able to evacuate from the city and stay with relatives in Baton Rouge prior to the storm, their home was completely destroyed from the storm surge flood that resulted when the Industrial Canal levee was breached in the aftermath of the hurricane. After several months in Baton Rouge, the Baptiste family returned to New Orleans to find that their home had been swept from its foundation in the flood. The family had limited insurance coverage on the house. They were, however, able to secure a trailer for "temporary" housing from the Federal Emergency Management Agency (FEMA) after a protracted struggle with social service agencies.

As the city of New Orleans began its slow recovery from Hurricane Katrina, André was able to put his mechanical skills to work on daily reconstruction projects while Willette again found employment as a maid in a French Quarter hotel. While there was a limited amount of money coming into the Baptiste household, the family was experiencing significant problems. In interactions with their insurance company they discovered that their policy did not cover the massive damage caused by the levee breach. Therefore, it would be impossible for them to rebuild their modest home. Significantly, the floodwaters destroyed much of the infrastructure of the Baptiste children's school, which was still closed months after the storm. This meant that the children's education had effectively come to a halt. Additionally, like many victims of the storm, the Baptiste family was waiting for a relief check from FEMA that would assist with their recovery from the disaster. However, government bureaucratic red tape at the local, state, and federal levels was needlessly delaying the receipt of these funds.

The months of living in the cramped confines of the FEMA trailer began to take their toll on members of the Baptiste family. Anger, frustration, fear, and depression started to manifest themselves in various ways. André, angered by his perceived loss of control over his life, started to drink heavily and commenced to abuse his wife and children verbally and physically. Willette, often tired from working long shifts at the hotel, became neglectful of the children. The children, who were not attending school, were left unsupervised for long periods of time. Significantly, the youngest child began wetting her bed and went into a panic every time she heard thunder because she feared that the storm was coming again. In addition, the entire family was experiencing allergic reactions from toxic mold that was growing in the trailer.

In a meeting with a FEMA official about the family's situation, André angrily stated, "I'm sick and tired of watching the French Quarter and the other rich White parts of this city doin' well after the storm and we poor folks still strugglin' and hustlin' to get by." He went on to say, "The government is for them, it don't work for me!"

Questions for Reflection and Discussion

In reflecting on the case of the Baptiste family, please consider the following questions:

1. What issues of social injustice can you identify in the case of the Baptiste family and how are they impacting the wellness and dignity of the family? According to the United Nations Declaration of Human Rights, which of the Baptiste family's human rights appear to be violated given the issues presented?
2. What counselor characteristics would be important prerequisites to address these identified injustices effectively?
3. While it would be important to work on the individual issues of each member of the Baptiste family in counseling, it is apparent that their issues are symptomatic of larger systemic dysfunction. Develop a counseling intervention for this family that demonstrates knowledge of advocacy processes that will promote their collective wellness and human dignity.
4. It has been argued that the concept of social justice is turning counselors into social workers. There are those who assert that social justice has been conceived as the identity of social workers, and that counseling is about producing change by promoting growth and development in clients. In reflecting on the Baptiste family, do you support this assertion or do you see the importance of counselors acting as agents of social change? Why or why not?

2009 CACREP standards addressed in case studies and questions:

Entry-level standard II.G.1.i; II.G.2.e
Doctoral-level standard II.C.1; C.4

## CONCLUSION

Social justice, a sometimes difficult and challenging notion to conceptualize, is considered to be the fifth force in counseling. Mastery of this concept is now an important learning outcome of counselor training as reflected in the 2009 CACREP standards. Professional counselors, therefore, are now expected to be able to intervene not only in the lives of clients to help them solve problems or make decisions, but also in the social context that affects those lives. Social justice rests on a premise that the environment is a key factor in determining wellness and human dignity. Problems and challenges that confront clients, therefore, can often be traced to negative environmental systems and their adverse impact on human development. This is particularly evident when these environmental effects are characterized by inequitable treatment, disregard for human rights, and an unfair allocation of societal resources.

As we reflect on the great social challenges of the twenty-first century, leadership in professional counseling must be centered on competency as agents of social justice. Professional counselors must be committed to employing their expertise to help individuals while they simultaneously challenge the profound social, cultural, and economic inequities that adversely impact the wellness and human dignity of scores of people. Through one's own sense of and commitment to social justice, a counselor can be a true advocate for wellness and human dignity and a leader in the quest for a better world.

# 8

# *Theoretical Foundations of Client Advocacy*

## Victoria E. Kress and Matthew J. Paylo

## INTRODUCTION

The intersection of leadership and advocacy is at the forefront of Chi Sigma Iota's philosophical view of the counseling profession. Chi Sigma Iota (CSI) leadership has always considered advocacy to be a two-pronged concept that includes both advocating for the profession and advocating for consumers of counseling services. It is difficult—if not impossible—to separate client and professional advocacy. In this text's introduction, the editors thoughtfully address this concept in stating:

> If we do not have a strong profession that is recognized, respected, and empowered, trained professional counselors will lack the right to practice what we have been trained to do. At the same time, if we fail to advocate for our clients, we risk losing the fundamental reason for entry into this profession—to help others achieve their optimum potential for human development and wellness.

As such, client advocacy is just as necessary as professional advocacy (Myers, Sweeney, & White, 2002); no discussion of advocacy would be complete without a focus on the ways that counselors can advocate for their clients.

In this chapter, we will focus on the theoretical foundations of client advocacy. As this chapter is intended to address foundational and theoretical issues, a discussion of important client advocacy-related concepts is provided. We will also present a model for addressing client advocacy. Finally, we will identify the ways that counselors can integrate client advocacy concepts into counseling practice and supervision.

Key Terms

**Client advocacy.** For the purposes of this chapter, client advocacy will be described as the intentional action—or actions—of a counselor to assist in removing external obstacles and barriers that impede clients' well-being or inhibit clients' growth and development (Toporek, 2000).

**Theoretical foundations.** In this chapter, theoretical foundations refer to the information that is important in conceptualizing counselor-initiated client advocacy efforts. The theoretical foundations addressed in this chapter include discussions of the following constructs: oppression and discrimination, empowerment, social action, the characteristics of effective client advocates, advocacy-related competencies, and finally, various professional counseling organizations' conceptualizations of client advocacy.

## CLIENT ADVOCACY-RELATED CONCEPTS AND FOUNDATIONS

In this section, concepts central to understanding client advocacy are addressed. The concepts of advocacy, oppression and discrimination, empowerment, and social action are discussed in terms of their relationship to client advocacy. All of these concepts are foundational to discussions about client advocacy.

### Advocacy

Advocacy, as it relates to counseling and clients, is an elusive term to operationalize, as it can relate to attitudes, attributes, behaviors, knowledge, or the skills needed for successful advocacy implementation. As such, the concept of advocacy may refer to a wide variety of activities and beliefs in which professional counselors could engage to assist clients. Most simply, advocacy is the endeavor or process of "arguing or pleading for a cause or proposal" (Lee, 1998, p. 8). Advocacy can also be the action of speaking on behalf of another person or group of individuals to bring about a desired change.

As related to counseling clients, advocacy is the intentional action or actions of a professional counselor to assist in removing external obstacles or barriers that impede clients' well-being (Toporek, 2000). Using the latter definition, advocacy addresses the inherent and assumed power and privilege of the professional counselor. Because of the counselor's role and stature, to intervene with clients and advocate for specific client issues is a counselor's professional responsibility. Inherent in this definition is the client's ability to participate in the advocacy process along with the professional counselor, and eventually for himself or herself, independent of the professional counselor. A client advocating on her or his own behalf is the eventual hoped for product of all professional counselor-generated advocacy initiatives.

Once defined, important questions related to client advocacy become "Who especially should we advocate for?" and "Who should benefit from counselors' advocacy initiatives?" Lewis and Bradley (2000) stated that we should focus on advocating for those who have been marginalized, denied the opportunity to be involved in making important decisions that impact their lives, and stigmatized. All of the aforementioned characteristics describe the experiences of those who are oppressed and discriminated against.

## Oppression and Discrimination

As previously stated, professional counselors should be advocating for those individuals who experience oppression and discrimination. Lewis and Arnold (1998) described oppression as being the "systematic disadvantaging" of one group by other groups who hold greater societal power (p. 55). According to Lewis and Arnold, internalized oppression and systemic oppression are two types of oppression that seek to maintain the status quo. Internalized oppression is the acceptance of the myth, misinformation, and stereotypes that the dominant culture constructs about its own cultural group. Internalized oppression can be debilitating to clients, consciously or unconsciously dictating thoughts, feelings, and behaviors.

Professional counselors need to be aware of oppression not only to support clients, but also to allow clients to process how that oppression influences their perception of self, their behaviors, and lost opportunities in a prejudiced society. Carlson, Sperry, and Lewis (1997) stated that clients who recognize the role of oppression in their lives are most likely to be able to move from self-blame to self-management, and to ultimately find their way past a theme of being less than or not good enough. Recognizing the debilitating role that oppression has on clients' lives does not take away their oppression; through the construction of a new narrative, it does provide clients with an opportunity to relate to their oppression in a new way.

The second type of oppression that Lewis and Arnold (1998) presented is systemic. All individuals live in a world full of oppression. Referring back to Lewis and Arnold's definition of oppression, everyone is implicated as either the oppressed or the oppressor. The ramification of such a statement is that all human beings are involved in one group or the other by their response to—or lack of response to—oppression. Such responses, whether active or passive, will either alter or maintain the status quo. Status quo pertains to the power hierarchy of the present social structure (Prilleltensky, 1994). Prilleltensky argued that oppression not only permeates our lives, but significantly constrains and thus limits all of our lives.

Oppression pervades our culture; it is present in our existence. Lewis and Arnold (1998) contend oppression is no one's fault, it predates our existence. Nonetheless, as we work with our clients, it is our responsibility to recognize our role as both a perpetrator and a victim while having the strength and courage to challenge oppression, attempting ultimately to end the debilitating use of it to hinder and control.

Professional counselors may find themselves in one of the previously mentioned oppressed groups. In advocating for clients, counselors' awareness of the power differential inherent in the structure of the helping relationship is imperative. Due to their role as counselors, they may have access to professional and institutional policy making out of the reach of clients (Toporek, 2000). This position affords professional counselors the privilege to intervene at levels that clients cannot access. This intervention can occur on multiple levels, but one of the ways that professional counselors can address oppression and discrimination is by empowering clients.

### Empowerment

Empowerment and social action, the following two concepts we will discuss, pertain to advocacy that has been historically associated with feminist and multicultural theories. Empowerment consists of the personal interaction between professional counselors and clients, which primarily attempts to validate the reality of clients while considering the sociopolitical, sociocultural, and socioeconomic contexts of their realities (Toporek, 2000). With empowerment, actions of the professional counselor remain on the individual system level and assist the client in the awareness and validation of the barriers that hinder his or her well-being and holistic wellness.

Empowerment has been discussed extensively in the literature, and McWhirter's (1994) definition is often stressed. McWhirter believed that empowerment is the process by which people, organizations, or groups who are powerless cycle through the following process: They become more attuned to the power dynamics that impact their life context, they develop the skills they need to gain reasonable control over their lives, they exercise this emergent power, they exercise this power without infringing on the rights of others, and thus they actively support the empowerment of others in their community.

This concept of empowerment is not a new concept, especially to scholars rooted in feminist (Enns, 1993) and multicultural theories (Sue, Ivey, & Pedersen, 1996). Empowerment philosophies emphasize client self-awareness and client skill acquisition, which is intended to help navigate oppressive systems, thus enhancing a sense of control over one's life. Empowerment then does not directly challenge the oppressiveness inherent in our social system, yet does so indirectly through the client's ability to manage or negotiate sociopolitical influences. Empowerment in this sense moves from the traditional sense of self-efficacy of the client to include the social aspects of the client's life. Professional counselors should not ignore this aspect of empowerment because dismissing substantial influences on their lives could significantly disempower clients (Toporek, 2000).

Social Action

Toporek (2000) noted that a model of client advocacy should also include a focus on social action. Social action is the implementation of an intervention, constructed by the professional counselor, that addresses macro-level, social change. This social action takes place on behalf of clients, client populations, or social issues within society, not necessarily with a specific client. This concept of social action is not new, and social action permeates human history. In practice, social action has myriad implementations. Enns (1993) provided a number of forms that social action can take. She suggested that social action can involve the following ideas: conducting action research to challenge reigning orthodoxies, providing pro bono services to institutions that extend services to women, engaging in primary prevention efforts and leading public education and support groups within the community, working to alter organizational climates to serve clients more effectively, influencing public policy, and working with grassroot organizations to promote social change. As can be seen by this list of suggestions, social action can take many forms, and serves an important function related to the client advocacy process.

## THE CHARACTERISTICS OF EFFECTIVE CLIENT ADVOCATES

Much has been written about how professional counselors might approach client advocacy. In this section, some of this literature will be discussed. Some suggest that when advocating for minority clients' needs and experiences, professional counselors need to be willing and able to function in a number of different roles using appropriate strategies. For example, Atkinson, Thompson, and Grant (1993) proposed a three-dimensional advocacy model for counseling racial/ethnic minorities. They proposed a schema grounded in the assessment of the variables of locus of etiology, level of acculturation, and the goals of counseling. Using these three variables in assessment, professional counselors can then determine the role they may choose to intervene. Atkinson et al. suggest the following roles: advisor, advocate, facilitator of indigenous healing methods, facilitator of indigenous support systems, consultant, change agent, and professional counselor.

Building on Atkinson's et al. (1993) advocacy model, Sue et al. (1996) discussed the commonalities among the alternative roles (e.g., advocate, change agent) assumed by professional counselors to address oppression and discrimination. Sue et al. outlined six distinct characteristics needed to engage in these roles, roles that they believe go beyond those defined in traditional counseling. These characteristics are (1) an active helping style, (2) an ability to work outside the conventional office setting, (3) an ability to focus externally to change environmental barriers, (4) a move from the mindset of internal pathology to one where the client is assessed as in a problematic situation, (5) an ability to assume a prevention-oriented approach, and (6) an increased recognition of the need to implement effective counseling strategies.

Kiselica and Robinson (2001) suggested that in order to advocate effectively for clients, counselors develop the following characteristics: (1) a capacity for commitment and an appreciation for human sufferings; (2) nonverbal and verbal communication; (3) a multisystemic perspective; (4) individual, group, and organizational interventions; (5) knowledge and the use of media, technology, and the Internet; and (6) assessment and research skills.

Goodman et al. (2004) suggested when advocating for their clients that counselors consider principles that can guide them in their advocacy efforts. For example, Goodman et al. contended that counselors need to possess and understand six essential principles: examination of the self, sharing power in the process, giving voice, raising consciousness, focusing on strengths, and leaving clients with tools. Goodman et al.'s suggestions are clearly influenced by feminist and multicultural theoretical influences. These theoretical principles provide professional counselors with essential characteristics needed to advocate for clients.

Finally, in considering necessary professional counselor characteristics, the American Counseling Association (ACA; Lewis, Arnold, House, & Toporek, 2002) has suggested requisite competencies needed by professional counselors interested in advocating for clients. The ACA advocacy model (Lewis et al., 2005) consists of 43 competencies among three levels of intervening: (1) the client/student, (2) the school/community, and (3) the larger public arena. A number of competencies appear within all three domains, providing a thorough presentation of advocacy competencies. Along these three levels, the competencies are divided into empowerment (i.e., the counselor is acting with the client) and advocacy (i.e., the counselor is acting on behalf of the client) activities. As explained in more detail in Chapter 6, the development of these advocacy competencies has lead to counseling associations and accreditation bodies adopting a position of counselor responsibility concerning culturally competent counseling as well as advocating for clients on the individual or systemic level.

## PROFESSIONAL COUNSELING AND CLIENT ADVOCACY

Professional counseling has a long tradition of advocating for client's rights and needs (Kiselica & Robinson, 2001). The ethical and professional standards of practice concerning advocacy in counseling continue to evolve. The American Counseling Association (ACA) and the American School Counselor Association (ASCA) are the two most represented national organizations within the counseling profession, and both project a stance that advocacy is a responsibility of professional counselors.

## ACA Code of Ethics

In their most recent version of the ethics standards, the ACA included advocacy as a role of the counselor. The ACA governing council approved this new Code of Ethics in 2005. Section A.6a. of the 2005 ACA Code of Ethics states, "When appropriate, counselors advocate at individual, group, institutional, and societal levels to examine potential barriers and obstacles that inhibit access and/or growth and development of clients" (p. 5). This standard is significantly different from the 1995 ACA Code of Ethics, which does not mention the word *advocacy* or *advocate* in the counseling relationship section. This change has significant ramifications for counselors, counselor educators, and counselors-in-training.

The Code of Ethics also requires professional counselors to be competent in all domains in which they practice. Due to the ACA Code of Ethics component that "counselors practice only within the boundaries of their competence based on education, training, supervised experience, state and national professional credentials and appropriate professional experience" (ACA, 2005, C.2.a), counselors must receive training and education in a supervised capacity to meet competency requirements concerning advocacy.

## ASCA Code of Ethics

The ASCA has taken a similar position to ACA in regards to the value it places on advocacy for clients as articulated in the ASCA (2010b) Code of Ethics preamble:

> Each person has the right to be respected, be treated with dignity and have access to a comprehensive school counseling program that advocates for and affirms all students from diverse populations regardless of ethnic/racial status, age, economic status, special needs, English as a second language or other language group, immigration status, sexual orientation, gender, gender identity/expression, family type, religious/spiritual identity and appearance. (Preamble, p. 1)

This statement essentially paves the way for school counselors to advocate for and empower students at the individual, school, community, state, and federal levels. Through the clarity of this requirement, the issue of whether to advocate for a client moves from that of a personal decision of the professional counselor, to an expected counselor role.

The school counselor is responsible to treat the student as the "primary obligation" in a respectful and culturally sensitive fashion (ASCA, A.1.a) and consider the development of the student's educational, academics, career, personal, and social needs (ASCA, A.1.b). The school counselor is also responsible to "collaborate with agencies, organizations, and individuals in the community in the best interest of students without regard to personal reward or remuneration" (ASCA, D.2.a) and to "extend his/her influence and opportunity to deliver a comprehensive school-counseling program to all students by collaborating with community resources for student success" (ASCA, D.2.b). These responsibilities are individual and systemic, leading the counselor to advocate on multiple levels as needed with each student, case, or issue.

### Council for Accreditation of Counseling and Related Educational Programs (CACREP)

The ACA's and ASCA's Codes of Ethics present advocacy as a responsibility of the counselor, and therefore competency and training are introduced as issues that need consideration. Competencies are based on education, training, and supervised experience. These components are regulated by the Council for Accreditation of Counseling and Related Educational Programs (CACREP, 2009). In the 2009 standards, CACREP clearly and concisely outlined the requirements for advocacy in counselor training regardless of specialization (e.g., school counseling, mental health counseling, community counseling, or career counseling). In the core requirements under professional identity, the CACREP standards state, "Advocacy processes needed to address institutional and social barriers that impede access, equity, and success for clients" (CACREP, 2009, G.1.i). In another core requirement, under social and cultural diversity, the standards state, "Counselors' roles in developing cultural self-awareness, promoting cultural social justice, advocacy and conflict resolution, and other culturally supported behaviors that promote optimal wellness and growth of the human spirit, mind, or body" must be included in counselor education programs (CACREP, 2001, G.2.d). The ACA's and ASCA's Codes of Ethics along with the CACREP accreditation standards work together to provide counselors with not only the expectation of advocacy, but also the means, through education and training, to be competent advocates.

### AN INTEGRATED MODEL OF CLIENT ADVOCACY

It is essential that a model of client advocacy be dynamic. To advocate optimally for clients, professional counselors need a model that incorporates multiculturalism, advocacy competencies, and a wellness focus. In this section, these three components are discussed.

### Multicultural Competencies

The multicultural movement has forced the counseling field to examine clients' lives within systemic contexts and to own the prejudice and oppression within our society and within traditional counseling theory and practice. Multiculturalism reorients the field of counseling by (1) increasing counselors' awareness of assumptions, values, and biases; (2) increasing counselors' understanding of the worldview of culturally different clients; and (3) increasing counselors' development and use of appropriate intervention strategies (Sue et al., 1998).

The awareness that comes from multiculturalism leads professional counselors to client advocacy and action. This directive for action dismantles the notion of counselors' neutrality and enables the profession to begin to break down the oppressive systems perpetuating our society. "Once we begin to notice systemic oppression, it is just one more short step to accepting our responsibility for social action" (Lewis & Arnold, 1998, p. 51).

Professional counselors must first become aware of their internal world before they are ever competent to work with clients. Lee and Hipolito-Delgado (2007) asserted that for counselors to be effective helpers, there must be an awareness of self, an interpersonal awareness, and a systematic awareness of the world around them. In other words, professional counselors must be aware of their own personality and how they contribute to the counseling process, must possess the awareness to enter the client's world, and must possess the ability to perceive accurately environmental influences and a means to intervene with the client or on the client's behalf.

Lee and Hipolito-Delgado's (2007) recommendations are congruent with the Association of Multicultural Counseling and Development's (AMCD) multicultural counseling competencies (Arredondo et al., 1996). The AMCD multicultural counseling competencies (Arredondo et al., 1996) consist of three components: (1) counselor awareness of cultural values and biases, (2) counselor awareness of the client's worldview, and (3) culturally appropriate strategies for intervention.

The counseling field appears committed to promoting multiculturalism. This commitment translates into the inclusion of social advocacy in our training programs and research. Whether building upon multicultural competencies or calling for social action, the profession has made numerous requests for the implementation of advocacy in counseling (Bemak & Chung 2005; Kiselica & Robinson, 2001; Lee & Walz, 1998b; Lewis & Bradley, 2000) yet a gap between these pleas and practice as well as research still exists (Bemak & Chung, 2005).

Advocacy Competencies

Through the introduction of the multicultural counseling competencies (Sue, Arredondo, & McDavis, 1992), the counseling profession established the need for professional counselors to acknowledge and become aware of the systemic and unjust conditions that permeate society and clients' lives. This awareness paved the way for the advocacy competencies. In 2000, Jane Goodman, ACA president at the time, appointed the Advocacy Competencies Task Force. This group was charged with developing a set of competencies for counselor advocacy (Toporek, Lewis, & Ratts, 2010).

As previously mentioned, the ACA advocacy competencies (Lewis et al., 2002) addressed numerous competencies. For the purposes of this chapter, we will focus on the client empowerment, community collaboration, and public information aspects of the competencies. Chapter 7 on social justice discusses advocacy efforts that focus on professional counselors acting on behalf of clients.

## Client Empowerment

The essential aspect of client empowerment relates to enhancing clients' awareness and wellness. What empowerment is not is the bestowing of power to those that lack power. Empowerment can be better conceptualized as a process by which the professional counselor and client endeavor together, with the aim being the fostering of clients' personal wellness through an increased sense of internalized power and control. Empowered clients can take action on their own behalf to improve their current situation while simultaneously fostering a greater sense of self-sufficiency and personal strength. According to Holcomb-McCoy and Bryan (2010), assisting clients in building their own power initially consists of (1) first recognizing the power differential that typically exists between counselor and client, (2) intentionally diminishing their own role as experts in the counseling process, and (3) including the client as a mutual expert in the process. Pragmatically, empowerment techniques applied by professional counselors are attempts to raise clients' level of awareness to situations, alternatives, and decision-making skills, as well as increasing clients' sense of responsibility to lean against oppressive societal entities. Ball (2000) conceptualized the process of empowerment as existing along a continuum consisting of three levels of client awareness: (1) increased awareness about alternatives and possibilities; (2) the process of questioning one's perception in the world, considering one's personal choices and capacities for accomplishing alternative possibilities; and (3) becoming a confident decision maker who challenges oppressive social forms for oneself and others. This process is a strength-based wellness approach to working with clients.

## Community Collaboration

Most clients, families, and communities have been in a struggle against oppressive structures, and as such, professional counselors should honor the strength, courage, resilience, tenacity, and perseverance of our clients; it is optimal to work from a strength-based wellness approach. This approach involves empowering clients, families, and communities to be joined with existing organizations that are already established, in the community (or surrounding community), and work toward change. The professional counselor is the connector, collaborator, and ally for these individuals and organizations. Professional counselors are innately positioned to become the first responders, as they become aware of situations in which oppression and discrimination impede clients, families, and communities from being able to function and live a life of optimal wellness.

## Public Information

Another level of advocating for clients relates to awakening the public's sense of humanity by exposing human indignities with the intent of igniting the public's sense of responsibility to deal with and address systematic oppression. By informing the public, counselors educate individuals about environmental factors that have impeded the development and optimal wellness of others. These obstacles need to be disseminated to the public through any means that a professional counselor deems necessary. Possibilities include community presentation, lobbying endeavors, written documentation, research endeavors, and any multimedia transmission of material.

## Client Wellness

The underlying aim in all advocacy efforts, whether it be client empowerment or social action, is to promote optimal client wellness and well-being. Myers, Sweeney, and Witmer (2000) defined wellness as "a way of life oriented toward optimal health and well-being, in which body, mind, and spirit are integrated by the individual to live life more fully within the human and natural community. Ideally, it is the optimum state of health and well-being that each individual is capable of achieving" (p. 252).

The wellness paradigm involves encouraging wellness, through prevention, development, and wellness-enhancing interventions. This paradigm has always been a core component of the counseling profession, and our professional identity (Myers & Sweeney, 2008). Conceptually, when considering the counseling literature, two models of wellness have the most empirical support: (1) the wheel of wellness (Myers, Sweeney, & Witmer, 2000) and (2) the indivisible self (Myers & Sweeney, 2005).

### Wheel of Wellness

The wheel of wellness (Myers et al., 2000) is a theoretical model utilizing Adlerian individual psychology as a means to organize (e.g., work, love, and friendship) components of wellness (i.e., gender identity, cultural identity, sense of worth, sense of control, realistic beliefs, emotional awareness and coping, sense of humor, nutrition, exercise, self-care, stress management, and spirituality). All 12 components are interrelated and impact each other. Additionally, this model is ecological in nature, considering society, government, global events, oppression, and discrimination as having a significant impact on peoples' overall wellness.

### Indivisible Self

The indivisible self (Myers & Sweeney, 2005) is an evidence-based model of wellness based on data studies based on the wheel of wellness model. This model was produced through structural equation modeling and consists of five second-order factors (i.e., creative, coping, social, essential, and physical) of selves. These second-order factors of self include the original wheel of wellness components as third-order factors that impact each other as well as the overall factor they are subsumed under. The creative self consists of the following third-order factors: thinking, emotions, control, work, and positive humor. The coping self consists of the following third-order factor: leisure, stress management, self-worth, and realistic beliefs. The social self consists of the following third-order factors: Friendship and Love. The Essential Self consists of the following third-order factors: spirituality, gender identity, cultural identity, and self-care. Lastly, the physical self consists of the following third-order factors: exercise and nutrition. The model is ecological and assumes that wellness is impacted by the environment (e.g., social events, society, oppression, and discrimination).

## CLIENT ADVOCACY APPLICATIONS

Armed with self-awareness of the impact of multiculturalism, knowledge of the advocacy competencies, and a dedication to wellness, professional counselors are ready to advance the call of advocacy within the profession and to enhance clients' overall well-being. Professional counselors can promote the advancement of advocacy in clinical practice and through supervision. Case examples are used to illustrate these applications.

### Client Advocacy Through Clinical Practice

In the following case, the professional counselor begins by exploring the client's microsystem (individual level; Bronfenbrenner, 1979) and the wellness associated with his or her sense of self (Myers & Sweeney, 2005). Further explorations reveal significant oppression and discrimination resonating from the classroom, the university, and the community (mesosystem), which are significantly contributing to the client's current wellness struggles.

Akins (a pseudonym) is a 21-year-old Egyptian American male earning a bachelor's degree in biology at a small, urban university. He has recently sought counseling services in the university outpatient clinic due to his overwhelming and sometimes debilitating social anxiety. He stated during the initial contact that he fears being evaluated/critiqued, and this appears to drive his desire to avoid certain situations. During the initial intake assessment, the professional counselor considered an evidence-based model of wellness, the indivisible self (Myers & Sweeney, 2005), to help make sense of Akins' presentation, symptoms, and his overall wellness. Following are the results of that inquiry:

1. **Creative self.** Akins identified himself as a "hard worker" who is extremely interested in what others think about him and how he is perceived. He described his humor as witty and smart, yet disclosed that he does not think that most people "get" him. He thinks that he will be successful and eventually be a molecular biologist after extensive training and education.

2. **Coping self.** Akins reported the need to be liked and to be exceptional at everything he does. He knows that this ideal is unreasonable, but lives

his life through the motto, "Never expect things to happen, struggle and make them happen." He views his life and accomplishments by the products that his endeavors and actions produce, and this is the most motivating influence on his life.

3. **Social self.** Akins reported that he is in a committed relationship that is fulfilling and that he intends to "marry this girl." He described a somewhat secure social support system involving a few friends, yet after further discussion it appeared that these individuals were more like acquaintances than friends and that he is rather isolated. He mentioned that he misses his family "a great deal" and sometimes feels "extremely disconnected" due the relatively long distance they live away from him (i.e., a five-hour car ride).

4. **Essential self.** Akins reported being a devout Muslim and expressed concerns for the narrowed thinking of the community that the university was within. With little to no opportunity to be around others who are like-minded, he reported feeling alienated at times. Additionally, Akins reported identifying as an Egyptian American, yet sometimes he desires to be like other Americans. He reported a strong sense of pride in his heritage, and yet discussed a host of past conflicts with his parents over their ideals for him. He stated that his parents grew up in Egypt and moved to the States in adulthood. His father come to the States primarily for the opportunity to complete a medical residency in pain management in the States, and eventually sought citizenship. Also, he identified himself as a heterosexual male and values the rights of others to practice whatever sexual orientation they desire.

5. **Physical self.** Akins reported that he exercises on a regular basis and that while not eating a particularly healthy diet, he has maintained a normal BMI for all of his life. He believes he is in good physical condition and that he takes care of himself.

6. **Ecological impacts.** Akins discussed feeling like an "outcast" and "different" from others within the university community. "I feel like I am being watched, judged, and not given the same freedoms that my peers are given." He stated, "After 9/11 sometimes the States feel like what I've read about those old witch hunts in New England or those communist trials. Society as a whole appears to lump all Muslims together with those extremists. Like at any moment, I might snap and strap a bomb to myself. Hey, I'm an American too. What gives you the right to be so presumptuous about me, someone you have never even taken the time to talk to?"

As the case unfolded, the presenting issue, which was dealing with his anxiety, appears to be relevant from an individual counseling paradigm, yet systemic influences immediately become apparent to the professional counselor. The increase in panic attack symptoms and generalized anxiety appears to be related to a civilization/history class that—due to the liberal arts nature of the university—is a requirement for all students. Akins reported feeling alienated in the classroom. He stated that on numerous occasions his professor was dismissive, confrontational, offensive, and highly critical of his worldview. He stated that he is treated differently and is not totally sure why this is the case.

After further exploration, it is apparent to the professional counselor that Akins is being discriminated against for his Muslim worldview. The continued deeming and shaming he has endured in the classroom is oppressive and is ultimately contributing to his increased social anxiety. He also reported a number of local hate crimes toward Muslims with little information being conveyed to the members of the community. The oppressive nature of the community appears to continually foster Akins' mindset that there is something inherently wrong with him.

The professional counselor is now at a crossroads. The professional counselor could conceptualize Akins' situation from an individual level of analysis. Helping him manage and reduce his own anxiety by developing coping skills and learning relaxation techniques, and applying cognitive-behavioral skills are examples of individual-level interventions. Additionally, at the individual level of analysis the professional counselor could encourage assertiveness training for Akins with the intent of him standing up for himself.

If the professional counselor is interested in advocating for Akins, the following interventions based on the model presented in this chapter are suggested:

Client empowerment (individual level):
  Provide openness, warmth, and positive regard, thus allowing Akins to be the expert on his life and current situation.
  Work with Akins to help him be aware of his anxiety and manage it in pro-social manners; develop his capacity to tolerate stressful situations and evaluations.
  Assist Akins in increasing components of his sense of wellness (e.g., social, coping) in an attempt to impact and increase his overall wellness.
  Empower Akins by increasing his awareness of his possibilities, and assisting him in making decisions that best fit with the outcomes he desires (e.g., Akins explores the idea of withdrawing from the class and taking the class in the future, possibly with another professor or just at another time).
  Support Akins and educate him on ways to advocate for himself on the individual, community, and public levels.
Community collaboration:
  Consult and connect Akins with existing resources within the university setting (e.g., diversity office, multicultural resources, student

affairs, housing/student life). Facilitating the connection between the client and these resources forces the counselor to be able to utilize technology, and to be open to exploring the resources available to each client. This can often be trial and error exploration requiring the counselor to attend meetings, presentations, and shadow existing organizations and resources.

Connect Akins with local and regional education resources, accreditation bodies, or university administration personnel to pursue mediation or action-orientated avenues.

Assist Akins at preparing media (e.g., letters, videos, multimedia) to educate and inform the university, administration, faculty, and students of the current oppressive situation both on the campus and within the community. This ideally would be in conjunction with another organization or student group, which would consist of other individuals, so as not to increase Akins' alienation and potential discrimination.

Work on existent university initiatives, committees on the campus to provide presentations, guest speakers, and rallies to increase awareness of the oppression felt by minority students, giving some individuals an opportunity to have their voices heard in a community setting.

Public information:

Support Akins in preparing media (e.g., letters, videos, proposals) to disseminate to local, state, regional, and national politicians or political bodies.

Connect Akins to regional or national associations (e.g., Islamic Society of North America) working toward reducing discrimination and prejudices toward Muslims.

Support Akins in preparing a video to send to media outlets educating individuals, discussing the oppression felt, and possible ideas for bridging differences in an attempt to alleviate oppression/discrimination of individuals within the local community.

Present at the local, regional, and national levels (e.g., meetings, forums, conferences) on behalf of marginalized populations within your communities.

Participate in state and national legislative lobbying endeavors for marginalized populations.

Conduct and publish research addressing oppression and discrimination of marginalized populations.

## Client Advocacy Through Supervision

Supervisors also have an important role to play in supporting client advocacy. In this section, issues that supervisors might consider in relation to advocacy are described. The case of Akins is used to contextualize the discussion of supervision-related advocacy issues.

Chang, Hays, and Milliken (2009) present a three-tiered model of promoting advocacy and social justice that can be used in supervision. The model is unique in that it challenges supervisors to develop their supervisees' client advocacy skills. The model consists of the following tiers:

Tier 1: Self-awareness
Tier 2: Client services
Tier 3: Community collaboration

According to Chang et al.'s (2009) model, the self-awareness tier refers to the supervisee's awareness of his or her own cultural values and biases. Self-awareness also includes the supervisee engaging in a self-analysis of his or her own values, personal philosophies, and action strategies regarding social change. As a part of these efforts, supervisees must be aware of their own biases so as to be optimally sensitive to their clients' social contexts. Supervisees are more likely to engage in client advocacy if they have an understanding of what advocacy means to them and how that relates to their own value system.

In the case of Akins, a supervisor might ask the professional counselor the following questions to encourage an enhanced self-awareness related to client advocacy: What are the social and political issues influencing Akins' circumstances, and how might his situation relate to this context? How does Akins perceive that these social influences relate to his experience? What impact did your cultural background have on this session, and how you perceive Akins' circumstances? What impact did Akins' cultural background—and your cultural background— have on your work in this session? These are just examples of questions that are intended to enhance supervisees' self-awareness. The aforementioned questions— if applied with care, and responded to thoughtfully—will likely uncover complex connections and relationships that impact the professional counselor's work with Akins. Ongoing discussions of this nature should help the supervisor come to understand a supervisee's level of awareness, and should theoretically contribute to the supervisee's enhanced self-awareness.

In Chang et al.'s (2009) model, the client services tier relates to the supervisees being taught to understand the complicated interactions of the various social, political, and educational systems that may impact their clients' lived experiences. As a part of this tier, supervisees consider the advantages and disadvantages of clients holding membership in various systems. Finally, client services relates to helping supervisees assist clients in gaining access to needed resources to help them navigate these systems.

With regard to the case of Akins and the client resources aspect of the model (Chang et al., 2009), the supervisor can invite the professional counselor to consider the ways that Akins can be empowered. A discussion of what resources could be useful to Akins would also be helpful. Finally, the counselor could be asked how he or she can promote this issue at the university level to create larger-scale change. A discussion of how this problem at the university can be prevented in the future, and what fears the professional counselor has related to serving as an advocate, may also be helpful (Chang et al., 2009). As many supervisees may struggle with understanding their role as a social change agent, processing their fears and ambivalence related to larger-scale client advocacy is important.

The final tier of Chang et al.'s (2009) model is entitled community collaboration. In this tier, supervisees assist clients in gaining access to resources, and educate the community about the relationship between oppression and mental health. In the case of Akins, the professional counselor could be encouraged to do research and develop a list of resources that include groups that work to address issues and agendas that relate to Akins' experiences. Chang et al. (2009) also suggested encouraging supervisees to volunteer at various community agencies to discover firsthand how they support the public. In this case, the professional counselor might be encouraged to volunteer with a Muslim or Egyptian American group.

## SUMMARY

In this chapter, we provided an overview of the theoretical foundations of client advocacy. The denseness of the information in this chapter highlights the importance of an advocacy approach that is integrated, dynamic, and comprehensive. The information in this chapter also points to the importance of professional counselors striving to develop their advocacy competencies by continually challenging themselves to learn more and develop their skills related to client advocacy.

We hope that this chapter's content provides a foundation upon which professional counselors can build in developing their personal advocacy style. While counseling and supervision case examples were provided to illuminate the chapter's content, we would be remiss if we did not emphasize that all counselor-generated client advocacy efforts are unique; typically, counselors' advocacy efforts will not look the same from client to client, or from counselor to counselor. Counselors' styles, theoretical approaches, resources, and experiences are a few aspects that will inform their advocacy approach, and the examples provided in this chapter were intended to serve as narratives that generate creative ways of thinking about client advocacy; the case examples were not intended to serve as templates that should be mimicked.

Professional counselors can reap many rewards secondary to client advocacy (Chang et al., 2009). For example, counselors' sense of personal satisfaction can be enhanced through helping others. Also, professional counselors are vulnerable to burnout and compassion fatigue, and any efforts to enhance professional counselors' personal satisfaction can be productive. Through client advocacy, counselors are also able to learn from their clients' difficult experiences, and this helps enrich their own lived experiences (Kiselica & Robinson, 2001). Finally, client advocacy efforts serve to inform counselors' knowledge and skill base, which can ultimately help professional counselors advocate for future clients.

## DISCUSSION QUESTIONS

1. Explain the role of professional counselors in advocating for clients. Additionally, provide a rationale for advocating for clients distinguishing between the differences of empowering clients and engaging in social action for clients. (CACREP, 2009; Section II, G2f)

2. Discuss the connection between promoting client wellness and advocating with or on behalf of a client when it is evident that external barriers prevent the client's optimal wellness. (CACREP, 2009; Section II, G2e)

3. **Case study 1:** Sandra is a 42-year-old woman with three children who immigrated into the United States illegally from Mexico. She reports that her husband has recently left the area to find work because unemployment has significantly increased over the past few months. She states that he hopes to return in the future when he has compiled some additional resources. Currently, she and her three children are alone in a menial home surviving on limited funds. She presents to you as wanting some job advice and direction because she is actively seeking employment but is totally unaware of any resources within the community. She speaks broken English and appears a little disheveled on her presentation. Sandra states that she has no external family support and has only a few friends within driving distance. She states that she received your name from an ER doctor during a recent crisis with her oldest daughter that resulted in eight stitches under her daughter's left eye. (CACREP, 2009; Section II, G1i, G2d, G2e, G2f)

   a. List some ways a professional counselor could intervene on the individual or micro-level?

   b. List some ways a professional counselor could intervene on the school/community level?

   c. List some ways a professional counselor could educate or increase understanding on the national or public level?

4. **Case study 2:** Mika is a 15-year-old Japanese American male who reports being bullied by a few of his peers. He comes to you, his school counselor, and reports the following information. He is a second-generation male from Japan. He perceives his family to be extremely strict. His father travels on business often and wants Mika to do something in the science or mathematic fields. His sister and mother offer some support but are

often preoccupied with their own hobbies and interests. He states only having a few close friends, which are females, and says he has always found it difficult to make male friends. He knows you somewhat well and discloses that he thinks he might be gay. He states that he is not really that attracted to girls and has found himself fantasizing about other males. He feels like the kids that are bullying him can tell that he is a little different. They have called him a "fag" and a "queer" and he is finding it tremendously difficult to just continue to "laugh it off." He comes to you for help and guidance on what he should do. (CACREP, 2009; Section II, G1i, G2d, G2e, G2f)

a.  List some ways a professional counselor could intervene on the individual or micro-level?

b.  List some ways a professional counselor could intervene on the school/community level?

c. List some ways a professional counselor could educate or increase understanding on the national or public level?

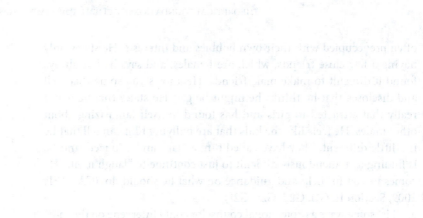

# 9

# Client Advocacy
## In Action

### Michael D. Brubaker and Rachael D. Goodman

## INTRODUCTION

Action is one of the essential cornerstones of client advocacy. It is not enough to talk about how injustices exist and that counselors are needed to promote client well-being; we must actually step forward out of the comfort of our offices and classrooms and strive to change our communities for the better. As Saul Alinsky (1971) wrote, "Change means movement. Movement means friction. Only in the frictionless vacuum of a nonexistent abstract world can movement or change occur without that abrasive friction of conflict" (p. 21). Like professional advocacy, it takes courage to step forward and challenge those structures that maintain their power by reinforcing the status quo.

Consistent with the overall philosophy of this book, we support the concept that client advocacy is interdependent with professional advocacy. When counselors are disempowered professionally, there are fewer resources available to help the communities where services are needed. Alternatively, when counselors are effectively impacting their communities, they have a stronger voice as they advocate for licensure and a broader scope of practice. Also, we support the core philosophy that advocacy is an act of social justice, a partnership between counselor and client, identifying racism, sexism, ageism, ableism, classism, heterosexism, and other forms of oppression, then addressing them within and outside of the therapeutic relationship. Lastly, we support the notion that the end goal of advocacy is not only to remove client barriers and other forms of oppression; rather, client advocacy must seek a positive end goal of wellness and human dignity, understood and driven from the client's perspective.

In this chapter, we portray the particular role for counselors, that of an advocate, inspiring active change with those individuals and communities we name as our clients. Throughout this chapter, we use a wider definition of the word *client*, which includes the many types of people counselors serve, including students, consumers, counselees, and communities. Following a brief explanation of our theoretical orientation, we will show four examples of client advocacy from different specialties, including clinical mental health counseling, trauma counseling and disaster response, school counseling, and counselor education and supervision. While reading each of these, we encourage you to think about how you could apply these principles and activities in your counseling settings. To facilitate the movement from reading to action, we will offer you some exercises and discussion questions along with some helpful resources.

Definitions of Key Terms and Concepts

**Critical consciousness:** A process of raising consciousness that focuses on personal awareness of oppression, dialoging with others, and taking action or praxis (Freire, 2001).

**De-ideologizing:** A process of deconstructing social beliefs and norms, critically analyzing the sources and impacts of these beliefs (Martín-Baró, 1994).

**Community engagement:** A collaborative process where counselors and community members identify, plan, and execute strategies that promote wellness and human dignity within the community.

**Servant leadership:** A leadership style where one focuses on service to others and may be contrasted with those where the needs of the leader are central (Greenleaf, 1970a). Servant leadership may still incorporate wellness practices for leaders.

**Nice counselor syndrome:** Possessing a desire to be "nice" and avoid conflict that prevents counselors from taking social justice action (Bemak & Chung, 2008).

## COUNSELING THEORY AND CLIENT ADVOCACY

For counselors, advocacy often begins with realizing the needs of a community and the individuals and families within this community. As Kiselica and Robinson (2001) noted:

> Perhaps the most important step we all must take in advocacy work is to look deep within ourselves and try to discover what forms of human suffering really move us to the point that we want to get up and fight—each of us in our own unique way—for other human beings. (p. 395)

Yet this awareness does not come as readily as we might expect. Indeed, in a profession where clients express great emotional pain and suffering, it would seem that counselors would quickly be moved to advocate for our clients and their communities. However, this is not always the case. Often, we encourage our clients to focus on *their* roles in *their* suffering and try to help them change any negative patterns in behavior and thought and develop positive coping strategies. The term *nice counselor syndrome* has been associated with a failure to identify and address the environmental and organizational causes of client suffering (Bemak & Chung, 2008); however, there may be more to the story.

If we look closely at the values and assumptions within our theoretical orientation, we are likely to see important indicators as to whether we choose to advocate with our clients or not. Our theory of choice reveals our assumptions about the human condition and how one's life may be improved (Archer & McCarthy, 2007). If we ascribe suffering primarily to the client's own choices, our advocacy efforts will likely remain limited and the "fight" will be focused on changing the client. Alternatively, if suffering is viewed as a result of social inequalities and injustices, then we may be inspired to challenge those systems as we strive for clients' and systemic change.

Prilleltensky (1997) illuminated this subject in his analysis of the primary theories found in the counseling profession. Categorizing them into four groups, he noted that each theory is based on a set of values that may perpetuate or ameliorate social injustices. The category that he most highly extolled was one he named *emancipatory communitarianism* (EC). EC was envisioned as an aspirational paradigm bringing together the best of empowering approaches, such as liberation psychology (Martín-Baró, 1994) and communitarian principles (Etzioni, 1991). In contrast to traditional theories that largely focus on the individual as cause and solution to presenting problems, EC is based on the assumption that social inequality and oppression are primary causes of suffering and psychological distress experienced by clients (Prilleltensky, 1997). Furthermore, this perspective promotes the recognition that solutions will not come by a single member or group in society; rather, the whole society carries a responsibility to promote wellness and human dignity for all. Freedom and responsibility are balanced, hand-in-hand.

We have found a number of theories that, in part, support the EC perspective. There are many empowering approaches, such as feminism, queer theory, and multicultural counseling, that have emerged in response to social oppression. Like liberation psychology, which shares common roots with the groundbreaking work of Paulo Freire (2001), a common goal of each of these is to raise consciousness among both the oppressed and the oppressors. Unfortunately, our sights can be too narrow and we may forget the fact that when we seek to promote the rights of one group, we may infringe on the rights of another. Yet, if we see our goal as the liberation of all from oppression, separate causes may join toward a common end. "We are caught in an inescapable network of mutuality, tied in a single garment of destiny" (King, 1964, p. 77).

Ecological counseling (Conyne & Cook, 2004) may prove to be a helpful way to understand the larger social systems and identify where society and individuals each need to change to promote overall well-being. Based on the work of Bronfenbrenner (1979) and Lewin (1936), ecological counseling takes a careful look at the many layers of an ecosystem, highlighting the importance of the health and wellness of both individual and community. When injustices and oppression occur, it is incumbent upon the whole system to change to promote greater health and wellness. When matched with the empowering approaches mentioned earlier, counselor and client may increase their critical consciousness of how the whole social system supports injustices and oppression, as well as what actions can be taken toward equality. In these cases, counselors are more likely to embrace *community engagement* approaches rather than relying on tradition individual interventions. Whole communities are approached through a variety of techniques to assess current needs and to strategize about ways to better the whole.

When advocating with clients, counselors may seek to better understand the multiple sources and factors that reinforce the assaults on wellness and human dignity. Clients and counselors are encouraged to challenge internalized messages that blame survivors of oppression for their condition. Additionally, counselors must often challenge their own beliefs that they lack power to create social change. Counselors who employ these theories in their advocacy practices will look honestly and directly at social injustices, co-creating strategies to address the most influential individuals and systems in order to move toward positive outcomes.

## CHALLENGING AND REFINING BEST PRACTICES
## FROM AN ADVOCACY PERSPECTIVE

Counselors are challenged to examine existing research and practices with a critical eye to determine their value and inclusion of social justice and advocacy principles. For instance, the Substance Abuse and Mental Health Services Administration (SAMHSA) provides best practices for disaster response work or Psychological First Aid (National Child Traumatic Stress Network and National Center for PTSD (NCTSN and NCPTSD), 2005). SAMHSA's Psychological First Aid (PFA) manual now contains information on culturally appropriate disaster response, including the importance of supporting cultural practices that may help in recovery from trauma. Furthermore, SAMHSA acknowledges that marginalized populations often have higher rates of predisaster trauma and face barriers during disaster recovery (NCTSN and NCPTSD, 2005). While such information is important for disaster responders, it is not sufficient. As Prilleltensky (1997) wrote, "Discourse without action is dangerous because it creates the impression that progress is taking place when in fact only the words have changed" (p. 530). Counselors truly working for the well-being of their clients will use advocacy and social justice as the foundation to their work. In disaster response, counselor functions should include the following: identifying barriers to resources, advocating for client-identified needs, and developing initiatives to support client self-advocacy.

Counseling practices that promote or fail to challenge social injustices that limit client well-being should be reconsidered. Alternatively, there are some recognized best practices that are consistent with advocacy principles. Counselors need to integrate the principles of social justice as a foundation for counseling practices that traditionally do not address issues of culture, oppression, and prevention. The multicultural counseling competencies (Sue, Arredondo, & McDavis, 1992) were a culmination of the work of the Association for Multicultural Counseling and Development (AMCD) that fought for cultural awareness, knowledge, and skill to be included as fundamental counseling practices. While clearly culture influences the formation of human interactions and worldviews, including counseling, the multicultural counseling competencies formally acknowledged this and required counselors to be competent in working within cultural value systems other than their own.

Recently, the American Counseling Association (ACA) advocacy competencies outlined practices that extend the traditional view of a counselor's role to include political and social advocacy, public information, and leadership in systems-level change (Lewis, Arnold, House, & Toporek, 2002). Given the barriers to enacting change within a system, the competencies and related resources provide guidance for altering the oppressive structures that negatively impact mental health (Ratts, Lewis, & Toporek, 2010a). Research on effective social justice advocacy practices shows the need for advocates to build purposeful relationships, educate and empower others to self-advocate, and understand power structures (Eriksen, 1999; Field & Baker, 2004; Singh, Urbano, & Haston, 2010). The following case examples depict the application of advocacy best practices and social justice theories by counselors in various settings.

## DIFFERENTIAL APPLICATIONS OF ADVOCACY BEST PRACTICES AND SOCIAL JUSTICE THEORIES BY COUNSELING SPECIALTY

Many counselors have been exposed to the principles of client advocacy in some form but have not seen how counselors implement these ideas in practice. For this reason, we offer four examples to demonstrate some of the ways that counselors are working in the field to change the lives of their communities. While not a focus of this chapter, it should also be noted that the lives of the counselors involved are also changed throughout this process. In each case, we provide an overview of key client advocacy issues in the specialty area, a description of a case that addresses these needs, the case outcomes, and suggestions for further applications. Our hope is that you, the reader, will be inspired to develop new, creative, and even better activities in your own setting.

Clinical Mental Health Counseling

The medical model has deeply influenced the specialty area of mental health counseling. Since the dawn of the psychotherapy movement, physicians have guided the paradigms and language that we use to describe the problems experienced by our patients and clients (Elkins, 2009). Being linked to medical establishments and medical managed care, mental health counselors are often required to use this language to support third-party payments and to interface with medical professionals who will often seek to address these problems with medical solutions. Although pharmaceutical support may be indicated in some cases, the process of therapy is not inherently medical (Elkins, 2009). In fact, this model of care can create a dehumanizing experience where clients are objectified by their diagnosis and the rigid treatment of what is often termed an illness.

There are a number of problematic assumptions supported by the medical model when used in counseling settings. First, counselors are expected to be trained as experts who will diagnose and treat clients with evidence-based practices, proven to work with the majority of persons experiencing this condition. Although appealing in many ways, this approach leads counselors to focus on specific therapeutic techniques, which actually account for a small portion of the factors that promote healing and overall wellness through the counseling relationship (Bohart & Tallman, 1999; Wampold, 2001). Second, when addressing problems from an evidence-based practices approach, counselors may find themselves addressing problems from a majority standpoint instead of understanding a client in his or her unique circumstances. If research does not exist for marginalized populations, counselors may default to majority practices that have not been proven with these individuals. Third, the medical model often assumes that the problem is located within the individual instead of the ecological system (family, society, and environment) around him or her. This individualistic perspective negates the importance of these broader factors. Furthermore, individual-focused practices run counter to many cultures that are more collectivistic in nature.

*Case Example*

Developed in 2005, the Ohio-based Wellness Management and Recovery (WMR) program was designed to empower clients diagnosed with severe mental illnesses (SMIs). With the objectives of increasing one's quality of life through personal and communal strengths, WMR seeks to empower clients, called consumers, to identify and pursue their own personal goals, use knowledge and skills to collaborate effectively with their mental health care providers, and live a healthier lifestyle (Bullock et al., 2009). Over 10 weeks, consumers meet in groups of 5–10 members, engaging an interactive curriculum where they learn to self-advocate with medical and mental health professionals using effective communication skills and information about their diagnosis, their medications, and the roles of their professional care team (Bullock et al., 2009). Using a communal wellness approach, participants learn how to use professional and natural (i.e., family and community) supports to improve their quality of life (Bullock et al., 2009). As these consumers often feel disempowered by the symptoms of their diagnosis as well as by their mental health providers, WMR provides a space to explore these experiences and to become informed, skilled, and empowered to become self-advocates. Where previously consumers were often passive recipients of standardized treatment plans from medical and mental health providers, they have become active co-creators of their treatment goals and positive life outcomes.

Theoretically, WMR is based on social learning theory and many of Prilleltensky's teachings that are consistent with emancipatory communitarianism (Wilcox, Wesp, Rich, & Watson, 2009). Recognizing the power of peer learning, the founders designed WMR groups to be led by two individuals, one mental health counselor and one program graduate peer leader. This approach provides an opportunity for group members to learn from the success of graduates and develop self-efficacy in a group structure where power is equalized and hierarchies and job titles may be deconstructed.

As indicated in the curriculum, one of the unique aspects of this approach is that clients are empowered to work with their health providers, understanding their professional roles, the medications they provide, and the communication skills to interact effectively with them (Bullock et al., 2009). Participants are encouraged to bring family members and other supporters to the groups to learn together, with the consumer at the center of the process. This communal approach utilizes many of the strengths available in both the natural and clinical environments. Furthermore, the program emphasizes cultural competency throughout, providing a safe space for all to participate, grow, and claim their power as consumers in the health care system (Wellness Management and Recovery, 2010).

Currently, WMR is used in 19 Ohio-based organizations by over 249 peer specialists, counselors, and other mental health providers. The leadership of WMR is comprised of both mental health counselors and consumers who have graduated from the program, modeling the shared leadership of the educational groups. Also unique was the fact that 3 of the 10 pilot sites where WMR was tested were run by consumers instead of the traditional professional agency structures (Bullock et al., 2009). Following this initial success of the pilot programs, WMR leaders have engaged other agencies, advocating for the use of WMR groups within their current practices. Within the agency setting, it is important to address management to garner their support and prepare them for the changes that will accompany consumer empowerment. Without the support of agency leadership, there are fewer opportunities to access the clients who can benefit from these groups.

*Outcomes*

From the beginning, WMR has been committed to measuring program effectiveness in changing the participant's quality of life. Tracking consumers from preprogram through a six-month follow-up, this advocacy-oriented approach has shown increases in many wellness measures, such as effective wellness planning, improved coping, participation in self-help activities, and the integration of social supports, all of which have helped to decrease life-interfering symptoms (Bullock et al., 2009). In total, 44% of WMR program graduates reported improvements in recovery measures in both consumer-operated and non-consumer-operated sites (Bullock et al., 2009).

In qualitative analyses of participant feedback, consumers reported many advocacy outcomes, including "finding a voice" and overall empowerment, seeing self as an advocate, redefining self as a person versus an illness, gaining social confidence, and overcoming the prejudice and stigma of being diagnosed with a mental illness (D. Wilcox, personal communication, May 26, 2010). WMR has proven itself as an effective way to engage mental health counselors, consumers, and other supporters in a transformation of attitudes and interpersonal communication where partnerships are forged to create wellness in the lives of many who have previously experienced disenfranchisement through the mental health system of care.

WMR is one example of how advocacy can be incorporated into a traditional system of care. Although not every agency is ready for this type of transformation, many are beginning to see the benefit of such practices that appear to have long-term benefits to their consumers. Other consumers, families, and agencies are likely to benefit from similar practices.

*Applications*

While WMR has been limited to agencies in the state of Ohio, it is likely that other consumers in hospital and community-based organizations would likely see similar gains in wellness behavior through greater advocacy. It is interesting that WMR has not thrown out the medical model; rather, it has adapted to this model, empowering clients to work effectively within it. Like WMR, others have suggested that counselors need to advocate for clients by providing complete information about medications and mental health counseling processes (Ingersoll, Bauer, & Burns, 2004). It is apparent that clients who are also under the care of a physician may benefit from increased knowledge and the communication skills to participate actively in goal setting and decision-making processes about their care.

Ideally, mental health counselors would have the support of the physician while their patients were attending an advocacy group like WMR. Even when this is not the case, counselors may work in centers outside of the medical setting to promote wellness through empowerment. With improved outcomes and additional documented research, there is hope that with more education, medical/health care professionals will recognize the benefits of such efforts and collaborate more readily.

Clients face many obstacles in their lives that can impair their overall health and wellness. For instance, clients who experience homelessness must negotiate a number of barriers in the mental health system, including social bias against "the homeless," high staff turnover, overworked employees, and long waiting periods to receive care. If these clients were supported through a group such as WMR, they may gain information, build self-esteem, and support one another in communication skill development as they role-play various scenarios. Other groups who experience disempowerment through our health care system would likely also benefit.

## Trauma Counseling and Disaster Response

Increasingly, counselors are involved in trauma and crisis counseling. The rise of disasters worldwide and the increase of counselors working around the globe are both factors in the greater need for counselors to be prepared to respond to crisis and trauma events. There is greater awareness too, that trauma has both immediate, short-term impacts and long-term effects for entire communities.

It is now understood that trauma can be transmitted intergenerationally, passed down from parent to child (Danieli, 1998). This concept of transgenerational trauma has been particularly helpful in understanding the long-term effects of past oppression, such as the Holocaust, slavery, and Native American genocide. Furthermore, recent research has solidified the finding that discrimination such as racism can also be a cause of trauma among marginalized individuals (Carter, 2007; Harrell, Hall, & Taliaferro, 2003). The effects of trauma caused by marginalization are multiplied when crisis or disaster events occur.

Marginalized communities are at greater risk to be negatively impacted by disasters for a variety of sociopolitical reasons (Farquhar & Dobson, 2004). The disparities in access to housing that force individuals and families with lower income to live in low-lying, flood-prone areas are one example. Limited access to resources may make individuals more vulnerable prior to the disaster and create more difficulty recovering postdisaster. Transportation and lodging are needed to evacuate an area that is expecting a flood or that is engaged in conflict, both of which are less accessible to those with fewer financial resources.

Counselors need to understand the complex contextual factors that create and influence trauma and have the advocacy skills to promote social justice effectively. Clearly, the issue of advocacy is central to effective disaster response and trauma counseling given the multiple systemic factors that are likely to impact clients before, during, and after an event. Advocacy plays a key role in helping clients access support for recovery.

*Case Example*

The earthquake in Haiti in January 2010 not only impacted Haitians living on the island, but also Haitians and those of Haitian descent living in the United States and around the world. In Florida, members of the Haitian community worried about their family and friends living in the devastated island nation. Many brought family members living in Haiti to live with them in Florida. This is often the case with disasters; the impact is not only on the immediate area, but is much more far-reaching than might be anticipated.

After speaking with colleagues within the Haitian community, the second author developed an outreach to provide postdisaster services to the Haitian community in Florida. The theoretical foundation for this outreach was based on prior counseling outreaches, such as those to post-Katrina residents in New Orleans and trauma survivors in Southern Africa using Paulo Freire's (2001) critical consciousness theory and emphasizing culture-centered techniques, empowerment, and sustainability (Goodman & West-Olatunji, 2009).

Within this model, counselors are trained to work collaboratively with the community to identify strengths and endemic ways of healing trauma. The goal is to empower community members to continue in the practices that have been effective in the past, while adjusting to the current situation and creating new strategies as necessary. There is a reciprocal exchange of information between community members and counselors so that both groups bring their own knowledge into the process. In addition to other areas of expertise, community members are the experts in the sociopolitical history of the group, relevant past traumatic experiences, effective healing practices, and cultural values and traditions. Counselors use their expertise to integrate this information with their knowledge of traumatic stress and their skills in interpersonal and group process to help the community maximize posttrauma healing.

The counseling outreach team worked with community members at two Haitian churches and provided consultations and other services whereby community members and counselors discussed and exchanged information about the impact of the earthquake in Haiti. The counselors facilitated discussion with a youth group as well as men's and women's groups. The conversations focused on deconstructing media images and negative stereotypes that had become more visible following the earthquake. The groups also discussed sources of strength, pride, and resilience, which aided them in healing from the trauma. The counselors facilitated discussions around providing support to community members in need, as well as finding ways to take action on behalf of the community.

One significant form of advocacy that the community discussed was a plan to raise money to send several church members to Haiti to provide needed support to their community. The counselors also provided a call-in radio show focused on psychoeducation related to trauma. Members of the community called in to the show to discuss their observations and concerns about how the earthquake was impacting friends and family both in Florida and in Haiti. The counselors provided information on trauma symptoms, including the presence of short- and long-term reactions and the impact of trauma on children. Discussion also focused on ways to support friends and family and the needs of the community. Emphasis was not only on providing information about trauma, but also on who in the community was already engaged in healing practices, how they could continue those practices, and what additional resources could be advocated for that would support healing.

Discussions on the radio as well as in other forums focused on advocacy—both by counselors for the community and by the community members themselves. The community clearly had a strong sense of self-advocacy as they discussed the needs of their loved ones in Haiti and how they would pool resources to meet these needs. The community also voiced concerns about grief and healing among both those in Haiti and those in the United States. One challenge identified by the community and the counselors was the significant lack of available resources for referral. The outreach team was unable to identify any Creole-speaking counselors in the area. Therefore, a focus of the conversations both on the radio show and in other forums was on how to bolster existing forms of support and healing, as well as how to increase resources via advocacy action.

### Outcomes

Throughout the process, the community identified needs and resources for the continued recovery effort. They identified individuals within their community and how these individuals might serve unique functions in the process. One young woman was identified as someone who was interested in psychology and counseling; the community discussed ways that they might collaborate with the counseling team to help her pursue this goal and also benefit the community with her future training.

The counselors were able to identify ways in which they might connect the community with resources and support the initiatives developed by the community. One example was the lack of counselors who speak Creole and who understand the Haitian culture. One member of the counseling team partnered with leaders in the church to develop plans for a counseling center within a new church building. The counseling team also planned to consult with professional organizations to find ways to support the training of Creole-speaking counselors and counselors familiar with Haitian culture, and to provide training on these issues to other professionals. As such, outcomes were very much focused on advocacy within and by members of the counseling profession.

### Applications

It is clear that counselors are needed to provide trauma and disaster response services to communities globally, and to advocate for the needs of often marginalized communities. A culture-centered approach is necessary in disaster and trauma work so as not to further exacerbate the trauma experienced by the individual or community. The case example presented demonstrates that counselors can create collaborative partnerships with communities in which they reinforce natural support systems and ways of healing, while also providing additional information and resources. This model can have applications in disaster response, but also in working with communities that have been marginalized due to racism, poverty, or other sociopolitical issues. Counselor-community partnerships can create opportunities for genuine advocacy that is generated from within the community, instead of imposed by outsiders.

## School Counseling

The role of school counselors is a topic of frequent discussion within the counseling profession. School counselors often face challenges within their work environment as they are tasked with functions that are outside of their training. Often they are asked to complete administrative tasks, taking time away from their important work with students, teachers, and parents. Under the American School Counselor Association (ASCA) National Model for School Counseling Programs' (ASCA, 2005), school counselors are encouraged to advocate that their professional role include counseling, consultation, and prevention, instead of paperwork, discipline, and administrative functions.

School counselors have a unique opportunity to provide not only counseling services but also much-needed consultation and advocacy to multiple stakeholders in the school. The achievement gap, or the disparate performance of lower-income and racial/ethnic minority students, is a consistent blight on the current state of education in the United States. Clearly, there is a critical need within the school setting to create an educational environment in which all students are able to succeed. In 2007, 43% of White students were found to be at or above proficient in reading, while only 14% of African American students and 17% of Latino/a students were at this same level according to the National Assessment of Education Progress (Aud, Fox, & KewalRamani, 2010).

Multicultural counseling and education scholars often point to the underlying prejudices and ethnocentric perspectives that create an environment that marginalizes individuals from non-European backgrounds. In education, prominent voices have underscored the biased teaching and testing practices that exclude culturally diverse students. Here are some common examples: lack of culturally representative images in the classroom, failure to select racial/ethnic minority students for leadership positions or awards, and teaching practices and behavior requirements that fit European American norms, namely individual, silent work (Hale, 2001). Counselors working in schools can add their expertise in cultural competence as well as group process and personal development to assist teachers in developing more culturally appropriate practices. School counselors have the opportunity to train teachers to advocate for their students and for the professional within the school setting.

*Case Example*

The second author served on a university-based counseling consultation team led by a counselor educator and multicultural counseling and education expert. The team was asked to provide services to increase the success of culturally diverse students, particularly African American and Latino/a American students, at a K–12 university laboratory school. Despite having many resources at their disposal, educators and administrators struggled with the common problem faced by schools across the nation—the underachievement of students of color.

The consulting team relied on positionality theory as well as critical consciousness theory to ground their interventions. Positionality theory refers to an individual's perception of social location, meaning how each individual is positioned by herself or himself and by others (Harley, Jolivette, McCormick, & Tice, 2002). Positioning is affected by many socially constructed factors, including gender, ethnicity/race, and socioeconomic status. In the educational environment, positionality will influence who is seen as powerful and capable and who is not. It was the intent of the consulting team to integrate positionality theory with critical consciousness in a way that allowed educators to understand how they might unintentionally position certain students as leaders, learners, and achievers, and other students as not. Critical consciousness theory emphasizes the deconstruction of oppression within a social context through personal reflection, dialogue, and action (Freire, 2001).

The counselors provided a variety of services, including whole staff trainings on positionality and issues of diversity and discrimination in education. They also offered consultations as requested to teachers, teaching teams, and school counselors. One intervention, a "story circle" group, offered school personnel the opportunity to explore diversity issues on a more personal level in a group setting. The participants were provided with directed readings on topics of multicultural education and spent time in the group reflecting on the readings as well as their experiences with students and personal biases. They also discussed their strengths and limitations as educators and of the educational system as a whole.

The objective of the group was to create greater awareness of disparities in education and identify ways in which educators could engage in advocacy action. While the counselors provided expertise in group process and educational hegemony, the educators provided expertise in instructional methods, pedagogy, and education policy and practice. Counselors and educators worked collaboratively to identify biases in the school setting that disadvantaged racial/ethnic minority students and to generate ideas for challenging the system and their own beliefs.

As with any training that engages issues of racism and discrimination, a challenge to the process is the aversion to admitting one's own biases. Mainstream society is ostensibly opposed to racism, making it very difficult for individuals to acknowledge their socialized racist beliefs. For this reason, a counselor-led group process can create a safe space for individuals to share biases and attempt to challenge these beliefs. Another challenge within the school setting is the difficulty of receiving support for social justice initiatives from educators and administrators. In an environment that is very much outcome focused, a counseling process group may be difficult to justify unless it can be linked to improving academic achievement and standardized test scores.

*Outcomes*

Outcomes from the counselors' work at the school included greater awareness and advocacy action on the part of administrators and teachers. For example, one administrator reported that while doing his regular classroom observations, he noticed that all of the racial/ethnic minority students were seated in the back of the room. He decided to advocate for these students by pointing this out to the teacher and suggesting an adjustment to the seating arrangements, which the teacher completed. Another teacher, also serving as curriculum coordinator, did research on her own and discovered a teaching technique that had been found to be effective with both racial/ethnic minority students and White students. She provided information to each of the teaching teams within the school on this research and the techniques, and offered to serve as a consultant to help them implement the techniques in their lessons. Several teachers described becoming more aware of their own biases when working with racial/ethnic minority students. One teacher noted that this inspired her to create a more affirming environment for all students by including images of scholars and scientists from diverse backgrounds in her classroom. She also took action by spending positive one-on-one time with each student, and telling them that she believed in their ability to succeed.

*Applications*

Certainly, a strength of counselors is the ability to facilitate growth groups among a variety of different populations. Furthermore, counselors have training in multicultural and social justice issues that other professionals may lack. This combination enables counselors to provide a greatly needed service within our nation's increasingly diverse schools and community settings (Sue, 2008).

For school counselors, this ability can make them a great asset to school staff. By enabling teachers to be more aware of their own biases, and therefore more effective and culturally appropriate in the classroom, they can reach more students than working on an individual basis, and can engage in prevention instead of remediation. Furthermore, empowering teachers to advocate for themselves as well as for their students creates an environment that supports all students instead of marginalizing those that do not fit European American norms for behavior.

## Counselor Education and Supervision

Within the specialty of counselor education and supervision, client advocacy takes on multiple meanings because of the multiple roles and relationships of a counselor educator. As in the case with school counselors, counselor educators may advocate for their students, targeting individuals and policies that marginalize and otherwise oppress students, keeping them from achieving their full potential as emerging counselors. Likewise, supervisors will likely find themselves in a position to advocate with supervisees, either students or fellow professionals who experience injustices while in practice. We must also consider the clients who are ultimately receiving direct services from the students and supervisees who counselor educators and supervisors indirectly impact. In these cases, counselor educators and supervisors are entrusted to protect the public interest, leading current and future counselors to treat clients equitably and promoting justice while offering their services. Indeed, counselor educators and supervisors who embrace social justice and advocacy principles are likely to see students, supervisees, and the community all as clients in some regard. It would be difficult to ask students and supervisees to promote social justice and advocacy with their clients without modeling this behavior themselves.

Most recently, counselor educators and supervisors have been called to infuse social justice paradigms throughout their pedagogical practices, helping students to grow in their self-awareness and advocacy skills (Constantine, Hage, Kindaichi, & Bryant, 2007; Steele, 2008). Educators who promote social justice and advocacy will create environments where power is shared between instructor and student, self-exploration is highly valued, and grounded knowledge is accessible to all (Guiffrida, 2005). Furthermore, students and faculty alike are called to engage their community, expanding the classroom to the world around them (Constantine et al., 2007).

### *Case Example*

As a doctoral student, the first author was invited to join a feminist, social justice-oriented counselor educator to be a teaching assistant in a master's-level theories course. The course was inherited from a retiring faculty member who had taught the course in a traditional manner, surveying various counseling theories and providing lab exercises for students to practice. Together, the teaching team incorporated Prilleltensky's (1997) emancipatory communitarianism (EC) and his analysis of the values, assumptions, and practices of various counseling theories in the course.

Because both had worked with a number of clients who experienced marginalization, the instructors felt it important for students to consider the impact of their theory of choice, in particular, how their theory would affect their practices with various types of clients. In addition, they sought to create a learning atmosphere where students would experience greater equality and where ideas could be freely explored and challenged. In this setting, power sharing created honest dialogue and a shared responsibility to learn and grow.

One of the central exercises conducted early in the course was a process of *de-ideologizing* the dominant paradigm. De-ideologizing, first identified by Martín-Baró (1994), is a process of deconstructing social beliefs and norms, critically analyzing the sources and impacts of these beliefs. Using Prilleltensky's (1997) analysis of values, assumptions, and practices, the first author developed a kinesthetic exercise where students could explore their own values and assumptions and determine what types of theories are likely to align with these values. After clearing away chairs and tables, the group established four points on the floor, where each represented one of the four categories of theories identified by Prilleltensky (1997): traditional, empowering, postmodern, and emancipatory communitarianism. A description of each was read aloud and students were invited to portray their resonance with the theories by positioning themselves within or outside of the points of the circle. The instructors joined the group and found each other in two different positions, indicating the multiplicity of options and diminishing the notion that there is only one correct, social justice-oriented theory, or that one remains stagnant over time. As such, students were encouraged to be honest and exploratory.

After all were given a chance to describe their own values and how they aligned with their respective theories, the class began to explore how one's choice of theory would impact various clients. From an individual standpoint, some clients would feel more comfortable with traditional theories that would support their personal goals of improved mental health. Others might be better served with empowering approaches that acknowledge the injustices they are overcoming, and finding new skills to grow and change. The group challenged each other to think about the greater social good and their responsibility as counselors to support this endeavor. If a theoretical approach supports one person or group but disregards the rights and responsibilities of others, is this a just approach? By engaging in this dialogue, the instructors were able to advocate not only for marginalized populations, but for society as a whole. Furthermore, students were provided an opportunity to voice when they experienced values being shaped by injustice and oppression.

This conversation was put into a different context when the students met as a class to talk with a group who had experienced homelessness. This panel of experts gave an idea of what it was like to live without housing, surviving day to day and being subjected to daily discrimination because of this status. The panel gave the students practical ideas about how they could be effective serving this population. The group then continued the conversation in the classroom, considering the efficacy of various theoretical approaches when working with those experiencing homelessness and other forms of oppression (see Brubaker, Puig, Reese, & Young, 2010, for more details about this case example).

*Outcomes*

Over the course of the semester, students actively engaged in the learning process, taking turns presenting material and sharing their perspectives on the benefits and limitations of each theory. Many students were actively involved in other advocacy initiatives related to local, national, and international projects, which inspired conversations about the relevance of counseling theories in various contexts. Following this course experience, students reported how their critical reflection continued into their practicum and internship experiences, where they developed community collaborations, organizational needs assessments, and student advocacy activities. Although some students became proponents of EC, others did not. This was important, as the course was not designed to convert students to a social justice, advocacy-oriented paradigm. Rather, the intent was to de-ideologize the dominant paradigms and create critical consciousness, so that students could make better informed decisions about their theory of choice.

*Applications*

Advocacy in the classroom begins with an awareness of social injustices followed by intentional community engagement (Steele, 2008). It may involve teaching advocacy skills such as effective communication skills (including media skills), understanding broader organizational systems, and advocacy-oriented clinical skills (Kiselica & Robinson, 2001). There may also be opportunities to advocate for particular groups of people who experience oppression or for the community as a whole. All of these projects can be reinforced when understood through a student's theoretical lens.

Counselor educators may also incorporate advocacy activities when teaching other classes outside of the counseling curriculum. In one such case in an undergraduate drugs and society course, the first author created an assignment for students to investigate the disparity in legal consequences between those caught with powder versus crack cocaine. They were then required to write a letter to their congressional representative, using their knowledge of the drug potency, the history of these laws, and a proposed solution. Sending the letter was optional; however, many indicated their intent to have it delivered. It should be noted that the law was modified to reduce these disparities in 2010 following this letter writing exercise. There are many other examples of opportunities for client advocacy that may be employed by counselor educators and supervisors, and in the exercises that follow we to encourage you to identify some of those.

## SUMMARY

Throughout this chapter, we have provided a number of examples of client advocacy across various specialty areas of the counseling profession. While examining these cases and engaging in the exercises and discussion questions, we have suggested ways that you might become a greater advocate for your own clients, which may include individuals or whole communities. Making the transition to becoming an advocate can be uncomfortable for some, but we must not shy away. It is our belief that taking this action-oriented role of building critical consciousness and standing up with clients for their rights begins with a critical examination of ourselves and our current practices. In fact, we may be contributing to the oppression that our clients experience. Through this greater awareness, we may then be able to step into the larger community with greater humility and understanding of how we may promote wellness and human dignity while engaging in acts of social justice. Through these small steps, we may begin to see the larger role that we may play as catalysts for change in our profession and in our communities.

## EXERCISES FOR APPLICATION

### From Past to Present

This activity focuses on increasing your knowledge of the historical factors that may influence your clients today. As discussed in this chapter, clients are impacted by oppression and inequities that may have been created many years or even centuries ago. One clear example is the impact that slavery and the legacy of racism may have on individuals of African descent in the United States (Cross, 1998).

For this exercise, select a film, book, or other resource that describes some historical event or aspect that impacts your client population or a population of interest. For example, prior to working with survivors of Hurricane Katrina in New Orleans, it was critical for disaster responders to be educated in the sociopolitical history of New Orleans and how that history had marginalized citizens. Viewing the documentary television series directed by Spike Lee, *When the Levees Broke* (Glover, Lee, Nevins, Pollard, & Robinson, 2006), gives an insight into the context in which citizens of New Orleans live.

Questions for reflection may include:

1. What historical events impacted or are impacting clients? How?
2. What historical political or legislative issues impacted or are impacting clients? How?
3. How are current counselor responses impacted by historical events, legislative issues, or marginalization/discrimination?
4. What are the current ways in which clients might benefit from advocacy, particularly with respect to disaster response counseling?
5. What are the avenues available for advocacy?
6. How might counselors engage in advocacy?

**(CACREP standards met:** I.4, G.4, J.2, H.3)

Community Resource Exercise

This exercise is designed for a classroom or local conference in order to gather multiple resources for client advocacy. Oftentimes the United Way or another local agency will gather information about resources to aid persons in need of care. Advocacy resources are not always as prevalent. Class or conference participants are invited to seek out community members, agencies, or other groups who advocate for clients and present this information on poster boards to share with one another.

To begin, participants should think of the population who they are serving (or will soon serve) and how they may experience marginalization. This activity will take some initial research in the field, talking with community members, counselors, and other professionals, as well as searching for information in both peer-reviewed and general resources, online and in print. It will be helpful to consider issues of stigmatization, economic oppression, legal disparities, and other ways that individuals, families, and communities are kept from reaching their full potential. The next step will be to locate those who are advocating for change. Some examples may be community centers, activists, politicians, religious leaders, and counselors. Finally, participants are invited to develop and share in a poster or other presentation format a list of these advocates, with contact information, and a brief summary of their current efforts to advocate for their population chosen for this exercise.

**(CACREP standards met:** J.2)

Adapting Your Current Practices

In this chapter, you have seen a number of examples where counseling practices have been infused with client advocacy. Each one of these situations could be addressed in a traditional manner where social justice and advocacy would be minimal. Consider your own theory and practices in your current counseling setting. Do you currently advocate with and for your clients? How might you alter your weekly activities to include greater client advocacy?

Begin with an analysis of your theory of choice. Consider the values and assumptions behind the theory that informs your practice. Does it take into account the ways that social systems impact individuals and communities? How does it empower or disempower clients? How do the related practices serve the greater good? Next consider your daily activities. On a sheet of paper, list your current activities performed each week and the degree of advocacy that is involved, on a scale from 1 to 10. For example, a mental health counselor in a community agency may include activities such as individual therapy, clinical rounds, peer consults, charting, and supervision, among others.

After rating each activity, consider the three most important that would favorably impact your clients if the amount of advocacy was increased. Describe in detail how these practices would look if there was greater advocacy and the difference this would make among your clients and the communities in which they live. Next, describe the necessary steps to reach this vision in an action plan. Share this with at least one person whom you identify as a competent client advocate to receive their feedback and begin to implement the plan.

**(CACREP standards met:** J.2, H.2)

### Counseling and Politics

Whether of interest to counselors or not, political issues do impact clients. Numerous examples abound, from stress caused by recent changes to immigration laws to government spending in education and mental health. In this exercise, you will identify issues that are relevant for you, your clients, or both. Step 1 will be to tune in to the political issues going on around you and take a critical look at how they might affect you and your clients, either positively or negatively, or both. Local, national, and international news broadcasts, lobbying and activist organizations, counseling organizations, and your clients can all serve to educate you about relevant issues.

Once you have identified an issue, reflect on who is impacted and in what ways. Try mapping out the impact, starting with those directly impacted and then extending to individuals who might be indirectly impacted. For instance, regarding changes to immigration laws that allow for racial profiling in Arizona (SB 1070, 2010), undocumented students who are fearful of being stopped by the police and deported would experience a direct impact of increased stress and anxiety. Indirect impacts might include the teachers and school counselors who see an increase in agitation and behavioral problems in the classroom among such students.

Finally, identify strategies for advocacy that you might use to make your voice heard on this issue. Letter writing to an elected official, as described earlier, is one option. You might choose to support an advocacy or lobbying organization. You might create a petition for a change in policy. Regarding the example of immigration and racial profiling laws, one opportunity for advocacy would be to support the overturning of SB 1070 or support such legislation as the DREAM Act (www. dreamact.info), which offers a pathway to citizenship for children who are undocumented. Such changes might reduce the fear and anxiety experienced by students, as well as the secondary stress on educators and counselors. See the list of websites provided at the end of this book for resources on counseling and politics, and then add your own local resources and share with your colleagues and peers.

**(CACREP standards met:** J.1, J.2)

## DISCUSSION QUESTIONS

1. This chapter described WMR as a means of augmenting the medical model to be inclusive of advocacy and empowerment. What are some of the traditional theories or models of counseling that you have come across (e.g., cognitive-behavioral therapy (CBT), medical model)? How does this theory/model address (or not address) advocacy? What limitations do you see to working within one of these theories or models with regards to client advocacy? How might you augment this theory/model to more fully address or include advocacy action?
2. This chapter described the instruction of a counseling theories course in which students and instructors de-ideologized theories. Reflect on your own counseling theory of choice. What are the tenets of that theory? Does it have potential to marginalize clients? If so, how? How might you incorporate social justice and advocacy in your case conceptualizations using your theory of choice? What is the role of the counselor according to your theory? Does it include advocacy? How might you augment your theory to include advocacy?
3. One example of client advocacy involves advocating with Haitians who are living in the United States. What are the wide-reaching effects of natural and human-made disasters that often go unnoticed by the general public and by counselors, in particular? What are the causes of this lack of attention? What role can counselors play in addressing this need?
4. There were many challenges to client advocacy mentioned in the beginning of the chapter, both internal and external to us as counselors. What barriers to client advocacy do you experience? What positive and negative messages do you have about advocacy and your role as an advocate? How might you change as a person if you were to advocate more fully for your clients? How might your relationships with your clients change?

# III

## LEADERSHIP AND ADVOCACY ROLES IN COUNSELING

# III

LEADERSHIP AND
ADVOCACY ROLES
IN COUNSELING

# 10

# Leadership and Advocacy in Counselor Education Programs
## Administration and Culture

CRAIG S. CASHWELL AND CASEY A. BARRIO MINTON

Education is not the filling of a pail, but the lighting of a fire.

—William Butler Yeats

Are leaders and advocates born or made? As with all questions of this nature, the answer is that both innate and developed knowledge, skills, and attributes are important. Some people seem to naturally possess an innate desire and skills to lead and advocate for disenfranchised individuals and groups. At the same time, leaders in the counseling profession seem quick to credit those who mentored them as a student. At its core, counseling is a developmental profession. In the same vein, the process of becoming a professional counselor is very much a developmental one, in which students build a range of knowledge and skills over time, including knowledge and skills related to leadership and advocacy. Increasingly, counseling students learn during their preparation that counseling and social justice are inexorably linked (Lewis, Toporek, & Ratts, 2010). Counselor educators, then, serve a vital role in advocacy and leadership training and development, including what/how they teach, how they organize and administer their program, and what they model for students. Leadership and advocacy efforts are necessarily directed to advocate for both (1) individual clients and marginalized groups, and (2) the counseling profession (Myers & Sweeney, 2004). Therefore, the authors in this chapter will explore a number of ways in which counselor educators can use administrative processes and program culture to develop leaders who advocate for clients, for the counseling profession, and against all injustices that harm society.

Throughout this chapter, the most compelling question is *how*. That is, how does an educator instill in a student a passion for his or her work, a selflessness that is not ego driven but longs only to do the next right thing? For in the end, true leadership is not about being a leader, but about being a servant, serving some cause beyond oneself in which one believes. Before reading further, take a few minutes to reflect on the following questions and either journal or discuss your thoughts with another:

- Who in your counselor preparation program are/were your professional mentors?
- What have they taught you?
- How did they teach you this?
- How does/did the overall culture of your training program enhance your leadership and advocacy knowledge and skills?

In the authors' personal experiences and in discussion with others, *never* has a counseling student or professional answered the *how* questions above with a memory of didactic teaching in the classroom. Instead, memories unfold of seeing the passion in their faculty, seeing the humility with which they approached their work, or of experiential work in the classroom that touched them far deeper than at an intellectual level alone. If all educators do is "fill the pail," to borrow from the Yeats quote with which we opened this chapter, the process is doomed to fail. That is, if all an educator can offer to students is knowledge, he or she offers little, if anything, not already contained in a textbook. Knowledge is vital, but it is only the beginning of counselor development. Indeed, counselor educators must always challenge themselves to offer themselves, their experiences, and their wisdom. If education is the lighting of a fire, educators must recognize that it is only *their* fire that can kindle a spark in others.

Because education is relational, students also play a key role in this developmental process. Through the educational process, students typically are given opportunities for self-examination and to learn about personal strengths and limitations. What students do with this information is critical. From an educational standpoint, students must ask themselves two relevant questions:

1. What is needed for me to grow personally and professionally? That is, what are my growing edges?
2. In the form of both support and challenge, what do I need from others to help me with this growth? And, from whom can I get this?

In many instances, the answer to the final question above may involve faculty or peers in the program. Often, students drawn to the counseling profession may have a personal culture of helping others. The shadow side of this, however, is that many counseling students lack critical skills of asking for help and support from others. The process of seeking mentoring, then, is critical for students to maximize their potential as leaders and advocates.

Counselor educators may utilize program administration and systematic methods for developing a culture of leadership and advocacy to kindle this spark within our ranks. Because the Council for Accreditation of Counseling and Related Educational Programs (CACREP) (2009) standards provide a foundation upon which counselor education programs and faculty can inspire leadership and advocacy, we begin this chapter with an exploration of the ways in which the standards provide a foundation for effective program administration processes. Later, we turn our attention to methods for developing a culture in which community members integrate, teach, practice, and supervise the development of leadership and advocacy skills.

## PROGRAM ADMINISTRATION: CACREP STANDARDS AND PROCESS CONSIDERATIONS

The curriculum within which counselor educators prepare professional counselors serves as a mold to shape the knowledge and skills of the student and to facilitate counselor development. As Sweeney discussed in Chapter 1, the overarching framework for counselor preparation standards is provided by CACREP. By establishing minimal standards for learning environments, program professional identity, standards of professional practice, and specialty program areas, CACREP promotes excellence within the profession. In fact, the eight core curricular areas, long a part of the CACREP standards, are now recognized within counselor licensure laws and regulations within many states; our standards have become a key resource for professional advocacy. Although most individuals who write and study the CACREP standards focus almost exclusively on curricular requirements, professional practice standards, or program area standards, the 2009 CACREP standards include a number of more specific criteria that call upon programs and faculty members to engage as leaders and advocates for the profession and model administrative leadership within their programs. In addition, core curricular requirements and program area standards ensure a degree of standardized attention to leadership and advocacy in our formal curricula.

### Leadership and Advocacy for the Profession

The 2009 CACREP standards include a number of items that were developed explicitly for ensuring leadership and advocacy for the profession. The acculturation and mentoring process of developing counselors is vital, and several standards ensure that program faculty members who are mentoring students have a clear and strong identity as professional counselors. For example, Standard I.W ensures that programs have sufficient numbers of core faculty members who have professional counseling identities and credentials; practice within their bounds of competence; and engage in professional counseling development/renewal, research and scholarship, and service and advocacy activities. Similarly, Doctoral Standards I.I and I.K require faculty member participation in professional counseling associations and scholarly pursuits. Standard II.C and Doctoral Standard II.B.3 require that counseling program students identify with the counseling profession and participate in professional organizations; further, Doctoral Standard I.C requires that "programs accept as primary obligations ... preparing students to assume positions of leadership in the profession and/or their area(s) of specialization" (p. 131). As we discuss next, adherence to standards regarding ratios, admissions, gatekeeping, and program evaluation provides administrative guidance for programs and ensures that programs are accountable to stakeholders within and outside of our profession (see Chapter 16 for an expanded discussion of accountability).

Administrative Leadership for Programs

The CACREP (2009) Standards Revision Committee developed a number of standards to enhance general administrative leadership and preparation quality for effective leadership. For example, Standards I.J and I.U ensure attention to student and faculty diversity and inclusion in program operations, and Standard I.X ensures appropriate "administrative and curricular leadership" (p. 86), including the appointment of an academic leader and field experience coordinator. In addition, Standards II.A and II.B require that program faculties be intentional about developing and disseminating program mission and objective statements. Similarly, Standard I.L recognizes the importance of an orientation as part of successful induction in the program and profession. As Myers discussed in Chapter 3, the ability to give voice to and operationalize one's mission and vision is key to effective leadership. As we illustrate below, additional CACREP standards provide additional administrative guidance around student-to-faculty ratios, admissions, gatekeeping, and program evaluation processes.

*Ratios*

Standard I.M ensures that core faculty will deliver the majority of the curriculum rather than overrelying on adjunct or affiliate faculty who bring their own strengths but may not have clear and strong professional counseling identities. Standard I.N restricts student to faculty FTE ratios to 10:1, ensuring that programs have sufficient resources to mentor students, and Standard I.O ensures that students have access to an advisor throughout their program. Standards I.Q and I.R acknowledge that clinical programs require intensive supervision and oversight and promote faculty to student ratios in individual (6:1) and group (12:1) supervision that allow faculty to mentor and support students adequately. These standards, taken together, generally provide an upper limit on admissions for a program based on faculty resources, preventing programs from becoming "diploma mills" in which large student-to-faculty ratios and large class sizes for practicum and internship prevent students from getting vital quality mentoring, training, and supervision throughout their studies. As we discuss later in the chapter, quality mentoring is essential to creating a culture of leadership and advocacy.

## Admissions

Perhaps no single task performed by a counselor preparation program is more important than the admissions process. It is at this decision point that the future leaders of our profession are chosen. The 2009 CACREP standards provide some important criteria for the admissions process. First, admissions decisions must be made by a selection committee (Standard I.K). This ensures that (1) decisions are made by a small group of individuals going through an established review process, including consultation with one another about who will be the most successful candidates, and (2) no single individual has responsibility and authority over the admissions decision process.

Additionally, CACREP Standard I.K provides minimal criteria that should be used to make admissions decisions, including "potential success in forming effective and culturally relevant interpersonal relationships in individual and small group contexts," aptitude for graduate study, and career goals (2009, p. 84). Noteworthy here is the fact that the interpersonal factor is given priority over aptitude for academic success and career goals. Although all are important, the order of these standards seems to point to the essence of interpersonal and emotional intelligence in the admissions process. Implicit in these standards is openness to self-exploration and personal growth, key features of a social justice orientation. Similarly, an important part of this process is assessing all students' potential for and commitment to leadership and advocacy for the profession. In that regard, Doctoral Standard I.D.5 requires explicit attention to "potential for scholarship, professional leadership, and advocacy" in the admissions process (p. 132).

## Gatekeeping

Gatekeeping, or the systematic and developmental review of student performance and appropriateness for the counseling profession, including but not limited to development of remediation plans for student deficiencies and, when necessary, the facilitated transition out of the program, is a foundational role within counselor preparation programs (Bernard & Goodyear, 2009). CACREP Standard I.P (2009) clearly outlines that

> program faculty conducts a systematic developmental assessment of each student's progress throughout the program, including consideration of the student's academic performance, professional development, and personal development ... [and] if evaluations indicate a student is not appropriate for the program, faculty members help

facilitate the student's transition out of the program and, if possible, into a more appropriate area of study. (p. 85)

In keeping with the American Counseling Association Code of Ethics (2005), it is imperative that counselor preparation programs have a clear policy and procedures on gatekeeping, and that students are informed of these policies and procedures at the outset of their training.

The importance of this gatekeeping function cannot be overstated. While sound admissions practices provide programs with access to students with the greatest potential for success as leaders and advocates for the counseling profession and marginalized clients, the tasks of gatekeeping protect the public from impaired professionals, including those who systematically impose values and oppress disenfranchised groups. Researchers have found that CACREP accredited programs and programs with formalized gatekeeping procedures more effectively follow through with concerns about student deficiencies than do non-accredited programs and programs with no formalized gatekeeping procedure (Gaubatz & Vera, 2002). Certainly, recent scholars have highlighted the importance of communicating clearly about expectations, remediation, and gatekeeping processes (Foster & McAdams, 2009; Kress & Protivnak, 2009; McAdams, Foster, & Ward, 2007).

*Systematic Program Evaluation*

CACREP (2009) Standard I.AA requires programs to be engaged in an ongoing process of systematic program evaluation. This standard goes on to indicate that program faculty must systematically review their programs, curricular offerings, and program applicant characteristics. Further, program faculty must conduct follow-up studies of program graduates, site supervisors, and program graduate employers. Ongoing assessments of student learning and performance in the areas of professional identity, professional practice, and the program area standards are also required. Additionally, these data must be distributed to program constituents and used to inform program modifications. That is, the 2009 standards require a program to develop an ongoing and systematic program evaluation to provide data to monitor program effectiveness and support the development of leaders and advocates within the profession. Additional standards related to evaluation of faculty (II.BB) and communication of evaluation results and procedures (II.CC and II.DD) also serve as accountability checks for program administrators.

Finally, a foundational shift in the 2009 standards occurred around the implementation of Student Learning Outcomes (SLOs) for the program area standards. Historically, both the core curricular experiences (Section II.G) and the program area standards (e.g., school counseling, clinical mental health counseling) were written as input-based standards, meaning that programs needed only to indicate where these knowledge-based standards were taught in the curriculum and document this, most commonly in course syllabi. With the implementation of the 2009 standards, however, programs must provide evidence of (1) student learning and (2) student skills and practices. The move to SLOs, including leadership and advocacy behaviors, heightens program awareness of student performance, clarifies expectations for students, and ensures that students have the requisite knowledge and skill sets to be competent professional counselors.

## Leadership and Advocacy in the Formal Curriculum

In addition to the above standards that ensure that professional counselors are well equipped to be leaders and advocates for the counseling profession, additional CACREP standards (2009) address the role of counselor training programs in preparing students to be leaders and advocates for marginalized individuals and groups. As mentioned previously, faculty members are expected to serve as role models for students. Standard I.W.5 specifies that all core faculty must engage in activities related to *service and advocacy* (e.g., program presentations, workshops, consultations, speeches, direct service)" (italics added, p. 86). In addition to this modeling, however, faculty members must provide training in leadership and advocacy. Specifically, Standard II.G.1.h requires students to be grounded in "the role and process of the professional counselor advocating on behalf of the profession" (p. 90). Standard II.G.1.i specifies that the counseling curriculum must train students in "advocacy processes needed to address institutional and social barriers that impede access, equity, and success for clients" (p. 90). The 2009 standards include a number of additional items that require students to address diversity at both micro and macro levels.

In addition to the core standards, diversity and advocacy are written into each of the entry-level program area standards, and leadership and advocacy appears as one of five essential learning outcome areas in the Doctoral Standards. Each of the program area sections is divided into "Knowledge" and "Skills and Practices" sections, highlighting that leadership and advocacy are ultimately about translating knowledge into action through a set of behavioral skills. Moreover, because the 2009 CACREP standards include SLOs for the first time, programs must provide evidence of student outcomes in these areas, placing the onus on training programs to demonstrate where and how content is being taught and how it is being assessed. In Chapters 14 and 15, you will read about specific CACREP curricular standards and SLOs related to leadership and advocacy and learn formal curricular methods for meeting and assessing the standards. For now, however, we turn our attention to ways in which counselor educators can inspire leadership and advocacy through program administration processes.

Process Considerations for Program Administration

Although the CACREP (2009) standards include specific items designed to ensure that accredited programs establish minimal foundations for effective program management and preparation in leadership and advocacy, these standards do not capture the essence of *how* programs go about doing so in a way that encourages excellence among faculty members and students. Previously, Lewis (Chapter 2) discussed theory and research as they relate to leadership in general. Similarly, Myers (Chapter 3) discussed qualities of professional counseling leaders and applied these qualities to Chi Sigma Iota's (CSI) Principles and Practices of Leadership Excellence (2009). Counselor education faculty members may build upon these foundations by exploring several questions.

### How Do Program Faculty Members Embody Characteristics of Effective Leaders and Advocates as They Administer Their Counselor Education Program?

First and foremost, counseling program leaders and faculty members must remember that actions speak louder than words, and that students will learn far more from their example than their teachings. Above all things, counselor educators can consider whether they are genuine and consistent in their personal and multiple professional roles. Consider the following true examples that we have heard from students in various settings:

- A student is encouraged to take the weekend off from studies to center herself and connect with family. The student asks the faculty member if she will be doing the same. The honest answer is no.
- A student attends a conference and meets her "hero" only to be dismissed with a sexist comment.
- Students who are taught in the classroom to emphasize servant leader philosophies also get caught in the midst of "ego wars" among their faculty.
- Students are encouraged to attend professional meetings and conferences but rarely see their program faculty at these meetings.

### How Do Program Administration Processes Demonstrate the CSI Principles and Practices of Leadership Excellence?

The Principles and Practices of Leadership Excellence (CSI, 2009) (see Chapter 3 for an in-depth discussion) provide concrete guidance regarding opportunities to evaluate program leadership processes. Whether part of a formal and informal leadership evaluation process, program faculty members may look for specific indicators of adherence to the principles, and they may invite key stakeholders to provide feedback on their perceptions of leadership process strengths and needs. Faculty members can, in turn, use feedback to propose changes to the administration process.

Imagine, for example, a program in which faculty members and students were active and productive in their professional pursuits; however, few were aware of what others are doing. After noting that the unit does not attend well to Principle 9, recognition of others, a faculty member asked the program coordinator to place a "good news" item at the beginning of every agenda. After each meeting, the recorder announced faculty member, student, and alumni recognitions and accomplishments to all members of the community, including academic leaders and university media. In addition to enhancing a sense of program cohesion and pride, the simple act resulted in a local news story regarding the accomplishments of the group and assisted the faculty in advocating for additional program resources for students.

### How Do Program Administration Processes Model Inclusive Social Justice and Advocacy Perspectives?

As noted previously, the CACREP standards (2009) require that programs attend to diversity among faculty and students. As program faculty members inspire students toward social justice and advocacy perspectives within the classroom and counseling room, we must remain aware of the potential for systematic inequities within our own programs. When attending to this issue, faculty members must ask difficult questions regarding which faculty member, staff, and student voices are heard and valued within program operations. Although uncomfortable for many, such a process provides an opportunity for social justice while modeling skills needed to address systematic inequities.

In addition to attending to communication processes, program faculty members may examine grade rosters, competency concern documents, program completion data, and comprehensive examination results to identify which students tend to be the most and least successful in the program. When program faculty members become aware that students from a particular group are not performing as well in the program or note high turnover among support staff or faculty members, they must explore potential reasons for the inequities and develop proactive strategies for addressing the concerns. The second author recalls a powerful moment in which an international student in a multicultural counseling course shared that the instructor's and program's expectation for mutual dialogue created dissonance between her cultural value of achievement and cultural beliefs regarding the nature of the student-teacher relationship. It was through such interactions that international students in the program came to establish an organization to reduce isolation and promote academic and clinical success among international students; each semester, several faculty members support the organization by attending events and presenting workshops responsive to the self-identified needs of members.

In addition to staying alert to issues of inequity within programs, counselor education faculty members must also attend to the social justice and advocacy role of the program in the larger community. In 2010, several counselor education programs made national news with regards to lawsuits in which students alleged religious discrimination and first amendment violations from counseling programs (McManus, 2010; *Ward v. Wilbanks et al.*, 2010). Although the courts rejected the cases or found in favor of the counselor education programs, these events highlight the importance of opening a dialogue with students and the public regarding the sensitive interplay between personal beliefs and professional standards and behavior. Certainly, program leaders may use mission statements, objectives, admissions processes, orientations, and handbooks (all required by CACREP standards) to give voice to the role of the social justice and advocacy orientation within the program while honoring constituents' cultural perspectives.

### How Can Administrators Engage Faculty, Students, and Other Constituents in Developing and Communicating Program Priorities and Practices Regarding Leadership and Advocacy?

As expressed earlier in this text, effective leaders involve others in establishing an organization's mission and vision. Certainly, the CACREP (2009) standards require that programs develop and disseminate a program mission (II.A) as well as objectives that "reflect current knowledge and projected needs concerning counseling practice in a multicultural and pluralistic society" (II.B.1, p. 89) and "reflect input from all persons involved in the conduct of the program, including program faculty, current and former students, and personnel in cooperating agencies" (II.B.2, p. 89). As administrators engage in this process, they may explore opportunities for creating shared vision and ownership within the program. As they do so, they also are modeling to students the ways in which agency, school, and professional organization leaders can garner support and buy-in from constituents. One way to do so is to facilitate a strengths, weaknesses, opportunities, and threats (SWOT) analysis (Hill & Westbrook, 1997) specific to program engagement in leadership and advocacy. Once constituents identify SWOTs, leaders may communicate several measurable leadership and advocacy objectives to students and alumni via program newsletters. In addition to coming together to determine where leadership and advocacy must be taught in the formal curriculum (see Chapters 14 and 15), program faculty members may choose to initiate curricular and co-curricular engagements in direct support of identified priorities.

Imagine, for example, that a SWOT analysis for one program leads to the realization that it had strengths in national leadership and publication engagements, weaknesses when it comes to local and state-level client and professional advocacy efforts, opportunities to apply national strengths to the weaknesses, and threats from a current legislative agenda proposing cutbacks in graduate programs requiring more than 36 credit hours. As a result of the analysis, the program faculty collaborates with the local CSI chapter to develop a special newsletter in which they highlight results of the SWOT analysis, challenge stakeholders to action, and provide a column specific to legislative advocacy recommendations. Future issues of the newsletter may include a column in which community members report updates, triumphs, and needs related to the program priorities.

### How Can Counselor Education Faculty Model, Teach, and Engage Students in a Shared Program Leadership and Advocacy Process?

Certainly, the last example includes concrete implications for engaging community members in establishing leadership and advocacy priorities. Students and faculty alike benefit when counselor education programs involve students in everyday program leadership processes. Programs may allow student representatives to attend nonconfidential portions of faculty meetings or appoint students to search committees or advisory councils. Similarly, programs may be transparent with students when communicating about program accountability measures and reasons for changes in curricula or policies. Finally, programs with active CSI chapters may establish formal methods for ensuring a student voice within faculty decisions and a faculty voice (beyond the chapter faculty advisor) within chapter engagements.

For example, a program that is adopting the 2009 standards for the first time will likely undergo a number of key changes in program operations as it attempts to assess SLOs. Faculty members may be asked to make significant changes to how they conduct courses, and students may be asked to purchase services or document their work in different ways. Rather than communicate grudgingly that the changes are a necessary evil imposed from the outside or place the evaluation report in a far-off corner of a program website, leaders might use results of the program evaluation report to facilitate honest discussions regarding learning opportunities. Similarly, faculty leaders can use adoption of SLO measures to engage constituents in discussions regarding accountability in their own practice and identification of ways the new data may help to strengthen the program and profession.

In the first half of this chapter, we explored the CACREP (2009) standards relevant to program administration in counselor education, and we discussed five key process questions when considering the role of leadership and advocacy in overall administrative functioning. Certainly, attention to these processes will provide a foundation for promoting a culture of leadership and advocacy within counselor education programs. In the next section, we attend more specifically to ways in which counselor educators can cultivate this culture through formal and informal program activities.

## CULTIVATING A CULTURE OF LEADERSHIP AND ADVOCACY

Themes related to program culture and mentoring arise consistently in studies regarding professional counseling leadership (Black & Magnuson, 2005; Gibson,

Dollarhide, & McCallum, 2010; Luke & Goodrich, 2010; Magnuson, Wilcoxon, & Norem, 2003; Meany-Walen, Barrio Minton, Pronchenko, & Purswell, 2010). In particular, consider the following two conclusions:

> It is clear from the responses that all participants were significantly influenced toward service by their doctoral adviser and/or faculty mentors, if not by the culture of the program. Although counselor educators may know that students are influenced by their teaching, this study highlights how profound that learning may be when combined with the passion for the profession articulated by these participants. (Gibson et al., p. 291)

> Many of the models were unaware of the influence they had on their protégés. From this we might assume that each class a counselor educator teaches, each supervision session a supervisor conducts, or each encounter between an experienced and novice counseling practitioner becomes an opportunity to model attributes that contribute to leadership. (Magnuson et al., p. 50)

Leadership and advocacy are promoted primarily through faculty-student interactive experiences via dissemination of information, modeling, and process discussions. As Magnuson and colleagues (2003) noted, this occurs through formal processes such as classroom teaching and counseling supervision. Equally as important, however, are the informal processes through which students are mentored. In many ways, this parallel curriculum is vital to our profession. The key question is how counselor educators can cultivate a culture of leadership and advocacy throughout program experiences. As mentioned at the outset of this chapter, it is through both formal and informal processes that the talents of future leaders and advocates are potentiated. In particular, we highlight three considerations: communication, curricula, and mentoring.

### Communicating and Modeling Professionalism

Each educational act has the potential to include mentoring. Even as an educator is determining *what* to teach, he or she must also grapple with *how* best to promote learning. Because teaching and counseling are both relational in nature, the model created by an educator in the classroom, individual and group supervision, and in advising and mentoring relationships is at the heart of the development of future leaders. Training students in leadership theory and advocacy competencies is important. It is inadequate, however, in and of itself to spark the passion for leadership and advocacy. This cannot be taught; rather, it must be modeled.

Students also learn from the model set by faculty of professional memberships and service. As faculty members are engaged in leadership opportunities and service, students observe an orientation to give back to the counseling profession and to advocate for disenfranchised individuals and groups. Disparities between what is being taught in the classroom and the professional behaviors of faculty create a disconnect for students. Actions do, indeed, speak louder than words.

Counselor educators have unique opportunities to communicate and model professionalism throughout the curriculum. As discussed previously, educators might communicate faculty, staff, and student accomplishments via a listserv or newsletter so that the leadership and advocacy work of community members is celebrated and highlighted by the group as a whole. Although we would like to believe that involvement in leadership and advocacy is internally motivated, researchers have found that recognition and encouragement by others is key to the developmental process (Gibson et al., 2010; Luke & Goodrich, 2010; Magnuson et al., 2003; Meany-Walen et al., 2010). Thus, these celebrations can serve as powerful reinforcers for community members' accomplishments while inspiring other community members to consider how they might become involved. Similarly, faculty members may take class time to discuss their own professional engagements and encourage students to attend conferences, workshops, or advocacy days. This modeling of professionalism may be particularly powerful when faculty members visit with students about their roles at upcoming events and take time out to guide students through their first conference activities or experiences.

An extension of faculty professional service is when faculty members encourage students to engage in positions of leadership and support them in finding opportunities for leadership. Often, this begins within the local Chi Sigma Iota chapter, as students assume leadership positions under the mentorship of a local chapter advisor. Faculty members can support and develop leadership skills among students as they provide students with concrete examples of opportunities for leadership and advocacy and allow class time to connect the opportunity with course materials. Often, students use these leadership experiences within their local chapter to springboard into leadership opportunities at the local, state, and even national levels (Gibson et al., 2010; Luke & Goodrich, 2010; Meany-Walen et al., 2010). Increasingly, professional organizations have student representatives on their governing or advisory boards, and students often gain rich experiences serving in this capacity. Faculty members serve an important role in helping students become aware of these opportunities and cultivating a culture of service and leadership within their academic community.

## Curricular Considerations

Within counselor preparation programs, there are a number of formal and informal mechanisms built in to the training process within which leadership and advocacy can be developed in students. Whether developed via formal classroom instruction, supervision, advising, or informal curricular processes, *how* programs go about establishing and implementing a cohesive, meaningful curriculum is key.

### Classroom Instruction

In addition to the ever-important dissemination of information, the classroom serves as a fertile environment for cultivating social justice and leadership orientations among students. There is an emergence of counseling theories and strategies that promote social justice advocacy (Brubaker, Puig, Reese, & Young, 2010; Crethar, Torres Rivera, & Nash, 2008). Additionally, educators can and should work within a constructivist and multicultural pedagogical framework to increase students' awareness of social injustices (Green, McCollum, & Hays, 2008; Steele, 2008). Taken together, content and pedagogy highlight the *what* and *how* of effective classroom strategies. What is taught within the classroom communicates to students the link between counseling, leadership, and advocacy. Moreover, however, *how* it is taught more clearly communicates the salience of the issues. Please consult Barrio Minton and Wachter Morris (Chapter 14) and Hill, Harrawood, Vereen, and Doughty (Chapter 15) for sustained discussion regarding recommendations for integrating leadership and advocacy in formal master's-level and doctoral curricula.

### Counseling Supervision

As Glosoff, Durham, and Whittaker discuss in Chapter 11, supervision of practicum and internship experiences affords another opportunity to promote social justice and leadership awareness among students. Counseling supervision provides a particularly unique opportunity to promote social justice, as it incorporates assessment of the individual student's cognitive complexity, cultural awareness, personal experiences of power and privilege, and focuses discussions based on these assessments (Glosoff & Durham, 2010). Although there is limited literature on social justice advocacy training within supervision (Durham & Glosoff, 2010; Glosoff & Durham, 2010), there are emerging models of supervision with a social justice advocacy orientation (see Chang, Hays, & Milliken, 2009). Through individual and small group supervision, then, educators can build on the classroom experiences of students to facilitate consciousness of social injustices and how counselors can address these injustices through leadership and advocacy.

### Advising

As discussed previously, the CACREP (2009) standards require that master's- and doctoral-level students have access to faculty advisors throughout their academic programs. Faculty members also mentor students in leadership and advocacy orientations within the formal advising process. Faculty members who take the time to really listen to students' professional goals and aspirations can help them make informed decisions, in particular, about electives and practicum and internship sites that will help them meet their career goals and facilitate a social justice orientation. Similarly, advisors can facilitate discussions about leadership interests and opportunities for engagement in professional counseling organizations.

Further, faculty availability for drop-in or impromptu meetings serves a key role in the advising and mentoring process. While many meetings are scheduled in advance because of busy schedules, some of the most impactful meetings (for both students and faculty) are more impromptu ones in a faculty member's office or in the hallway. Throughout their training programs, most, if not all, counseling students have key and pivotal impactful moments and events. Sometimes these are occasioned by something in the classroom, a discussion with a peer, or a challenging client or supervisee. These moments provide rich windows of opportunity, true "teachable moments," and represent key exchanges between faculty and students in which students are particularly open to learning, growing, and being mentored.

*Informal Curricula*

Just as formal classroom, supervision, and advising curricula are key to establishing a culture of leadership, program faculty members can be intentional about developing informal or co-curricular opportunities to provide professional development opportunities for community members while cultivating a culture of leadership and advocacy. Indeed, Luke and Goodrich (2010) identified CSI chapters as pedagogical tools key to socialization to professional identity, and they suggested that programs employ CSI chapters as co-curricular partners in the process.

> Thus, CSI-sponsored activities (e.g., professional development workshops, conferences, newsletter articles and resources) can serve to supplement departmental efforts to fulfill CACREP standards by providing further education and experiences to members of the department related to counselor professional identity and leadership. Furthermore, one way to consider intentionally using CSI would be to situate chapters more centrally within the curriculum to increase both faculty member involvement and student engagement around professional counseling issues, including advocacy, leadership, and professional identity. (Myers et al., 2002, p. 74)

When program faculty members maintain active membership, attend chapter events, mentor student engagements, and offer their leadership and advocacy services to student members, they model professionalism and send powerful messages regarding the value of these activities and student leaders to the program and profession. In addition, program faculty members may encourage student leaders to develop annual leadership and advocacy themes or events. In so doing, chapter members create co-curricular opportunities for dialogue regarding the role of both within the counselor education program. In the next section, we explore the role of mentoring for creating a culture of leadership and advocacy.

Mentoring

Whereas curricular considerations include structuring classroom, supervision, advisory, and co-curricular opportunities to maximize meaningful attention to leadership and advocacy throughout programs, mentoring is

> a nurturing, complex, long-term, developmental process in which a more skilled and experienced person serves as a role model, teacher, sponsor, and coach who encourages, counsels, befriends a less skilled person for the purpose of promoting the latter's personal and/or professional development. (Black, Suarez, & Medina, 2004, p. 46)

Certainly, the counselor education literature includes many discussions regarding the critical role of mentorship in one's professional development (e.g., Benishek, Bieschke, Park, & Slattery, 2004; Black et al., 2004; Casto, Caldwell, & Salazar, 2005; Walker, 2006), especially for women and students of racial and ethnic minorities. Similarly, mentorship has emerged as a central theme in literature related to professional counseling leadership (e.g., Black & Magnuson, 2005; Gibson et al., 2010; Luke & Goodrich, 2010; Magnuson et al., 2003; Meany-Walen et al., 2010). In addition to ensuring that students have access to advisors throughout their programs, counselor education programs must attend to the ways in which they are mentoring master's- and doctoral-level students across their programs. Certainly, programs wishing to develop a strong culture of leadership and advocacy must also consider ethical considerations (see Warren, 2005) as they engage in intentional mentoring processes (Black et al., 2004).

### Master's-Level Students

One of the essential arenas for mentoring of master's-level students surrounds professional identity. Healthy developmental progression through the program of study seems to be that students move from external authority (the "experts") to an internalized expertise surrounding a personal definition of counseling, areas for personal growth, and indeed, the transition to recognizing that change happens not only at individual levels but also at systemic levels, leading to a system-level identity (Gibson et al., 2010). Such development can be facilitated by faculty members, including the CSI chapter faculty advisor, who take the time to help students articulate and work through their professional developmental struggles. In programs that house both master's-level and doctoral-level students, the mentoring and modeling processes can be enhanced by intentionally using doctoral students in the role of mentors. Some master's-level students, in particular, may relate more readily to the influence of other students.

### Doctoral-Level Students

Given that primary obligations of counselor education programs are to develop scholars and leaders for the profession (CACREP, 2009), counselor education programs may derive opportunities for doctoral-level mentorship from the five doctoral student learning outcomes areas: supervision, teaching, research and scholarship, counseling, and leadership and advocacy. Although some mentoring relationships fulfill multiple functions for an individual, one relationship need not satisfy all areas. Indeed, a number of professional counseling leaders reported benefiting from multiple mentors who modeled multiple paths to excellence (Meany-Walen et al., 2010). Regardless, programs can be intentional and systematic about evaluating whether all students' personal and professional mentoring needs are being met throughout their developmental process.

In preparation of doctoral students, mentoring of teaching must be an intentional process. Doctoral students do not learn to be good teachers by being teaching assistants (TAs), giving guest lectures, and handling the more mundane tasks of the teaching process. Instead, they must first observe faculty who are passionate about teaching within a social justice paradigm. This serves to fuel the second part of the mentoring process, whereby students gain supervised teaching experiences in which they engage in behavior rehearsal, feedback, and additional rehearsal in their journey toward empowering others toward a strong professional identity inclusive of leadership and advocacy. We wish to emphasize here that we consider the developmental process of becoming a clinical supervisor to fit within this framework. That is, observation, modeling, didactic training, and behavioral rehearsal with systematic and intentional feedback are all vital to developing as a clinical supervisor. As with all tasks, becoming an excellent educator is a developmental process that requires support, encouragement, and challenges.

Of particular importance in the current milieu is strong mentoring in research, resulting in the Association for Counselor Education and Supervision (ACES) endorsement of Guidelines for Research Mentorship in Counseling/Counselor Education (ACES Committee for Research Membership, 2009). To remain viable as a profession, continued growth must be made in the quality and rigor of research being produced by faculty and students (Briggs & Pehrrson, 2008). In an economy where educational academies are increasingly reliant upon external funding for support, counseling programs must respond. Research self-efficacy does not occur, however, solely through didactic instruction. Instead, counselor programs must engage students in the process of conducting quality research throughout their training program through collaborative research projects and the establishment of research teams. In particular, faculty mentors can ensure that students are selecting research topics necessary for the advancement of the profession through leadership and advocacy. For an expanded exploration of these dynamics, please consult Hays, Wood, and Smith (Chapter 13).

Finally, the parallel curriculum also includes mentoring students about how to create a holistically well approach to life, one that incorporates all facets of personal wellness (physical, emotional, spiritual, interpersonal) as well as meaning making through one's career. An educator plays a key role in student development when he or she both models an approach to personal wellness and continues to challenge students to engage in self-care, develop a wellness plan, and live a balanced, healthy, and productive life.

## CONCLUSION

In this chapter, we have explored ways in which professional counseling programs can use administrative processes and program culture to cultivate a spirit of leadership and advocacy in professional counselors and counselor educators. In particular, we discussed how the CACREP (2009) standards model leadership and advocate for the profession; ensure a strong professional identity of faculty members; include administrative safeguards that require accredited programs to engage in enrollment, admissions, gatekeeping, and program evaluation procedures that protect our profession; and require attention to leadership and advocacy in the formal curricula. In addition, we proposed process questions that program faculty members can utilize to evaluate the degree to which their program administrative processes model strong leadership and advocacy. Finally, we discussed the importance of cultivating a culture of leadership and advocacy, including communicating and modeling professionalism; attending to classroom, supervision, advising, and co-curricular curricula; and mentoring master's- and doctoral-level students. It is with intentional and ongoing focus to these areas that a culture of leadership and advocacy can flourish.

## EXERCISE FOR APPLICATION

The following activity is intended to raise your awareness around the educational and developmental aspects of leadership and advocacy. Prepare for the activity by placing a journal or something on which to write nearby. If the activity is done in a group, a facilitator can lead the process, but the activity is easily done individually as well.

First, take a few minutes to just "center down" by bringing your awareness to your breath. As thoughts enter your awareness, just gently allow them to float away as you return your awareness to your breath (if facilitating others in this process, pause here for about three to five minutes).

Now, think of a long time (pause).

Now, double that time (pause).

And double it again (pause).

Now, think of eternity (pause).

From this perspective, reflect upon this thing each of us calls "my life" and reflect on the following questions:

1. Who are my most important teachers? What have they taught me? How have they taught me?
2. What gifts as a leader and advocate do I already possess?
3. What are my internal barriers to being an effective leader? What steps can I take to reduce these barriers?
4. In what should I be engaged more fully?
5. In what should I be engaged less?
6. What do I want my professional legacy to be?
7. What do I want my personal legacy to be?

After a period of internal reflection, create an external process to help anchor your reflections. If you are doing this activity individually, journal your reflections. If you are in a group, you can either discuss in small groups or journal first and then process in small groups. Some form of external process is important, as it gives added clarity to the next steps in your developmental process.

## DISCUSSION QUESTIONS

1. In your formal education, who have been your most important teachers and mentors? What did they teach you and, equally important, how did they teach you?
2. What are some creative ways that faculty members can promote a culture of leadership among students?
3. How can local chapters of Chi Sigma Iota promote leadership and advocacy among their members?
4. John, a counseling student, is a strong student academically, making a grade of A or A– in all of his counseling coursework. He is adamant, however, in his unwillingness to counsel same-sex couples because of his personal religious beliefs. From an advocacy perspective, how can/should counseling faculty address this issue with John?
5. Imagine you are applying to be a doctoral student or faculty member in a counselor education program. What elements of program culture are most important to you? How will you assess which programs provide the best fit?

# 11

# Supervision
## Promoting Advocacy and Leadership

HARRIET L. GLOSOFF, JUDITH C. DURHAM,
AND JILL E. WHITTAKER

## INTRODUCTION

As discussed throughout this book, theories of leadership and research support exemplary leadership practices. There also is a well-developed body of literature on theories of counseling supervision, and several authors have written about the need for supervisors to address issues of culture in both supervisory and counseling processes (Chang, Hays, & Shoffner, 2003; Glosoff & Durham, 2010; Hays & Chang, 2003). More recently, there has been an increased focus in the professional literature on using supervision to help professional counselors develop the skills necessary to recognize and address societal factors that impact the mental health needs of clients, especially those from marginalized groups. In this chapter, we discuss ways in which counseling supervision can be used to facilitate the development of leadership and advocacy skills in professional counselors.

Both the Code of Ethics of the American Counseling Association (ACA, 2005) and national standards for the preparation of counselors published by the Council for Accreditation of Counseling and Related Educational Programs (CACREP, 2009) require that professional counselors demonstrate diversity and advocacy knowledge and skills or competencies. CACREP also requires that graduates of counselor education programs understand and can apply leadership theories to their work. Unfortunately, counselor preparation programs have not traditionally addressed leadership and advocacy competencies in their master's curricula (see introduction). In addition, as the editors also present, although doctoral programs offer courses in which advocacy and leadership theories and practices are discussed, few comprehensively address these issues. When preparing professional counselors to be leaders in the field, it is necessary to provide opportunities for them to become exemplary practitioners and effective supervisors.

The assumption that well-trained professional counselors are able simply to translate counseling skills into effective supervision is an inaccurate and potentially misleading notion. Bernard and Goodyear (2009) described supervision with an untrained supervisor as similar to participating in counseling or therapy with a paraprofessional who has only learned some rudimentary relationship skills but who lacks a broader conceptual understanding of the counseling process. Supervision requires its own proficiencies that need to be taught, practiced, and developed (McMahon & Simons, 2004). Because of this, CACREP (2009) requires that students from master's programs have knowledge of counseling supervision models, practices, and processes (II.G.1.e), that site supervisors have training in counseling supervision (III.C.4), and that doctoral students exhibit the ability to apply theory to the provision of clinical supervision.

In reality, however, many counseling professionals who provide supervision to practicum and internship students or new professionals are master's-level clinicians who have never received formal supervision training themselves (Studer, 2005). In holding with Chi Sigma Iota's (CSI) principle of Vision of the Future, ongoing training opportunities in supervision are critical in the development of counselor leaders. Appropriately trained professionals providing academic and nonacademically based supervision, reinforcing supervisees' leadership growth, and offering opportunities for advocacy and leadership skills to be practiced will result in more competent counselor advocates in the field.

This chapter fits with the overall philosophy and schematic presented in the introduction of the book. Supervision is one of the four external arrows in the model presented by the editors in the introduction. Some authors have noted that supervision is an optimal forum for empowerment, developing cultural competence, and training professional counselors in advocacy (e.g., Bradley, Lewis, Hendricks, & Crews, 2008; Chang, Hays, & Milliken, 2009; Durham & Glosoff, 2010; Glosoff & Durham, 2010). As we strive for excellence in the counseling profession, it is important that we ensure that developing counselors receive supervision and that such supervision assists them in critically examining how they can be effective agents of change on behalf of underserved individuals and groups (social justice counseling advocates), on behalf of the counseling profession (professional advocacy), and leaders in their work settings, their communities, and in the counseling profession.

We begin this chapter with brief definitions of some key terms and concepts that apply to advocacy, leadership, and supervision upon which we expand throughout the chapter. These definitions are followed by a brief discussion of leadership and counseling, and similarities of essential qualities and skills (e.g., cognitive complexity and flexibility) used by effective leaders and counselors. This is followed by an overview of the supervisory theories and practices related to the development of cognitive complexity and a discussion of their relationship to preparing counselors to become effective leaders and advocates for clients and the counseling profession. Relevant research is included in these discussions. We conclude with examples of activities and strategies that supervisors can use in individual, triadic, and group supervision to enhance cognitive complexity, flexible leadership, and social justice advocacy. We end with questions for continued discussion.

## Definitions of Key Terms and Concepts

**Advocacy** is defined by ACA (2005) as "promotion of the well-being of individuals and groups, and the counseling profession within systems and organizations. Advocacy seeks to remove barriers and obstacles that inhibit access, growth, and development" (p. 20).

**Cognitive complexity** is the ability to absorb, integrate, and make use of multiple perspectives at the same time. Labouvie-Vief and Diehl (2000) described it as involving a high use of reflection, "and integration of contextual, relativistic and subjective knowledge" (p. 490).

**Supervision** is a distinct professional activity in which a more senior member of a profession monitors and evaluates the services provided by a more junior member of that same profession (Bernard & Goodyear, 2009). Supervision is "used to promote and protect the welfare of the client, the profession, and society at large" (Falender & Shafranske, 2004, p. 30).

## LEADERSHIP

The model of leadership espoused by CSI is one of the "servant leader" (Greenleaf, as cited in Herr, 2010), or one whose drive to leadership is propelled by a primary desire to serve or effect change through interactions on a systemic or organizational level to promote a greater good (Herr). Leadership from this perspective is a "process whereby an individual influences a group of individuals to achieve a common goal" (Northouse, 2004, p. 3). Issues of context, culture, equity, and justice have only recently come to be included in conversations and definitions of leadership (Chin, 2010).

Models of leadership and the characteristics or qualities necessary for effective leadership are also evolving. Valued characteristics of leadership typically noted in the professional literature now include flexibility in thinking (Yukl & Mahsud, 2010), the ability to form collaborative relations to effect change reflective of mutual purpose (Graen & Uhl-Bien, 1995), and the ability to adapt and change as the situation dictates (Yukl & Mahsud). The qualities of flexibility and adaptation have become increasingly necessary given the diversity and changes in our society and cultural contexts. The flexible and adaptive leader can respond appropriately to the changing needs of society and organizations by being responsive to the current needs of the community, group, or clients being served. The flexible leader can balance competing values and manage difficult trade-offs (e.g., reliability or efficiency versus the need for innovation and change) as well as the competing needs of different stakeholders (Yukl & Mahsud).

Leaders must inspire with vision and direction in order to enhance growth and expansion (Kaiser & Overfield, 2010). According to Kaiser and Overfield, "flexible leadership is conceptualized as the mastery of opposing but complementary behaviors in terms of *how* one leads, as well as in terms of *what* organizational issues a leader focuses on" (p. 105). Flexibility in leadership means that one has a high tolerance for and is able to embrace ambiguous situations and demonstrate comfort and curiosity with multiple realities. Leaders need to be able to approach the unknown with intellectual curiosity while seeking better solutions (White & Shullman, 2010). Such flexibility requires an interpersonally flexible style in which an individual can respond to changing conditions and multiple demands. The characteristics of successful leaders are similar to those of effective counselors in that they must be able to hold multiple perspectives and, when needed, make choices among seemingly competing perspectives in determining the best way to move forward. A flexible, adaptive leader is one who is responsive to change and also able to make use of a variety of behaviors, choosing what is most relevant for any specific situation (Yukl & Mahsud, 2010).

There are numerous traits associated with the quality of flexible leadership described in the literature, including social intelligence, together with the capacity for systems thinking; emotional intelligence, including the capacity for empathy, self-awareness, and self-regulation; and cognitive or behavioral complexity (Yukl & Mahsud, 2010). In their discussion of necessary leadership characteristics, Hooijberg and Quinn (1992) offered the concept of *behavioral complexity*, or "the ability to act out a cognitively complex strategy by playing multiple, even competing roles, in a highly integrated and complementary way" (p. 164). This is very similar to Labouvie-Vief and Diehl's (2000) definition of cognitive complexity, which has been linked to flexibility in choosing counseling techniques and advanced counseling skills (Ober, Granello, & Henfield, 2009).

Although research regarding strategies that promote the development of flexibility in leaders is limited, Nelson, Zaccaro, and Herman (2010) reviewed the literature and provided examples of two techniques, experiential variety and strategic feedback, that have been shown to enhance the development of what they label *adaptive expertise*. They described adaptive expertise as enabling leaders to change their responses to be in alignment with unanticipated, unfamiliar, or uncertain information, hence flexibility. They discussed a component of adaptive expertise as cognitive frame changing, or "the capacity to switch among various perspectives or frames of reference" (p. 132). Again, this is a concept that presupposes flexibility as well as cognitive complexity. We now discuss cognitive complexity in relation to counseling supervision.

## COUNSELING AND COGNITIVE COMPLEXITY

The notion that more successful counselors operate at higher levels of cognitive complexity has long been hypothesized and supported within the literature (Fong, Borders, Ethington, & Pitts, 1997; Holloway & Wampold, 1986; Ladany, Marotta, & Muse-Burke, 2001; Stoltenberg, 1981). Cognitive complexity has been linked to (1) the development of more complex clinical hypotheses and case conceptualizations (Ladany et al.), (2) greater objectivity within the counseling session (Borders, 1989), (3) the use of more complex and effective verbal skills and higher levels of confidence (Fong et al.), (4) avoidance of stereotyping (Sprengler & Strohmer, 1994), and (5) demonstration of greater empathy, less prejudice, more sophisticated descriptions of clients, lower levels of anxiety, and greater tolerance for ambiguity (Jennings & Skovholt, 1999). Thus it is not surprising that many have noted that one of the primary goals of counselor education and supervision should be to enhance students' reflectivity and critical thinking skills (Bernard & Goodyear, 2009; Falender & Shafranske, 2004; Owen & Lindley, 2010). As cognitive and behavioral complexity are essential characteristics or qualities associated with both effective leadership and successful counseling, it seems imperative that professional counselor training programs facilitate cognitive development.

## SUPERVISION

Because of the overlapping skills and characteristics essential to both counseling and leadership, supervision offers a natural vehicle to prepare professional counselors who are not only effective clinicians, but who are also able to assume leadership roles and advocate for the counseling profession and for those seeking counseling services. The ability to deal effectively with complex and sometimes conflicting information seems to be a key to effective leadership, advocacy, and counseling. Owen and Lindley (2010) noted that "cognitive complexity can influence a variety of clinical and educational processes, from how they [counselors] make decisions to their engagement in classes and supervision" (p. 128). Research indicates that cognitive complexity may be domain specific and the ability to think deeply in one domain does not necessarily translate to another domain. In other words, the ability to think in a complex manner in one area (e.g., counseling) may not be correlated with the ability to think complexly in another domain (e.g., political policy) (Welfare & Borders, 2010). The counseling profession needs to develop a testable model that can be used to assess and increase cognitive complexity in counseling, a model that enhances reflective thinking, and the ability to choose among multiple, and at times opposing, alternatives as part of the therapeutic process.

Owen and Lindley (2010) presented a therapists' cognitive complexity model (TCCM) that frames three distinct aspects of cognitive complexity that mirror specific elements in counselor training. These include (1) in-session thoughts, or those things that counselors tell themselves about the client during the session (e.g., he is really depressed); (2) metacognitions that reflect the ability of counselors to monitor their progress within the session and to evaluate their own thoughts and reactions as they occur in the session (e.g., I felt very close to my client at the beginning of the session, but I am aware that the more we discuss her divorce, the more distance there is between us); and (3) epistemic cognitions or counselors' views about the nature of knowledge reflective of a movement from dualistic or relativistic thinking to constructivist beliefs about knowledge. These epistemic beliefs directly inform how counselor trainees interact in classes as well as with supervisors and shape trainees' conceptions about what they learn. For example, students who believe that knowledge is relative may view all suggestions as equally valid and therefore may not embrace their supervisors' suggestions. Likewise, they may not be able or motivated to discriminate between sound and unsound therapeutic practices and recognize the need for and opportunities to engage in leadership and professional advocacy activities.

In the next section, we briefly present key components of four models we believe are readily applicable for preparing counseling leaders and advocates with regards to the concept of cognitive complexity. These include the four following models: Bloom's Taxonomy of Educational Objectives (Bloom, Engelhart, Furst, Hill, & Krathwohl, 1956), the Heuristic Model of Nonoppressive Interpersonal Development (HMNID; Ancis & Ladany, 2001), the Synergistic Model of Multicultural Supervision (Ober et al., 2009), and Chang et al.'s (2009) three-tiered model for integrating a social constructivist framework for addressing social justice and advocacy issues in supervision. These models provide supervisors with a strong foundation for using supervision to promote the development of the cognitive and behavioral complexity that is essential for counselors to be effective leaders and advocates.

### Bloom's Taxonomy of Educational Objectives

Although not a model of supervision, Bloom's Taxonomy of Educational Objectives (Bloom et al., 1956) is one of the most widely accepted models for enhancing cognitive complexity. Bloom's Taxonomy includes six cumulative levels of instructional outcomes, each building on the previous level. Briefly, the six levels are as follows: Knowledge, or merely recalling information; Comprehension, or being able to grasp the meaning of the information; Application, or the ability to use the information in new situations; Analysis, or the ability to break the information into component parts; Synthesis, or the ability to integrate the material or information into a new whole; and finally Evaluation, or the ability to judge the value of the material or information based on defined criteria. In regard to supervision, supervisors can assess where on the taxonomy supervisees are operating (Glosoff & Durham, 2010). In addition, Granello (2000) noted that Bloom's Taxonomy "could be a useful learning schema for supervisors to encourage cognitive growth in their supervisees in an intentional manner" (p. 33). We present concrete suggestions for the use of Bloom's Taxonomy in the section of this chapter on strategies for application.

### Heuristic Model of Nonoppressive Interpersonal Development (HMNID)

The Heuristic Model of Nonoppressive Interpersonal Development (HMNID) (Ancis & Ladany, 2001) offers a model of supervision in which supervisors are taught to assess and understand patterns of thoughts, feelings, and behaviors about themselves, their supervisees, and their clients across various demographic variables, which include race, ethnicity, sexual orientation, gender, disability, and socioeconomic status. As indicated by the word *heuristic*, this is a problem-solving method that leads to learning and discovery for supervisors and supervisees through looking at the development of multiple identity variables across multiple dimensions, much in the same way that racial identity development models have been expanded to include other demographic dimensions, such as issues of gender and sexual orientation. For any given demographic variable, people can belong to one of two groups: socially oppressed group (SOG, or target group) or socially privileged group (SPG, or dominant group). For each demographic variable, people progress through phases called means of interpersonal functioning (MIF). It is not the demographic variable that accounts for one's behaviors, thoughts, and actions. Rather, it is how one perceives oneself and interacts with others due to the environmental press.

Ancis and Ladany (2001) described four phases of development of MIF: adaptation, incongruence, exploration, and integration. In the *adaptation* phase there is complacency, apathy, and conformity to socially oppressive environments and only a superficial understanding of differences often reflecting stereotypic attitudes. In the *incongruence* phase, previously held beliefs about oppression and privilege seem incongruent, dissonant, and inconsistent with newly experienced life events. The *exploration* phase includes active exploration of the meaning of membership in one's SOP or SPG; this often includes anger, shame, or guilt for not previously recognizing oppressive situations. The *integration* phase is marked by multicultural awareness and integration, proficiency in interactions with SOGs, insight regarding oppressive interactions, and a commitment to nonoppressive environments.

### Synergistic Model of Multicultural Supervision

The Synergistic Model of Multicultural Supervision (Ober et al., 2009) is an integration of the HMNID (Ancis & Ladany, 2001) and Bloom's Taxonomy of Educational Objectives (Bloom et al., 1956) with the addition of the multicultural counseling competencies (Sue, Arredondo, & McDavis, 1992). This model attends to both the process and content of supervision and promotes multicultural competence through increasing cognitive complexity, self-reflection, and structured interventions. This model provides two important reminders for supervisors. First, Bloom's Taxonomy addresses "only the cognitive processing portion of cognitive complexity" (Granello, 2000, p. 33). Second, it reminds supervisors about the need to model exploration of cultural issues that may influence clients and the counseling and supervisory processes in an integrative manner; attend to the cognitive, affective, and behavior domains; and develop the knowledge necessary to work with clients from diverse backgrounds.

### Chang et al.'s Social Constructivist Model

Chang et al.'s (2009) social constructivist model applies constructivist tenets to the process of supervision for the purpose of assisting and expanding supervisees' awareness of their own and their clients' contextual issues as they impact the counseling process. According to social constructivism, multiple realities exist and are derived from interaction with one's environment. Cognitive functions also exist and are a function of social or interpersonal interactions with one's environment. Therefore, reality is flexible, changeable, and a function of one's environmental interactions. When applied to supervision, the model asserts that learning takes place in the interactive process between the supervisor and supervisee, and the general goal is for the supervisor to facilitate the supervisee's constructions of meanings related to self-awareness, client issues, and community collaboration for the promotion of client and professional advocacy. Since multiple realities are considered normative, it is the supervisor's task to assist the supervisee in contemplating issues from individual, social, and cultural constructs.

## SUPERVISION STRATEGIES FOR THE DEVELOPMENT OF FLEXIBLE LEADERSHIP, COGNITIVE COMPLEXITY, AND COUNSELING ADVOCACY

In this section, we present strategies for assisting professional counselors in assuming leadership roles for the profession, for professional advocacy in their work settings and communities, and for individual and group advocacy to minimize the negative effects of societal conditions on the wellness and human dignity of those served. The overarching goal of these strategies is to help supervisees increase their cognitive complexity and to, in turn, develop more flexible leaders. There are myriad such interventions, and in this chapter we will focus on those that are related to professional counselors as advocates and leaders (versus general supervision). Throughout this section, we reference in parentheses the CACREP standards (2009) that are most relevant to the strategies, citing core standards that apply to all professional counselors (regardless of area of specialization) and those standards specific to knowledge and skills required for effective supervision. Please note that we believe professional counselors and supervisors have an ethical responsibility to be self-aware and to be effective advocates and leaders (ACA, 2005). Because of this, we include CACREP standard II.G.1.j. as relevant to all strategies.

## Assessing Cognitive Complexity

Higher levels of cognitive complexity have been associated with advanced counseling skills (Ober et al., 2009) as well as skills necessary to be effective leaders and advocates (Kaiser & Overfield, 2010; Yukl & Mahsud, 2010). As such, we recommend getting a baseline of supervisees' cognitive level. Having the ability to process complex material is necessary to be able to recognize client characteristics and other issues that may influence the counseling process. In addition, cognitive complexity is essential for differentiating and integrating relevant information and determining how different pieces of information form a dynamic whole (Owen & Lindley, 2010; Welfare & Borders, 2010). By beginning with a baseline assessment, supervisors and supervisees can co-create goals that help supervisees build on their current level of functioning, increase their ability to "absorb, integrate, and use abstract information and integrate multiple perspectives" (Glosoff & Durham, 2010, p. 119), and thus deal effectively with the ambiguity inherent in their roles as counselors, leaders, and advocates.

Regardless of the developmental level of the supervisee, it is important for supervisors and supervisees to form a working relationship by getting to know one another, their respective cultural backgrounds, and their related expectations regarding clinical skills and issues of leadership and advocacy competence. For example, asking supervisees in what ways they believe they are privileged, and in what ways they are oppressed or marginalized, serves multiple functions depending on the theoretical basis from which the supervisor is working. In terms of the HMNID (Ancis & Ladany, 2001), such questions offer a framework to assess the level of identity development of supervisees. It not only helps supervisors understand how supervisees may view themselves as members of target and dominant groups, but also affords an opportunity to begin to assess where supervisees are functioning in terms of the four phases or means of interpersonal functioning. For example, supervisees in the adaptation phase may not have considered such questions and may become anxious when such discussions arise. This has implications for how able they will be to recognize and work with clients on issues of culture, power, and privilege as well as their capacity for managing cognitively complex information. This also has implications for how effectively counselors can assume leadership roles, as flexible and adaptive leaders must be cognizant of and responsive to diversity and cultural contexts. Supervisors can use this initial assessment to develop interventions to help supervisees deepen their understanding of self and others, and broaden dichotomous thinking, both critical factors in effective counseling and flexible leadership. These interventions lay the foundation for supervisees to also identify ways in which they can counsel clients from diverse cultural heritages, to identify systemic and sociopolitical barriers to client growth and well-being, and consider what their leadership roles may be in effecting change. Following, we present specific types of activities that can be used in supervision to enhance the development of leadership, and advocacy skills, as well as the critical element of cognitive complexity.

Examination of Systems

The HMNID (Ancis & Ladany, 2001), the Synergistic Model of Multicultural Supervision (Ober et al., 2009), and Chang et al.'s (2009) three-tiered social constructivist model all speak to the need for professional counselors to be able to deal with complex issues (cognitive complexity), be aware of cultural factors that may influence growth and development of individuals, and recognize that there are multiple ways to consider what is normal (cognitive flexibility). Additionally, these models identify ways in which professional counselors can work outside of the counseling room to promote client well-being through leadership and professional advocacy activities. Following are examples of supervisory strategies to these ends.

*Using the ACA Advocacy Competencies*

The ACA advocacy competencies, developed by Lewis, Arnold, House, and Toporek (2002), are organized around two different but intersecting dimensions: (1) the extent to which clients may be involved in advocacy efforts, and (2) the level of intervention or the focus of the advocacy interventions (from focusing on work directly with an individual, to the community, to the societal level). During discussions related to clients, ask supervisees to address what they see as the issues related to each level of the competencies. For example, a supervisee presents a client who seeks counseling to deal with the stress he is experiencing because he is being bullied in school because he is gay. He reports that his teachers are aware of the bullying but that they do not intervene. Begin by having the supervisee present her or his counseling plan. Then have the supervisee, as well as other members of the supervision team, identify what actions might be most helpful for the client to take. How might counselors provide leadership as advocates with teachers related to this issue without identifying the client? Are there policies and programs that might be effective? In addition to exploring the types of advocacy efforts in which the client and the counselor may engage, it is important that supervisees identify their own comfort level in terms of being advocates and leaders, and also learn to expand and work beyond their present comfort zones. The following questions may be helpful in this regard:

- What does being a counselor advocate (or counseling leader) mean to you? (Knowledge on Bloom's Taxonomy)

- How comfortable are you in terms of working one-on-one with your client to empower her to address her issues? (Knowledge)
- How do you think your personal comfort level with advocacy (or leadership) affects whether you are willing to talk with teachers or try to get policies instituted to make the school a safer place? (Application)

In addition to asking questions, have supervisees in triadic and group supervision role-play being the client who is being bullied, the counselor advocate, a teacher or group of teachers, and a principal. Ask supervisees to role-play how they might actually approach such a situation. In our experiences, this often helps supervisees feel better prepared to do this in real life and allows them to make connections between the "language" of advocacy and leadership and things that supervisees are already thinking and doing. This is similar to when supervisees may describe how they approach a clinical situation but may not yet be able to identify the corresponding theory. (CACREP II.G.1.e, h–j; II.G.2.a–f; II.G.3.b, d, f, h; II.G.5.a, b, d, e; II.G.7.a–c, f; Doctoral II.C.2, 4, 7; IV.A.1, 2, 4; IV.B.1, 2; IV.G.1, 2; IV.H.2, 3; IV.I.1–3)

*Examination of Intakes and Counseling Processes From a Cultural and Social Lens*

The purposes of this activity are to help supervisors assess the case conceptualization abilities of supervisees, as well as assess how supervisees may see their own strengths and limitations as advocates and leaders (Glosoff & Durham, 2010). This is a multitiered activity that can be used in individual, triadic, or group supervision.

- In individual supervision, have supervisees critique a request for service forms used at their work site from a cultural lens. Ask them to identify indications of assumptions of cultural bias (e.g., classism, heterosexism) [Multicultural Counseling Competencies] and ways in which the materials or process invite or further marginalize certain clients. One purpose of this activity is to have supervisees identify core knowledge about the process by which clients enter the system and begin to apply what they have learned about culturally competent counseling (Bloom et al., 1956; Granello, 2000). In addition, to complete this exercise, supervisees must learn about the communities in which clients are being served, talk with community members to gain a better understanding of why some people do not take advantage of available services, consider multiple perspectives by analyzing how others may interpret forms and procedures, and then adapt to better serve individuals who may need services. This exercise, although simple on the surface, is meant to help supervisees with cognitive complexity and leadership flexibility.

- In triadic and group supervision ask supervisees what changes they think would make the materials and processes more inviting for the clients being served in their school or agency. Have them relate these to the ACA advocacy competencies.

Follow up on the last activity by asking what roles supervisees see themselves play in effecting the changes they identified; specifically, ask them to identify the processes for effecting changes in the intake materials or procedures and what they see as their roles in facilitating those processes. These activities are aimed at helping supervisees analyze and synthesize information from a variety of sources, including their own thoughts, feelings, and competence in relation to advocacy and leadership. (CACREP II.G.1.e, h–j; II.G.2.a–f; II.G.3.b, d, f, h; II.G.5.a, b, d, e; II.G.7.a–c, f; Doctoral II.C.2, 4, 7; IV.A.1, 2, 4; IV.B.1, 2; IV.G.1, 2; IV.H.2, 3; IV I.1–5)

*Identification of Players and Politics*

Very often, especially when supervising counseling students as compared to postacademic staff members, it is easy to spend the majority of time focused on review of cases, matters of logistics and paperwork, and addressing specific client-oriented questions brought up by supervisees (Glosoff & Durham, 2010). Effective leaders, however, recognize the importance of understanding organizational structures and how decisions are made. We recommend that supervisees present an organizational chart or explain to their supervisors and other supervisees the responsibilities of various staff members (knowledge on Bloom's Taxonomy). Ask what roles professional counselors play in their organizations and how those roles are determined. This can help supervisees begin to understand the social constructs and contextual issues that influence their work (Chang et al., 2009).

Professional counselors very often work on interdisciplinary teams. Such teams offer opportunities for misunderstandings or conflicts, and the potential for collaborative work based on the knowledge and level of respect that team members have for the roles each play in relation to services being provided. We suggest using discussions and role-plays in group supervision to help supervisees clearly articulate not only their own theoretical orientation, but also who professional counselors are and what they can do in relation to the mission of the organization. Ask them if they have experienced any situations in which other professionals may have made disparaging remarks (subtle or overt) about the profession of counseling. Discussing and role-playing such situations can promote cognitive complexity and help supervisees develop the confidence they need to respond as leaders and advocates in a nondefensive, pro-active manner.

Clients are affected not only by the direct actions of those serving them, but by policy makers at a variety of levels. As supervisees identify themes in their work with clients or how professional counselors are and are not utilized, have them explore the types of regulations that may be influencing what they are experiencing. Encourage supervisees to take action, using information provided by professional counseling associations. For example, have supervisees draft and critique each other's letters to policy makers about specific issues, such as the recognition of professional counselors as service providers in various systems, or the need to advocate for appropriate caseloads for professional counselors in schools. In addition, assist in the development of their leadership abilities by having them articulate what they can do to organize others in these efforts, both individually and through leadership roles in counseling associations. This facilitates cognitive complexity, as it requires counselors to synthesize and integrate information from a variety of sources and then to discern what information policy makers may deem most relevant/important. We also suggest that supervisors can share with supervisees what leadership roles they have assumed and invite them to join them in activities such as participating in leadership and advocacy efforts (e.g., participating in legislative day). (CACREP II.G.1.b, c, h–j; II.G.2.a–f; II.G.3.b, d, f, h; II.G.5.a, b, d, e; II.G.7.a–c, f; Doctoral II.C.2, 4, 7; IV.A.1, 2, 4; IV.B.1, 2; IV.G.1, 2; IV.H.2, 3; IV.I.1–5)

*Identification of Data and Themes and Self as Advocate and Leader*

In group supervision, have each supervisee present data on the types of issues presented by their clients over a certain period of time and identify themes that may exist. Once everyone has had the opportunity to contribute to the development of a co-constructed list of themes, have the members of the supervision team share what they see as external barriers to client growth and identify at least one thing each member can do to advocate with or on behalf of clients, at the larger systemic level, or on behalf of the counseling profession. Encourage supervisees to think about themes and barriers in relation to the missions of professional associations such as the ACA and its divisions, Chi Sigma Iota, and national credentialing bodies. In addition to reviewing themes that may relate directly to issues presented by clients, have supervisees discuss patterns of funding for services (regardless of the type of work site) as well as any patterns regarding the clients seen by professional counselors as compared to those seen by psychologists, social workers, and other mental health professionals. If there are patterns, have supervisees discuss their hypotheses as to the reasons behind these differences (e.g., Are these based on skill, titles, or credentials held, or on funding sources?) and how valid those reasons may be. For example, do those assigning clients understand what professional counseling is and how professional counselors are prepared to work with the clientele being seen in that setting?

In our experience, supervisees may or may not identify themselves as leaders. It is helpful to ask them about what leadership means to them and how they may assume leadership roles in their own lives. For example, are they the ones who organize their friends and try to resolve or mediate differences? Have they ever seen anything that they thought needed to be changed (e.g., when they were in high school or college or in their community) and then spoke up about it, or in some other way volunteered? Sometimes supervisees think of leadership and advocacy efforts as being "grand" or require them to be very vocal and "out front." Supervisors can help professional counselors recognize that they may approach leadership in a variety of ways, sometimes quietly behind the scenes collecting data and organizing people. For example, have supervisees share with each other how they view being accountable and using data in their work as a form of advocacy or how they think they can use their membership in an organization to have that organization take action or create policies related to the data and themes supervisees identified as important. Part of leadership is recognizing that one has a voice. This exercise and associated questions can help supervisees who may not already think of themselves as leaders begin to use their voices, while also requiring that they use higher levels of thinking to process what may be conflicting information and cognitively and emotionally complex reactions. (CACREP II.G.1.e, h–j; II.G.2.a–f; II.G.3.b, d, f, h; II.G.5.a, b, d, e; II.G.7.a–c, f; Doctoral II.C.2, 4, 7; IV.A.1, 2, 4; IV.B.1, 2; IV.G.1,2; IV.H.2, 3; IV.I.1–5)

### *Identification of Resources Needed*

Have supervisees identify when it might be most effective to develop alliances with other professionals and members of the community. Individually have supervisees develop resource lists that include potential referral sources, such as community organizations, religious or faith-based institutions, and other groups that may be allies in developing and supporting programs that promote social justice and the well-being of individuals (Chang et al., 2009). Chang et al. recommended that supervisees volunteer at community agencies to get a better understanding of how these agencies serve the public. We also see volunteering as an important way to form collaborative relationships, understand the politics of the agencies, evaluate which agencies might be the most helpful to different clients, and to identify professional leadership needs and opportunities as they relate to practice. (CACREP II.G.1.e, h–j; II.G.2.a–f; II.G.3.b, d, f, h; II.G.5.a, b, d, e; II.G.7.a–c, f; Doctoral II.C.2, 4, 7; IV.A.1, 2, 4; IV.B.1, 2; IV.G.1, 2; IV.H.2, 3; IV.I.1–5)

### Self-Awareness as a Critical Tool

Self-awareness is essential to effective counseling and leadership. In terms of the models of both leadership and supervision presented earlier in this chapter, self-awareness includes an understanding of one's own cultural background, privileges, positionality, values, and biases. It also promotes the development of a strong identity as a professional counselor and leader. In addition, the ACA Code of Ethics (2005) delineates that ethical "counselors are aware of their own values, attitudes, beliefs, and behaviors" (A.4.b, p. 4). Many authors have noted that both supervisors and supervisees, therefore, must be aware of how their own backgrounds and beliefs systems, and their understanding of power, oppression, advocacy, and leadership, affect how they think of counseling and supervision (e.g., Ancis & Ladany, 2001; Chang et al., 2009; Durham & Glosoff, 2010; Estrada, Wiggins Frame, & Braun-Williams, 2004; Glosoff & Durham, 2010). Supervisors can use many activities to increase self-awareness focused on advocacy and leadership. We present just a few examples and would like to note that although the implementation of the activities may look different depending on the developmental levels of the supervisees involved, we have used these activities to both assess and advance the cognitive developmental level of master's students, doctoral students, and postmatriculate supervisees.

### Focused Questions Related to Culture, Advocacy, and Leadership

The development of cultural awareness is essential for counselors to work ethically and effectively with clients and as advocates and leaders. Having focused discussions related to culture, power, and privilege is essential to enhancing the critical consciousness and cognitive complexity of supervisees (Glosoff & Durham, 2010; Vera & Speight, 2003). Following are examples of questions that require supervisees to think beyond a surface level or a simple "knowing":

- How do you think your cultural background affects how you interpret and apply counseling theories? How about how you view your role as a leader?
- What is it like for you to receive feedback from and give feedback to members of this team who are culturally different from you? How do you think this translates to your role as a member or leader in professional counseling organizations?
- When you think of advocates and leaders in your community, who do you most admire and why? How do you see your work as similar to that person?

Such questions are particularly relevant for assessing the self-awareness component of multicultural competence (Sue et al., 1992) as well as supervisees' identity and development of means of interpersonal functioning (Ancis & Ladany, 2001). In addition to increasing self-awareness, such questions also help supervisees view their own world in relation to others, including clients (Chang et al., 2009), and call for them to reflect on complex issues that involve emotional as well as cognitive components (Bloom et al., 1956), essential in the development of leadership and advocacy skills. (CACREP Section II.G.1.e, j; II.G.2.b, e, f; Doctoral II.C.2, 4, 7; IV.A.1, 2, 4; IV.B.2; IV.I. 1–3)

### Genograms

Have supervisees create cultural genograms (Estrada et al., 2004) of their families (as defined by the supervisees). In general, the use of genograms helps both supervisees and supervisors understand how supervisees have constructed meaning and values in their own lives. In individual supervision, have supervisees denote the cultural traditions they associate with each of their family members and discuss how they think these traditions have ultimately influenced the supervisees' identity (Glosoff & Durham, 2010).

Asking reflective questions related to power dynamics in families can help supervisees examine how beliefs and practices in their families influence their work with clients, as well as their perceptions of leadership and advocacy roles. We suggest beginning with a question focused at the knowledge level of Bloom's Taxonomy (Bloom et al., 1956), such as "Who made important decisions in your family?" To move to higher-ordered or more cognitively complex thinking, at an appropriate time, supervisors can follow up with questions such as:

- What, if any, patterns do you see when you look at the relationships across generations and who had the "final say" in important decisions?
- How do you think those patterns influence you in your counseling relationships and how you view yourself as a leader?
- How have the teachings of the religion/spiritual beliefs practiced in your family influenced your beliefs about the role of advocacy in professional counseling?
- Were there family members who advocated for you or other family members (e.g., did anyone stand up for a sibling who was having difficulties at school)? If so, how were advocacy efforts rewarded or punished by parents or other important adults?

Throughout the process, Glosoff and Durham (2010) suggested that supervisees explore their own reactions to what they learn about their family and identify the messages they received about advocating for oneself and others, and about leadership roles. For example, ask supervisees to reflect on how factors in their own lives may help them move from a knowledge level of thinking (e.g., What leadership roles did your grandmother play in her neighborhood?) to an application level (e.g., How might the stories you heard about your aunt or uncle being in a union and getting arrested for picketing while on strike influence what types of actions you are willing to take with or on behalf of client Z [specific client]?). This activity can be used to help assess how supervisees are able to reflect (higher-order skill on Bloom's Taxonomy) on one's own values and lay the foundation for supervisees to apply similar processes to their work with clients (e.g., case conceptualization and treatment plans) and in their roles as leaders and advocates (e.g., What leadership or advocacy roles might supervisees adopt to ensure that services provided by professional counselors are available to individuals seeking counseling?). (CACREP II.G.1.e, h, j; II.G.2.b, e, f; Doctoral II.C.2, 4, 7; IV.A.1, 2, 4; IV.B.2; IV. I. 1–3)

Case Presentations

Asking supervisees to present on how they conceptualize client issues as well as their counseling or treatment plans is a very common practice. There are several ways to structure case presentations to assess and enhance supervisees' level of cognitive complexity (using Bloom's Taxonomy), their level of means of interpersonal functioning (Ancis & Ladany, 2001), and their cultural and advocacy competencies (Ober et al., 2009), as well as their potential to assume leadership roles. Regardless of how supervisors structure case presentations, in addition to having supervisees report on basic information about clients, it is helpful to ask even beginning counselors how they will evaluate progress and how they assess their effectiveness as counselors, advocates, and leaders in the counseling profession (evaluation on Bloom's Taxonomy). Following are examples of exercises that can be included or structured around case presentations to increase cognitive complexity and flexibility of thought with a focus on developing advocacy and leadership.

*Triadic and Group Supervision*

Triadic and group supervision offer ideal venues to help supervisees recognize how they approach their work as counselors, advocates, and leaders, and to help them consider multiple perspectives. Asking supervisees to share how they might approach clients or other situations from varying theoretical bases can help them expand or hone their understanding of the theoretical basis of their work. It also offers an opportunity to have supervisees discuss how approaching clients from varying theories does or does not influence the types of advocacy and leadership efforts in which they might engage. We further suggest that supervisees challenge themselves to reflect on their leadership and advocacy actions in relation to all case presentations. For example, have supervisees discuss clients or situations that could potentially benefit from their advocacy efforts and note what actions they may have taken. If they did not take any, have them discuss what stopped them from engaging in advocacy efforts at that time. Such discussions set the expectations that they should be including advocacy interventions in their work with clients. (CACREP II.G.1.e, h–j; II.G.2.b–f; Doctoral II.C.2, 4, 7; IV.A.1, 2, 4; IV.B.1, 2; IV.G.1, 2; IV.H.2, 3; IV.I.1–3)

*Consideration of Salient Demographics of a Particular Client*

Ask supervisees to consider what they know about the cultural background of the client, including where and under what conditions the client lives and how the client gets to the counseling sessions. The purpose of this activity is to have supervisees understand what they may take for granted and how this can influence counseling relationships. For example, a supervisee may report that his client is "typically at least 15 minutes late for sessions" and that he [the counselor] feels that this is a sign that the client "does not take counseling seriously." In asking how the client gets to the counseling session, the counselor may discover the client has to take two buses to get there, that the buses are often late, and that the client is actually highly motivated. This is operating first at a knowledge level (Bloom et al., 1956). The supervisee may also discover that the client misses sessions because of lack of child care. In discussing the lack of affordable child care, the supervisor can assist supervisees in exploring the role counselors may play in addressing such situations, moving beyond knowledge to action. For example, a similar discussion that took place between the first author and a group of doctoral students led to a deep exploration of professional identity. Students questioned whether assuming leadership roles to institute and obtain funding for child care in a community mental health center is "bordering on what social workers do," how they might empower clients to find possible solutions to their problems, and so on. (CACREP II.G.1.e, h–j; II.G.2.b–f; Doctoral II.C.2, 4, 7; IV.A.1, 2, 4; IV.B.1, 2; IV.G.1, 2; IV.H.2, 3; IV.I.1–3)

*Ask Questions*

Supervisors can use questions to both assess and enhance supervisees' cognitive complexity. For example, when supervisees give diagnostic impressions of their client, supervisors can ask a question such as, "What does the data indicate about the prevalence of clients from the _____ cultural background (e.g., clients who identify as Hispanic; clients who practice Catholicism) being diagnosed as _____ (having oppositional defiant disorder) as compared to clients from other racial, ethnic, and religious groups?" This assesses knowledge on Bloom's Taxonomy (Bloom et al., 1956; Granello, 2000; Ober et al., 2009). Asking "What evidence exists for the diagnosis you made?" (Granello, p. 37) assesses for and encourages the ability of supervisees to apply what they have read. Asking supervisees about how the diagnostic criteria were determined, and how this relates to the developmental and wellness models promoted by the counseling profession, helps them understand how diagnoses have been constructed and to reflect on how professional counselors can be leaders in constructing diagnoses to be used to promote well-being. A key in all of these discussions is to help supervisees explore how their concepts of normalcy and abnormal behaviors are constructed; examine how their own culture, experiences, and beliefs influence how they conceptualize and work with clients; identify external factors that may affect clients' well-being; and identify how they can most effectively advocate for and on behalf of clients, communities, and policies to effect change. (CACREP II.G.1.e, h–j; II.G.2.a–f; II.G.3.b, d; II.G.5.a, d, e; II.G.7.b, c, f; Doctoral II.C.2, 4, 7; IV.A.1, 2, 4; IV.B.1, 2; IV.G.1, 2; IV.H.2, 3; IV.I.1–3)


CONCLUSION

To summarize, according to the ACA Code of Ethics (2005) all professional counselors have an ethical responsibility to be culturally competent and to enhance the well-being of clients from diverse backgrounds. They must be able to identify obstacles that interfere with human development or growth and engage in advocacy with and on behalf of clients. Supervisors, therefore, have an ethical obligation to help supervisees be able to "focus beyond interventions that take place directly with clients during counseling sessions" (Glosoff & Durham, 2010, p. 127). This often involves changing schemas so that supervisees integrate the role of advocate and leader in their identities as professional counselors, rather than seeing these as functions separate from counseling. Supervision provides a natural venue for professional counselors to explore not only clinical issues, but issues of culture, power, oppression, and privilege experienced by and between clients, supervisees, and supervisors. For professional counselors to address these issues with clients effectively they must be self-aware and able to recognize and address complex, sometimes conflicting cognitive and emotional information. This requires cognitive complexity, the ability to differentiate and integrate information about themselves, their clients, and the myriad external factors that may influence client well-being and growth.

In this chapter, we discussed the similarities of essential characteristics of effective leaders, advocates, and professional counselors and provided an overview of supervisory theories and practices related to the development of cognitive complexity. In addition, we offered concrete strategies that supervisors can use to promote self-awareness and higher-order thinking and to prepare professional counselors who are culturally competent social justice advocates and leaders within the profession. Finally, we offered questions for continued discussion. We believe it is essential that supervisors help supervisees recognize that whatever their work setting, they have opportunities to empower their clients, to advocate with and on behalf of clients, and to assume positions of leadership to promote human dignity and wellness for all. As we previously noted, however, not all professional counselors (and supervisors) identify themselves as advocates or leaders. We entreat supervisors to assist supervisees to develop the critical consciousness and courage it takes to examine how they can be effective agents of change and leaders in the counseling profession.

## DISCUSSION QUESTIONS

Following are questions for further consideration and discussion:

1. Sam is a Latino (male) who is currently supervising master's students in their first semester of a two-semester internship. Several of his supervisees admit to having had very few interactions with racial or ethnic minorities until arriving at graduate school. They all have a very empathic manner with their clients and also seem to see presenting problems as being totally intrapsychic, while Sam sees these as contextual issues and

related to poverty and class. Sam raises the idea that external factors may greatly influence clients' presenting problems and the resolution of those problems. In addition, he refers the supervisees to the ethical issues of self-awareness and advocacy.

a. What is your hypothesis about the supervisees' level of cognitive complexity?

b. How might Sam assess their level of cognitive complexity?

c. What might Sam do to increase their level of cognitive complexity?

d. How might Sam assist his supervisees in understanding and designing advocacy interventions for their clients?

e. Sam would like to help his supervisees see their roles as advocates and leaders as core parts of their identity as professional counselors. What would you suggest he do in working with the supervisees mentioned?

2. Freida is the coordinator of counseling services in an urban high school district. She supervises counselors in three different schools. Two issues that the counselors continually bring up are that (a) demands to engage in noncounseling activities (e.g., overseeing testing programs) take away time from their counseling duties, and (b) the student/counselor ratio greatly interferes with their effectiveness in helping students address personal and social issues that may be affecting their academic success. Although the counselors complain on a regular basis, they do not seem to be able to identify what they can do individually and collectively to effect changes.

a. Develop at least one strategy, based on any of the models of supervision presented in this chapter and the ACA advocacy competencies, that Frieda can use to help the counselors identify what roles they can assume as advocates and leaders in their own schools and at the district level.

b. What, if anything, would you do differently if Frieda was a supervisor at a clinical mental health center?

3. Are there cultural value systems or worldviews that might be at odds with enhancing cognitive or behavioral complexity? In other words, is the ability to hold a constructivist or postmodern perspective that embraces holding multiple truths a culturally bound phenomenon?

4. Researchers have consistently documented that students from marginalized and disenfranchised populations are less likely to complete high school, go on for advanced degrees, or enter professional careers. What strategies might counselor leaders use to advocate for a greater representation of marginalized and underrepresented groups within the counseling profession?

5. All professional counselors are challenged to be effective leaders and advocates for our profession. What role does supervision have in training professional counselors as effective leaders and advocates? How has supervision helped you in developing your leadership and advocacy skills?

# 12

# *Counseling Practice*
## Schools, Agencies, and Community

Andrea L. Dixon and Brian J. Dew

## INTRODUCTION

The leadership and advocacy roles we exhibit on behalf of the counseling profession and the diverse clientele professional counselors serve are of utmost importance in the clinical work we do daily in schools, mental health agencies, and our communities. In our clinical settings, injustices experienced by many groups of individuals are omnipresent and create the need for advocacy and leadership from professional counselors in all specialty areas. Although our roles as professional counselors require numerous activities, the Council for Accreditation of Counseling and Related Educational Programs 2009 standards (CACREP, 2009) highlight leadership and advocacy as critical in the training of professional counselors.

Today, it is not just enough for professional counselors to have knowledge of advocacy and leadership principles. Rather, it is essential that professional counselors ascertain and implement the targeted skills needed to put these principles to work in their practices. Fortunately, many national counseling organizations such as the American Counseling Association (ACA) and its divisions, the National Board for Certified Counselors (NBCC) and Chi Sigma Iota, include the ideals of advocacy leadership in their models of best counseling practice; and although it takes fortitude for professional counselors to act as leaders and advocates on behalf of diverse client populations, it is now no longer just a call to the counseling profession. Today, as discussed in Chapters 1 through 9, leadership and advocacy are expected in our daily clinical work with clients across counseling settings.

We strongly believe that every professional counselor must be prepared to advocate and lead through example. Therefore, the purpose of this chapter is to build upon the concepts presented in former chapters by offering examples for advocacy and leadership application in K–12 schools, mental health agencies, and within communities. Throughout this chapter, we use the terms *student* and *client*, depending upon the specific counseling practice setting we are discussing. In addition, we discuss how leadership and advocacy roles are presented in the counseling profession, and we offer strategies for professional counselors to lead by example as advocates in schools, mental health agencies, and within communities on behalf of students/clients and the profession as a whole. We also address specific knowledge and skills with examples of these by work setting. Finally, we provide examples that represent the numerous and diverse manners in which professional counselors can be leaders as they serve K–12 students in schools and clients in mental health agencies as advocates in their clinical settings, and how they combine their efforts both inside and outside of their respective interdisciplinary clinical settings.

Consistent with the advocacy competencies endorsed by the ACA's Governing Council in 2002 (see Appendix D), we view advocacy as a two-pronged concept, including both advocacy for the profession and advocacy for the K–12 students in schools and clients in agencies we serve. The focus of our advocacy efforts should center on the recognition and culturally appropriate treatment of client needs and emphasis on one's optimal human wellness and dignity, empowerment, and social equality. As referenced in the ACA advocacy competencies, professional counselors are to "recognize the impact of social, political, economic, and cultural factors on human development" as well as identify obstacles to the client's well-being, develop and implement a plan of action, and seek out potential allies to confront potential barriers (Lewis, Arnold, House, & Toporek, 2002, p. 1). These advocacy strategies are presented as leadership acts focused within a social justice framework that allows counselors to act on behalf of traditionally marginalized groups of students and clients. Essential to these strategies is the process through which counselors learn about these roles and practice specific applicable strategies in their training (i.e., applicable counselor education ideas for the CACREP core curriculum, as described in Chapters 14 and 15). Through consultation and collaborative processes, professional counselors can act as leaders and social justice advocates in their daily clinical work.

Social justice-focused leadership, counseling, and advocacy are the current expectations in contemporary counseling practice in the United States (Dixon, Tucker, & Clark, 2010). As noted by Dr. Lee in Chapter 7, a call to professional counselors to work as advocates and leaders on behalf of the counseling profession and the K–12 students and clients we serve is not sufficient to meet societal needs; socially just advocacy and leadership is an imperative and a daily reality for professional counselors in the field. This tenet is especially relevant to school counselors and their work with students and their families. Today, the ACA-endorsed advocacy competencies (Lewis et al., 2002) and the Chi Sigma Iota Principles and Practices of Leadership Excellence (CSI, 1998, 2011) offer frameworks for guiding professional counselors in their roles as advocates and leaders, in both mental health agency and school counseling settings. In the next section, we explore leadership and advocacy roles within twenty-first-century school counseling.

## LEADERSHIP AND ADVOCACY IN TWENTY-FIRST-CENTURY SCHOOL COUNSELING

School counselors work within a microcosm of society in which they serve students from a variety of diverse backgrounds who live with a variety of social, emotional, academic, familial, and psychological concerns that come with them when they enter the educational environment (Stone & Clark, 2001). Because students may present with these concerns when they arrive at school, providing only reactive counseling services is no longer enough. Today, advocacy principles such as equity of services for *all* students, uniform access to services, and impartial participation (Crethar, Torres Rivera, & Nash, 2008; Marsella, 2006) are evident in daily professional school counseling practice. Professional school counselors act as leaders who implement these advocacy principles in U.S. schools in order to promote access and opportunities for all K–12 students (American School Counselor Association (ASCA), 2005; Education Trust, n.d., 2003, 2010). In addition, as Drs. Kress and Paylo emphasized in Chapter 8, school counselors are equally challenged to implement strength-based interventions to promote wellness and positive mental health for students and their families (Myers, Willse, & Villalba, 2011). These leadership and advocacy efforts extend to educating others on the roles of the school counselor and advocating for the profession as a whole.

### School Counselors' Roles as Leaders and Advocates

Leadership and advocacy roles have long been a part of school counselors' daily work tasks in the K–12 schools (Trusty & Brown, 2005). School counselors are called upon regularly to exhibit advocacy efforts in order to promote the academic and personal/social success of every student, which in turn places them in a primary leadership role within their schools. According to the ASCA (2005) national model, school counselors should focus their leadership and advocacy efforts toward (1) eliminating barriers impeding students' development, (2) creating opportunities to learn for all students, (3) ensuring access to a quality school curriculum, (4) collaborating with others within and outside the school to help students meet their needs, and (5) promoting positive, systemic change in schools. Therefore, as advocates, school counselors are natural leaders within the schools as they collaborate with other leaders and work toward systemic change and social justice (ASCA; Trusty & Brown).

Through their training and the multiple expectations they fulfill each day, school counselors are uniquely equipped to become strong leaders in their schools. As the only professionals in schools that are trained in mental health counseling techniques (Clark & Stone, 2007), school counselors act as the primary liaisons for all individuals in the school and community members and stakeholders. They work to facilitate communication among and between students, parents, other family members, teachers and staff, administration members, mental health agencies, and other community-based organizations (Clark & Stone). Additionally, school counselors maintain ongoing leadership roles through educating staff, parents, and community members regarding the roles school counselors can play in their students' lives and in the maintenance of all K–12 students' academic and personal/social success. They also plan, implement, and evaluate school counseling programs that utilize proactive versus reactive individual and small group counseling approaches for overall student development and wellness (ASCA, 2005). More specifically, school counselors create programs that aid K–12 students in their acquisition of knowledge, skills, and awareness around such topics as bullying prevention, substance use and abuse, and many others (ASCA). Other leadership roles include serving on community-based profit and nonprofit boards in order to have a voice in the service delivery gaps that can exist between home and school (Trusty & Brown, 2005). Finally, school counselors have the unique ability to be visible at a variety of school functions (i.e., PTA meetings, school board meetings, students' sports functions, etc.) that allow them to be seen as leaders on behalf of school reform and student development (Clark & Stone). Therefore, not only do school counselors provide leadership for their entire communities and schools, but they are also able to exhibit their leadership roles by advocating on behalf of the school counseling profession, and K–12 students' educational and personal/social needs (ASCA).

*Advocating for the School Counseling Profession*

Within the counseling profession, school counseling has a tremendous history of defining and redefining itself, creating the opportunities for school counselors to have voice as leaders and advocates for the profession. According to ASCA, advocacy is a complex process; however, the ASCA national model states, "Advocating for the academic success of every student is a key role of school counselors and places them as leaders in promoting school reform" (2005, p. 24). As the school counseling profession has developed, school counselor national training initiatives and standards emerged in response to the ever-changing needs of K–12 students and their families and the roles that school counselors are expected to play in their schools. Today's national models and training standards (the Education Trust's National Center for Transforming School Counseling (NCTSC), the ASCA's 2005 National Model for School Counseling Programs, and the 2009 Council for the Accreditation of Counseling and Related Educational Programs (CACREP) standards) include expectations that professional school counselors act as leaders and social justice advocates for students in K–12 schools in relation to closing achievement gaps between groups of advantaged and disadvantaged students regardless of race, ethnicity, income, or background (ASCA; CACREP, 2009; Dahir & Stone,

2009; Dixon et al., 2010; Education Trust, 2002, 2010). In fact, the NCTSC declared social justice advocacy as a moral imperative for school counselors (Martin, 2002), and the 2009 CACREP standards include leadership and diversity/advocacy as key domains of learning outcomes for school counselors.

The NCTSC, ASCA, and CACREP each purport differing foci in the field of school counseling, and each has made significant contributions to defining the roles of school counselors as leaders and advocates. The NCTSC believed that school counselors were left out of the education reform discussion in the United States and witnessed many new school counselors feeling unprepared to serve as effective advocates for all students (Education Trust, 2002). Therefore, the NCTSC created a network of organizations, state departments of education, school counselor professional associations, higher education institutions, and school districts dedicated to transforming school counselors into leaders and agents of change in their schools and in the lives of students (Education Trust, 2002, 2010). The ASCA worked to create the National Model for School Counseling Programs (2005) in order to provide frameworks for K–12 school counselors to be leaders in creating counseling programs in which they can create standards of practice for counseling activities, consultation, collaboration, and advocacy efforts. Following suit, within the 2009 standards, the CACREP included leadership and advocacy standards for the specialized training of school counselors who work with diverse K–12 students in schools.

These national movements were developed in part to lend cohesion to the school counseling profession whose practices varied widely across the United States and to advocate for school counselors engaging more in leadership and advocacy, counseling, and community outreach efforts (ASCA, 2005; Education Trust, 2002, 2010). These organizations' efforts now guide school counselors in their attempts to be leaders and advocate for the profession through educating students, parents, teachers, administrators, other school personnel, community mental health counselors, and a wide variety of community members regarding what counselors do and can offer to their schools in daily practice (ASCA; Education Trust, 2002, 2010). Because the ASCA national model suggests that school counselors be leaders in K–12 schools that consistently collect data on the numerous services they provide to students and their families, counselors can use this information to advocate for themselves within their schools and school districts when national and state budget cuts may threaten their professional positions. We highly encourage school counselors to find ways to have a voice as leaders in their schools and communities when it comes to promoting the profession that supports our children's education, wellness, and development. In addition to school counselors providing leadership within their communities and schools and acting as advocates on behalf of the profession, it is imperative for school counselors to also advocate for their primary "clients" in schools, their students.

### Advocacy for K–12 Students

Beyond advocating for the school counseling profession at macro levels, school counselors are leaders and advocates on a daily basis, working on behalf of their student clients in schools. The primary focus of school counselors' work is to provide clinical and educational services to students in order to promote their academic, career, and personal and social development, or wellness (ASCA, 2005; Dixon et al., 2010). School counselors are called upon to advocate on behalf of students with teachers and administrators regarding equitable academic services and, at times, parents and community-based social service agencies outside of the educational environment. In this section, we review strategies for advocating with and on behalf of students who are living in high-poverty home environments or facing various types of discrimination in the school setting, including racial/ethnic minority students; lesbian, gay, bisexual, and transgendered (LGBT) students; students with disabilities; and immigrants and students who speak English as a second language.

### *Advocating for Students in Poverty*

Within the schools, school counselors are working with students who come from homes with diverse socioeconomic conditions. Despite an increasingly diverse population, schools continue to be segregated by class, particularly in inner cities (Moody, 2001). The National Center for Education Statistics (NCES) reported that in 2007–2008, 16,122 schools were considered high-poverty schools in the United States (2010). Within these schools, 76–100% of the student enrollment was eligible for free or reduced-price meals. In addition, the percentage of high-poverty schools increased from 12% in 1999–2000 to 17% in 2007–2008 (NCES). High-poverty schools also have higher rates of special education student populations and greater numbers of racial/ethnic minority students. As a result, teachers and school counselors work with larger numbers of traditionally marginalized groups in schools.

K–12 students who live in poverty or at the poverty level often experience a range of personal/social concerns that can directly affect their success at school (Thomas, 2010). Accordingly, it is critical that school counselors develop advocacy and community outreach skills in order to assist these students in overcoming barriers associated with poverty. These students can be members of homeless families or nontraditional family structures (i.e., families of divorce, stepfamilies, families with same-sex parents, etc.), and they may have parents or guardians who are not as able or willing to be involved in their students' academic lives as other parents and guardians who have the resources their families and children need (Thomas). Students living in poverty may believe that they are not worthy of some of the other students' benefits in schools because of the internalization of negative messages about what it means to be poor in this country and the lack of resources compared to their peers. These internalization processes can result in students not receiving the academic services and equitable treatment within schools to which they are entitled. School counselors have the opportunity to work with these students as advocates for academic and personal/social needs, while teaming with other leaders and mental health professionals in the schools, such as school psychologists for assessment of undiagnosed emotional or learning disorders. Ultimately, school counselors serve as leaders as they collaborate with social workers to advocate on behalf of students living in poverty by reaching out to them and their families and linking them with services in the community.

Another important leadership role for school counselors involves how they connect with students' parents and guardians to offer support to the family on behalf of the student and his or her academic success. This may include advocating for transportation being offered to families to be able to attend conferences and school activities or leading fund-raising activities for students needing computers or other academic support at home. Finally, this creates a need for school counselors to have a working knowledge of community resources, such as hospitals, clinics, mental health agencies, and social service agencies, and maintain openness to collaborating with other professionals in order to advocate for students living in poverty.

*Academic and Social Advocacy for Students Facing Discrimination in Schools*

Along with students who live in poverty, several additional groups of students are considered traditionally marginalized in K–12 schools (Thomas, 2010). Some of these groups include racial/ethnic minority groups; students who are LGBT; students with physical, emotional, behavioral, or cognitive disabilities; and immigrant students and others who speak English as a second language (ESOL) (Harry & Klingner, 2006). These groups of students may experience varying forms of discrimination while at school in terms of academic services available or not available to them, lower levels of social acceptance and tolerance from other students and teachers, and potential accommodations needed for assessment and testing in the U.S. school system.

The goals of the ASCA national model suggest that school counselors are central in schools and should be most concerned with the positive academic and personal/social development for *each and every one* of their students, regardless of their backgrounds or needs (ASCA, 2005; Bryan, 2005). School counselors are in prime positions to serve as leaders and advocates for these different groups of students who may not have a voice for themselves in the educational environment. Primary to school counselors' roles as advocates on behalf of these students is acknowledgment and understanding of historical barriers faced by these groups of students in the K–12 schools and leadership roles school counselors can play in addressing these oppressive experiences with the schools (Bryan). Racial and ethnic minority and LGBT students, students with disabilities, and immigrant and ESOL students may feel powerless in a majority-dominated school culture where characteristics such as nondominant language skills, lower socioeconomic class, and cultural variations are viewed as deficit based and do not allow for students to have equal access to services and opportunities. Nonmajority students in such schools may also experience oppression and a lack of privilege that perpetuates the negative stereotypes often associated with these groups of students and their families.

Through their knowledge, awareness, and the skills they implement through strengths-based school counseling programs, school counselors can advocate for students who experience different forms of academic and social discrimination at school by offering individual counseling and small group counseling to students who may have similar needs, such as students with disabilities and ESOL and immigrant students. Individual counseling may allow for students to voice their concerns in a private setting, and counselors can aid students in locating services within and outside of the school. Small groups can be formed around specific topics that students may be experiencing and can involve helping students to learn how to advocate for themselves in appropriate manners, both academically and socially. In addition, school counselors are leaders who can offer in-service trainings for teachers regarding some of the specialized academic needs for students from underrepresented groups, such as ESOL, newly immigrated students, and students with disabilities. In addition, school counselors can offer ideas for how teachers can be advocates on behalf of these students in their classrooms.

Academically, students may need school counselors to advocate for their equal access to tutoring and accommodations through special education opportunities, individualized education plans, and mentoring possibilities (Bryan, 2005). Counselors should be active participants in special education and student assistance teams because it is often likely that they have knowledge of certain students' home lives, educational plans, and academic accommodation needs. For students with disabilities, this can mean advocating for special testing and homework accommodations. For immigrant and ESOL students, this can mean advocating for language interpreters for students and parents/guardians and connecting these students with one another through small group experiences. In addition, school counselors can advocate for students by facilitating tutoring and peer counseling programs that offer social connections and academic support. Finally, school counselors may connect families with community-based social agencies that offer support to immigrant and ESOL families.

Although the U.S. educational system has made strides in equalizing opportunities for traditionally marginalized student groups in schools, school counselors are still called upon to be advocates for students in social as well as academic situations. In order to be ethical leaders who advocate on behalf of students who experience social discrimination, school counselors should acknowledge their own biases and stereotypes around groups of racial and ethnic minority youth,

LGBT students, students with disabilities, and immigrant and ESOL students. The ASCA (2010a) maintains numerous positions statements that guide school counselors in their work with these groups of students and aid school counselors in understanding their leadership roles in the school setting. Once school counselors address their own biases, they can illustrate their leadership when collaborating with other school professionals to advocate for students experiencing discrimination in academic, co-curricular, or social scenarios.

School counselors can be proactive by providing educational large group guidance lessons around diversity, tolerance, acceptance, privilege, and oppression within classrooms. Sponsoring cultural diversity days and events in schools throughout the year is another way in which school counselors can be leaders and advocate for social acceptance and tolerance of groups of students represented in the school. Students can be invited to present to others in the school regarding their backgrounds, cultures, values, and other diverse components of their lives. Most importantly, school counselors are called upon to be academic and social advocates for groups of students who experience varying forms of discrimination within the K–12 schools. The roles of advocate and leader are ones that are expected on a daily basis as school counselors offer voice to many students and families who may need support in equalizing the social injustices that can occur in schools.

It is an exciting time in the school counseling profession as school counselors create new ways to lend their professional voices to their students as advocates and leaders in their schools and communities. Whereas school counselors provide leadership and advocacy for and on behalf of K–12 students and their families, communities remain reliant on multiple sources to meet the increasing mental health needs of their residents. Therefore, counselors who are employed in community-based mental health agencies provide critical service delivery and serve as important advocates for persons across the life span and leaders for their communities and profession in creating systemic change.

## ADVOCACY AND THE MENTAL HEALTH AGENCY COUNSELOR

Professional counselors employed by mental health agencies provide essential services to their community members, many of who are unable to attain counseling services from private or other public locations. Given the increased demands placed onto community mental health agencies as a result of decreased funding of state hospitals, a broadening of service delivery options, population growth, and reduced stigma surrounding mental illness (Mazade & Glover, 2007), professional counselors who work in these settings must be capable of working with diverse populations and knowledgeable of an array of therapeutic issues. Individuals who obtain counseling services at mental health agencies report high prevalence of multiple and complex co-occurring conditions, are at high risk for multiple health issues such as obesity, diabetes, coronary heart disease, and smoking-related illnesses (McCann, 2010), and may also present with legal issues as a result of being referred by corrections, juvenile justice, and other judicial systems (Theriot & Segal, 2005). While these multiple psychosocial and legal issues may seem daunting to some mental health clinicians, counselors, with their emphasis on assessment, diagnosis, treatment, and prevention, are well trained to serve as frontline service providers. Yet, simply providing effective counseling services to mental health agency clients and their family members is not sufficient. The counseling profession demands that mental health agency counselors be advocates for both the profession and their clients (Lewis, Toporek, & Ratts, 2010).

## Advocating for the Counseling Profession

Advocacy on behalf of the counseling profession is essential, especially for mental health agency counselors who often work alongside individuals with other professional identities, such as psychiatrists, psychologists, social workers, and clinical nurses. Mental health agency counselors are well suited to help their community members cope with a variety of issues. Professional counselors employed in mental health agencies perform a range of important responsibilities, including screening; individual, group, and family counseling; documentation; the development, initiation, and evaluation of treatment planning; and referral making (West, Hosie, & Mackey, 1987). The counseling profession's emphasis on looking at pathology from a developmental or wellness perspective is also crucial, due in part to the diverse sociodemographics (e.g., age, race/ethnicity, sexual orientation, class, etc.) found among clients seeking counseling services at mental health agencies. A prevention and wellness model of counseling, given the increased linkage between physical and mental health, is especially relevant in helping counselors be effective in mental health agency settings.

Finally, the counseling profession's increasing recognition of the importance of evidence-based treatment outcomes, as confirmed by the revised 2009 CACREP standards and the revision of the ACA Code of Ethics (2005), has and will continue to strengthen the training and preparation of mental health agency counselors (Hennessy & Chambers, 2009). Competent and well-trained professional counselors are needed to provide high-quality, culturally relevant, and effective services to individuals who are seeking clinical services at community mental health agencies. As a result, professional counselors are increasingly being recognized as effectively providing these services, as recently evidenced by the Veterans Administration's inclusion of licensed mental health counselors (Office of Veterans Affairs, 2010). Yet, more work is needed. Mental health counselors are still excluded from certain public (Medicaid and Medicare) and private third-party reimbursement plans, or if they are covered, mental health counselors are often compensated at much lower rates. Professional counselors who are employed in mental health agencies possess a unique perspective in detailing the varied roles and responsibilities that they fulfill in order to meet the needs of a community. It is essential that these perspectives be shared with local, state, and federal political leaders, local officials, and other mental health professionals in order for policy makers to understand the critical role that professional counselors employ in their communities.

### Advocating for Clients of Community Mental Health Agencies

Using advocacy as a mechanism to address oppressive social structures as well as to improve the conditions for those who have been historically disenfranchised is especially relevant for mental health agency counselors. While professional counselors in these settings work with a broad range of clinical issues experienced by individuals, couples, and families, certain therapeutic factors commonly serve as barriers to our clients' individual and systemic well-being. In this section, we review strategies for advocating with and on behalf of persons who suffer from addiction, live in poverty, and face various types of discrimination. Professional counselors who work in mental health agencies can also advocate for the physical well-being of our clients. Therefore, we also explore methods in which mental health counselors can advocate for health promotion, including prevention and screening.

#### *Advocating for Addicted Clients*

Substance dependence, and to a lesser degree process-related addictions (e.g., sex, food, and pathological gambling), remain among the most common mental illnesses seen by counselors who are employed in community-based mental health agencies (Rose, Brondino, & Barnack, 2009). Yet, it has been our experience that resistance to working with addicted clients is high among counseling students compared to clients presenting with other issues. The first step toward advocating for addicted clients is for the counselor to examine her or his own bias related to this population. As mental health agency counselors, do we believe that persons with addictions are capable of change and do we place higher (or lower) stigma on certain types of addictive behavior compared to others? The 2009 CACREP standards, including specific foci on core and program specialty areas, contain the strongest emphasis on counselor training with regards to working with persons experiencing addiction than ever before. Specifically, counselors are encouraged to examine bias and understand how counselors' stereotypes impact the clinical relationship with a client living with an addiction and her or his family members.

Second, advocating on behalf of addicted clients may require that mental health agency counselors stress a harm reduction approach, rather than a consistent, abstinence-based model (Bonar & Rosenberg, 2010). Given the significant bias toward abstinence-based treatment and recovery programs, many of which are now housed in mental health agencies, many professional counselors feel pressured to endorse an all-or-nothing approach to recovery. Some clients of mental health agencies will resist abstention from *all* mood-altering substances. The professional counselor's ability to display empathy, work together to create, implement, and evaluate therapeutic goals, and promote facilitative behaviors that reduce at-risk behaviors is critical. Third, professional counselors in mental health agencies must assess for multiple oppressions that an addicted client may experience. Realizing that our society and its legal system unfairly treat drug use and its consequences differently based on the gender, ethnicity, and age of the user, it is common for addicts to internalize these messages. Often, these beliefs will serve to intensify the guilt and shame associated with recreational or dependent use of a drug. Next, professional counselors can advocate for their addicted clients by being knowledgeable of and having direct access to information related to effective referral sources. Mental health agency counselors can assist their clients by providing the names, locations, and meeting times of recovery-oriented groups, halfway housing, shelters, medical services, family and couples counseling, and employment agencies (Simmons et al., 2008). Professional counselors can also advocate for their addicted clients by volunteering to serve on community-based, nonprofit boards that promote the prevention of drug use or the reduction of risks associated with drug using behaviors. Finally, mental health agency counselors can serve as educators within a community, especially related to changing drug trends, the escalation of process-oriented addictions, specifically sex and food addiction, and the impact of addiction on family and friends.

*Advocating for and Providing Leadership on Behalf of Clients Living in Poverty*

Persons living in poverty, if they do obtain mental health services, are more likely to seek out counselors at community-based mental health agencies than persons who report higher income levels. Consequently, it is imperative that counselors employed in mental health agencies develop advocacy skills in order to assist their clients in overcoming barriers associated with poverty. Clients from impoverished backgrounds or who are currently living in poverty may have internalized the notion that they are inferior to others, unworthy of success, and incapable of making changes. Researchers have found that this negative belief system leads to low self-esteem and feelings of powerlessness, potential barriers to counselors' advocacy efforts (Liu & Ali, 2008).

When working with clients in poverty, Liu, Pickett, and Ivey (2007) suggested that professional counselors focus on a phenomenological approach to issues of social class and the client's experience rather than on implied stereotypes related to the individual. Next, professional counselors must examine their own stereotypes and biases around persons living in poverty. Has the professional counselor internalized the same messages as the client with regards to one's ability to make significant changes in one's life? A professional counselor can advocate directly with the client to develop a more inclusive and truthful assessment of one's financial condition and help the individual, couple, or family to differentiate between a situational versus permanent circumstance. Upon arriving at the mental health agency, clients from impoverished backgrounds may not be aware of how classism and other types of discrimination (e.g., racism and heterosexism) could be impacting them (Liu, 2001). While serving as advocates, professional counselors can help their clients to recognize and confront how other societal beliefs can be hindering their success. Persons living in poverty will often lack important assertiveness, empowerment, and resiliency skills (Liu & Ali, 2008). Professional counselors employed in mental health agencies can work on advocacy strategies with clients that will help them to identify their needs and to develop effective behavioral efforts in confronting oppressive conditions.

Professional counselors can display leadership within their agencies and communities by linking services and sharing of client information, essential steps in mainstreaming mental health and medical service delivery and reducing costs. As leaders, mental health agency counselors can also educate and encourage their clients throughout the process of identifying and accessing existing social service systems. Knowledge of community resources such as hospitals, clinics, schools, and other mental health agencies and a willingness to collaborate with other professionals is essential in advocating for clients who live in poverty.

Mental health agency counselors can exhibit critical leadership skills by assuming active roles in community-based organizations or groups and developing relationships with other professional allies. As a result of these leadership efforts, counselors can identify and access advocacy networks as well as ascertain potential sources for collaboration. Counselors who are employed in mental health agencies do not always have to look outside their place of employment in order to provide leadership for educating others. Professional counselors must be willing to voice their opposition to agency policies and procedures that may be discriminating against those persons without transportation or access to particular programming.

## Issues of Discrimination Among Women and LGBT Clients

Professional counselors at mental health agencies will often assist clients who have experienced various types of discrimination and who are seeking to address impaired coping mechanisms associated with being different than the dominant or majority culture. Professional counselors can serve as advocates for women as well as LGBT persons by acknowledging barriers faced by members of each group and by actively working to address these oppressive attitudes and policies within a community. Women face myriad challenges that serve as barriers to optimal well-being. Pay inequality, limited career advancement opportunities (e.g., the glass ceiling), and sexual harassment combine to impact a woman's financial condition (Berdahl & Moore, 2006; Wrigley, 2002). The multiple roles a woman performs and the excessive pressure to present one's self as altogether can have negative consequences on her physical, emotional, spiritual, and mental well-being (Barnett,

2004). In fact, some women will be reluctant to seek out counseling services at a mental health agency because of this reluctance to admit fallibility. One of the most destructive threats to wellness among women of all ages is the direct and indirect threat of violence, including but not limited to intimate partner violence, sexual assault, and dating violence (Tjaden & Thoennes, 2006).

Professional counselors at mental health agencies can advocate for their female clients by offering gender-specific groups that address such topics as misogynic concerns, violence, and parenting skills. Having current knowledge of existing referral services for shelters (especially ones that will accept a mother and her children), legal and financial advisors, and gender-specific community resources such as 12-step fellowships is useful. Professional counselors from mental health agencies can provide leadership within their communities by volunteering to educate members of their communities via speaking at various religious, school, and other local events. As leaders, it is important for both female and male mental health agency counselors to recognize their leadership potential in educating their community members about gender-specific risks.

Even though acceptance of gay men and lesbians has become more common-place than at any time in our nation's history (Saad, 2010), many LGBT persons will seek out counseling at mental health counseling agencies. In order to advocate for persons with a nonheterosexual sexual orientation or a nontraditional gender identity, counselors must be willing to address heterosexual privilege and its costs to LGBT persons. The inability to express one's affections toward the person with whom you love and society's minimization of the validity of the same-sex relationship combine to influence the internalization of negative cognitions about what it means to be nonheterosexual. This internalization process contributes to the elevation of shame and guilt as has been considered the most significant impediment to wellness among LGBT persons (Newcomb & Mustanski, 2010). Professional counselors can advocate directly with their LGBT clients by challenging these self-limitations. Professional counselors must also be knowledgeable of sexual minority identity development and its importance in advocating with clients. Clients in the earlier stage of identity development may not be capable of advocating for themselves to the degree that clients in the latter stage of development are.

Not only can professional counselors advocate for and on behalf of their LGBT clients and loved ones, but also their training in and adherence to ACA's 2005 Code of Ethics and the ACA advocacy competencies (Lewis et al., 2002) provide the impetus for leadership in their communities. Mental health counselors can identify and collaborate with other leading community officials to address systemic and other community-based obstacles to optimal well-being for LGBT persons. Professional counselors employed in mental health agencies can convey leadership within their job setting by being proactive in removing barriers within one's place of work, including the redesign of agency screening

forms to reflect relationship status other than single and married and the inclusion of transgender as an option for gender. In addition, leadership efforts for
LGBT clients require that counselors know of resources that are supportive of
nonheterosexual persons. Through their work in the community, such as volunteering for an AIDS fund-raiser or the support of a lesbian health initiative,
counselors can build networks of support while simultaneously advocating for
their LGBT clients.

Advocating for transgender clients requires professional counselors in mental
health agencies to recognize the multiple risk factors experienced by members
of this population, including the threat of physical violence, lack of employment opportunities, high rates of homelessness, and elevated rates of depression,
anxiety, and isolation (Kenagy, 2005; Sangganjanavanich & Cavazos, 2010). For
transgender persons who are taking or considering taking hormones, it is essential that mental health agency counselors be able to recommend endocrinolo-
gists and other medical professionals that are knowledgeable and supportive of
persons with nontraditional gender identities. Public advocacy and leadership
on behalf of transgender clients is critical to raising community awareness to
the unique and often challenging needs of this community. Results from local
needs assessments examining the transgender community consistently show
that transgender persons are not often embraced by a community's lesbian, gay,
or bisexual community, and therefore are often socially and politically isolated
(Kenagy & Hsieh, 2005). Mental health agency counselors can display leadership
within their communities and by educating community members, including
mental and public health professionals, medical staff, religious leaders, and law
enforcement officials, to the unique needs of the transgender community.

### Advocating for Mental and Physical Health and Wellness

The gap between community-based need and sufficient service capacity continues to widen for many mental health agencies. As a result, greater emphasis on
mental health screening is impacting the work of counselors employed in these
settings. Increased focus on screening for mental illness allows professional
counselors to expand the number of persons serviced via public services, com-
bat the potential stigma (although lower than in the past, stigma still remains
a barrier to mental health services, especially for racial and ethnic minorities)
of receiving mental health services by entering specific at-risk communities and
provide screening outside the agency setting, prevent risk associated with serious mental illness from developing, and enhance the potential of at-risk persons
being placed on psychotropic medications, especially the second-generation psy-
chotropics (Provan, 1997).

A mental health agency counselor can utilize this screening and prevention
approach to advocate more effectively for his or her clients. Professional counselors can lend leadership to community-based health initiatives by serving as

pivotal members of teams that assess, select, and implement screening of at-risk populations. Through previous leadership and advocacy work within the community, a counselor can utilize existing relationships with medical, mental health, legal, and religious leaders to conduct effective community-based outreach efforts. The counselor, when out in the community, can provide a list of resources and referrals to at-risk persons. Mental health counselors can also team up with other nonprofit organizations, such as HIV/AIDS service organizations, to carry out free or low-cost testing.

In addition to screening, professional counselors employed in mental health settings can advocate for their clients and provide leadership for their agencies and communities by integrating a holistic health promotion approach into their individual and group counseling services. Given the rate of unemployment and the increasing number of persons living without insurance (medical, dental, or vision), mental health agency counselors are increasingly having to address physical health concerns among their clients. Professional counselors should utilize these opportunities to advocate for and on behalf of their clients. First, professional counselors should emphasize routine medical screenings for both their female and male clients. Identifying low-cost, community-based medical providers who conduct gynecological, breast, colon, and rectal exams and providing this information to colleagues and clients is pivotal. Second, clients will often need assistance in navigating through complex medical systems. Professional counselors can assist their clients in organizing paperwork, communicating with, making, and attending scheduled appointments with medical officials, and identifying potential transportation and child care issues. Third, professional counselors must be knowledgeable of free or low-cost support group or related sources of support. Persons who are confronting issues related to grief/loss, cancer, HIV/AIDS, addiction, and smoking cessation can find support in community-based groups. When these groups do not exist, mental health agency counselors can first recognize the community's need and second, organize efforts to launch such a support system. Finally, professional counselors employed in mental health agencies can provide leadership by encouraging state and national political leaders to adopt policies that will make health care more affordable and accessible. Because of their experiences with persons who have minimal health care coverage as well as with individuals who have no health insurance, professional counselors are uniquely positioned to lobby government officials on behalf of clients who have experienced financial, mental and public health, and medical suffering as a result of the existing health care system.

## CONCLUSION

In this chapter, we discussed how leadership and advocacy roles are illustrated in the counseling profession and described strategies for professional counselors who lead by example as advocates in K–12 schools, mental health agencies, and within communities on behalf of students/clients and the profession as a whole. We also illustrated the numerous and diverse manners in which professional counselors are serving their students and clients as advocates in their clinical settings, and we discussed how they combine their efforts both inside and outside of their respective settings. We believe it is an exciting time in professional counseling, during which professional counselors in *all* clinical settings are afforded the privilege to act as leaders on behalf of our profession and implement social advocacy for students and clients from a variety of diverse backgrounds who may truly benefit from our advocacy efforts as leaders in our field.

## DISCUSSION QUESTIONS AND ACTIVITIES

1. a. Discuss the various methods in which school counselors employed in K–12 school settings in the United States can offer academic and social advocacy for students and their families.
   b. Discuss the various methods in which mental health counselors who are employed in community-based agency settings can advocate for their clients.
2. Design a six-week advocacy project for school counselors to implement in either an elementary or secondary school setting that involves individual, small group, and large group guidance efforts that bring diverse students, teachers, and families together in educational and experiential encounters. (CACREP 2009; Section II.C.4; IV.J.1)
3. How have mental health agencies changed over the past 20 years? What are the implications of these changes on our profession's call for leadership and advocacy?
4. **Case study 1:** Maria is a Mexican student who recently moved to the United States with her father, mother, and two younger brothers. She entered into eighth grade at an inner city middle school in the Midwest United States. During her first semester, Maria struggled in her academic coursework due to her lack of skills in being able to read and understand English; however, she did not seek out help and her parents do not speak English. Her teachers have shown little empathy because Maria's oral language skills in English appear to be excellent. She is able to express herself orally and understand others' spoken English. She is called into her eighth grade school counselor's office due to her failing all of her coursework. Maria presents as a happy eighth grader who enjoys school and has also made several good friends in the school; however, she is very concerned about her schoolwork and performance in school and does not know how to seek help and support. (CACREP,

2009; School Counseling Section III.O.2, O.3; E.1, E.2, E.4; Doctoral Standards IV.I.2)

   a. How might Maria's school counselor demonstrate leadership by advocating for and on behalf of Maria's academic achievement?

   b. Maria's school counselor does not speak Spanish. What are the in-school and out-of-school resources her school counselor can pull upon to help get Maria the services she needs as well as consulting with her parents about her academic issues?

5. **Case study 2:** Brenda is a recent graduate from a CACREP-accredited mental health counseling program and has obtained a counselor position in her local community mental health center. During her first week of employment, Brenda is provided a caseload of over 20 clients. One of her clients is a 36-year-old, white, gay, HIV+, methamphetamine addict who has been a client at the agency for over 2 years. During the initial interview, the client acknowledges binging on methamphetamine over the past two months. (CACREP, 2009; Addiction Counseling Section III.E1, E3, E4; Clinical Mental Health Section III.E.6, F.1; Doctoral Standards IV.J.2)

   a. What types of issues would Brenda be most concerned about obtaining more information?

   b. What is the impact of drug use on this client's psychosexual functioning and his medical condition? In what ways could Brenda advocate for and on behalf of this client?

6. **Case study 3:** Juan is a 58-year-old immigrant from Mexico who has lived in the United States for over 40 years. He has been employed in the construction business for nearly all of his adult years but was laid off from his work approximately one year ago. Juan is seeking mental health counseling at the local agency. At his intake, Juan acknowledged being depressed and incredibly anxious due to the possibility of having to foreclose on his home. He reports his financial outlook to be bleak and believes he has let his family of three daughters down. Juan has a 10-year history of high blood pressure that has recently been causing Juan problems due to his anxiety. (CACREP, 2009; Clinical Mental Health Section III.D.3, F.3; Doctoral Standards IV.I.2)

   a. Which of Juan's issues are most pressing?

   b. To what kind of community resources might you, the counselor, attempt to link this client?

   c. How might you involve his family in your advocacy efforts?

7. **Case study 4:** Richard is a 32-year-old, gay, white male who has been partnered for nearly 8 years. He has always wanted to father a child but admits to his counselor, "I just don't think it's meant to be for me to become a dad." When probing this statement, the client justifies such

a comment by referring to his sexual orientation. (CACREP, 2009; Clinical Mental Health Section III.D.3, F.3; Doctoral Standards IV.I.2)

a. How might Richard's internalized homophobia be impacting his decision to become a father?

b. What types of community collaborations could the counselor employ to help his or her client overcome the stigma attached to parenting by nonheterosexual persons?

c. Describe various manners in which Richard's counselor can demonstrate leadership within his or her agency and community on behalf of LGBT clients.

# 13

## Advocacy and Leadership Through Research Best Practices

Danica G. Hays, Chris Wood, and Jayne E. Smith

## INTRODUCTION

There is increasing public demand that counseling practices be evidence based, creating "best practices" for counseling that are intended to provide information about the most effective interventions for specific conditions and populations (Gelso, 2006; Shapiro, 2009; Wester, 2007). Best practices for the counseling profession involve the integration of research and practice with an ultimate goal of accountability to clients and the general public. Through intervention and programmatic research, professional counselors and counselor educators demonstrate an integration of advocacy and leadership as they identify effective and ineffective—or even harmful—interventions and dialogue with scholars to advance the knowledge base of the profession (see American Counseling Association (ACA), 2005).

Professional counselors are part of a growing profession that values designing, conducting, and evaluating research using a variety of approaches, including quantitative, qualitative, and single-subject design, to name a few methods (Hays, 2010). Establishing best practices allows for greater reliability in case conceptualization, intervention, and prediction (Shapiro, 2009). Moreover, best practices with respect to evaluation and assessment can be a means of promoting social justice within the profession and society (Wood & D'Agostino, 2010). Because sound and culturally relevant research fosters more effective clinical practice, counselors and counselor trainees are encouraged to adopt a scientist-practitioner perspective, even before they begin seeing clients.

How do the concepts *best practices* and *scientist-practitioner* relate to leadership and advocacy in counselor preparation? As the editors of this text discuss in the introduction, the mission of Chi Sigma Iota International involves a commitment to advocacy for counseling professionals and their clients. Further, the CSI Principles and Practices of Leadership Excellence (CSI, 2009) indicate that leaders endorse and apply the mission and vision of CSI and provide a framework for understanding characteristics of effective leaders (see Chapter 3).

Toward this objective, leadership and advocacy are interdependent yet interrelated constructs, and both are needed in the counseling profession. We agree that advocacy is a critical focus of leadership efforts, and we would add that advocacy efforts facilitate leadership skill development. Since part of the vision of CSI and the counseling profession in general relates to supporting research and best practices, we will discuss in this chapter how professional counselors may use research for leadership and advocacy.

Infusing best practices as a foundation for advocacy and leadership involves three key efforts: extending existing knowledge relevant to the counseling profession, identifying best practices, and disseminating current knowledge to shape counselor preparation and practice. After providing professional organizations' calls for best practices, we define and review characteristics of best practices, discuss the state of the literature concerning the "evidence" of evidence-based practices, and outline some strategies for increasing knowledge of best practices in training programs and the counseling profession. We will end the chapter with case examples to illustrate a five-tier developmental taxonomy for integrating advocacy and leadership in counseling research. In order to understand the symbiotic relationship of research to leadership and advocacy in the counseling profession, it is important to define key terms and concepts associated with best practices in research.

## Key Terms and Concepts

**Best practices** are those practices guided by and that contribute to clinical research; they are the outputs counselors reflect upon and integrate into interventions with their clients and those that are updated based upon a practitioner's research activities. To this end, best practices involve using science to guide practice as well as making efforts in practice to engage in research. A term often used interchangeably with best practices is **evidence-based practice**, which typically refers to data generated from randomized clinical trials to address a specific client problem. However, we conceptualize best practices to incorporate idiographic aspects of clinical practice (i.e., what type of counseling would be most helpful for a specific client) in addition to nomothetic qualities typically identified in clinical trials (i.e., what works for most individuals in a well-defined client population; Shapiro, 2009).

The Institute of Medicine (2001) defined best practice as the "integration of best researched evidence and clinical expertise with patient values" (p. 147). Expertise is assumed to be built on empirical knowledge that leads to a more universal understanding of what clients need. Best practices are important to leadership and advocacy, as they guide us in identifying effective interventions, theories, and models that validate the counseling profession. Like other health-related professions, best practice research in counseling provides a foundation from which leaders in the profession may advocate for the betterment of individuals, communities, and the general public.

**Accountability** refers to a standard of quality to ensure best care or best practice to a third party. It involves being responsible and transparent to an external party (typically the general public) when engaging in or choosing an intervention. In leadership and advocacy, counselors display accountability as they implement policies and practices that empower and serve clients.

**Outcome research** relates to empirical findings, falling on a continuum of highly controlled designs, such as randomized clinical trials, to more flexible single-subject and case study designs (Hays, 2010). As such, outcome research and evaluation may serve as a basis for treatment planning. Erford (2008) suggested three methods used in outcome research: clinical trial studies, qualitative analysis, and meta-analysis. **Clinical trials**, also known as randomized clinical trials, have comparison groups, standardized treatment protocols, and outcome measures. **Qualitative analysis** involves researchers summarizing robust trends and findings across studies, clients, and contexts. **Meta-analysis** is a quantitative summary of the effect size of numerous studies to demonstrate the strength of the findings, in this case, on the effectiveness of counseling. We recommend reviewing Whiston and Campbell (2010) and Erford, Savin-Murphy, and Butler (2010) for additional information on these types of outcome research.

The key terms presented above are just a few of those connected to best practices and counseling research. To be effective leaders and advocates, practitioners and counselor educators are to engage in several types of research in ways that contribute significantly to the profession. In the following section we highlight how research and best practices are emphasized throughout professional organizations and associations.

## PROFESSIONAL ORGANIZATIONS' CALL FOR BEST PRACTICES

Professional counselors have a moral and ethical responsibility to provide effective services to clients, to bring the best of science and practice to the "table." The mission of the ACA includes language pertaining to advocacy: promoting professional development of counselors, advancing the profession, and providing culturally sensitive services to clients. One method of professional counselor advocacy is attending to research best practices in evaluating interventions, and is alluded to in several areas of the ACA Code of Ethics (2005): Counselors are to attend to the effectiveness of services (A.1.c, C.2.d), practice within the boundaries of their competence (C.2.a), and maintain knowledge of current research and professional information (C.2.f). Additionally, professional counselors and counselor educators are to introduce techniques and individual and programmatic interventions with an empirical basis, or at least acknowledge when techniques are "unproven" or "developing," and take cautions to avoid harming clients involved in them (C.6.e, F.6.f). Further, ACA calls upon counselors to be involved in research that benefits practice:

> Counselors who conduct research are encouraged to contribute to the knowledge base of the profession and promote a clearer understanding of the conditions that lead to a healthy and more just society. Counselors support efforts of researchers by participating fully and willingly whenever possible. Counselors minimize bias and respect diversity in designing and implementing research programs. (Section G, p. 16)

While there are some public and private entities that only reimburse evidence-based services, there is not yet a universal mandate to use formal research to justify services (West & Warchal, 2009). The ACA Code of Ethics (2005) speaks to the importance of seeking effective practices and helping develop the profession through greater public accountability. Interestingly, only 11 of ACA's 19 divisions (58%) include "research," "best practice," "scholarship," or "knowledge" in their mission, vision, values, or purpose statements. Some examples of statements from ACA divisions and other counseling organizations are provided in Table 13.1.

Table 13.1 reflects several mission and vision statements that indicate a collective assumption that research for leadership and advocacy is an important aspect of the counseling profession. Given its importance, practitioners and counselor educators must review what counseling and counseling-related studies

**Table 13.1** Selected ACA Division and Professional Counseling Organization Best Practices Statements

### ACA Divisions

1. Association for Assessment in Counseling and Education: "The Association for Assessment in Counseling and Education (AACE) is an organization of counselors, educators, and other professionals that advances the counseling profession by providing leadership, training, and research in the creation, development, production, and use of assessment and diagnostic techniques." "The mission of AACE is to promote and recognize scholarship, professionalism, leadership, and excellence in the development and use of assessment and diagnostic techniques in counseling" (www.theaaceonline.com).

2. American College Counseling Association: "The mission of the American College Counseling Association is to be the interdisciplinary and inclusive professional home that supports emerging and state of the art knowledge and resources for counseling professionals in higher education" (http://www.collegecounseling.org/about/mission-statement).

3. Association for Counselor Education and Supervision: The Association for Counselor Education and Supervision vision statement includes four bullets, one of which is "provide and disseminate premier research and scholarship" (http://www.acesonline.net/vision.asp).

**Table 13.1 (continued)** Selected ACA Division and Professional Counseling Organization Best Practices Statements

4. Association for Multicultural Counseling and Development: The mission statement indicates and emphasis on research: "Providing global leadership, research, training and development for multicultural counseling professionals with a focus on racial and ethnic issues" (http://www. amcdaca.org/amcd/default.cfm).

5. American Rehabilitation Counseling Association: This association includes five key points in the mission statement, one of which states: "Provides research findings with direct application to the current and future practice of rehabilitation counseling" (http://www.arcaweb.org/).

6. American School Counseling Association: "ASCA provides professional development, publications and other resources, research and advocacy to more than 27,000 professional school counselors around the globe" (http://www.schoolcounselor.org/).

7. Association of Specialists in Group Work: "The purpose of the Association shall be to establish standards for professional and ethical practice; to support research and the dissemination of knowledge; and to provide professional leadership in the field of group work" (http://www.asgw.org/purpose.asp).

8. Counselors for Social Justice: Mission statement includes: "Disseminating social justice scholarship about sociopolitical and economic inequities facing counselors and clients/students in schools and communities" (http://counselorsforsocialjustice.com/mission.html).

9. International Association of Addictions and Offender Counselors: Vision statement indicates: "Our vision is to be a high quality resource organization which supports prevention, treatment, research, training, and advocacy for the addicted and forensic/criminal justice populations" (http://www.iaaoc.org/mission.asp).

10. National Career Development Association: "NCDA provides service to the public and professionals involved with or interested in career development, including professional development activities, publications, research, public information, professional standards, advocacy, and recognition for achievement and service" (http://associationdatabase.com/aws/NCDA/pt/sp/about).

11. National Employment Counseling Association: NECA has eight key points, of which one states: "Showcasing Best Practices" (http://www.employmentcounseling.org/).

## Professional Organizations in Counseling

1. Chi Sigma Iota International: The mission of CSI is to "promote scholarship, research, professionalism, leadership, advocacy, and excellence in counseling, and to recognize high attainment in the pursuit of academic and clinical excellence in the profession of counseling" (www.csi-net.org). To this end, CSI provides grants to individuals and chapters that promote these constructs.

2. Council for the Accreditation of Counseling and Related Educational Programs: The vision, mission, and core values of CACREP reflect a commitment to professional competence through providing standards for excellence in professional training programs. One of the five core values states: "Creating and strengthening standards that reflect the needs of society, respect the diversity of instructional approaches and strategies, and encourage program improvement and best practices" (http://www.cacrep.org/template/page.cfm?id=40).

3. National Board for Certified Counselors: The mission of NBCC is to promote quality assurance, value of counseling, public awareness of quality counseling practice, professionalism, and leadership (http://www.nbcc.org/whoWeAre/About.aspx).

are available to understand the scope of best practices research today. In doing so, the mission and vision statements are reflected in practice, which in turn promotes integrity throughout the field and accountability to the public. In other words, conducting and reviewing research for leadership and advocacy demonstrates how to be leaders and advocates in the field. Thus, it is crucial to increase the integration of advocacy and leadership through research in practice.

Some research in clinical effectiveness has been conducted for general psychotherapy (e.g., Lambert & Ogles, 2004; Smith & Glass, 1977; Wampold, 2001), children and adolescents (e.g., Kazdin & Weisz, 2003), and families and couples (e.g., Shadish, Montgomery, Wilson, Wilson, Bright, & Okwumabua, 1993). Sheperis, Young, and Daniels (2010) provided a list of 18 journals from the ACA and its associated divisions, which were used to search for articles related to "counseling effectiveness," "outcomes research," "best practice," "counselor preparation," "trauma interventions," and "trauma research." Of the 9,444 articles listed in EBSCO (Elton B. Stephens Company, a subscription agency) from 17 of these journals, search results yielded only 171 articles with these terms. However, after reading the abstracts, only 11 articles provided clinical trials, meta-analyses, qualitative analyses, or an interdisciplinary literature review examining studies over the course of 1 year to 40 years. The topics covered included multicultural competency (D'Andrea & Heckman, 2008), school counseling outcome research (Whiston & Sexton, 1998), relevance of counseling outcome research (Sexton, 1996), child group psychotherapy (Shechtman, 2002), outcome research on psychotherapy with children and adolescents (Eder & Whiston, 2006), evidence-based effective practice with older adults (Myers & Harper, 2004), marriage and family therapy (Baldwin & Huggins, 1997), relationship enhancement couples and family outcomes research (Accordino & Guerney, 2003), review of clinical mental health practices (Kelly, 1996), clinical trials of vocational rehabilitation (Rogers, Anthony, Lyass, & Penk, 2006), and spirituality in counseling (Hage, Hopson, Siegel, Payton, & Defanti, 2006). Clearly there is a need for more research on best practices specific to counseling beyond the 11 articles noted above, so that counseling leaders and advocates can promote the profession and the clients they serve and strengthen the demonstration of the mission and vision statements of our professional organizations.

## BEST PRACTICES: A BRIEF OVERVIEW

What makes a best practice in counseling a best practice? How are professional counselors trained to identify a best practice? How do counselor preparation programs train counselors to use existing research in practice or develop best practice research in the field? To answer these questions, we must first describe how best practices in research are requisite to identify best practices in counseling. Then, we will discuss how to integrate research of best practices into counselor training programs in efforts toward developing scholarly leaders to advocate effectively for clients, interventions, and the profession.

We believe a best practice in counseling has three requirements: clinical utility, counselor competency, and client characteristics, which include the interplay among counselor, client, and scientific literature. The purpose of establishing best practices in the counseling profession is to advance knowledge to improve client services, thereby embodying leadership in the profession. With this knowledge, we are equipped with evidence to advocate for the betterment of our clients, practice, and profession. Best practices in counseling are also informed by and guide counselor training programs. Counseling curriculum can be reflective of best practices in counseling and research, by exploring the three components.

As indicated by calls from professional organizations and accrediting bodies, establishing best practices in research is an ethical issue that relates to practitioner, client, trainee, and public accountability. Council for Accreditation of Counseling and Related Education Programs (CACREP) standards address the importance of outcome research and evaluation in training. Specifically, CACREP (2009) calls for counseling faculty members and students to contribute to scholarship within the profession at large and through individual programs and with clients in a professional, ethical, and culturally relevant manner. Students are to be prepared to evaluate research relevant to their respective specialty areas critically and understand best practices and outcome research data to apply findings to practice. Additionally, the standards speak to the need for faculty to produce and integrate research in their instruction as well as create a culture of scholarship in doctoral programs.

Figure 13.1 shows that, using three criteria as indicating best practices in counseling (i.e., clinical utility, counselor competency, attention to client characteristics), counselors can engage in three ways to establish best practices in research that impact training programs, services, and the professional literature.

**Figure 13.1**    Establishing best practices model.

## LEADERSHIP AND ADVOCACY IN RESEARCH: IMPLEMENTATION IN PREPARATION PROGRAMS

Thus far we have defined various types of research, summarized the call from ACA and its divisions as well as other professional organizations in counseling, identified a gap in the literature, provided a conceptual overview of best practices in counseling and research, and discussed the integration of the two in order to enhance leadership and advocacy. We now turn to recommendations for implementing leadership and advocacy in research through counselor preparation programs. Specifically, we discuss organizational culture, recommend activities integrated throughout the curriculum, and provide a developmental taxonomy to address implementing leadership and advocacy in research.

### DEVELOP A CULTURE OF BEST PRACTICE RESEARCH

Developing a culture in counselor education programs that supports the development of the scholar-leader is an important step in implementing the leadership and advocacy standards. What do we mean by culture? Edgar H. Schein, a leading scholar in the field of social psychology and expert consultant in organizational culture and development, stated this:

> The culture of a group can be defined as a pattern of shared basic assumptions that was learned by the group as it solved its problems of external adaptation and internal integration, that has worked well enough to be considered valid and, therefore, to be taught to new members as the correct way to perceive, think, and feel in relation to those problems. (2004, p. 17)

In this case, a *shared basic assumption* in research is crucial to the development and accountability of the profession to the public. This assumption is met through developing scholar-leaders who understand the importance of advocacy for the individual, community, and profession. CACREP (2009) emphasizes that programs acknowledge this assumption by publicizing a comprehensive mission statement that attends to advocacy and leadership (see Section II.A) and infuses current *quality* counseling-related research in teaching practice (see Section II.E). Additionally, CACREP asserts that programs are to create learning environments that prepare students to contribute to the profession and inform practice as scholars and leaders (see Doctoral Standards, Section I, C.3 and C.4). Counselor educators are to prioritize this assumption by establishing accountability measures within the department that integrate best practices research throughout the curriculum with an emphasis on developing leaders and advocates (see Chapters 10, 14, and 15 for further discussion). In particular, programs are to attend to research and evaluation as a core curriculum requirement and continually assess student learning outcomes across the CACREP program areas, as these actions reflect a commitment to advocacy and leadership through research best practice. The remaining sections provide specific recommendations for application.

Opportunities to Integrate Best Practice Research Throughout the Curriculum

In this section, we provide recommendations for integrating best practice research throughout the curriculum. We know there are many examples of this across counselor preparation programs and encourage departments to build on these existing elements. Additionally, we encourage departments to continue sharing best practices in leadership and advocacy research through publications, presentations, and other methods. As we shift from conceptual to application, we hope readers will initiate and build upon these recommendations and those already in practice.

*Develop Critical Consumers of Research (CACREP, 2009; Section II, Professional Identity, B.1)*

One way to help counselors-in-training avoid "blind acceptance" of all scholarly articles is to teach students to investigate the design characteristics and how findings are being applied through an assignment where they must present a critical analysis of an article relevant to their specialty area or to the focus of the class. For instance, in a human development class, students might be given an article related to different life span development theories and asked to critique the design and findings and recommend how they might use that article to advocate for the population represented in it. In so doing, future counselors are being prepared to integrate research as a key component to their advocacy practices. In developing recommendations for applying the research to advocate for their clients, they are practicing leadership.

*Become Skilled in Identifying Best Practices (CACREP, 2009; see Doctoral Standards, Section IV, I.4, I.5, J.2)*

To help students become skilled in identifying best practices, counselor educators can provide assignments where students must arrive at consensus for a best practice using several sources. In groups, students may be challenged with attempting to determine whether an intervention or strategy used to respond to multicultural issues, community, national and international crises, or current topical and political issue is, in fact, a best practice. Students could do this through replication of the study, multiple evaluations and assessments, community involvement, and analyzing the intermediate and long-term effects of the study through multiple data sources. In becoming skilled in identifying sound best practices, students are strengthening their advocacy competencies, which enhances their ability to be leaders within their work setting and community.

*Integrate Research in Fieldwork (CACREP, 2009; see Doctoral*
*Standards, Section II, B.2, B.4, C.5, and Section IV, J.2)*

Fieldwork provides a rich environment for training practitioners to be scholar-leaders. The practice of helping students integrate research in fieldwork may take many forms. An assignment might include analyzing the fieldwork site using Figure 13.1 as a guide. Another assignment might be to collaborate with a program faculty and site supervisor to conduct a needs assessment in the organization or an action research project that will enhance the site's services. Students could be asked to work within CSI chapters to provide grant awards to fund this research. The key in these types of assignments is to instill the practice of research in action, which reflects effectively using advocacy and leadership in the field. Much like we instill treatment planning, these types of assignments provide a foundation for how to integrate advocacy and leadership through best practice research in the daily functions of a counselor. The hope is research will move from being an extra activity in the already busy life of a counselor to being ingrained in daily practice.

*Provide Research Mentorship to Fieldwork Sites (CACREP, 2009;*
*see Doctoral Standards, Section II, B.2, and Section IV, J.2)*

Student groups, guided by program faculty, can provide research mentorships through existing fieldwork sites. The Association for Counselor Education and Supervision (ACES) provides a helpful set of guidelines for research mentorship (ACES Committee for Research Mentorship, 2009). Mentorship, in and of itself, is a key component of developing strong leaders. Furthermore, when faculty and students provide mentorship to community organizations aimed at increasing the use of research best practice, they model advocacy and leadership.

*Create Graduate Research Teams for Community Partners (CACREP,*
*2009; see Doctoral Standards, Section II, B.1, B.2, B.4; Section IV, J.2)*

Many community partners, including nonprofits, K–12 schools, agencies, and governmental departments, might have an unmet research need. Graduate research teams could be assigned to work with the community partner to develop and implement a research study based on their needs. Similar to the recommendation above, this reflects the commitment to the profession to advocate on behalf of community partners and help community partners advocate for themselves. Students are given an opportunity to provide team leadership with the community partners, hence enhancing their experience with integrating advocacy and leadership through research best practice. In many universities, community partnership grants are available to support such outreach and community partnership efforts.

A Developmental Taxonomy for Integrating Advocacy and Leadership

Figure 13.2 illustrates a way to conceptualize advancing knowledge and identifying best practices in the counseling profession. This conceptualization can provide a way of understanding the development of best practice from a general knowledge of what works to a sophisticated understanding of how to evaluate the effectiveness of one's counseling interventions in practice. This also demonstrates the progression of a counselor trainee to a leader and advocate for clients, the community, and the profession. It serves as a potential developmental taxonomy for teaching counselors-in-training (as will be illustrated in case examples).

At a base level, a professional counselor or counseling student knows the transtheoretical and theory-specific elements of counseling that are conducive to positive counseling outcomes (*knowledge guiding the profession*). The professional counselor or trainee uses this basic knowledge as a foundation for interacting with clients and the community, which will assist counselors or trainees in

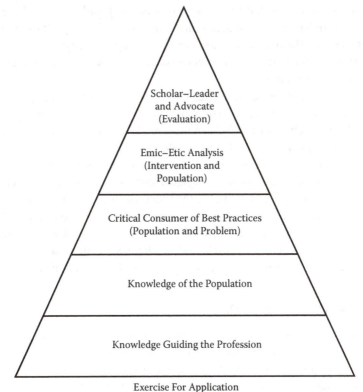

Figure 13.2    A process for integrating advocacy and leadership in research.

becoming aware of multicultural, topical, and political issues where they might utilize advocacy and leadership skills.

Building on this, the professional counselor must gain a deep knowledge of the population(s) being served—this includes the requisite knowledge for multiculturally competent practice as well as the most prevalent problems/phenomena and treatment challenges of the specific population (*knowledge of the population served*). The professional counselor continues to gather data through interaction with the population(s) being served. Again, this information will inform the advocacy strategies developed in higher tiers.

The third tier of Figure 13.2 represents where practitioners must become critical consumers of research. They must become informed of best practice for the given problem (e.g., what treatment modalities have evidence of the most positive outcomes). A practitioner also needs to become knowledgeable about specific counseling interventions that are most effective for the given population (e.g., individual vs. group, home visits). The challenge, then, is to determine the degree to which the existing research for a client problem fits with the population the counselor is serving (*best practices (problem and population)*). If there is no existing research on the best practice intervention(s) with the specific population in question, then the counselor/counselor-in-training must engage in an analysis to determine if the best practice intervention is universal or if a more culture-specific intervention is warranted.

Finally, the culminating knowledge in this hierarchy is developing a methodologically sound strategy for evaluating the efficacy of one's current practice (*evaluation*). Is the specific problem being remediated in the specific population by the current interventions? This evaluation might also be formative in nature, seeking to improve the quality of interventions provided for the population. This corresponds to our recommendations to engage in collaborative research in fieldwork and with community partners. This is the point where the practitioners or counselor trainees become advocates and scholar-leaders in the field as they take the information they have gathered, through effective counselor-client relationships, critical analysis of existing research, and development of necessary research, in support of the effective intervention with or on behalf of the population.

### EXERCISES FOR APPLICATION

In this section, we provide two case studies to illustrate the conceptual model in Figure 13.2 and demonstrate how the recommended activities can be integrated into the curriculum. There are guiding questions that counselor educators may assign to students to assist in training scholar-leaders and advocates. Further, the case studies can be helpful to practitioners who are interested in developing research competencies related to advocacy and leadership.

Case Study 1: Counseling Practitioner (CACREP, 2009; see Doctoral
Standards, Section II, B.1 and C.5; Section IV, I.4, I.5, and J.2)

You are one of several counselors recently hired in the mental health division
of a community services agency. The agency has recently been awarded a federal grant to provide services to a growing population of Sudanese refugees
in the area. (The hiring of additional counselors at the agency is a result of
the new funding from the grant.) You have limited experience working with
refugees and want to learn about critical concerns and effective interventions
for this population. You have read that language barriers create obstacles to
accessing resources for relocated populations, and you wonder how advocacy
might play a part in your work. Additionally, you will be asked to contribute to
quarterly and annual reports required by the grant, including reporting treatment effectiveness related to specific benchmarks. As you prepare to serve this
population as a professional counselor, how can research guide your professional practice?

1. Knowledge guiding the profession: Explore the research on the effectiveness of counseling as a mental health intervention. What implications does this research have for your work in the case study? (For this
   question, as with the questions below, students can be either required to
   find research on their own or given key studies to read.)
2. Knowledge of the population served: What does the research indicate
   are the essential experiences of Sudanese refugees? What mental health
   issues might they likely experience? How might these differ from the
   concerns of other refugee populations?
3. Critical consumer of best practices (problem and population): Research
   at Step 2 will lead a student to explore treatment for posttraumatic stress
   disorder (PTSD), as an example. In turn, research at Step 3 may lead students to the International Society for Traumatic Stress Studies (ISTSS)
   and the best practice guidelines for PTSD, as examples.
4. Emic-etic analysis: This step in the activity requires students to determine whether best practice guidelines are appropriate for the given
   population. Given the information from Steps 2 and 3, the counseling
   researcher can assess the following: What gaps exist in the best practice
   guidelines? In light of your research on the Sudanese refugee population, how do the recommended treatments fit or not fit with this population? What other practices might be appropriate for this population,
   given the knowledge of their needs? This step is not intended to be a
   philosophical debate on the epistemological origins of research, but
   rather an applied learning activity giving students a heuristic for professional decision making.

5. Scholar-leader and advocate evaluation: Given your knowledge of counseling practice, effective best practices for PTSD (including how to measure client change regarding this phenomenon), and the population in the case study, describe an appropriate evaluation strategy for the agency. This is intended to become a performance-based learning activity that requires students to apply learning from evaluation coursework in combination with the learning from the above steps.

Case Study 2: Counselor Trainee (Section IV, Doctoral Learning
Outcomes, J.2; Section II, Professional Identity, B.2, B.4, C.5)

Your fieldwork site is a clinical mental health clinic within a work-learn program for young adults who did not earn a high school diploma at the traditional age of 18. This program gives them another chance to earn their high school diplomas while working. In addition, the program participants experience high rates of teen pregnancy, court involvement, homelessness, substance abuse, and domestic violence. Your site supervisor mentions that the retention rate for female participants is much lower than for male participants. You noticed that as well, since your caseload consists of only one female. Your site supervisor says there isn't enough time in the day to identify reasons for this issue. You have an assignment to develop a research project for one of your classes. You wonder if your program faculty will work with you on developing a project to meet this need. How would you implement this project?

1. Knowledge guiding the profession: Explore research on effective needs assessment strategies used in alternative school settings. What implications does this research have on developing a strategic plan to meet the organization's needs? How might you collaborate with your site supervisor, faculty, and fellow students?
2. Knowledge of the population served: What else do you know about the population being served at your site? Based on that knowledge, what does the research indicate are the essential experiences of your female participants? What mental health issues might they likely experience? What research methods are recommended for working with your population?
3. Critical consumer of best practices (problem and population): Research at Step 2 will lead to the exploration of participatory action research, as an example. Students may also identify the need to develop empowerment programs for the participants. In turn, research at Step 3 may lead students to review participatory action research projects in the literature.
4. Emic-etic analysis of the population and problem: This step in the activity requires students to determine whether best practice guidelines are

appropriate for the given population. Given the information from Steps 2 and 3, you can assess the following: What gaps exist in the best practice guidelines? In light of your research on the needs assessments and your female participants, how do the recommended treatments fit or not fit with this population? What other practices might be appropriate for this population, given the knowledge of their needs?

5. Scholar-leader and advocate evaluation: Given your knowledge of effective needs assessment strategies and the population in the case study, describe an appropriate plan to assist your supervisor in identifying the reasons for low retention rates of female participants. What predicted results do you think your needs assessment will yield? How might you recommend intervening to meet those needs?

The above case studies and subsequent questions walk readers through the process of progressing from practitioner and trainee to scholar-leader and advocate. The parsimonious examples could be rewritten around a variety of topics or populations in order to illustrate the same principles and guide students through the requisite learning. Different assignments (e.g., papers, small group discussions, presentations) might be used at any of the five tiers/steps in order to give feedback to students or help students synthesize their learning. The hope is that this strategy for teaching how to integrate best practice research to develop scholar-leaders and advocates in and of itself becomes something of a guideline or standard for counselor education programs.

## CONCLUSION

Determining best practices research is a complex process whereby professional counselors and those who prepare them are faced with a number of important considerations. In this chapter we presented a rationale for attending to a more comprehensive notion of best practices, using criteria such as client utility, counselor competency, and client characteristics that apply to a variety of delivery contexts. Infusing best practices research in advocacy and leadership efforts involves three main areas: extending existing knowledge relevant to the counseling profession, identifying best practices, and disseminating current knowledge to shape counselor preparation and practice.

We discussed various professional organizations' positions on the role of outcome research in counseling and highlighted available studies and resources. Additionally, we provided key terms associated with best practices research. We concluded the chapter by describing three ways to address the integration of best practice research in training programs—developing an organizational culture, integrating activities throughout the curriculum, and using the five-tiered model.

## DISCUSSION QUESTIONS

1. How do advocacy, leadership, and research connect to inform ethical and professional imperatives of the counseling profession?
2. Using the components of the establishing best practices model, describe how advocacy and leadership relate to best practice and vice versa.
3. What is the difference between best practices in counseling and best practices in research?
4. Apply the five-tiered model to a CACREP standard.
5. Identify three strategies for increasing your knowledge of research regarding best practices.

# IV

## *FUTURE DIRECTIONS FOR COUNSELING LEADERSHIP AND ADVOCACY*

# 14

# *Leadership Training*
## Entry-Level and Doctoral Curricula

Casey A. Barrio Minton and
Carrie A. Wachter Morris

## INTRODUCTION

In previous chapters, authors discussed key elements of leadership theory, practice, and research and provided recommendations for enhancing professional counselors' leadership development in a variety of settings and situations. As Sweeney illustrated so poignantly in Chapter 1, leadership has been critical to the development of the counseling profession. In Chapter 2, Lewis summarized how key theoretical, philosophical, and research foundations of leadership as a concept connect with the specific orientations and skill sets of professional counselors. Next, Myers provided specific discussion and illustration of Chi Sigma Iota's (CSI) Principles and Practices of Research Excellence (2009). Part I of this text concluded as the editors reflected on their varied leadership journeys and urged readers to do the same.

Throughout Part III, leaders discussed specific leadership and advocacy roles for professional counselors. In particular, Cashwell and Barrio Minton (Chapter 10) discussed key elements for counselor education program administration and mentoring, focusing particularly on how CACREP standards highlight faculty involvement in leadership and help advocate for the profession. Other chapters included more specialized attention to professional counselors' leadership and advocacy roles in supervision (Chapter 11), practice (Chapter 12), and research (Chapter 13).

Across chapters, authors came to very similar conclusions: It is both possible and critical to develop leaders for the counseling profession. To demonstrate ways to develop leadership, most authors provided several applications and recommendations for leadership exploration, including activities appropriate to counselor education settings. In this chapter, we build upon these foundations by illustrating opportunities for integrating leadership into formal entry-level and doctoral counselor education curricula. First, we prioritize leadership knowledge and skills from the literature that we believe are most essential to entry-level counselors. Then, we explore opportunities to integrate attention to leadership in each of the core curricular areas of the Council for Accreditation of Counseling and Related Educational Programs (CACREP) 2009 standards. Next, we discuss leadership knowledge and skills essential to doctoral-level counselor educators and supervisors and provide recommendations for attention within each of the five CACREP doctoral-level knowledge and skills domains. Finally, we end with a discussion of next steps for evaluating student learning outcomes related to leadership competencies and, in turn, developing an evidence base for professional counseling leadership training methods.

Definition of Key Terms and Concepts

**Leadership curricula:** Formal classroom activities, experiences, and assignments designed with the intention of augmenting students' leadership knowledge, skills, and practices.

**Student learning outcome** (SLO): "A stated expectation of what someone will have learned" (Driscoll & Wood, 2007, p. 5). SLOs answer the question: "What do our students need to be able to DO 'out there' (in the rest of life) that we are responsible for in this classroom?" (Stiehl & Lewchuk, 2008, p. 6).

## ENTRY-LEVEL PROFESSIONAL COUNSELING PREPARATION

When developing leadership curricula for entry-level programs, we recommend counselor education faculties come together to assess current programmatic foci, priorities, and opportunities related to leadership. As Cashwell and Barrio Minton argued in Chapter 10, formal and informal mentoring and modeling are key factors in helping students internalize the central role of leadership and advocacy in their daily activities. Key questions for faculty consideration may include: (1) In what ways are program faculty members and students involved in local, state, and national leadership? (2) How are we modeling leadership to students? (3) How we are supporting students' engagement in leadership? (4) How do we address and assess leadership knowledge and skills in our formal and informal curricula? (5) What leadership knowledge and skills do employers expect from our candidates? (6) What are the pressing professional or client advocacy opportunities in our area, and in what ways might we use a grounding in these issues to inform leadership opportunities? Although specific to school counseling, counselor educators who are interested in a more sustained exploration process may consult House and Sears (2002) for an extensive listing of questions for exploring opportunities for leadership and advocacy in curricula. After developing an understanding of current program priorities, strengths, and needs related to leadership, counselor educators will be in better positions to articulate specific student learning outcomes (SLOs) related to leadership.

## CACREP SLOs Related to Leadership

Most master's-level students are preparing for careers in which they will spend the majority of their time in direct service to clients/students, and learning outcomes at this level must be focused on helping candidates develop leadership knowledge and skills that will help them be more effective in their daily practice. In particular, students may need assistance disputing myths about leadership in general and understanding the many facets and methods of leadership. Because Dixon and Dew discussed professional counselors' roles for leadership and advocacy in Chapter 12, we will focus our attention on direct and indirect mentions of leadership in the SLO sections of the CACREP 2009 standards.

All CACREP (2009) program areas include SLOs that require candidates to understand history, philosophy, and trends; roles, functions, settings, and relationships with other professionals; and professional organizations, competencies, preparation standards, and state credentials. Most program areas also include SLOs regarding understanding professional issues and public policies relevant to their settings. Because leadership is critical to the development of our profession and serves as an essential role of the professional counselor, such standards imply attention to leadership even if they do not use the word *leadership* specifically. Certainly, an understanding of the professional issues and methods for interacting with other professionals is critical to the *what*'s and *how*'s of leadership.

### Educational Settings

To date, most literature regarding professional counseling leadership has focused on professional counselors who work in educational settings. Indeed, both the American School Counselor Association (ASCA) National Model for School Counseling Programs (2005) and the National Center for Transforming School Counseling (http://www.edtrust.org/dc/tsc/vision) describe school counselors as leaders of the educational team and advocates for systemic change. In turn, a number of counseling scholars have explored leadership roles and experiences of professional school counselors (e.g., Briggs, Slaton, & Gilligan, 2009; Dollarhide, Gibson, & Saginak, 2008; Janson, Stone, & Clark 2009; Mason & McMahon, 2009; McMahon, Mason, & Paisley, 2009). Thus, it is not surprising that the CACREP 2009 standards include several direct mentions of leadership-related SLOs for professional counselors who work in educational settings. The school counseling (SC) leadership SLOs are as follows:

- Knows the qualities, principles, skills, and styles of effective leadership (O.1)
- Knows strategies of leadership designed to enhance the learning environment of schools (O.2)
- Knows how to design, implement, manage, and evaluate a comprehensive school counseling program (O.3)
- Understands the important role of the school counselor as a system change agent (O.4)
- Understands the school counselor's role in student assistance programs, school leadership, curriculum, and advisory meetings (O.5)
- Participates in the design, implementation, management, and evaluation of a comprehensive developmental school counseling program (P.1)
- Plans and presents school counseling-related educational programs for use with parents and teachers (e.g., parent education programs, materials used in classroom guidance and advisor/advisee programs for teachers) (P.2)

Although not expressly mentioned elsewhere in the SC SLOs, other SLOs require that school counselors use leadership skills to build collaborative teams, engage others in school counseling programming, and utilize literature and data to "design, implement, manage, and evaluate" (SC C.4) various programs. Together, these standards illustrate the importance of leadership competency for school counselors who serve as educational leaders in their schools. Albeit critical, we cannot let this focus eclipse the importance of school counselors as leaders in their communities and within professional counseling associations.

Similarly, the Student Affairs and College Counseling (SACC) SLOs include three direct mentions of leadership:

- Understands organizational, management, and leadership theory and practice (A.8)
- Understands strategies and leadership required for services encompassed by college student development in postsecondary education, such as admissions, financial aid, academic advising, judicial services, recreational sports, disability services, international student affairs, and health services (A.9)
- Demonstrates an understanding of leadership, organization, and management practices that help institutions accomplish their missions (B.5)

*Community Settings*

Although CACREP (2009) does not use the word *leadership* explicitly in SLOs for clinical mental health; addiction; or marriage, couple, and family counselors, leadership is implied in SLOs that require candidates to draw from professional literature to design, implement, and evaluate counseling and advocacy programs. These standards are parallel to the school counseling leadership standards regarding comprehensive developmental school counseling programs. One career counseling SLO requires that the career counselor "understands leadership theories and approaches for evaluation and feedback, organizational change, decision making, and conflict resolution" (K.3). In addition, SLOs such as "understands management of mental health services and programs, including areas such as administrative, finance, and accountability" (CMHC A.8) and "understands organizational theories, behavior, planning, communication, and management useful in implementing and administering career development programs" (CC K.1) are centered on leadership competencies.

## Formal Leadership Curricula

Because most counselor education curricula are already saturated with content and practice-related requirements in fulfillment of CACREP 2009 standards and state-specific credentialing requirements, we suspect that most master's-level programs will not have the luxury of a dedicated course in professional counseling leadership knowledge and skills. Thus, attention to leadership will need to be integrated into existing curricular and practice experiences, starting with foundations and setting-specific professional orientation courses and revisited at other points in the core curriculum. In the following sections, we highlight a number of ways in which counselor educators may attend to leadership competencies within the eight CACREP core curricular areas and professional practice experiences. For each area, we provide a targeted discussion of leadership learning objectives and then present a table in which we propose more specific leadership learning objectives and connect those to potential course readings, activities, and assignments. For additional curricular ideas, please refer to practice exercises and recommendations found throughout earlier chapters of this text.

### Professional Orientation and Ethical Practice

More than any other core curricular area, professional orientation and ethical practice is ripe with opportunities for sustained attention to leadership theory, skills, and practices. As discussed previously, leadership has been fundamental to the history and philosophy of our profession (II.G.1.a) and serves as a critical professional role and function of counselors (II.G.1.b). Counselor educators may highlight opportunities and skills for leadership when addressing content related to professional organizations and issues (II.G.1.f); professional credentialing, accreditation, and public policy (II.G.1.g); and advocacy on behalf of the profession (II.G.1.h) and clients (II.G.I.i). Certainly, attention to appropriate use of power and our responsibilities as leaders belongs in the discussion of counseling ethics (II.G.I.j). Taken together, these foundations will provide a context and grounding for the *why*'s, *what*'s, and *how*'s of leadership (see Table 14.1).

**Table 14.1**    Professional Orientation and Ethical Practice and SLOs

| Leadership Learning Objective | Course Readings, Assignments, or Activities |
|---|---|
| Identify characteristics and accomplishments of historical and emerging leaders in the profession (II.G.1.a, II.G.1.b; AC A.1; CC A.1; CMHC A.1; MCFC A.1; SC A.1; SACC A.1) | • Chapter 1<br>• West, Osborn, and Bubenzer (2003b)<br>• Magnuson, Wilcoxon, and Norem (2003)<br>• Interview or create a profile of a professional counseling leader<br>• Create a panel presentation in which professional counseling leaders discuss their leadership experiences and development |
| Identify current strengths, weaknesses, opportunities, and threats to our profession (II.G.1.g, II.G.1.h; AC A.1, C.7, E.3, E.4; CC A.1; CMHC A.1, A.7, C.9, E.6; MCFC A.1, C.4, E.5; SC A.1, E.2; SACC A.1, B.4) | • Construct an executive summary of a current issue in one's setting with concrete attention to leadership needs and opportunities |
| Understand fundamental elements of leadership theory and philosophy, skills, and development (CC K.1, K.3; SC O, P; SACC A.8, A.9, B.5) | • Chapters 2–4<br>• West, Bubenzer, Osborn, Paez, and Desmond (2006)<br>• Attend CSI day at ACA convention |
| Identify opportunities for involvement in professional counseling and interdisciplinary organizations related to one's setting (II.G.1.b, II.G.1.f; AC A.4, E.4; CC A.4; CMHC A.4, E.4; MCFC A.4, E.5; SC A.4; SACC A.5) | • Luke and Goodrich (2010)<br>• Create a profile regarding key philosophies, needs, leadership structure, and opportunities for student and new professional involvement within a local, state, regional, or national professional association |
| Develop skills for administrative leadership in one's setting (II.G.1.b; AC A.3, B.2; CC A.3; CMHC A.3, A.8, B.2; MCFC A.3; SC A.3, B.2, M, N, O, P; SACC A.4, A.9) | • Herr, Heitzman, and Rayman (2006)<br>• Interview administrative leaders in desired counseling setting about how they developed their leadership skills, how they implement leadership, and strengths and challenges of their approaches |
| Communicate with key interdisciplinary stakeholders and players regarding counseling in one's setting (II.G.1.b, II.G.1.g; AC A.3, E.4; CC A.3, F.3; CMHC A.3, E.4; MCFC A.3, E.5, F.3; SC A.3, B.2, F.2, F.3, M, N; SACC A.4, F.6) | • Create a panel presentation consisting of an intact interdisciplinary team from settings specific to student interests<br>• Have students interview different professionals that work in or with counselors in their setting of choice about methods for encouraging effective interdisciplinary communication |

*(continued)*

**Table 14.1 (continued)**    Professional Orientation and Ethical Practice and SLOs

| Leadership Learning Objective | Course Readings, Assignments, or Activities |
|---|---|
| Understand the role of leadership in the professional requirements of counselors in one's setting (II.G.1.b; AC A.3; CC A.3; CMHC A.3, A.8; MCFC A.3; SC A.3, O, P; SACC A.4, A.9, B.5) | • Dollarhide et al. (2008)<br>• Janson et al. (2009)<br>• Mason and McMahon (2009)<br>• Interview professional counselors in anticipated counseling setting regarding their work functions and roles; require students to attend to leadership and involvement in professional organizations explicitly<br>• Construct a critical analysis of the role of school counselor as leader throughout the ASCA (2010a) position statements |
| Provide a leadership role within committees and task groups (II.G.1.b, II.G.1.f; SACC A.9) | • Parr, Jones, and Bradley (2005)<br>• Provide opportunities in class to take leadership responsibilities (e.g., lead a class discussion of a reading assignment; select a group advocacy activity) |
| Understand role of leadership in one's professional development (II.G.1.b; AC A.3; CC A.3; CMHC A.3; MCFC A.3; SC A.3, O, P; SACC A.4) | • Write an autobiography regarding the role of leadership in one's own career development and aspirations. Conclude with a discussion regarding leadership as part of a professional development plan |

*Social and Cultural Diversity*

CACREP (2009) standards regarding social and cultural diversity require that students have sufficient grounding in multicultural and pluralistic trends (II.G.2.a), cultural experiences (II.G.2.b), multicultural and social justice theories (II.G.2.c), strategies for working with diverse populations (II.G.2.d), and counselors' roles in facilitating others' cultural competence (II.G.2.e) and eliminating oppression and discrimination (II.G.2.f). These standards are intricately connected to counselors' advocacy and social roles as discussed throughout Parts II and III of this text. Lewis, Arnold, House, and Toporek (2002) highlighted this connection in the ACA advocacy competencies when they stated, "Change is a process that requires vision, persistence, leadership, collaboration, systems analysis, and strong data. In many situations, a counselor is the right person to take leadership" (p. 2). They go on to discuss how counselors can "awaken the general public to macro-systemic issues regarding human dignity" (p. 3). Although written with a focus on counseling practice, students need to understand how the multicultural counseling competencies (Arredondo, Toporek, Brown, Jones, Locke, Sanchez & Stadler, 1996) can make them more effective professional counselors *and* leaders. Leadership curricula within the social and cultural diversity area may include attention to two broad areas: (1) understanding cultural elements within leadership styles and development, and (2) engaging in local and organizational leadership regarding social justice issues (see Table 14.2).

**Table 14.2**    Social and Cultural Diversity and SLOs

| Leadership Learning Objective | Course Readings, Assignments, or Activities |
| --- | --- |
| Understand methods for developing a culturally responsive leadership style (II.G.2.d; AC F.3; CC K.3; CMHC F.3; MCFC F.4; SC E.3; O.1; SACC A.8, B.5) | • Explore ways in which media figures demonstrate culturally linked leadership styles; ask students to compare and contrast with their own leadership preferences and styles |
| Understand how definitions, understandings, and reactions to leaders and leadership are shaped by cultural beliefs, values, and experiences (II.G.2.b) | • Portman and Garrett (2005)<br>• Black and Magnuson (2005)<br>• Create a panel presentation in which professional counseling leaders discuss cultural elements of their leadership journeys<br>• If requiring interviews with culturally diverse individuals, require attention to definitions and experiences with leadership<br>• In cultural exploration papers, require inclusion of a subsection regarding cultural elements of students' leadership development |
| Understand how privilege, prejudice, discrimination, and oppression influence how one's voice is heard, acknowledged, valued, and accepted (II.G.2.f; CC E.2; CMHC E.2; MCFC E.4; SC E.2; SACC E.6) | • View and discuss *Color of Fear* (Lee, 1995)<br>• Facilitate an experiential exercise in which students identify and challenge automatic tapes regarding leadership style and abilities |
| Lead others in exploring opportunities for multicultural or social justice programming within one's work setting (II.G.2.d, II.G.2.e, II.G.2.f; AC F.2, F.3; CC E.2, E.3, F.2; CMHC E.2, E.5, F.2; MCFC E.4, F.3; SC E, F, O, P; SACC F) | • Identify a social justice-related need for leadership in one's anticipated work setting and create a plan for facilitating change |

## Human Growth and Development

The human growth and development standards focus on "understanding the nature and needs of persons at all developmental levels and in multicultural contexts" (CACREP, 2009, p. 10). Although these standards do not address leadership explicitly, effective leaders understand human development (II.G.3.a) and customize their style and approach to the needs of their constituents (II.G.3.e) (See Table 14.3).

## Career Development

Because we addressed professional counselor career development issues in the professional orientation section, this section is specific to the ways counselor educators can help professional counselors develop leadership skills to promote

**Table 14.3**  Human Growth and Development and SLOs

| Leadership Learning Objective | Course Readings, Assignments, or Activities |
| --- | --- |
| Understand how leadership style, skills, and focus change as individuals develop (II.G.3.a) | • Girl Scouts of America (2008)<br>• Read Chapter 4 or selections from West et al. (2003b) and discuss how accounts of leadership development incorporate attention to other developmental life themes and roles<br>• Construct a lifeline with attention to one's own leadership roles, perceptions, and activities throughout key developmental periods |

optimal career development for clients/students. In particular, CACREP 2009 standards require that programs include attention to a broad range of career counseling knowledge, including attention to career counseling processes, techniques, and resources (II.G.4.g). Because leadership is essential to many individuals' success in the workplace, counseling students may benefit from curricular coverage of organizational leadership initiatives and priorities. Like the CACREP SLOs for career counseling, the National Career Development Association multicultural career counseling and development (2009) competencies include attention to the importance of career counseling program promotion, management, and implementation. Certainly, it appears as if attention to leadership skills for career counseling programs is an essential part of the curriculum (see Table 14.4).

*Helping Relationships*

The human relationships standards include attention to a number of areas critical for leadership competency. Just as professional counselors must understand how their characteristics and behaviors influence the helping process (II.G.5.b), leaders should understand how their characteristics and behaviors influence their effectiveness. As Lewis discussed in Chapter 2, essential counseling skills (II.G.5.c) are fundamental to effective leadership skills. Further, Myers (Chapter 3) illustrated how systemic perspectives (II.G.5.e) are critical to effective leadership. Finally, standards require an overview of consultation methods (II.G.5.f); by definition, consultants are leaders. Although few counselor education programs will wish to replace attention to in-session helping relationships with essential skills for leadership, educators can work with students to help them understand how this skill set is nearly identical to that needed for effective leadership (see Table 14.5).

*Group Work*

The core curricular standards for group work (CACREP, 2009) are the only core curricular standards in which leadership is mentioned directly. Whether attending to group dynamics, stages, processes, and roles (II.G.6.a), leadership styles

**Table 14.4**    Career Development and SLOs

| Leadership Learning Objective | Course Readings, Assignments, or Activities |
|---|---|
| Understand leadership styles and skills needed for work in a variety of settings (II.G.4.b, CC D.4) | • Create an interdisciplinary employer advisory panel in which a variety of employers discuss leadership needs for work within their discipline<br>• Attend a university-sponsored career fair; ask employers regarding leadership expectations of candidates |
| Develop and implement culturally responsive career development programs (II.G.4.c, II.G.4.g; CC F; SC C.4; SACC D.1, D.2) | • Plan a guidance unit, small group curriculum, or other program appropriate for anticipated counseling setting, including attention to culturally appropriate assessment instruments or interest inventories<br>• Partner with a field experience site or other relevant group (e.g., freshman experience on campus, residence hall, boys and girls club, etc.) and deliver and evaluate a career development program tailored specifically to the needs of that group |
| Develop and implement leadership development programs (II.G.4.c, II.G.4.g; CC D.4; SC C.2; SACC D.2) | • Plan a leadership development activity for your population of interest, giving particular attention to helping develop leadership skills and contact with role models<br>• Partner with a field experience site or other relevant group (e.g., freshman experience on campus, residence hall, boys and girls club, etc.) and deliver and evaluate a leadership development program tailored specifically to the needs of that group |

and approaches (II.G.6.b), theories (II.G.6.c), methods (II.G.6.d), or students' direct experiences in growth groups (II.G.6.e), leadership is inherent throughout the standards. By definition, group workers are leaders, and organizations are groups. Thus, students in group courses may benefit by understanding how they can apply skills

**Table 14.5**    Helping Relationships and SLOs

| Leadership Learning Objective | Course Readings, Assignments, or Activities |
|---|---|
| Understand relationship between essential counseling, consulting, and leadership skills (II.G.5.c, II.G.5.f) | • Identify counseling and consulting skills that may support and hinder effective leadership<br>• Observe a professional meeting (staffing, business meeting at conference, faculty meeting, CSI chapter meeting) and attend to the ways in which effective leaders use essential counseling and consulting skills |
| Understand parallels between characteristics of effective helpers and characteristics of good leaders (II.G.5.b) | • Assign readings regarding leadership characteristics<br>• Reflect upon characteristics of helpers and leaders in one's own life |

**Table 14.6**   Group Work and SLOs

| Leadership Learning Objective | Course Readings, Assignments, or Activities |
|---|---|
| Apply group counseling concepts and skills to leadership or organizations and professional counseling associations (II.G.6) | • Observe business meetings at professional conferences, programs, agencies, or schools; connect leader/member skills and processes with group counseling content<br>• Identify one's group leadership style and areas for development<br>• Require students to participate in a task group as part of group counseling course requirements; require analysis of leadership role and contributions of each member |
| Recognize group roles and power in action within organizations and professional counseling associations (II.G.6.a) | • Observe business meetings with attention to group dynamics. Ask: Who's listening? Who has power? How are decisions made? |

beyond the traditional counseling group to effectiveness as leaders within schools, agencies, and professional counseling associations (see Table 14.6).

*Assessment*

Although CACREP (2009) standards related to assessment are focused on technical assessment aspects such as standardized and nonstandardized testing (II.G.7.b), statistical concepts (II.G.7.c), reliability (II.G.7.d), and validity (II.G.7.e), they also provide an opportunity for identifying instruments related to leadership style and understanding how one might utilize them to maximize organizational functioning (see Table 14.7).

*Research and Program Evaluation*

The CACREP (2009) standards related to research and program evaluation are critical for effective leadership. In particular, effective leaders must be able to understand the importance of research (II.G.8.a) for evidence-based practice

**Table 14.7**   Assessment and SLOs

| Leadership Learning Objective | Course Readings, Assignments, or Activities |
|---|---|
| Understand instruments and assessment methods related to leadership style (AC G.1; CC G.1, H2; CMHC G.2; MCFC G.1; SC G.1, H.1, H2; SACC H.1) | • Complete MBTI, NEO, or related instrument and discuss connections between results and one's leadership style<br>• Complete a test review of an instrument related to leadership (e.g., Kouzes & Posner's (2007) *Leadership Practices Inventory*)<br>• When discussing semistructured qualitative assessments (e.g., lifelines, genograms, or ecomaps), ask students to focus on leadership applications |

(II.G.8.e) and utilize research methods (II.G.8.b) and statistical methods (II.G.8.c) to inform needs assessment, program evaluation, and modification processes (II.G.8.d). Certainly SLOs discussed earlier regarding counselors in educational and community settings highlight this critical role in program leadership. As discussed in Chapter 13, such knowledge will ensure that future leaders can communicate with key administrators and stakeholders to secure funds, advocate for the profession and programs, and utilize a data-driven process to guide assessment and decision-making processes regarding organizational and program effectiveness (see Table 14.8).

Professional Practice

As a capstone experience, students in CACREP-accredited counselor education programs must complete at least 700 hours of practicum and internship activities (CACREP, 2009). By definition, the counseling internship must include

**Table 14.8** Research and Program Evaluation and SLOs

| Leadership Learning Objective | Course Readings, Assignments, or Activities |
| --- | --- |
| Utilize professional literature to guide decision making about counseling programs and services (II.G.8.a, II.G.8.e; AC I.1, J.1; CC I.1, J.1) | • Develop a white paper or proposal regarding how to augment or improve counseling programs or services based on a review of relevant literature |
| Conduct a needs assessment regarding organizational members to guide priorities and decision making (II.G.8.d, SC G.3, SACC F.2) | • View CSI's reports regarding the 2008 member survey and data; identify ways in which the leadership team utilized data from members to guide organizational initiatives<br>• Conduct a needs assessment of organizational members and report data trends |
| Develop and evaluate programs for empowering client populations toward leadership (II.G.8.d; CC F.1, I.1, I.3, I.4; CMHC C.3, I.2, I.3; MCFC I.2, J.3; SC C.2, D.2, I.2, I.4, J.3, K.3, P.1; SACC D.6, I.2, I.3) | • Briggs, Slaton, and Gilligan (2009)<br>• Develop a formative and summative evaluation plan for a proposed leadership development program |
| Understand role of counselors as leaders in program development, implementation, management, and evaluation (II.G.1.b, II.G.8.d; AC A.3; CC A.3; CMHC A.3, A.8; MCFC A.3; SC A.3, O, P; SACC A.4, A.9, B.5) | • If requiring a program development proposal as a part of course requirement, require attention to leadership roles and skills needed for successful implementation |
| Communicate to key stakeholders regarding program needs and plans (II.G.1.b, II.G.1.g; AC A.3, E.4; CC A.3, F.3; CMHC A.3, E.4; MCFC A.3, E.5, F.3; SC A.3, B.2, F.2, F.3, M, N; SACC A.4, F.6) | • Require students to "pitch" a program proposal to a hypothetical board or other decision-making entity |

**Table 14.9**  Professional Practice and SLOs

| Leadership Learning Objective | Course Readings, Assignments, or Activities |
|---|---|
| Discuss leadership dynamics and roles at play within one's practicum or internship site (II.G.1.b; AC A.3; CC A.3; CMHC A.3, A.8; MCFC A.3; SC A.3, O, P; SACC A.4, A.9, B.5) | • Provide a site presentation in which the student attends to a variety of aspects of counseling practice within the site; require specialized attention to organizational structure and analysis, including leadership style, strategies, and roles of counselors and administrators |
| Demonstrate professional leadership skills within practicum and internship activities (see above) | • Ensure that practicum and internship rating forms include explicit attention to assess SLOs related to leadership practice within one's counseling setting<br>• Require students to submit a reflection and recording or other evidence of engagement in a leadership at the internship site (e.g., leadership workshop, leading a meeting, conducting a needs assessment, proposing a modification of practices) |

"opportunities for the student to become familiar with a variety of professional activities and resources" (III.G.4). Because leadership is an essential component of professional counselors' roles, the counseling internship should include opportunities for candidates to observe leadership and engage in leadership activities. Such a continuous link may help counselors understand how what they learned about in their coursework applies to counseling practice in a very real way (see Table 14.9).

## DOCTORAL-LEVEL COUNSELOR EDUCATION AND SUPERVISION PREPARATION

We opened our section on master's-level curricula by discussing the importance of exploration by program faculty and agreement regarding the role and place of leadership in the formal curricula. Because future doctoral-level counselor educators and supervisors will provide leadership and preparation for our profession, an expanded conversation is essential for all doctoral programs. Only after agreeing upon programmatic priorities, foci, and needs can counselor educators construct meaningful doctoral-level curricula.

### CACREP SLOs Related to Leadership

In addition to requiring that professional leadership roles be reflected in doctoral program objectives (II.A), CACREP (2009) identifies "preparing students to assume positions of leadership in the profession and/or their area(s) of specialization" as a primary obligation of accredited doctoral programs (I.C.4). Further, programs must consider candidates' potential for professional leadership and advocacy in admissions decisions (I.D.5). In the most recent standards revision, CACREP identified five primary SLO areas: supervision, teaching, research and scholarship, counseling, and leadership and advocacy. In addition to having the knowledge and skills of master's-level professional counselors discussed previously, doctoral-level candidates must demonstrate competency in the following SLOs expressly dedicated to leadership:

- Understands theories and skills of leadership (I.1)
- Understands models, leadership roles, and strategies for responding to community, national, and international crises and disasters (I.4)
- Understands current topical and political issues in counseling and how those issues affect the daily work of counselors and the counseling profession (I.5)
- Demonstrates the ability to provide leadership or contribute to leadership efforts in professional organizations or counseling program (J.1)

Given the primary emphasis on leadership within the doctoral standards, some doctoral programs may develop a course or seminar specific to leadership and advocacy. In the absence of existing literature regarding doctoral-level leadership curricula, we propose a CACREP-compliant syllabus with recommendations for a leadership course. Alternatively, the proposed curriculum may be adapted as part of a major unit within a doctoral-level professional issues course. In the remainder of this section, we highlight opportunities for attending to leadership within each of the remaining CACREP areas: supervision, teaching, research and scholarship, and counseling. For discussion regarding leadership within the informal counselor education curriculum, consult Cashwell and Barrio Minton (Chapter 10).

### Leadership Course Syllabus

Whether serving as a stand-alone seminar or integrated unit, counselor educators will likely attend to four primary content areas within a formal leadership course: theories and skills of leadership; leadership roles of professional counselors, counselor educators, and supervisors; current leadership context and priorities; and methods for facilitating others' leadership development. Table 14.10 includes a summary of SLOs related to each of the four proposed content areas; when appropriate, we cite related doctoral-level CACREP SLOs at the end of the item.

### *Methods of Instruction*

Although some counseling courses lend themselves more to lecture, and some counselor educators may rely upon lecture from time to time, for the purposes of leadership skills training, we believe doctoral students may learn best from interactive seminar discussion in which they are called upon to provide critical reflection of course-related readings and take leadership of elements of course discussion and exploration. In particular, students may benefit from participating in

**Table 14.10**   Leadership and SLOs

| Content Area | Knowledge and Skills Outcomes (SLOs) |
|---|---|
| A. Theories and skills of leadership | 1. Understands theories and skills of leadership (I.1)<br>2. Demonstrates the ability to provide leadership or contribute to leadership efforts in professional organizations and counseling programs (J.1) |
| B. Leadership roles of professional counselors, counselor educators, and supervisors | 1. Understands the interrelationships among leadership and advocacy for clients and for the profession<br>2. Understands role of leadership in development of the counseling profession<br>3. Understands roles and functions of professional counselors for influencing public policy and credentialing on state and national levels<br>4. Understands roles and functions of professional counselors as leaders in educational and community counseling settings<br>5. Understand roles and functions of professional counselors as leaders of scholarly and professional counseling organizations<br>6. Understands models, leadership roles, and strategies for responding to community, national, and international crises and disasters (I.4)<br>7. Understands the major roles, responsibilities, and activities of counselor educators (C.1) with regards to providing leadership for the profession |
| C. Current leadership context and priorities | 1. Understands current topical and political issues in counseling and how those issues affect the daily work of counselors and the counseling profession (I.5) |
| D. Methods for facilitating leadership development of student counselors, professional counselors, and students/clients | 1. Understands characteristics, qualities, and development of professional counseling leaders<br>2. Understands entry-level SLOs related to leadership<br>3. Demonstrates course design, delivery, and evaluation methods appropriate to course objectives (D.2) related to leadership<br>4. Demonstrates the ability to assess the needs of counselors in training and develop techniques to help students develop into competent counselors (D.3) and leaders |

panel presentations or interviews with professional counselors who have served as leaders in programs, local communities, and state and national professional counseling associations. These structured learning experiences provide an opportunity for students to see leadership theory and skills in action, and understand the ways in which the lived experience of leadership is related to professional identity. Further, they can help students identify with leaders, understanding how even the most influential leaders started as students and went through their own leadership development process. Finally, we believe applied service learning and engagement activities are critical for helping students move from understanding literature to taking leadership action. Service learning is a type of experiential education "in which students engage in activities that address human and community needs together with structured opportunities intentionally designed to promote student learning and development" (Jacoby, 1996, p. 5). For example, instructors may team with local agencies, residence halls, student organizations, local K–12 schools, or CSI chapters to form relationships that are mutually beneficial—providing leadership skill training to organizations while helping doctoral students address developmental needs and organizational concerns of the partnering organization. Examples of engagement activities that might be useful, but not as structured and reciprocal as a service learning component, might include facilitation of others' engagement in legislative activity or advocacy (e.g., organization of support for a bill that would benefit counselors, mental health, or education) or contribution to a local, state, or national professional counseling association. These provide students an opportunity to learn about leadership, practice leadership skills, and contribute to the leadership development of others at the same time.

### Required Texts and Readings

We hope counselor educators will find this text suitable as a primary text in a course regarding professional counseling leadership. Counselor educators may wish to supplement this text with readings cited previously in this chapter or book, West, Bubenzer, and Osborn's (2003b) *Leaders and Legacies: Contributions to the Profession of Counseling*, and Gibson, Dollarhide, and McCallum's (2010) qualitative study regarding nontenured assistant professors as division presidents. Finally, instructors may require students to visit or review leadership resources offered on the CSI website (www.csi-net.org), materials on the ACA public policy website (www.counseling.org/publicpolicy), or position statements on the ASCA website (www.schoolcounselor.org).

### Student Performance Evaluation Criteria and Procedures

Depending on doctoral students' grounding and foundations in leadership, instructors may wish to incorporate some of the master's-level activities and assignments discussed earlier in this chapter. Instructors may find the following five potential course assignments appropriate for facilitating and assessing the doctoral-level leadership SLOs outlined earlier in this chapter. Of course, we encourage counselor educators to adapt assignments so they are relevant to local context and program focus.

### Self as Professional Leader: Reflection and Development Plan

In this reflective paper, students submit a current curriculum vitae and a brief self as professional leader reflection and development plan. In the paper, students should include reflection upon their leadership experiences to date, their leadership styles and characteristics, and a five-year plan for growth as a professional leader. To ensure that students are able to integrate leadership theory and skills, we recommend that instructors require students to cite literature regarding theories and skills of leadership and detail concrete action steps regarding their involvement in specific professional associations and initiatives. This learning activity is designed to meet SLOs A1, A2, B7, and D1 in Table 14.1 and Table 14.4.

### Leadership in Daily Life Reflections

Just as students who engage in multicultural learning activities may report seeing culture wherever they look, students who are learning about leadership should begin to see leadership skills and practices in their daily lives. This assignment is designed for sensitive students to leadership by asking them to "tune in" and find leadership in their daily lives. Whether requiring students to observe official leadership activities (e.g., conference activities, legislative discussions, agency staffing meetings) or find leadership in everyday moments (e.g., family outing, class project), this assignment will help to assist students to identify and name leadership in a variety of settings. Instructors may ask students to submit daily, weekly, or monthly journals in which they share how they observed or connected with leadership in daily life; as an alternative, instructors may simply ask students to share their observations at the beginning of each class period by asking, "How did you see or do leadership this week?" Instructors who wish to ensure students are able to connect observations with leadership literature may require a formal summary in which students connect observations with assigned course readings. Depending on how the observations are structured, this learning activity may meet SLOs A1, B1–7, and D1.

### Leadership Issues Analysis

In this primarily academic assignment, students conduct a critical analysis of a professional counseling issue (e.g., counselor-first identity, counselors' roles in responding to and preventing bullying, licensure or certification requirements) of their choice. In particular, students provide an overview regarding the impact on professional counselors and clients/students, professional leadership and activities related to the identified issue, and recommendations for leadership and advocacy. The analysis should demonstrate an understanding of the ways in which leadership is connected to, but distinct from, advocacy. Counselor educators may encourage students to select an issue from ACA's legislative agenda (www.counseling.org) or CSI's advocacy themes (www.csi-net.org).

### Service Learning Engagement

Because we believe leadership training must be applied to be effective, we recommend that instructors require students to engage in a number of hours of a leadership activity throughout the semester. We conceptualize leadership activity as consultation related to leadership (e.g., with a CSI chapter, local school, or agency), participation in professional organizations, or engagement in legislative leadership or activity (e.g., mobilizing others to advocate). Instructors may identify an engagement in which the entire class may collaborate (e.g., developing a leadership development curriculum for use with counselors across the state) or allow students to identify their own engagements for the semester. In final reports of their engagements, students may provide evidence of the activity, discuss learning regarding their leadership styles and skills, and make connections between literature, course discussions, and leadership practice. Depending on focus, this assignment is designed to facilitate and evaluate SLOs A1, A2, B1–7, and D1.

*Leadership Development Activity*

Doctoral-level counselor educators and supervisors are responsible for facilitating others' leadership development; the purpose of this assignment is to help candidates use their understanding of leadership to inform leadership development activities. Whether creating and demonstrating a one-hour leadership training module or proposing a small group curriculum for use in master's-level counseling settings, schools, or agencies, this assignment requires application and synthesis of leadership skills. To ensure grounding with the evidence base for leadership, we recommend that instructors require narrative rationale, connections with master's-level leadership SLOs, and support for method and focus. This assignment is designed to facilitate and evaluate SLOs A1, A2, and D1–4.

Other Formal Leadership Curricula

Although we hope that doctoral-level counselor education programs find ways to offer a course or major unit regarding leadership, we are aware that many programs will chose to integrate attention to leadership throughout the curricula. In this section, we summarize opportunities for formal leadership curricula in the remaining four CACREP SLO areas: supervision, teaching, research and scholarship, and counseling.

*Supervision*

CACREP 2009 standards require that doctoral-level candidates demonstrate knowledge regarding purposes of supervision (A.1), theoretical frameworks (A.2), roles and relationships (A.3), and ethical, legal, and multicultural issues (A.4), and demonstrate both application of supervision theory and skills (B.1) and a personal style of supervision (B.2). We believe candidates must be able to conceptualize the development of supervisee skills in leadership as an essential component of their job function. In Chapter 11, Glosoff, Durham, and Whittaker discussed specific strategies for supervision at it relates to leadership and advocacy. Thus, we recommend instructors of supervision courses find ways to integrated their reading and recommendations.

## Teaching

CACREP 2009 standards require doctoral students to understand roles, responsibilities, and activities of counselor educators (C.1), instructional theory and methods (C.2), and instruction-related ethical, legal, and multicultural issues (C.3). Further, candidates must develop a teaching philosophy (D.1), engage in course design, delivery, and evaluation (D.2), and assess needs of student counselors (D.3). Cashwell and Barrio Minton addressed administrative aspects of counselor educator roles and leadership in Chapter 10. In addition, we recommend that counselor educators attend specifically to ways in which candidates can develop learning experiences for helping entry-level professional counselors maximize their leadership potential. In this case, the leadership development activity assignment discussed previously may provide a perfect opportunity. In addition, counselor educators may find ways to involve doctoral students in designing, implementing, and evaluating formal entry-level leadership curricula discussed earlier in this chapter.

## Research and Scholarship

The CACREP 2009 standards mandate understanding of quantitative (E.1) and qualitative (E.2) design and analysis, instrument design (E.3), and program evaluation (E.4). In addition, candidates must demonstrate skills in developing research questions (F.1) and designs (F.2), writing for publication (F.3), generating presentation proposals (F.4) and grant applications (F.5), and evaluating programs (F.6). As Hays and colleagues demonstrated in Chapter 13, research serves as the foundation of our profession and can play a critical role in leadership and advocacy; counselor educators may find their recommendations and activities helpful when considering opportunities to attend to leadership during research courses. Given the troubling absence of literature to support leadership development activities, counselor educators who implement formal research curricula can involve doctoral students in research designed to evaluate their effectiveness.

## Counseling

Finally, CACREP 2009 standards require that students know details regarding major counseling theories (G.1), methods for evaluating effectiveness (G.2), research base for theories (G.3), and effectiveness of crisis, disaster, and trauma models (G.4). In addition, students must demonstrate a personal theoretical orientation (H.1), apply multiple theories (H.2), and conceptualize across populations and settings (H.3). In Chapter 12, Dixon and Dew discussed opportunities to integrate leadership and advocacy into counseling practice. Certainly, counseling practice is the heart of our profession. As such, our leadership and advocacy methods are ways to ensure we are able to do our work well. Counselor educators may consult Chapter 12 for ideas regarding attention to leadership in doctoral-level counseling theory and practice courses.

## CONCLUSION

In this chapter, we discussed entry- and doctoral-level SLOs directly and indirectly related to leadership, and we provided concrete examples of opportunities to attend to leadership in formal counselor education curricula. Because we do not yet have outcome-based literature regarding leadership development or training activities, we drew from our understanding of the leadership development process, the foundations presented throughout this text, and our own experiences as professional counselors and counselor educators. As counselor educators find innovative ways to bring leadership training into the formal and informal doctoral curricula, we need to be intentional about developing and communicating an evidence base for best practices regarding leadership curricula and development within counselor education programs.

We hope individuals who develop and implement curricula will post them in common sharing venues (e.g., ACA/ACES Syllabus Clearinghouse) and present them at professional conferences. Similarly leaders of ACES or CSI may dedicate forums for posting leadership development exercises, activities, and assignments on websites or sponsor conference opportunities for discussing leadership training activities. These sharing activities may include discussion of methods for assessing and documenting CACREP (2009) SLOs related to leadership and may be used to inform more broad outcome-based research regarding the ways in which leadership training activities are associated with enhanced leadership self-efficacy, skills, short-term engagements, and long-term leadership contributions. In so doing, we can prepare a new generation of counselors and counselor educators who will lead our profession into the next stages of its development.

## DISCUSSION QUESTIONS

1. If you had to identify just three leadership learning outcomes for counselors across settings, which learning outcomes would you prioritize? Why?
2. Reflect upon the leadership development activities in which you have been involved. Which have been most meaningful and effective? As a counselor educator, how will these experiences inform your leadership development priorities?
3. Select one entry-level leadership development exercise specified above. Develop a lesson plan, including rationale, methods, resources, and learning outcome evaluation plan.
4. Imagine you are asked to present a half-day continuing education workshop regarding professional counseling leadership to a group of

professional counselors. Your host wants to ensure you include opportunities for practicing skills. What leadership approach will you take to the workshop? Why?

5. You are affiliated with a counselor education program that has recently adopted a series of leadership development activities across the curriculum. Develop a proposal for evaluating the program's effectiveness.

# 15

# *Advocacy Training*
## Curriculum for Professional and Client Advocacy

Nicole R. Hill, Laura K. Harrawood,
Linwood G. Vereen, and Elizabeth A. Doughty

## INTRODUCTION

Advocacy is fundamental to counseling and transcends specialty areas and professional settings (Eriksen, 1997; Myers & Sweeney, 2004); thus, counselor education programs need to design their curricula in ways that foster the development of emergent identities as advocates and promote the implementation of advocacy skills by students. It is imperative that emerging professional counselors, counselor educators, and supervisors gain experience and training in professional, sociopolitical, and client advocacy (Lewis, Arnold, House, & Toporek, 2002). The American Counseling Association's (ACA) advocacy competencies, as outlined by Lewis et al., have three foci: client/student advocacy, community/school advocacy, and sociopolitical advocacy. Within the field of counseling, there is strong endorsement of a fourth advocacy focal point, specifically professional advocacy (Chang, Hays, & Milliken, 2009; Myers & Sweeney, 2004; Myers, Sweeney, & White, 2002). Counselor training programs need to encompass all four areas of competence, while ensuring that emergent professional counselors and counselor educators are translating advocacy consciousness and insight into skills and actions. Counselor educators, therefore, have a responsibility to integrate advocacy-oriented experiences and assignments into the training curriculum.

Designing curriculum to incorporate advocacy-oriented training standards requires the use of transformational teaching strategies. Creating assignments that are experiential, reflective, and community grounded encourages advocacy consciousness among students as they translate knowledge into action. Bain (2004) asserted that "the best teachers...create...a natural critical learning environment in which they embed the skills and information they wish to teach in assignments . . . that will arouse curiosity, challenging students to rethink their assumptions and examine their mental modes of reality" (p. 47).

It is our belief that curricular initiatives within counselor education that integrate the knowledge and skills of advocacy require a framework of reflective, applied, and transformational learning. Given that the competencies required to be an effective advocate are both intrinsic and extrinsic, we assert that students need to have pedagogical experiences that challenge them to develop a professional identity grounded in advocacy and the skills necessary to manifest such a professional role and responsibility. Opportunities for self-reflection, experiential learning, and practical application heighten the impact of curricular practices by encouraging students to construct knowledge that translates into action. In this chapter, we overview transformational learning constructs related to advocacy to serve as a framework for integrating advocacy into master's- and doctoral-level curricula. The chapter continues with us presenting curricular activities and assignments across each of the entry-level CACREP core curricular areas, identifying potential advocacy assignments at the doctoral level, and posing reflective questions to encourage the integration of advocacy training into counseling programs.

### Definition of Terms

**Advocacy consciousness.** We define advocacy consciousness as an active and engaged recognition, awareness, proficiency, and competence related to advocacy. It requires an ongoing commitment to and exploration of knowledge and skill related to advocacy.

**Service learning.** Service learning is a type of experiential learning in which students interact with the community through structured and intentional activities to enhance student learning (Jacoby, 1996).

**Transformational learning.** Transformational learning focuses on creating change within the student that impacts the larger community context. Several factors define transformational learning, including an emphasis on reflexivity, commitment to community engagement, encouragement of dialogue, and translation of ideas and knowledge into action and application (Arman & Scherer, 2002; Barbee, Scherer, & Combs, 2003; Murray, Lampinen, & Kelley-Soderholm, 2006).

### Transformational Learning Related to Advocacy

Discourse related to pedagogy within counselor education has consistently espoused the integration of constructivist, dialogic, experiential, and reflexive teaching approaches (Arman & Scherer, 2002; Barbee et al., 2003; Dollarhide, Smith, & Lemberger, 2007; Guiffrida, 2005: Murray et al., 2006; Sexton & Griffin, 1997). Effective teachers focus on creating a learning environment in which knowledge is constructed and students are transformed by the experience (Bain, 2004).

Students learn content through dialogue and application so that they undergo qualitative changes in how they perceive the world (Bain, 2004). Contextualizing knowledge in the realities of counseling and community transforms students as they apply their learning to concrete sociopolitical issues and challenges.

Advocacy competence requires that student comprehension of professional, client, and sociopolitical issues serves as a building block for developing intervention skills. Thus, counselor education programs must generate creative teaching approaches that encourage transformational learning for students in relation to advocacy competence. Such learning requires a high level of engagement and creativity by the student (Shor & Freire, 1987). There are two factors that can facilitate transformational learning: personal experience and community connections. First, counselor educators can encourage students to make meaning of their learning through their own personal experiences (Moore, 2005; Ropers-Huilman, 2001). Not only does encouraging self-reflection coupled with self-awareness broaden students' understanding of advocacy issues, but also introspection prepares them to function beyond the classroom as professional counselors and educators. Students should critically examine their worldviews and experiences, and such critical examination is accomplished through discourse being valued in the classroom and through class assignments (Taylor, 2009). Taylor postulated three forms of critical reflection: content, process, and premise. Content reflection relates to focusing on what one thinks and feels, while process reflection involves assessing how individuals engage in perceiving. The final form, premise reflection, speaks to a consciousness of why individuals attend to elements of the world. Reflecting within oneself and dialoging with others can likely transform the field of counseling and our communities (Shor & Freire, 1987).

A second factor of transformational learning is building connections between the classroom and the community (Ropers-Huilman, 2001). Advocacy competence requires the translation of values and philosophies into interventions that shape the client/student, community, profession, and sociopolitical arena (Lewis et al., 2002). There should be an emphasis on creating change through one's advocacy training. One pedagogical approach utilized to ground students in the community is service learning (Murray et al., 2006). Service learning cultivates a sense of social responsibility, enhances knowledge through application to real-world dilemmas, and provides a forum for exploring critical reflection (Guiffrida, 2005; Snowman, McCown, & Biehler, 2009). Integrating service learning into advocacy training creates a tangible connection between classroom content and application (Barbee et al., 2003). Community-based learning opportunities can encourage critical thinking, role exploration, community collaboration, alliance building, self-awareness, and significant systems involvement (Burnett, Hamel, & Long, 2004). All of the identified outcomes of service learning are among ACA's advocacy competencies (Lewis et al., 2002).

Transformational learning provides a framework for creating advocacy training initiatives at the master's and doctoral levels. Across the chapter, specific curricular assignments will be presented that highlight the facets of transformational learning as a vehicle for enhancing students' advocacy consciousness. Both entry-level and doctoral-level CACREP 2009 standards will serve as the context for exploring assignments that foster advocacy awareness, knowledge, and skill.

## ADVOCACY TRAINING ACROSS THE CACREP COMMON CURRICULAR EXPERIENCES

### Curricular Framework

Within this section, we overview each of the core areas of the Council for Accreditation of Counseling and Related Educational Programs (CACREP) 2009 standards (CACREP, 2009) and articulate how to design pedagogical experiences to enhance master's- and doctoral-level students' advocacy competence (Lewis et al., 2002). We emphasize transformational learning because it fosters the intrinsic and extrinsic elements of advocacy consciousness. We also describe potential class assignments that are contextualized in terms of the factors of transformational learning.

### Professional Orientation and Ethical Practice

Professional orientation and ethical practice are the cornerstone of professional counselor identity (Ponton & Duba, 2009). Ponton and Duba articulated that a profession develops out of an existential need of a society; a central element of a profession is the collective and individual relationship between the profession and society. To define that relationship, and subsequently engage in transformational learning, counselors ask, "Who am I?" and "Who are we called to be by the society that has created us?" (Hendricks, 2008; Ponton & Duba, 2009). To be able to answer these questions, we must articulate our origin as a profession, define our professional role and responsibilities, identify how we function within a larger system, and demonstrate our knowledge of ethical and legal concerns in relation to the counseling profession. In other words, we must be advocates on both the individual and systemic levels (Chang et al., 2009; Lewis et al., 2002; Myers et al., 2002).

#### *Key Curricular Factors*

Professional orientation and ethical practice is a CACREP (2009) entry-level core curricular area that addresses a wide range of a counselor's professional functioning. Expectations of counselor trainees include that they are aware of the history and philosophy of the counseling profession, learn how to collaborate with other human service providers, be knowledgeable about emergency response, learn self-care strategies, understand supervision models, recognize the benefits of professional association membership and credentialing, and be aware of all ethical standards and legal aspects related to the counseling profession. Specific to leadership and advocacy, CACREP's (2009) professional orientation and ethical practice guidelines explicitly instruct that counselor trainees advocate on behalf of the counseling profession. Counselor trainees should also advocate for clients by recognizing "institutional and social barriers that impede access, equity, and success for clients" (p. 90).

*Creation of Syllabus*

Master's-level counseling programs that are CACREP accredited require curricular experiences that address professional orientation and ethical practice. The objectives found in the syllabus should directly reflect the key curricular factors outlined above. Incorporating language that includes direct phrases from the CACREP standards (2009) ensures that the standard is clearly addressed within the construction of the syllabus. The following are examples of observable objectives: Students will demonstrate that they understand "professional roles, functions, and relationships with other human service providers"; students will analyze "interagency/interorganization collaboration and communications"; and students will assess the "role and process of the professional counselor advocating on behalf of the profession" (CACREP, 2009, p. 90).

*Integration of Advocacy Into Class Assignments*

To address the current core area and raise advocacy consciousness, counselor educators may assign students an experiential activity that entails interaction with a multidisciplinary team of service providers. The community crisis response drill is an assignment instructors can use in a professional orientation and ethical practice class or crisis course in order to address CACREP (2009) entry-level core standards II.G.1.b, h, and i. Many communities continually implement crisis response drills to increase the likelihood that a crisis in the community will be addressed efficiently. The goal is to decrease response time, thereby mitigating loss of life. Professionals who typically participate are first responders (e.g., police, fire, and emergency medical technicians), nurses, physicians, and other support staff who may include mental health professionals (U.S. Department of Homeland Security, 2010).

This assignment requires prior collaboration with local first responders. The instructor for the class should become familiar with community response drills and be clear as to what role counselor trainees might play. If mental health roles are limited, students can learn valuable information from playing various roles during the mock disaster. The written assignment that accompanies this experiential activity reflects the students' experiences and addresses a number of CACREP (2009) areas within professional orientation. The following questions for the assignment reflect CACREP entry-level core standards II.G.1.b, c, h, i, and j: "What professional role did you play in the emergency community response drill?" "What responsibilities did you have during the mock disaster?" "How did you see various human service providers working together?" "What institutional or social barriers did you see that might prevent victims from receiving mental health services either during or after the crisis?" "In what ways would you envision you could advocate for the profession related to community crisis response?" and "Given your experience during the mock disaster, how might counselors find themselves practicing outside the scope of their training?" The reflective component of the assignment enhances the students' integration of their experiences and increases the transformational learning of the community-based assignment (Ropers-Huilman, 2001). Focusing the reflective questions on interprofessional collaboration, advocacy strategies, and obstacles to seeking services connects the experience directly to advocacy competencies (Lewis et al., 2002).

## Social and Cultural Diversity

The continual change and evolution in the cultural composition of the United States and the world at large has required professional counselors and counselor educators not only to be aware of social and cultural issues, but also to assist counselor trainees as they navigate the myriad social and cultural issues present in the world today (Hill, 2003; Vereen, Hill, & McNeal, 2008). In light of the cultural pluralism that is evident within our global society, it has become critical that professional counselors and educators take on leadership roles in advocating for the diverse needs of their clients and provide evidence through practice, advocacy, and scholarship of how professional counselors answer this professional calling. Professionals who acquire and develop skill in leadership, advocacy, and practical application will be better able to work effectively with individuals from diverse groups and populations (Green, McCollum, & Hays, 2008).

### Key Curricular Factors

The 2009 entry-level CACREP standards require that an academic program "provide an understanding of the cultural contexts of relationships, issues, and trends in a multicultural society" (p. 90). This edict requires that educators provide students with a variety of educational experiences to allow for the development of knowledge, individual growth, and practical skill (Green et al., 2008; Hill, 2003). As an educator, it can be challenging to help students at both the master's and doctoral levels embrace a present-focused ideology of multiculturalism or social justice in a world where the definitions of both are fluid and can appear to lack concrete operationalization that is equally embraced by all (Hill, 2003). As is outlined in the CACREP entry-level 2009 standards, the curricular experience for students must include the development of strategies for working with individuals, groups, and communities. Counselor educators need to structure classroom experiences and assignments in order to increase student understanding of socio-political issues. Instructors can use this increased comprehension as a spring-board for developing advocacy competencies (Eriksen, 1997).

## Creation of Syllabus

The creation of a syllabus for a course in social and cultural foundations requires the instructor to assess the cultural climate of the surrounding community, examine the current literature, and have knowledge of how best to provide a transformative experience for the students (Vereen et al., 2008). To do so, the instructor must balance the integration of CACREP 2009 standards with a philosophical ideology that ensures counselor trainees are presented with an experience that entails multiple methods of learning. Ideally, a series of course assignments will engender a multifaceted approach to learning by challenging the students to simultaneously be consumers of the literature, to learn through service and advocacy, and to engage in a transformative experience.

## Integration of Advocacy Into Class Assignments

The integration of advocacy into classroom assignments will require a multi-faceted approach to provide an experience where students can conceptualize, contextualize, and experience advocacy as it relates to cultural foundations and social justice (Lewis & Bradley, 2000). For example, the provision of a writing assignment or exam based on required reading only assesses a miniscule portion of the learning process for students. Additionally, asking students to conceptu-alize how advocacy relates to social and cultural foundations and social justice based solely on lived life experience provides a myopic context for understanding the role of advocacy in the life of a professional counselor or counselor educator. Counselor trainees need the opportunity to translate their lived experience and awareness into tangible actions in the sociocultural context.

In response to the present entry-level CACREP 2009 core, one classroom assignment at the master's level would require students to engage in a service learning project to provide mental health screening to individuals who identified as being homeless. The provision of mental health screening would afford a ser-vice to the individual, community, and profession, thereby addressing the mul-tiple foci of advocacy competence (Chang et al., 2009; Lewis et al., 2002; Myers & Sweeney, 2004; Myers et al., 2002). In addition, such a service would directly address a number of CACREP core issues while simultaneously providing a criti-cal learning experience for counselor trainees. The service to the individuals in the community would include the identification of the need for services and an identification of the systemic and institutional constructs that are present bar-riers within the world of the client. This type of service learning project would provide the students with the opportunity to collaborate with other helping pro-fessionals in order to advocate for community services that better meet the needs of the homeless population. Through interview strategies, the students could gain a more complete personal understanding of the variables and life experiences that have left many people homeless.

Such a service learning project engenders a sense of social responsibility about a social group, people who are homeless, which is largely overlooked in society (Murray et al., 2006). It also builds a tangible connection between the ideas of social justice and oppression discussed in the classroom and the realities of individual experiences in the community (Barbee et al., 2003). Adding a written narrative can enhance critical thinking and reflection. Instructors would ask students, within their written narrative, to provide an outline of systemic and institutional barriers experienced by the individual who was homeless and also identify avenues of advocacy and resources for the client. Additionally, the written narrative would include the identification of collaborative outreach, advocacy, and counseling services that counselors could provide for the client. Finally, the written narrative would provide an outline of personal and professional growth that would include an action plan of advocacy and service that counselors could offer.

## Human Growth and Development

As counselor educators, we are called to help our students understand how individuals grow and develop across the life span. Instructors present theories of human development to students in an attempt to help counselor trainees better conceptualize the issues individuals face across life transitions (Green & Piel, 2002). As with all new concepts, experience assists in solidifying learning, and therefore, class assignments should be geared toward helping students learn first-hand about issues facing individuals at specific developmental stages of their lives (Moore, 2005). In addition, students should have the opportunity to understand what challenges face these populations and how best to advocate for more effective care and services.

### Key Curricular Factors

CACREP's (2009) third entry-level core standard, human growth and development, invites instructors to "provide an understanding of the nature and needs of persons at all developmental levels and in multicultural contexts" (p. 91). Counselor educators can address criteria for this standard in a variety of classes; however, courses focusing on counseling and developmental theories often meet such criteria. Unfortunately, as we delve into the theoretical, we so often fail to provide students with opportunities to put these ideas into action. So much can come from allowing students to actually experience the ideas in their texts. Classroom experiences and class assignments should focus on transforming the theoretical into the practical (Ropers-Huilman, 2001).

## Creation of Syllabus

The syllabus for the human growth and development entry-level curricular core area needs to include course objectives and assignments that are connected directly to the relevant standards (CACREP, 2009). Providing ways for students to reflect with themselves and others about their understanding and application of developmental theories and models is important (Shor & Freire, 1987). Applying theoretical learning to the realities of individual experience will be helpful in creating transformational learning (Moore, 2005).

## Integration of Advocacy Into Class Assignments

One potential assignment to translate the theoretical into the practical is the developmental conceptualization and advocacy interview. The assignment will be multiphased with an initial interview that is conceptualized in terms of developmental theories and then used as a springboard for identifying potential advocacy strategies. The first phase of the assignment is to interview an individual about the challenges he or she currently faces in life. Organizations that serve the public or are associated with specific age groups, such as Big Brothers/Little Sisters, American Association of Retired Persons, Meals on Wheels, or local after-school programs, can select potential interviewees. Participants must be willing to be open about personal challenges they are experiencing. Potential interview questions for the first phase of the assignment include:

1. Tell me about yourself. Who are the most important people in your life?
2. How have things changed for you as you've gotten older?
3. What do you believe have been the biggest transitions you've experienced in your life? How did you adapt to those transitions?
4. What do you see as the major challenges you are currently facing in your life?
5. As you face these current challenges, how do you see your life changing?
6. What frightens you most about life? About change?
7. Where do you find the most joy? Where do you find the most support?
8. What community services do you utilize? What community services do you wish were available to you?
9. What should someone like me know about you? How could someone like me help you the most?
10. Please tell me anything else you'd like to share about yourself or the issues you are currently encountering.

The potential interview questions are purposive in their focus on the individual developmental process (CACREP entry-level standards II.G.3.a, b, f) and the impact of the system and community on such individual experience (CACREP entry-level standards II.G.3.d, h). The objective from this phase of the assignment is to have students increase their advocacy consciousness related to how individuals and systems interact (Lewis et al., 2002).

The second phase of the developmental conceptualization and advocacy interview is to have students complete a paper that identifies a developmental theory and applies it to the interviewee. Topics to be addressed within the conceptualization paper include (1) discuss human development according to your theory, including all major theoretical underpinnings, (2) identify the strengths and criticisms of your chosen theory, (3) articulate the multicultural implications of the theory, (4) define the types of issues you would conceptualize your interviewee to be experiencing according to your selected developmental theory, and (5) describe the next developmental transitions that you would expect for your interviewee.

The third phase of the developmental conceptualization and advocacy interview is to develop an advocacy plan for the interviewee based upon the interview and knowledge of developmental theory. Within the advocacy plan, students should include a discussion of philosophical needs and provide potential solutions within the community in which they live. If the community does not currently have appropriate supports, students should theorize how they could act as change agents to help create services related to the needs of the interviewee. The development of an advocacy plan based on the interview encourages students to connect experiences to potential areas of influence in the community (Barbee et al., 2003; Lewis et al., 2002). It also facilitates the recognition that there are individual and systemic initiatives to enhance optimal development across the life span, thereby addressing CACREP 2009 entry-level core standards II.G.3.a, d, h. In addition to the identified CACREP standards 2009, the assignment can also reflect the following standards, depending on the specifics of the interviewee and theory chosen: entry-level core standards II.G.3.c, e, g.

Use of personal reflection, a factor of transformational learning, enhances student learning (Taylor, 2009). Students can respond to questions such as: (1) What were your expectations going into the interview? (2) How were these expectations met or changed as you got to know your interviewee? (3) What surprised you most about your interview? and (4) How have your perceptions changed following the interview? Students can process these amongst themselves verbally within class or complete a reflective paper.

## Career Development

Counselor trainees need only reflect on their own journey of choosing a career path to counseling to understand the impact of occupational choice on life satisfaction. A career, if it is in line with our personality type (Holland, 1985; Holland & Gottfredson, 1976; Myers, 1987) and our chosen life roles (Nevill & Super, 1986; Super, 1980), can be a significant source of personal achievement. A professional counselor's role may consist of understanding and assisting clients in understanding their career paths. Professional counselors may advocate for clients as they explore career options by supporting clients as they address their self-concepts in relation to career choice and their exploration of nontraditional gender role careers (Super, 1990).

## Key Curricular Factors

The CACREP 2009 entry-level career development core area charges counselor trainees to understand the impact of their clients' careers on various aspects of life. To be competent in the area of client career development, counselor trainees must be proficient in theory that relates to career development and decision making, labor market information and career information systems, all aspects of career development programs, the impact of work on life roles, career, and educational planning, career assessment and techniques, and all facets of the career counseling process (CACREP, 2009).

## Creation of Syllabus

Courses in career development provide counselor trainees with a framework to understand the impact of career choice on client life satisfaction. Based on the CACREP 2009 entry-level core standards for the career development core area, objectives for the course may include: (1) Students will apply "career development theories and decision-making models," (2) students will interpret "labor market information resources and career information systems," (3) students will process the relationship between work and life roles, (4) students will review all aspects of career assessment and demonstrate skill in communicating assessment results in clear oral and written language, and (5) students will analyze the role of multicultural issues on career planning (p. 92).

## Integration of Advocacy Into Class Assignments

To address the objectives outlined above, a career service learning assignment may be used as a service learning activity that requires students' participation in a local career fair (Barbee et al., 2003). Near the completion of a three-credit career theory course, students may participate in a local career fair that is sponsored by career services on their university campus. Prior to the career fair, students should spend a minimum of 10 clock hours at the campus career services familiarizing themselves with procedures and career resources. Students will attend the career fair to offer the following services: individual one-on-one career counseling with referral to the campus career center if appropriate, explanation of online career information sites, and administration and interpretation of select career assessments. This assignment addresses the CACREP (2009) career development entry-level core standards II.G.4.a, b, d, e, f, and g. It also harnesses the power of service learning by translating classroom teaching into experiential community-based learning and by increasing students' recognition of the functioning of career services within the community (Guiffrida, 2005).

### Helping Relationships

Helping relationships are a fundamental focus of counselor education preparation programs because they encompass counseling skills, process, theories, frameworks, and models (CACREP, 2009). Skill development among counselor trainees serves as the implementation component of program training as students develop the qualities and interventions that will best serve clients needing prevention, intervention, and remediation. Advocacy training is critical within this domain of counselor preparation because it encourages students to develop counseling models and skills that reflect the diverse needs of individuals, families, communities/schools, and societies (Lewis et al., 2002). Advocacy consciousness, within the context of helping relationships, enhances students' abilities to connect content to application (Ropers-Huilman, 2001).

### *Key Curricular Factors*

As a CACREP 2009 entry-level core curricular area, helping relationships identifies models, skills, and processes that are critical for counselor trainees to develop. Instructors expect that counselor trainees will endorse wellness and prevention as appropriate counseling goals and will develop a systems perspective that recognizes the familial, social, and cultural contexts of clients. Further, curricular factors include the knowledge and understanding of counseling theories, interviewing and counseling skills, and effective helper characteristics. This core curricular area also addresses consultation, crisis intervention, and suicide prevention. Opportunities to integrate advocacy training permeate the helping relationships CACREP entry-level core area. Examples of integrating advocacy training include enhancing the wellness and prevention domains of counselor preparation, emphasizing the research bases to counseling theories, and encouraging the funding and support of crisis intervention models into communities.

### *Creation of Syllabus*

Multiple classes within a master's-level program typically address the curricular emphases within the helping relationships standards (CACREP, 2009). Syllabi across classes should clearly articulate the course objectives that reflect the specific language of the CACREP standards. The course content should parallel the course objectives, so there is a high level of consistency within the syllabus. Contextualizing the CACREP standards in advocacy training opportunities will enhance the students' experiences as they develop an understanding of how to initiate change effectively at the individual, family, and community levels from multiple roles and perspectives.

*Integration of Advocacy Into Class Assignments*

One class assignment that will enhance advocacy consciousness within the CACREP 2009 entry-level core standard of helping relationships is to have students complete a prevention project. The primary objective of assigning a prevention project is to encourage students' increased understanding that prevention is a goal of counseling (CACREP, 2009, entry-level standard II.G.5.a). Additional potential outcomes include students gaining an increased systems perspective as they implement a group-based intervention (CACREP entry-level standard II.G.5.f), increasing their counseling skills as they actively engage the community (CACREP entry-level standard II.G.5.c), and enhancing counselor characteristics that are most effective (CACREP entry-level standard II.G.5.b).

The syllabus can describe the assignment details for the prevention project as follows: "Each student will propose and conduct a prevention project. Students will submit evidence of the completion of the project on or before the end of the semester. The students will assess the outcome of the project including challenges and future directions. A reflective narrative about the experience will be included in the final product. The specific product to be turned in will vary based on the type and focus of the prevention project." Combining the reflective narrative with the prevention project itself harnesses the reflexivity of transformational learning and increases the students' likelihood of developing advocacy consciousness (Taylor, 2009). The community-based nature of the prevention project increases advocacy consciousness by encouraging a realistic perspective of prevention needs in communities and translating knowledge into action (Guiffrida, 2005; Ropers-Huilman, 2001; Snowman et al., 2009).

The prevention project has two phases. The first phase is a proposal process that asks the students to articulate the following: (1) targeted population, (2) targeted issue, (3) rationale for prevention project, (4) program setting, (5) prevention strategy, (6) necessary resources, (7) potential obstacles, and (8) timeline. Including a proposal process provides an opportunity for the course instructor to provide important feedback about the feasibility of the project, potential resources that may not be known to the students, and realities of obstacles. The instructor can also monitor the types of prevention strategies that will be implemented in the community, so that they appropriately represent the profession of counseling. Students share their prevention projects in class, so they receive feedback from their peers and can benefit from the vicarious learning of hearing about others' planned projects. Reflection emerges through class discussion and instructor feedback before the students implement the project.

The second phase of the prevention project is implementation and reflection. The implementation process provides students with an opportunity to meet both educational and community objectives as they are actively applying their learning to the community setting (Jett & Delgado-Romero, 2009). The reflective narrative that is connected to the prevention project encourages critical reflection, role exploration, and self-awareness (Shor & Freire, 1987; Taylor, 2009), thereby increasing the transformational impact of this assignment. Furthermore, because the CACREP entry-level core standards 2009 for the helping relationships tend to be spread out across multiple classes, the prevention project is a flexible assignment option because it could be focused in one specific content area if preferred.

Group Work

While learning the art of group work involves many critical facets, the development of core skills serves as the springboard for allowing counselor trainees to evolve as practitioners (Association for Specialists in Group Work (ASGW), 2000; Thomas & Pender, 2008). The development of these core skills will allow for growth and the further development and incorporation of advanced interventions (Wilson & Newmeyer, 2008). Oftentimes, individuals struggle in the transition from an individual counseling orientation and find it challenging to facilitate groups effectively. Transitional challenges for counselor trainees include performing individual counseling within the group setting or a pointed focus on content at the expense of process. Inherently, the role of the counselor educator is to assist the counselor trainee in the development of skills and an understanding of the role of the group facilitator (Wilson & Newmeyer, 2008).

*Key Curricular Factors*

Key curricular factors include the integration of CACREP 2009 entry-level core standards of practice for group work, ASGW's (ASGW, 1998, 2000; Thomas & Pender, 2008) standards of practice, and ACA's advocacy competencies (Lewis et al., 2002). Counselor educators and supervisors are charged with the challenge of helping counselor trainees integrate all aspects of these standards into the professional context of their work as group leaders. Specifically, the CACREP standards ask that students have curricular experiences that are not only didactic in nature, but also allow them an opportunity for practical application of their learning. Additionally, advocacy consciousness and transformational learning requires that in- and out-of-class learning be synergistically experienced (Dollarhide et al., 2007; Ropers-Huilman, 2001).

*Creation of Syllabus*

The creation of a dynamic group syllabus that strives to evidence adherence to standards established by CACREP (2009), ASGW (2000), and ACA (Lewis et al., 2002) asks the counselor trainee to assume a greater role in his or her learning process. A challenge for the counselor educator in the development of a course syllabus is the integration of both in- and out-of-class experiences. Students can complete these experiences in a manner that enhances the educational experience while they gain an understanding that the development of advocacy conscious-ness is an active process requiring alternative ways of learning and engagement.

*Integration of Advocacy Into Class Assignments*

One potential group development and implementation assignment that would integrate advocacy into the classroom would be to have students perform a group advocacy project. Such an assignment would have students conduct a commu-nity needs assessment and, based on the evidence emergent in the assessment, propose a group work intervention that would address the critical needs of a spe-cific population. The design of this assignment explores the resources available and barriers to access within the community in which the student intended to work as a professional counselor. It requires students to focus on an underserved population, thereby fostering the knowledge and awareness dimensions of advo-cacy consciousness.

The assignment can be detailed as the following statement: Students will develop for implementation, a group proposal relevant to their current intern-ship or practicum setting. These proposals should include the following infor-mation: (1) an underserved/underrepresented clientele population and a relevant issue or cluster of issues a counseling group might address; (2) a discussion of the type, format, and duration of the group, along with a rationale for each; (3) the goals and a detailed description of the procedures to be used (e.g., structured experiences, process focus, skill development, a combination of procedures); (4) a description of the primary group process issues that are likely to be encoun-tered in the group you propose (e.g., shame, anger management, lack of inter-personal skills, self-disclosure issues); (5) a detailed description of the topics to be discussed within group, as well as any and all experiential activities that you plan to integrate into the group setting; (6) a description of the procedures for recruiting, selecting, and preparing members; (7) group evaluation procedures; and (8) ethical concerns relevant to this group and to the setting and population it will serve. Each element of the group advocacy proposal reflects the entry-level CACREP 2009 standards related to group work (specifically, standards G.6.a–d) and contextualizes such standards in terms of advocacy.

To increase students' level of knowledge and understanding, students should use a multitude of resources, such as reference articles, books, and interviews with members of the identified underserved population. Not only does the group advocacy project require community-based exploration and critical thinking about client needs, but it also provides a foundation for counselor trainees as they prepare to facilitate groups in community and school-based sites (Barbee et al., 2003; Murray et al., 2006). The proposed group can be implemented within the context of clinical experience, thereby adding the crucial skill and practice component to advocacy consciousness.

Assessment

Advocacy is a vital part of counseling and counselor educators should incorporate it throughout the curriculum (Eriksen, 1997; Lewis et al., 2002). CACREP's (2009) entry-level core assessment standard provides an avenue for students to combine hands-on assessment while advocating for underserved populations. Additionally, in keeping with the spirit of social justice, counselor educators can help students understand how various assessment tools are biased and advocate for change (Green et al., 2008).

*Key Curricular Factors*

The CACREP 2009 entry-level core curricular area of assessment charges counselor educators to "provide an understanding of individual and group approaches to assessment and evaluation in a multicultural society" (p. 93). The specific content areas include the following: history of assessment, types of testing, statistical concepts, and ethical issues. An important additional aspect of these standards includes uncovering and recognizing bias within assessments that could skew scores for marginalized groups. CACREP entry-level core standard II.G.7.f provides an opportunity to increase advocacy consciousness by creating specific learning experiences and assignments related to the sociocultural factors present in assessment.

*Creation of Syllabus*

Within the curriculum for assessment, it is critical that instructors do not relegate the sociocultural context of assessment to a one-class topical discussion. Such a myopic focus does not encourage the development of advocacy consciousness adequately. Integrating such discussions across the academic term and connecting them explicitly to assignments and critical discourse will increase the student learning process (Hill, 2003).

*Integration of Advocacy Into Class Assignments*

One potential assignment that increases advocacy consciousness while attending to the entry-level core assessment standards (CACREP, 2009) is a critical assessment analysis. Students will conduct an in-depth review of an assessment used within counseling and highlight any bias it may contain. Students may choose potential assessments from those discussed in class. Students should address three primary domains in their critical analysis of the assessment tool: statistical information, sociocultural implications, and implications for advocacy. Within the domain of statistical information, students review and evaluate the following: (1) history of the assessment, (2) description of the intent of the assessment, (3) statistical information relating to the assessment, and (4) description of how scores are used and interpreted.

The emphasis on sociocultural factors in assessment and advocacy conscious-ness emerges in the remaining two domains. Within sociocultural implications, students must review and evaluate the following: (1) social and cultural factors related to the assessment, (2) description of bias inherent within the assess-ment, and (3) discussion of how the assessment could be marginalizing to cer-tain groups. The implications for advocacy domain focuses student attention on potential areas to advocate for ethical and cultural competent use and interpreta-tion of assessment instruments. Students respond to the following questions: (1) What potential changes would you recommend to help eliminate bias? (2) How could you advocate for these or other changes to be made? (3) What other actions could you take to bring awareness to the bias within this and other assessments?

Engaging students in a critical assessment analysis attends to CACREP entry-level assessment standards while also fostering advocacy consciousness. Such an assignment harnesses the reflexive and critical thinking domains that are neces-sary for the development of advocacy awareness, knowledge, and skills (Guiffrida, 2005). Asking students to apply their learning to potential advocacy strategies and interventions builds advocacy competence (Lewis et al., 2002).

## Research and Program Evaluation

Research has the potential to transform the profession because it defines how coun-seling develops and interprets its research base (Heppner, Wampold, & Kivlighan, 2008; LaFountain & Bartos, 2002). Curriculum related to research and program evaluation encourages counselor trainees to become active consumers and produc-ers of research. From a consumer perspective, counselors need to make informed assessments about the credibility and meaningfulness of research (LaFountain & Bartos, 2002). Professional counselors also need to generate research as a mecha-nism for protecting the credibility of the profession and the best interest of clients. Professional counselors must ask themselves, "What kind of knowledge must a profession be based on to succeed?" (Heppner et al., 2008, p. 3). Thus, the cur-riculum within counselor preparation programs needs to address foci within the research domain while advocating for the equitable and ethical use of research for culturally diverse groups (CACREP, 2009; Lewis et al., 2002).

### Key Curricular Factors

Research and program evaluation is a CACREP 2009 entry-level curricular core area that addresses research methodology, analysis, and interpretation. The CACREP entry-level standards include models of needs assessments and pro-gram evaluations. There is a level of advocacy consciousness reflected in CACREP entry-level core standard II.G.8.f, which asserts that students gain understand-ing of "ethical and culturally relevant strategies for interpreting and reporting the results" (p. 94). The emphasis on needs assessment, program evaluations, and culturally relevant interpretation of such studies provides an opportunity to integrate such learning into the course syllabus.

### Creation of Syllabus

Syllabi that reflect the 2009 CACREP standards for research and program evaluation include knowledge components as well as experiential components. Experiential components increase students' application of content and translation into practice (Nelson & Neufeldt, 1998). Course objectives reflect the language of the CACREP standards explicitly and link them to classroom experiences and class assignments.

### Integration of Advocacy Into Class Assignments

Students need to be able to develop a needs assessment and then apply it to the development of programs (CACREP, 2009). One potential assignment that will simultaneously meet the CACREP standards for research and program evaluation and ACA's advocacy competencies (Lewis et al., 2002) is to have students complete a community-based needs assessment. Stewart (1979) defines a needs assessment as a process of identifying community challenges and resources to meet those challenges in an effort to decrease the difference between the actual and ideal. For the class assignment, instructors ask students to work in collaboration with a clinical site already established in the community. For the planning phase of the community-based needs assessment, students will review research articles on a particular topic. They then use that information to inform their discussions with the service providers at the specified clinical site. Students follow consultation and collaboration with service providers with the development of a field survey or structured interview questions for a focus group to explore the perceived needs of the targeted population. Students conduct the formal needs assessment with a sample from the targeted population. Then, they analyze and disseminate the results to the clinical site. Students interpret results from the perspective of cultural relevance, and students use the results to create a series of recommendations to address the perceived needs.

The community-based needs assessment addresses multiple CACREP 2009 standards (such as entry-level core standards II.G.8.a, b, c, d, and f), while situating student learning within the community itself. Requiring students to consider the cultural relevance of the data analysis and recommendations encourages the development of an advocacy perspective. Transformational learning of advocacy consciousness is enhanced by adding a reflective component to the assignment in which students must respond to the following questions through journaling or group discussion: (1) What were critical moments of learning for you across the needs assessment? (2) How do you conceptualize the community's response to the population's identified needs? (3) What advocacy opportunities currently exist in the community based on your needs assessment? (4) How will you use needs assessments in your work as a counselor?

In summary, a multitiered community needs assessment follows the best practices outlined by Finifter, Jensen, Wilson, and Koenig (2005). It provides an opportunity for students to apply their learning associated with research in the context of needs assessments. It also develops a rich opportunity to identify advocacy needs within communities and strategies to address them.

## ADVOCACY TRAINING ACROSS THE DOCTORAL-LEVEL PREPARATION STANDARDS

Transformational learning can also provide a framework for addressing the knowledge, skills, and practices required at the doctoral level (Arman & Scherer, 2002; Barbee et al., 2003; Murray et al., 2006). Emergent counselor educators, supervisors, researchers, and practitioners at the doctoral level need to develop areas of professional expertise, cultivate a leadership identity, demonstrate competence as a supervisor, develop proficiency in teaching, evidence scholarly engagement and contributions, and model advocacy consciousness (CACREP, 2009). Given the program's specific mission, areas of emphasis and primary foci may vary across institutions. Thus, doctoral-level assignments need to provide flexibility and individuality, so they can allow programmatic and student individuation while meeting accreditation standards.

### Key Curricular Factors

The doctoral-level CACREP 2009 standards identify particular learning outcomes in the domain of leadership and advocacy. At the knowledge level, doctoral students need to demonstrate an understanding of advocacy models, leadership theories and skills, political context of counseling, interventions for responding to crises and disasters, and social change theories (Doctoral Standards IV.I; CACREP, 2009). The knowledge domain is coupled with a skills and practices emphasis as doctoral students are required to evidence "the ability to advocate for the profession and its clientele" (CACREP, 2009; Doctoral Standard IV.J.2). This particular accreditation standard reflects the dual focus of advocacy, namely, client-based advocacy and professional advocacy (Chang et al., 2009; Myers et al., 2002). Another important focus of the doctoral-level CACREP 2009 standards is the development of leadership skill influencing professional associations and counseling programs (CACREP, 2009; Doctoral Standard IV.J.1). The leadership skill requirement parallels the professional advocacy initiative mandated by accreditation and espoused by leaders in the counseling field (Chang et al., 2009; Myers et al., 2002).

### Creation of Syllabus

Syllabi that reflect the 2009 CACREP Doctoral Standards emphasize the application (namely, skills and practices) and understanding (namely, knowledge) facets of advocacy consciousness. We believe that integrating assignments into course syllabi needs to provide a level of individuality, so that students can develop their professional areas of expertise while fulfilling accreditation standards. Course objectives need to highlight the reflexivity, intervention orientation, and community focus inherent in the transformational learning approach (Arman & Scherer, 2002; Barbee et al., 2003; Murray et al., 2006).

*Integration of Advocacy Into Class Assignments*

A potential doctoral-level assignment is community mapping designed to explore the resources and barriers within the community in which students intend to work as a counselor or counselor educator. Through community mapping, students can assess the current programs in the community that serve clients. Assessing the community resources facilitates our awareness of what is available to clients in our communities, our understanding of what is needed to serve the clients in the community, and our recognition of what type of issues and services need to be a focus of advocacy. Such an emphasis encourages doctoral students to develop their leadership and advocacy competencies within the context of an informed understanding of their communities.

The goal of the community mapping assignment is for doctoral students to develop a better understanding of a particular community's assets, needs, and characteristics. The purpose of this assignment is to get students out into the community, increase their understanding of resources that are available, enhance critical thinking related to the community's ability to meet the needs of clients, and focus on their role of advocacy and leadership. The process of engaging the community would increase social responsibility, interprofessional engagement, and role definition (Guiffrida, 2005). The goals of the community mapping assignment reflect the hallmarks of transformational learning (Arman & Scherer, 2002; Barbee et al., 2003, Murray et al., 2006) as well as the accreditation standards articulated in doctoral-level learning outcomes (CACREP, 2009).

The community mapping assignment has a conceptual, information focus and an analysis, critical thinking focus. Students are required to explore the types of programs and resources available in their communities. The conceptual, information gathering focus is guided by questions such as: What mental health agencies exist? Who do they serve? What is their mission? On what issues do they focus? To what community resources do they make referrals? In what kinds of outreach are they engaging? How available are the services and programs? What are the specialty areas of practitioners? What are the professional credentials of the staff? What is the fee structure for services? Topics central to this exploration include the community's current strengths, local assets, resources, and activities. This component of the community mapping helps doctoral students to understand the context in which families and individuals function. Information that is relevant to describe thoroughly the community can be gathered in multiple modalities, such as through research, phone contact, phone interviews, and face-to-face interviews.

The analysis, critical thinking component of the community mapping assignment includes an examination of the current needs and available resources. Such analysis can be framed by questions such as: Who are we serving as a community? What opportunities and services do families, children, and adults want most? What are the demographics of the community? What are particular issues that are significant within the community? What are the political issues impacting the daily experience of clients and counselors in the community? As doctoral students consider the current needs of the community and the current available resources, it is important for them to critically consider current barriers, gaps in services, and other concerns. Discussion of these issues should generate a set of recommendations related to the community's emerging needs, potential to tap into underused resources, and need for advocacy. Doctoral students would then articulate leadership and advocacy strategies to address the gaps.

The format of the assignment is flexible in that there is an opportunity for students to creatively present their information in the most beneficial manner. There does need to be a narrative component that summarizes the following: (1) parameters of community mapping (What was mapped and assessed? Where?), (2) sources of information and methods for gathering information, (3) community population (Who needs to be served? What issues are present in the community?), (4) current resources, assets, and strengths, (5) current barriers and gaps, and (6) emerging needs and recommendations. Again, the focus of information gathering is on the current community demographics and needs and on current community services and resources. The focus of the analysis component is on assessing how well the needs of the community are currently being met. The implications component focuses on gaps and emerging needs in the community and how to address those on the individual, agency, and community levels. Doctoral students can also be asked to reflect on and articulate how they would integrate their enhanced knowledge and understanding into their classrooms and supervision sessions. The community mapping assignment demands that doctoral students engage the knowledge and skill domains of leadership and advocacy.

Another potential doctoral-level assignment is an individualized action plan with specific requirements related to the CACREP 2009 doctoral-level standards. For the class assignment, doctoral students are required to propose and complete an individualized action plan across the semester. It will be clearly articulated that the nature of the completed action plan will vary based on the individual focus of the plan, yet the structuring of the assignment will ensure an attention to relevant advocacy and leadership competencies. The proposal needs to include both a critical self-assessment and a detailed plan for further developing leadership and advocacy initiatives. Within the critical self-assessment, doctoral students would review their current level of multicultural competence (strengths related to knowledge, awareness, and skills and areas of improvement related to knowledge, awareness, and skills), current level of advocacy consciousness (strengths and areas of improvement related to knowledge, awareness, and skills), and current level of leadership skills (strengths and areas of improvement related to models, roles, and strategies). The critical self-assessment component of the individualized action plan encourages a high level of reflexivity and awareness, both of which are cornerstones of transformational learning (Moore, 2005; Taylor, 2009).

The proposal aspect of the individualized action plan would then detail goals, objectives, strategies, and methods for assessing success in two primary domains, namely, leadership and advocacy. Some example action goals could be planning a community-based mental health initiative that addresses an identified client need, developing a marketing plan to increase membership and engagement in a state professional association, or creating a leadership workshop that encourages counselor trainees and practitioners to further cultivate their leadership skills and contributions. At the completion of the academic term, doctoral students would be required to submit a narrative evaluating their action goals, objectives, and strategies coupled with evidence of their successful completion of the action plan as detailed in their proposed assessment process. The individualized action plan could be integrated into doctoral classes such as doctoral seminar, advanced multicultural, leadership in counselor education, or their programmatic equivalents. The assignment would address both the knowledge and skills and practices standards related to the leadership and advocacy learning outcomes (CACREP, 2009, Doctoral Standards IV.I.1, 2, 3, 4, 5 and IV.J.1 and 2).

## CONCLUSION

Advocacy consciousness requires the integration of knowledge and understanding into action and application. Developing class assignments across the CACREP 2009 entry-level curricular core areas and the doctoral-level standards provides an opportunity to enhance advocacy competence while simultaneously meeting the core area standards. The factors of transformational learning, namely, experiential learning, reflective, and community grounded, can facilitate the students' abilities to translate knowledge into action. The dual goal of advocacy is to create a professional identity as an advocate and to develop skills and competence. Transformational learning across curricula encourages the attainment of such a dual emphasis.

## DISCUSSION QUESTIONS

1. Consider a class that you are currently teaching or plan to teach in the near future. How could you develop assignments that foster transformational learning?

2. Within a master's-level program, how could you encourage critical self-reflection and experiential learning? How might that be different or similar in a doctoral-level program?

3. What do you perceive as the most critical advocacy competencies? How would these best be developed across a master's-level curriculum? A doctoral-level curriculum?

4. You have been assigned to teach the career development course. How will you integrate advocacy training while meeting the accreditation standards for this core curricular area?

5. You are designing a course at the doctoral level that focuses on leadership and advocacy. How will you build upon competencies already developed at the master's level in terms of advocacy models, social change theories, sociopolitical issues influencing counseling, and community response skills? What would be examples of classroom experiences and assignments to integrate into this course?

# 16

## *Future Needs*
## Accountability

LARRY C. LOESCH

Evident in the preceding chapters, as well as in the Chi Sigma Iota (CSI) position paper on leadership (Herr, 2010), is that there are myriad definitions, understandings, interpretations, philosophies, and belief systems about leadership. The CSI-endorsed advocacy of the servant leader perspective (Herr, n.d.) narrows the range of interpretations of what leadership should be and how leaders should act, but does not narrow them enough to indicate specifically how a counseling professional should actually *behave* so as to be a leader. CSI's (2009) Principles and Practices of Leadership Excellence help to clarify the CSI position paper on leadership, point to necessary perspectives on various aspects of leadership performance, and identify rather generalized guidelines for appropriate leadership behaviors, but again do not point to specific behaviors that would allow a professional counselor to manifest those principles in a way that would necessarily be deemed effective leadership practice. Ultimately, as Herr (n.d.) noted, leadership is whatever each individual counseling professional interprets it to be in regard to specific behaviors (i.e., concrete actions) intended to be leadership behavior.

A similar situation exists for *advocacy*. Interpretations of the word and opinions about behaviors appropriate and necessary to manifest it again are as diverse and individualized as those for leadership. Similar to the CSI resources relative to leadership, the advocacy competencies of the American Counseling Association (ACA) (2002) provide a comprehensive model for integration of advocacy activities across the counseling profession, identify professionally significant contexts in which advocacy activities are important, delineate domains in which advocacy activities are appropriate and relevant, and are instructive about advocacy practices in which professional counselors should engage. However, here too the specific *behavioral* manifestations of the recommended practices are left to the interpretation of each counseling professional attempting to implement them.

In this chapter, I explore underlying assumptions and the nature of leadership and advocacy accountability, what is good accountability information, how it can be obtained, and how it can be shared. I also present examples of accountability practices. As space permits, I provide comments about the relative qualities of various accountability practices.

Clearly the CSI and ACA positions on leadership and advocacy are important information that should be absorbed thoughtfully by all counseling professionals. Further, these position papers do *point toward* a basis for accountability for engaging in the recommended leadership and advocacy practices. However, they neither dictate nor delineate a specific basis for accountability. For example, the practice statement for CSI leadership principle 8 states, "Leaders assure that members are provided with opportunities to develop and apply their unique talents in service to others, the profession, and association." But *how exactly* does one *do* that? If one CSI "leader" writes an announcement about the needs of the membership committee for CSI's *Exemplar* and another makes a similar announcement at a CSI annual business meeting, have either or both fulfilled the practice stipulation, and if so, how effectively? For another example, consider the statements within the ACA advocacy competencies for social/political advocacy that stipulate, "In influencing public policy in a large, public arena, the advocacy-oriented counselor is able to: . . . 37. Distinguish those problems that can be best resolved through social/political action." But *how exactly* does one *do* that? If one advocate reflects on a problem and then makes a personal decision about whether to advocate in regard to the problem and another polls professional colleagues and goes with the majority opinion, have either or both fulfilled the advocacy competency, and if so, how effectively?

Given this muddled interpretive situation, how then can anyone determine if a counseling professional has been, or is, an effective and successful leader and advocate? In a professional context, the question becomes how can substantive and valid accountability information about leadership and advocacy activities be obtained? This question *can* be answered, but some assumptions are necessary before meaningful accountability information can be achieved.

Leadership and advocacy are integrated and *inseparable* concepts. If a person engages in *leadership* behaviors, she or he is *acting on behalf of* one or more people, that is, is attempting to change *something* (presumably for the better) for one person or a group of people. Substituting *advocacy* for *leadership* in the preceding sentence leads to an equally appropriate and valid statement. Therefore, it can be readily assumed that accountability considerations nominally associated with either one are necessarily associated with the other. The importance and benefit of this assumption is that a distinction does not have to be made, at least in regard to the nature of accountability determination processes, between leadership and advocacy as distinct professional activities. This means that the same, or highly similar types of, strategies and techniques can be used to develop accountability information for leadership or advocacy activities.

A second important assumption is that leadership and advocacy behaviors can be *taught* through relatively commonly used educational techniques, such as classroom instruction, modeling, mentoring, shadowing, and tutoring. Obviously this assumption is reflected in the new Council for Accreditation of Counseling and Related Educational Programs (CACREP, 2009) standards by virtue of inclusion of reference to leadership and advocacy development in those standards. As Solmonson (2010) noted, "The integration of advocacy competencies in the initial training of counselors incorporates the advocacy role as an essential element of professional identity" (p. 1). The importance and benefit of this assumption is that evaluation strategies and techniques proven to be effective when applied to other educational endeavors or enterprises can be applied to development of accountability information for leadership and advocacy instructional activities in the counseling profession. In general, there is no need to develop new and different methods for evaluation of leadership and advocacy instruction (although new methods are always welcome). However, there is a need to select and apply thoughtfully and carefully whatever data gathering method is to be used, an admonition no different than what is appropriate for evaluation of any professional counseling activity.

A third important assumption is that so-called hard data are likely the *strongest* type of accountability information for leadership and advocacy activities. For many, this assumption is easily accepted because it is in line with the litany of recommendations, calls, and demands for evidence-based counseling practice. West and Warchal (2009) wrote, "The call for greater accountability in counseling has resulted in attempts to include outcomes research as a component of clinical treatment. 'Evidence-Based Practice' has become the accepted term used to describe the integration of research and practice" (p. 291). Most commonly, outcomes research in this context means research that yields *numeric* data about *behavior change* resulting from application of some specific therapeutic treatment or intervention. Historically, what little professional counselor accountability information was available was comprised primarily of professional counselors' clinical impressions or clients' testimonials, both of which clearly are subjective data. Encouragement and support for evidence-based counseling practice is widespread because the "evidence" is presumed to be [more] objective, and thus more easily understood by people both within and outside of the counseling profession. However, limitations of evidence-based counseling practice, such as difficulties in generalizing from research studies in relatively controlled conditions to actual counseling practice settings, have been identified (e.g., Messer, 2004). Therefore, it remains an assumption that presumably objective behavior change data provide the best type of accountability information for various professional counseling activities. Nonetheless, it is the perspective espoused here as most appropriate for developing accountability information relative to leadership and advocacy because it is in concert with current trends and movements within the counseling profession.

## THE NATURE OF LEADERSHIP AND ADVOCACY ACCOUNTABILITY

*Accountability* is essentially synonymous with *responsibility* because it reflects the attribution of causation to a person's actions. Thus, when a person *does* something, there is a result of the action/behavior directly attributable to the person, and the person is presumed to have *caused* the result, regardless of whether the person wants to be held accountable for the result. Most commonly, professional leadership and advocacy activities are undertaken voluntarily. But whether engaging in a leadership and advocacy activity is assigned (e.g., by a professional organization officer), ascribed (e.g., as part of a professional role), or voluntary, there is an associated responsibility for the subsequent results of the activity. This means that all professional counselors who engage in leadership and advocacy activities will, and more importantly should, be held responsible for the results of their activities.

The critical foundation for any accountability process is determination of effective answers to the questions (1) *for what*, (2) *to whom*, and (3) *how* is the leader/advocate accountable? (Loesch & Ritchie, 2009). Because they are seemingly easy questions to which to respond, they are often, indeed far too often, not give appropriate attention, which in turn yields poor results for an accountability effort. Consider, for example, a student in a leadership and advocacy class in a counselor preparation program who is assigned in the context of the course to engage in an advocacy activity on behalf of homeless persons in the local community. In regard to evaluation of the student's performance, is the student to be held responsible (e.g., graded) for the overall result of the activity (i.e., some degree of benefit achieved for homeless persons), the extent to which the student effectively engaged in prescribed (e.g., taught or assigned) behaviors regardless of the overall result, or some combination thereof? Similarly, is the student primarily accountable to the course instructor or to the homeless persons, or possibly even to some local legal authority/agency?

Answering the *for what* question involves delineation of the (1) the specific desired outcomes expressed as measurable criteria or (2) the behaviors to be implemented and conducted expressed as observable and measurable criteria or (3) some combination thereof. Basically, needed are statements of what is to be accomplished or how something is to be done, both expressed in straightforward, objective language that all involved interpret in the same way. Similarly, answering the *to whom* question involves clear specification of who is to receive and use the resultant accountability information. Typically, these people are the "stakeholders," that is, the people who have a vested interest in the activity being successful (Erford, 2010). There are four major stakeholder groups for professional counselors: (1) the people they serve (e.g., clients), (2) members of the counseling profession, (3) the general public, and (4) funding providers. However, there may be other relevant stakeholders. For example, faculty instructors or supervisors also are an important stakeholder group for students. It is important to realize that not all identified stakeholder groups are equally important across situations, and therefore that prioritization is essential in answering the *to whom* question, in part because accountability information should be presented in a manner specifically, and likely uniquely, for each particular stakeholder group.

Psychologist/author Dr. Laurance J. Peter noted, "If you don't know where you are going, you will probably wind up someplace else" (Peter, 1977). This quip is entirely applicable to accountability activities. It is essential that answers to the three fundamental accountability questions be determined *before* any leadership or advocacy activity and associated accountability activity are begun. Unfortunately, all too often, an accountability process is imposed upon some professional activity after it has begun or even after it has been completed, which likely leads to invalid information and is unfair to the counseling professional being evaluated.

The a priori determination of *for what, to whom*, and *how* a counseling professional will be held accountable for a leadership or advocacy activity has several benefits. First, it informs the professional counselor of expectations for effectiveness and success in the activity as well as which and whose expectations are primary. Second, this information is important for effective planning; it should provide guidance for how the leadership or advocacy activity is actually to be conducted. Third, this information is essential to selection of appropriate and effective data gathering techniques and procedures. Finally, this information is important for deciding how the accountability information will be disseminated.

Astramovich and Coker (2007) echoed an oft made comment that professional counselors, unfortunately, infrequently engage in accountability activities, and lamented the pitfalls inherent in such behavior:

> Although counselors may be hesitant or unwilling to evaluate the effectiveness of their services because they see little relevance to their individual practice, the future of the counseling profession may well be shaped by the way practitioners respond to accountability demands. (p. 165)

Comparatively, rarely have professional counselors been criticized for failing to *plan* for provision of professional services. However, as indicated, by virtue of merely providing professional services, professional counselors are held accountable for their actions regardless of whether they want to be. Why not be accountable in ways over which professional counselors have at least some degree of control? In simple terms, professional counselors should integrate accountability planning into their planning for service provision, thus saving time, potentially improving service delivery, and perhaps even benefiting the counseling profession.

## LEADERSHIP AND ADVOCACY ACCOUNTABILITY DATA

Writing regarding counseling practice, Herr (2004) stated:

> Evidence-based practices are in contrast to earlier approaches that focused on process-based or function-based counseling programs. The latter emphasized checklists of counselor roles and functions, which if undertaken were assumed to be appropriate for all counselees and would yield successful outcomes. Evidence-based practices do not accept such assumptions; instead the intent is to identify interventions that empirically demonstrate successful outcomes for particular types of client problems under specific conditions. (p. 10)

While Herr's comment relates specifically to the counseling process, it is equally applicable to accountability activities. In brief, Herr's comment means that simply providing proof of having engaged in (conducted) a counseling or leadership or advocacy activity does not mean, or prove, that the activity was successful. Thus, even though there is considerable *historic* endorsement for them, professional counselor activity calendars, schedules, time logs, and the like are not sufficient or effective accountability data.

From a similar perspective, Hiebert (1997) wrote:

> What is needed is an evaluation system that has a broader definition of acceptable evidence and a model that promotes all players being involved in making the decisions about what evidence will be acceptable and what will not. I deliberately use the word "evidence" rather than "data," to emphasize that the basis of counsellor and client perceptions of counselling success are often, perhaps even most often, not based on test scores. (p. 114)

Presumably, Hiebert's contention is based in the difficulty, and relative rarity, of finding relatively substantive changes in test scores immediately following counseling or in the inherent limitations in various types of psychological (or other) assessments.

The question then becomes, what are good, substantive, appropriate, and acceptable data (evidence) for evaluating leadership and advocacy activities for accountability purposes? Loesch and Ritchie (2009) offered that:

> The word data usually connotes "numbers." However, technically, data are defined simply as "factual information," which allows data to be factual information in many different forms. Further, data can be generated in different ways (i.e., through different types of processes), so relatively simultaneous consideration must be given both to what and how data are generated. (p. 38)

Simply put, the best data (evidence) for leadership and accountability purposes are those for which there is shared and *essentially consensual agreement* about what the data are, mean, and represent. For example, if an organizational leader requests that another counseling professional develop a no more than 500-word article that addresses five specific events forthcoming for the organization, to be submitted by a specific date, then the evaluation criteria are clear: (1) How many words are in the article? (2) How many events were addressed in the article? (3) When was it submitted? The answers to these questions (i.e., the data) are "facts" because the vast majority of counseling professionals would interpret the numbers and date in the same way. Note that in this example the leader's request must be clearly stated so as to communicate the accountability evaluation criteria, which again reinforces the idea that accountability concerns must be addressed *before* an activity is initiated.

Notably absent from the preceding example is evaluation of the quality of the article submitted by the counseling professional. Quality is a highly subjective term, one not easily measured. Perhaps the best way to evaluate the quality of a behavior (action), process, or product is through determination of degree of opinion consensus. For example, a group of counseling professionals could use a rating scale to express their respective opinions about the quality of the article submitted and then the average rating computed. However, in accordance with good assessment practice, each rating element (i.e., level or category) of the rating scale would have associated with it as complete and informative description as possible of what the specific element represents to facilitate appropriate and valid use of the rating instrument. Also, a relatively large group of raters would have to be involved. And of course, in keeping with good professional and accountability practices, the leader, contributing counseling professional, and raters would have the rating scale at the time the leader's request was made.

Accountability processes, including those for leadership and advocacy, are *consumer driven*, which means that they are conducted to inform one or more identifiable stakeholder groups. The *best* accountability data are those readily understood by, and therefore best serve the needs of, the relevant stakeholder group(s). For example, a typical professional journal article (replete with theory and data analyses) about a research study of selected leader behaviors and associated changes in a professional organization structure likely would inform counseling professionals, but also likely would not be well understood by the general public. However, in general, (1) *behavior change* or (2) *product-developed* factual information is the type most easily understood across stakeholder groups. For example, if a counseling professional (leader) enlists professional counselors in a state to go to the state capital to meet with their respective legislative representatives to talk about changing a counselor licensure law, the number of professionals who actually go to the state capital for that purpose is the obvious accountability data (i.e., behavioral outcome). Similarly, if professional counselors "lobby" a legislature to create a new law, there is apparent accountability by virtue of a new law coming into existence, or not (i.e., product outcome).

Wall (2004) wrote, "Basing judgments, decisions, and interventions specifically on information acquired in some systematic and objective way is of major importance in the life of a practicing counselor" (p. 69). Although Wall was writing in regard to use of tests in counseling in particular, her comment applies across the realm of leadership and advocacy accountability. Acquiring accountability data in a systematic and (relatively) objective way can involve use of *any* validly and appropriately conducted measurement procedure because, again, the best data are those that best serve the stakeholders. Standardized and nonstandardized tests, checklists, rating scales, behavior observation records, opinion polls, performance records, questionnaires, surveys, structured interviews, professional records, sociograms, large-scale and single-subject research designs, Delphi studies, focus groups, needs assessments, goal attainment strategies, cognitive mapping, and (so-called) authentic assessment techniques are among the possible methods for generating leadership and advocacy accountability data. The oft cited dictum "form follows function" certainly applies in this context. Once well-considered, carefully expressed, and definitive answers have been developed for the questions "Who needs to know what?" and "How do they need to know it?" the needed, appropriate data will be evident. From that point, potentially and likely appropriate measurement techniques and procedures can be selected from among many known to be effective measurement techniques, and the accountability process will have been essentially planned out in regards to what needs to be done.

## ACCOUNTABILITY FOR LEADERSHIP AND ADVOCACY IN COUNSELOR PREPARATION

Professional preparation for counselor leadership and advocacy activities received far greater emphasis and attention in the 2009 CACREP standards (CACREP, 2009) than it did in previous versions of those standards. Such increased attention is warranted given the corresponding current emphasis on leadership and advocacy in the counseling profession. But just as there is variation in the extent to which current counseling professionals endorse or engage in leadership and advocacy activities, so too is there variation in the relative emphases on leadership and advocacy in the 2009 CACREP standards. A subsection entitled "Diversity and Advocacy" that presents pertinent and requisite knowledge and skills and practices is found in each of the six counseling specialty entry-level preparation program standards descriptions. Advocacy also is addressed specifically in the "Professional Orientation and Ethical Practice" subsection of the entry-level program core curriculum standards. However, standards specifically relative to professional preparation for *leadership* are rare in the 2009 standards for entry-level programs. The entry-level program standards for school counseling do contain a subsection entitled "Leadership," and specify pertinent and requisite knowledge and skills and practices. However, leadership in that context is restricted to the school counselor's role as a leader in the school, and not as a leader in other, broader areas of professional functioning. The 2009 doctoral-level preparation standards include several standards specifically related to leadership and a subsection entitled "Leadership and Advocacy" that present pertinent and requisite knowledge and skills and practices. Unfortunately, this imbalance suggests that professional leadership is appropriate and important only for counseling professionals holding a doctoral degree. Clearly that is not a perspective endorsed by either CSI or ACA. Level of academic preparation is *not* included in either CSI's or ACA's position statements on leadership and advocacy, ostensibly because the vast majority of both CSI and ACA members do not hold a doctoral degree.

In one sense, the leadership-advocacy attention disparity in the 2009 CACREP standards confounds accountability for leadership and advocacy preparation. Advocacy accountability activities likely can be associated directly to one or more specific CACREP standards, which facilitates clearer focus in instructional accountability. Conversely, because there are few direct allusions to leadership in the 2009 standards, connecting particular preparation activities specifically to leadership preparation is more difficult. However, remembering the first assumption presented relative to leadership and advocacy accountability may provide some resolution. That is, again, if leadership and advocacy are indeed inseparable constructs, then evaluation of preparation for one is evaluation of preparation for the other.

Counselor preparation is obviously an *educational* enterprise and encompasses and includes all variations of instructional methodologies, and therefore allows any of the myriad appropriate, valid, and effective instructional evaluation strategies and procedures to be employed to evaluate counselor preparation activities. Addressing counselor preparation program evaluation, which of course includes evaluation of specific instructional activities within a program, Liles and Wagner (2010) wrote, "When thinking about assessment, we cannot separate ourselves from the notion of accountability. The beauty of assessment planning is that it ensures counseling programs remain true to the CACREP standards, which, in turn, protect the student learning environment" (p. 4). Thus, obtaining leadership and advocacy instruction accountability information also contributes to counselor preparation program accountability.

In developing leadership and advocacy accountability data for counselor preparation instructional activities, it is best to "tie" the accountability strategy and applied procedures to a particular CACREP standard. For example, the CACREP Section II, Knowledge, G, 1, h standard stipulates that students achieve knowledge of "the role and process of the professional counselor advocating on behalf of the profession" (CACREP, 2009, p. 10). The appropriate and pertinent instructional *content* for this standard would be to a great extent established by the instructor. However, regardless of the content selected, for accountability purposes that instructional content would have to be described and delineated as specifically and extensively as possible. Further, because it is likely that the instructor would deem some content to be more important than other content, the relative values of various components of instructional content also would have to be specified. In accord with both good instructional and good accountability practices, the instructional content, including priorities, would be presented to the students *before* the instructional activity is begun. Traditionally, the instructor would then give an instructor-developed examination to determine the extent to which the students had "learned" the content relative to counselor advocacy in the profession. This procedure would yield instructional accountability data. However, instructor-developed examinations are notoriously lacking in psychometric quality, so the resultant accountability data probably would be considered very weak.

Better accountability data for this example might be obtained by using a different data gathering technique. For example, the Counselor Preparation Comprehensive Examination (CPCE) is developed and administered by the Center for Credentialing and Education (a corporate affiliate of the National Board for Certified Counselors). The CPCE is a very credible examination and is widely administered across counselor education programs. Pertinent here is that it contains some items relating to knowledge of counselor advocacy activities. Data from student performance specifically on those items would yield stronger accountability information because the assessment measure has greater psychometric credibility than do most instructor-developed tests.

A third possibility would be to have the accountability data generated by people not directly involved in the instructional activity. For example, the students could be assigned to develop a written presentation about "what they would do to advocate for the counseling profession in their first year as a professional counselor." Importantly here too, the assignment would have to include specification of which elements of the instructional content in particular were to be addressed in the presentation. The students' papers could then be evaluated as to whether they (sufficiently) addressed instructional content or perhaps "rated" for quality by a relatively large group of counseling practitioners. Obviously such a process would be fraught with practical problems, but it would yield *strong* accountability data because of the presumed objectivity of the external evaluators.

Amazingly, the word *accountability* occurs only twice in the 2009 CACREP standards, once each in the entry-level standards for clinical mental health counseling and school counseling programs, respectively, but then only as an element of a series for a larger idea. However, it *is* an important topic, and therefore, one about which students in counselor preparation programs should know. There are other important topics (e.g., counseling and technology) not receiving much

attention in the standards but which are significant aspects of counselor preparation. Developing advocacy and leadership accountability information for those
types of topics is more difficult, but possible. Consider doctoral-level standard
IV, leadership and advocacy, I, 1, stated as: "Demonstrates the ability to provide
leadership or contribute to leadership efforts of professional organizations and/
or counseling programs." Given the previously described admonitions about
instructors, students, and evaluators all operating a priori from a well-defined
explanation of the instructional content and, specifically to this type of standard,
clear delineation of the skills requisite for effective performance, students might
be asked (as before) to (1) develop a written presentation of how they will provide
leadership in the counseling profession during the first year after graduation and
(2) develop an accountability plan for that first-year leadership activity. And as
before, either the instructor or external professionals would have to evaluate the
extent to which the presentation addressed appropriate content, especially requisite skills, or evaluate the quality of the plans proposed. Although complicated,
the benefit of this approach is generation of accountability for elements of professional preparation beyond the obvious or minimally essential.

In general, obtaining good, strong accountability data for leadership and
advocacy preparation activities involves going beyond traditional, rather mundane student performance evaluation procedures. Results of instructor-made
tests, instructor's grading of students' papers, individual supervisors' opinions
of student performance, mere counts of students' professional involvements, and
the like simply are too subjective or vague to be considered good accountability data for leadership and advocacy preparation. Needed is some creativity and
extra effort to achieve accountability data that will be interpreted as relatively
objective and credible by the relevant stakeholders.

## ACCOUNTABILITY FOR LEADERSHIP AND ADVOCACY
## IN THE COUNSELING PROFESSION

The demand and need for accountability in educational endeavors, such as professional counselor preparation, is widely recognized and almost always endorsed.
After all, either public or private financial sources are *paying* for educational
enterprises, and it is reasonable that those sources, as *stakeholders*, should know
to what extent they are "getting what they paid for." But what about *professional*
leadership and advocacy activities? Are not most leaders and advocates in the
counseling profession "volunteers" (which includes, for example, *volunteering* to
be a candidate for election to an organizational leadership position)? Is it not
entirely reasonable to assume that these volunteers have the best interests of an
identifiable group or the counseling profession at heart. Why then should they be
held accountable for their leadership and advocacy actions?

The reason that counseling professionals should be held accountable for their leadership and advocacy activities is that they *may not* have the best interests of a group or the counseling profession at heart, but are instead promoting agendas that may not be widely endorsed, or are possibly even opposed, by a large group of professional counselors. For example, Smith, Reynolds, and Rovnak (2009) wrote, "On the surface, the social advocacy movement in counseling appears to be a called-for mandate" (p. 483), but continued by suggesting that the underlying "mandate" assumption needs to be examined carefully:

> Such an examination . . . is required to firmly establish the movement in the profession and to understand its impact on the profession, individual members, and distinct groups. Only after undergoing such scrutiny can the mandate of social action indeed be justly determined, particularly as a professional and/or personal mandate.
>
> We believe that the social advocacy movement lacks sufficient moderation and sometimes attempts to promote various agendas (e.g., personal, political) under the guise of "social action." It makes bold claims for which it has little or no evidence. (p. 483)

Accountability for leadership and advocacy activities in regard to social advocacy is clearly an essential part of the needed scrutiny to which these authors refer. Various societal groups are usually considered the primary stakeholders for professional counselors' social advocacy activities, but professional counselors also are primary stakeholders because the nature and results of those activities have significant implications for the entire counseling profession. Professional counselors do indeed need to hold their leaders and advocacy representatives accountable.

Establishing accountability for leadership and advocacy in counselor preparation is facilitated by the existence of the CACREP standards because they provide a relatively large pool of statements of what knowledge and which skills students are expected to gain as a result of their preparation. Although the standards are often promulgated as outcome based, the specific standards themselves are not presented as *behavioral* outcomes (i.e., do not specify exactly what the student should be able to do). However, for the most part they are specific enough such that the instructional activities associated with each standard can be translated into specific behaviors, which in turn facilitate measurement and subsequent evaluation of those instructional activities. Unfortunately, the so-called action statements in professional position or competency papers relative to leadership and advocacy (as well as many other professional topics) are even less behaviorally specific than are the various CACREP standards. Most often, the lack of behavioral specificity or behavior association is attributable to the fact that the included statements are *compound* sentences, ones that encompass a rather global *set* of ideas and activities rather than a single behavior. Thus, more complete explanation and justification of the behaviors and outcomes to be associated with each statement and more work are needed to relate the respective statements to a specific accountability activity. Nonetheless, such statements likely provide the best bases for accountability efforts for professional leadership and advocacy accountability activities.

Consider, for example, CSI's Principle (of Leadership Excellence) 8: mentoring, encouragement, and empowerment. The associated practice (presumably action or behavior) statement is: "Leaders assure that members are provided with opportunities to develop and apply their unique talents in service to others, the profession, and association [i.e., CSI]." Obviously this statement reads as a good idea. Unfortunately, it is at best complicated, as something to which to hold the leader accountable, and presents problems for developing an appropriate accountability process. Exactly *how does* a leader "assure" (guarantee) that members are provided those opportunities? Who is supposed to provide the opportunities? How many opportunities need to be provided? What are "unique" talents and how will they be determined to be unique? What are the contexts in which the unique talents are to be developed or applied? And so on. However, although difficult, it is not impossible to create an accountability plan for this statement.

In order to hold a leader accountable for this particular leadership practice statement, a relatively focused perspective, some definitions, and some delineations would have to be developed. Importantly, these process components also would have to be agreed upon and accepted by the leader, whoever is conducting the accountability procedure, and (representatives of) the stakeholders before the leadership *and* accountability processes are begun. For example, this statement *could* be interpreted to mean that the leader is responsible for informing members on a periodic basis and using different modalities of opportunities for the members to become involved in various professional activities (e.g., elected or appointed organizational positions, committee memberships, or work groups) in the association and the counseling profession. Further, it might be clarified that the leader is responsible for communicating the pertinent specific characteristics, experience, or skills a member would need to possess as well as the requisite behaviors in which the member would need to engage to have the potential to be successful in each announced opportunity. The resultant accountability data would then include how frequently the leader disseminated the information, what modalities were used to disseminate the information, and the extent to which the announcements included personal and professional requirements. These data would be relatively easy to generate, thus simplifying the accountability process. Again, however, these procedures do not address the quality aspect of the communications; evaluating quality would necessitate a more complicated evaluation procedure.

The accountability procedure briefly described for this example requires the accountability evaluators basically to engage in counting and check-off behavior. Although simple and quick, these procedures lead to relatively weak accountability data. Better data would result from (additional) evaluation of the quality of the communications. However, the ultimate goal of all leadership and advocacy is to bring about behavior change, that is, to get people to behave differently in readily apparent ways. Therefore, the strongest accountability data that could be developed for this example would result from determination of how many counseling professionals were actually moved to and did indeed volunteer for a new activity as a result of the announcements. Space limitations prohibit explanation of approaches that might be used to obtain such data; interested readers are referred to the literature on evaluation of advertising and marketing activities for adaptable guidelines and examples.

The biggest problem in evaluating *quality* of leader performance lies not in the complexity of the methods that can and should be used. Rather, it lies in the brevity of the time period in which most leaders in the counseling profession serve. For example, most elected positions (e.g., association officers) in professional counselor organizations serve for a one-year period. Similarly, many "appointed" positions are of relatively short duration because they are made by professional leaders elected to short-term positions. A counseling professional elected or appointed to a short-term professional position rightfully must be afforded *some* time before he or she can be expected do much of anything that can be evaluated. Quality-focused accountability evaluation procedures take some time to conduct, as do information dissemination procedures. The unfortunate result of all this is that in the vast majority of cases an elected or appointed counseling professional has been "replaced" before the accountability information can be used! The primary implication is that evaluation of quality of performance for accountability purposes is usually most beneficial in situations in which leaders or advocates will be or are in a position long enough for good accountability information to be both generated *and* used.

The most common method of obtaining indication of consensus (or lack of it) about the quality of a counseling professional's performance, result(s) achieved, or product(s) developed is through use of a rating scale. The key to effective evaluation through use of a rating scale is careful delineation of what aspects of performance are to be evaluated and accurate reflection of those aspects in the rating scale. In general, the more specific, the better. For example, asking respondents to rate a leader/advocate's performance on a scale ranging from 5 = good to 1 = poor makes for easy assessment, but the results aren't very helpful to informing or directing the leader/advocate's (or successor's) subsequent behavior. A better item might be to have respondents indicate (perhaps using a Likert-type scale) the extent to which they agree with (or endorse or support) a particular action taken by the leader/advocate. Although rating scales need careful development, current technologies, such as Internet-based surveys, allow such evaluations to be conducted quickly and easily, and thus allow the information to be used in a timely manner.

Even better quality of performance indicators may be achieved through the use of an iterative rating process such as the Delphi method. Iterative rating processes typically involve anonymous presentation of other respondents' previous ratings so that each rater will be "better informed" in making subsequent ratings on the same items. The eventual result (usually after at least three iterations) is presumed to provide high consensus about the ratings assigned. Iterative methods take longer to complete than single-event rating methods, but again, iterative methods are facilitated and response times diminished by Internet-based communication methods.

Methods for developing accountability data for leadership and advocacy activities range from the simple to the complex. Which type of procedure is best depends on the needs, purposes, and human, material, and time resources available for whoever is conducting the accountability process. Above all else, however, the accountability process must yield data that informs and can be used by stakeholders so that needed changes (if any) can be implemented to improve leadership and advocacy activities in the counseling profession.

## DISSEMINATING LEADERSHIP AND ADVOCACY ACCOUNTABILITY DATA

An important but often overlooked part of the *how* question in accountability is determination of the best method(s) to disseminate the results of an accountability process. An accountability process is successful only to the extent that the results are actually used (i.e., something actually happens as a result of having the data), and the results can only be used if the appropriate stakeholders receive them and can understand them (Loesch & Ritchie, 2009). The choice of dissemination method(s) depends on the specific stakeholders to be served.

It bears repeating that in an effective leadership and advocacy accountability process, the stakeholders will have been identified before the process was begun because such identification might influence the nature and conduct of the process implemented. Subsequently, that identification should point to *in what form* and *how* the information will be disseminated to (at least the primary) stakeholders. In general, the rule of thumb is to communicate the accountability information in ways that each respective stakeholder group is used to receiving important information. For example, professional counselors are relatively educated individuals who are used to receiving information that contains relatively sophisticated information (e.g., results of relatively complex data analyses). Thus, accountability data presented in a professional counseling journal article or newsletter may be an appropriate communication modality for them. Other educated professionals might also understand such sophisticated information. However, they likely will not be familiar with common counselor terminology, so communications to them should avoid use of "counselor speak." For consumption by susbsections of the general public, accountability information probably will have to be "boiled down" to be expressed in language understood by a wide range of people. Additionally, the length of the communication is an important consideration. Some stakeholders, such as legislators, may want brief summaries, while others, such as journalists, may want complete descriptions so that they can determine what is most important and useful. And finally, careful thought should be given to the actual *mode* used for dissemination, which again should be in accord with how the stakeholder group usually receives information. Written, verbal, and electronic (e.g., webpage, blog, e-mail attachment, or multimedia presentation) are the most common modes used, but others (e.g., product or process demonstration) may be appropriate. Thus, the whole leadership and advocacy accountability process comes down to thoughtful and careful planning from the very beginning to the very end.

## CONCLUSION

Myers, Sweeney, and White (2002) wrote, "A comprehensive national plan for advocacy, prepared and implemented through a coalition of counselors and counseling organizations, is needed and is, in fact, a professional imperative" (p. 401). Clearly such a movement requires leadership to become manifest. And just as clearly, as a significant professional endeavor, leadership and advocacy accountability are required to and for stakeholders both within and outside of the counseling profession. The means to achieving such accountability are available, and the entire counseling profession will benefit from achieving it.

## DISCUSSION QUESTIONS

1. In what areas or ways other than regarding leadership and advocacy has the counseling profession benefitted from the accountability activities of professional counselors? What was the nature of the accountability data and what were the benefits achieved?
2. What should be done to achieve greater acceptance of generating accountability information as an integral part of the work of professional counselors?
3. What criteria should a professional counselor apply to determine if she or he will implement a leadership or advocacy accountability activity?
4. Among the various stakeholder groups to which professional counselors might be accountable for leadership and advocacy activities, what criteria should be applied to determine situational order of priority among those stakeholder groups?
5. In what ways could the CACREP 2009 standards, CSI Principles of Leadership Excellence, and ACA advocacy competencies be integrated into more complementary or coherent professional statements?

How would they have to be modified to facilitate easier accountability practices?

6. What are the major similarities and differences between leadership and advocacy instructional and professional practice accountability?

7. Is being accountable (i.e., generating and disseminating accountability information) for any of your activities as a professional counselor also leadership and advocacy accountability? If so, how and why? If not, why not?

# *Appendix A: Selected Web Resources*

**2-1-1 Information and Referral Search** (http://www.211.org/). The 2-1-1 Information and Referral Search website provides free and confidential information and referrals for specific areas, including help with food, housing, employment, health care, counseling, and more.

**ACA/ACES Syllabus Clearinghouse** (www.counseling.org/Resources/TP/SyllabusClearinghouseHome/CT2.aspx). This website provides sample syllabi across counselor education programs. The website allows you to search by content area and to review syllabi uploaded by various counselor educators. You must be a member of ACA to search the clearinghouse.

**Aids Coalition to Unleash Power/New York (ACT UP/NY)** (www.actupny.org/). A diverse, nonpartisan group of individuals committed to direct action to end the AIDS crisis.

**American Counseling Association** (www.counseling.org). The ACA website includes links to the ACA Code of Ethics, the ACA advocacy competencies, the AMCD multicultural counseling competencies, the ACA job center, and several resources that counselors can use in their advocacy and leadership efforts (e.g., data on the effectiveness of counseling, public policy and legislative updates, etc.). In addition, there are links to all ACA divisions, which also have advocacy and leadership resources related to areas of counseling specializations.

**American Counseling Association advocacy competencies** (www.counseling.org/Resources/Competencies/Advocacy_Competencies.pdf). Adopted by ACA in 2003, this document provides counselors with a set of dispositions for affecting change at both the individual and systems level.

**American Counseling Association multicultural counseling competencies** (www.counseling.org/Resources/Competencies/Multcultural_Competencies.pdf). This document provides a set of counselor dispositions that characterize the awareness level, knowledge base, and skill set that are necessary for competent counseling intervention into the lives of clients from diverse cultural backgrounds.

**American Counseling Association public policy website** (http://www. counseling.org/PublicPolicy/). This website provides essential information related to ACA's professional advocacy initiatives, including legislative updates, current issues, methods of communicating with Congress, action steps you can take, and a list of resources.

**American Mental Health Counseling Association** (www.amhca.org). This official website of the American Mental Health Counseling Association (AMHCA) provides current information regarding training, malpractice protection, networking, and employment opportunities for mental health counselors.

**American School Counselor Association** (www.schoolcounselor.org/). This official website of the American School Counselor Association (ASCA) provides information on K–12 school counselors' efforts to help students focus on academic, personal/social, and career development, including an overview of the ASCA's National Model for School Counseling Programs®.

**Amnesty International** (www.amnesty.org/). Seeks to promote the human rights included in the Universal Declaration of Human Rights, focusing especially on prisoners of conscience, ending the death penalty, and combating torture.

**Association of Community Organizations for Reform Now (ACORN)** (www.acorn.org/). A national organization of low- and moderate-income families, mostly people of color, working together to make their communities a better place.

**Association for Counselor Education and Supervision (ACES)** (http:// www.acesonline.net). The ACES website includes resources specific to supervision, including suggested readings on advocacy and social justice, the ACES Standards for Counseling Supervisors, and a curriculum guide that can be applied to a variety of supervisor training programs.

**Association for Lesbian, Gay, Bisexual, and Transgender Issues in Counseling (ALGBTIC)** (http://www.algbtic.org). In addition to the competencies for counseling gay, lesbian, bisexual, and transgendered (LGBT) clients and the ALGBTIC competencies for counseling transgender clients, this website provides a multitude of resources designed to help counselors and supervisors most effectively serve individuals who are LGBT (and questioning).

**Association for Multicultural Counseling and Development (AMCD)** (http://www.amcdaca.org/amcd/default.cfm). In addition to the AMCD multicultural counseling competencies (also in the appendices section of this book), this website provides resources on global leadership, training and development, and research related to multicultural issues, with a focus on race and ethnicity.

**Association for Spiritual, Ethical, and Religious Values in Counseling (ASERVIC)** (http://www.aservic.org). To be a culturally competent counselor and supervisor, one must be able to recognize and address issues of spirituality and religion in counseling. ASERVIC has recently (2009) revised the competencies for addressing spiritual and religious issues in counseling, which have been endorsed by ACA.

**CAPWIZ public policy** (http://capwiz.com/counseling/home/). This website includes critical public policy issues that inform advocacy initiatives and could serve as a catalyst for developing timely assignments in a variety of courses.

**Center for Creative Leadership** (www.ccl.org). Nonprofit organization focused on leadership education and research; site includes information regarding leadership development trainings and the opportunity to sign up for free e-newsletter, *Leading Effectively*.

**Center for Ethical Leadership** (www.utexas.edu/lbj/research/leadership). Website for the Center for Ethical Leadership at University of Texas provides sample publications and syllabi related to leadership development.

**Center for Leadership and Ethics** (http://www.leadershipandethics.com/). The Center for Leadership and Ethics is committed to developing character and promoting ethics in daily life.

**Center for Third World Organizing** (www.ctwo.org/). A racial justice organization led by people of color whose mission is to achieve social and economic justice.

**Chi Sigma Iota** (www.csi-net.org). This official website of Chi Sigma Iota includes access to leadership resources, chapter information, a calendar for upcoming events, global networks, and a library of books and movies relevant to professional counseling via the "counselor's bookshelf."

**Chi Sigma Iota advocacy site** (www.csi-net.org/advocacy). This website has useful resources for counselors related to both professional and client advocacy.

**Chi Sigma Iota International** (csi-net.org/international). This website includes an extensive bibliography of published articles about counseling in countries around the globe and forums organized by continent where counselors can post information about their experiences with counseling and counselors around the world.

**Chi Sigma Iota leadership** (www.csi-net.org/leadership). Resources on this website include the CSI Principles and Practices of Leadership Excellence, essays on leadership excellence, and other information to assist counselors in developing leadership competence.

**Children's Defense Fund** (www.childrensdefense.org/). A child advocacy organization that champions policies and programs that lift children out of poverty, protect them from abuse and neglect, and ensure their access to health care, quality education, and a moral and spiritual foundation.

**Corporation for National and Community Service** (www.learnandserve. org). The website offers information about service learning opportunities across the nation and also details initiatives within higher education and grant opportunities.

**Council for Accreditation of Counseling and Related Educational Programs** (www.cacrep.org). The official website of the Council for Accreditation of Counseling and Related Educational Programs (CACREP) includes a full downloadable version of the 2009 standards, which for the first time specify essential leadership skills and abilities, news and events, information for students, information for programs, benefits of securing CACREP accreditation, and attending a CACREP accredited program.

**Education Trust: National Center for Transforming School Counseling** (http://www.edtrust.org/dc/tsc). This official website of the National Center for Transforming School Counseling (TSC) illustrates the work the TSC does with a network of organizations, state departments of education, school counselor professional associations, higher education institutions, and school districts dedicated to transforming school counselors into powerful agents and advocates of change in their schools and in the lives of students.

**European Association for Counseling** (http://www.eac.eu.com). This site reviews information about European national counseling associations, resources, standards, certification, and accreditation in the European continent. Includes information about obtaining a European certificate in counseling.

**Family Violence Prevention Fund** (http://endabuse.org). This website addresses domestic abuse—prevention for victims and perpetrator intervention—and child abuse violence prevention.

**GLSEN: The Gay, Lesbian, and Straight Education Network** (http://www. glsen.org/cgi-bin/iowa/all/home/index.html). This official website of GLSEN (The Gay, Lesbian and Straight Education Network) provides resources to ensure that each member of every school community is valued and respected regardless of sexual orientation or gender identity/ expression.

**GovTrack** (www.govtrack.us). Started in 2004, this citizen-based website promotes transparency in government by highlighting current legislative issues, voting records, and other important government information.

**Greenleaf Center for Servant Leadership** (www.greenleaf.org). This website introduces the reader to many facets of Greenleaf's leadership philosophy and work, including a definition of service leadership, information on conferences and training dedicated to this topic, and Greenleaf's essay on servant leadership that provided the foundation for its continued development and growth.

**Human Rights Campaign** (www.hrc.org/). The largest civil rights organization working to achieve equality for lesbian, gay, bisexual, and transgender Americans.

**International Association of Addictions and Offender Counseling** (www.iaocc.org). This official website of the International Association of Addictions and Offender Counseling (IAAOC) division of the American Counseling Association provides useful information about issues facing persons living with addictions or criminal behaviors.

**International Association for Counselling** (http://www.iac-irtac.org/Welcome.html). This site includes membership information, affiliate organizations, conference information, and connections to international research groups. This organization's journal is the *International Journal for the Advancement of Counselling.*

**International Registry of Counselor Education Programs** (http://www.ircep.org/ircep/template/index.cfm). This site aims to develop training curricula that integrate country-specific values and culture with ethical and excellent counseling practice across the globe.

**Jobs with Justice** (www.jwj.org/). Engages workers and allies in campaigns to win justice in workplaces and in communities where working families live.

**Library of Congress: Thomas** (http://thomas.loc.gov/home/thomas.php). This site provides updated contact information for your senators and representatives. You can also use this site to search for bills by topic, bill number, or bill title.

**Mental Health Liaison Group** (www.mhlg.org). This group provides its members "the opportunity to exchange political intelligence, form cooperative advocacy efforts, coordinate strategies and discuss public policy issues related to mental health" (http://www.mhlg.org/history_2010.pdf).

**National Alliance on Mental Illness** (www.nami.org). NAMI is dedicated to improving the lives of individuals and families affected by mental illness. NAMI focuses on awareness, education, and advocacy efforts that support those with mental illness.

**National Board for Certified Counselors** (http://nbcc.org). This certification agency provides resources for counselors and counselors-in-training. It directs counselors regarding national and state licensure, examination processes, advocacy efforts, and continuing education units (CEUs).

**NBCC International** (http://www.nbccinternational.org/). NBCC International works with other agencies across the globe to promote the counseling mission and expand counseling practice in culturally appropriate ways.

**National Coalition Against Domestic Violence** (www.ncadv.org). This website addresses domestic abuse and sexual assault treatment, prevention, and education and connects people with local domestic violence resources.

**National Coalition on the Homeless** (www.nationalhomeless.org/). A national network of people who are currently experiencing or who have experienced homelessness, activists and advocates, community-based and faith-based service providers, and others committed to ending homelessness.

**National Office for School Counselor Advocacy** (http://advocacy.collegeboard.org/college-preparation-access/national-office-school-counselor-advocacy-nosca). This website provides a variety of resources with a goal of promoting the value of school counselors as leaders in school reform, student achievement, and college readiness.

**National Organization for Women (NOW)** (www.now.org/). NOW's goal is to take action to bring about equality for all women by ending all forms of violence against women; eradicating racism, sexism, and homophobia; and promoting societal equality and justice.

**Rape, Abuse, Incest National Network** (www.rainn.org). RAINN connects victims of sexual assault with treatment and legal resources, while also providing sexual assault education and prevention, and a toll-free call-in number for victims.

**Southern Poverty Law Center** (www.splcenter.org/). A civil rights organization dedicated to fighting hate and bigotry, and to seeking justice for the most vulnerable members of society.

**Teaching Tolerance: A Project of the Southern Poverty Law Center** (www.tolerance.org). This website provides educational resources related to advocacy and social justice, and provides thought-provoking news, conversation, and support for those who care about diversity, equal opportunity, and respect for differences in schools.

**The Trevor Project** (http://www.thetrevorproject.org/). This website overviews programs identified with The Trevor Project, focused on ending suicide among LGBTQ youth by providing life-saving and life-affirming resources, including a nationwide, 24/7 crisis intervention lifeline, digital community, and advocacy/educational programs that create a safe, supportive, and positive environment for everyone.

**United Nations International Children's Emergency Fund (UNICEF)** (www.unicef.org/). The United Nations agency that helps build a world where the rights of every child are realized by influencing decision makers and a variety of partners at the grassroots level.

**Universal Declaration of Human Rights** (www.un.org/en/documents/udhr/index.shtml). Proclaimed by the United Nations on December 10, 1948, this document presents 30 articles that form the basis of human rights for all people.

**U.S. Senate** (http://www.senate.gov/index.htm). This is the official site for the U.S. Senate and provides information about pending legislation and the voting records of individual senators.

**White House** (www.WhiteHouse.gov). This site provides updates on featured legislation. You can also search this site by issue, including education and health care.

**World Health Organization** (http://www.who.int/en). This site includes information about WHO's mission, resources, and publications. It also includes links to the Department of Mental Health and Substance Dependence.

**Workshop exercises** (www.workshopexercises.com). A fun website designed to help individuals across any discipline boost their leadership training. The 15 leadership activities, developed by scholars and business leaders, are free and can be accessed on the website, which also includes team-building exercises, leadership insights, tips for running a smooth meeting, and how to focus a team.

# Appendix B:
# Chi Sigma Iota—Principles and Practice of Leadership Excellence

### PRINCIPLE 1: PHILOSOPHY OF LEADERSHIP

Exemplary leaders recognize that service to others, the profession, and the associations are the preeminent reasons for involvement in leadership positions.

**Practice:** Leaders recognize that service to others is a hallmark for effective leadership that requires:

- careful consideration of the magnitude of their commitment prior to accepting a nomination for a leadership role;
- acceptance of leadership positions primarily for the purpose of service rather than personal reward; and
- willingness to seek counsel prior to decision making that affects others.

### PRINCIPLE 2: COMMITMENT TO MISSION

Exemplary leaders show evidence of a continuing awareness of and commitment to furthering the mission of their organization.

**Practice:** Leaders maintain a continuing awareness of and dedication to enhancing the mission, strategic plan, bylaws, and policies of the organization throughout all leadership functions. They work individually and in teams to fulfill the objectives of the organization in service to others.

### PRINCIPLE 3: PRESERVATION OF HISTORY

Exemplary leaders respect and build upon the history of their organization.

**Practice:** Leaders study the history of their organization through review of archival documents (e.g., minutes of meetings, policies) and other resources, and discussions with current and former leaders, and they act to build upon that history through informed decision making.

## PRINCIPLE 4: VISION OF THE FUTURE

Exemplary leaders use their knowledge of the organization's history, mission, and commitment to excellence to encourage and create change appropriate to meeting future needs.

**Practice:** Leaders draw upon the wisdom of the past and challenges of the future to articulate a vision of what can be accomplished through imagination, collaboration, cooperation, and creative use of resources.

## PRINCIPLE 5: LONG-RANGE PERSPECTIVE

Exemplary leaders recognize that service includes both short- and long-range perspectives.

**Practice:** Leaders act to impact the organization before the year of their primary office, during the year of their primary office, and beyond that year, as appropriate, to assure the ongoing success of the organization.

## PRINCIPLE 6: PRESERVATION OF RESOURCES

Exemplary leaders act to preserve the human and material resources of the organization.

**Practice:** Leaders assure that policies and practices are in effect to assure financial responsibility and continuing respectful treatment of human and other material resources of the organization.

## PRINCIPLE 7: RESPECT FOR MEMBERSHIP

Exemplary leaders respect the needs, resources, and goals of their constituencies in all leadership decisions.

**Practice:** Leaders are deliberate in making decisions that are respectful of the memberships' interests and enhance the benefits to them as active members in the organization.

## PRINCIPLE 8: MENTORING, ENCOURAGEMENT, AND EMPOWERMENT

Exemplary leaders place a priority on mentoring, encouraging, and empowering others.

**Practice:** Leaders assure that members are provided with opportunities to develop and apply their unique talents in service to others, the profession, and association.

## PRINCIPLE 9: RECOGNITION OF OTHERS

Exemplary leaders assure that all who devote their time and talents in service to the mission of the organization receive appropriate recognition for their contributions.

**Practice:** Leaders maintain records of service to the organization and provide for public recognition of service on an annual basis, minimally (e.g., letters of appreciation, certificates of appreciation).

## PRINCIPLE 10: FEEDBACK AND SELF-REFLECTION

Exemplary leaders engage in self-reflection, obtain feedback on their performance in leadership roles from multiple sources, and take appropriate action to better serve the organization.

**Practice:** Leaders seek feedback, for example, from members of their leadership team, personal and leadership mentors, and past leaders of the organization. Exemplary leaders experiencing significant life transitions or crises actively and regularly seek consultation from such mentors regarding their capacity to continue the work of the organization during such duress. Leaders take action congruent with that feedback, which reflects their commitment to these Principles and Practices of Leadership Excellence.

Developed by the CSI Academy of Leaders for Excellence and approved by the CSI executive council for distribution to its members and chapters (1999). CSI © 2011. All rights reserved.

Chi Sigma Iota. (2009). *Principles and Practices of Leadership Excellence.* Greensboro, NC: Author. Retrieved from http://www.csi-net.org/leadership. Reprinted with permission.

# Appendix C:
# Counselor Advocacy Leadership Conferences I and II

## May 27–29, 1998 and December 11–12, 1998

### PREFACE

Chi Sigma Iota (CSI), the counseling honor society, instituted a new advocacy initiative that has long-term implications for leadership training through CSI chapters on university campuses throughout the world. The CSI Executive Council decided to make advocacy for counselors a long-term, sustained commitment. CSI leaders wish that this effort be as broadly based and inclusive as the profession itself. As a consequence, in May of 1998, an invited group of leaders in the profession met in Greensboro, NC, to share, discuss, and compare perceptions on a common vision for the advocacy of counselors and the services that they provide to others. The outcomes of the meeting were so positive that the participating organizations asked that a follow up conference be held in December in order further on the work underway.

ACA immediate Past-President Courtland Lee accepted the original invitation to collaborate with CSI in instituting this new initiative in May and ACA President Loretta Bradley offered her support to ensure that the results of these efforts are made available during the ACA 1999 World Conference in San Diego in April.

### ADVOCACY

All counselors entered the counseling profession with a desire to help others. Client advocacy feels right as a consequence. Counselors advocating for counselors and the services they provide may seem selfish or self-serving. However, a counselor does not need to be in the field long before realizing that in the absence of advocacy for the profession, the right to be a counselor serving any particular population would be very severely limited.

Every occupational group must be proactive in the marketplace or they will become extinct over time. Counselors must not only believe in their profession's preparation standards, graduate programs, credentialing requirements, and scope of services, but they must educate, inform, and promote them to legislators, employers, third party payers, and the public at large. This can be done most effectively, however, while addressing advocacy for our clients as well.

While CSI has implicitly supported both client and counselor advocacy by the very nature of its mission and purpose, CSI leaders were left wondering if there was more they could do for counselor advocacy through our almost 200 chapters and more than 8,000 active members. Learning how to advocate for the counseling profession is a leadership competence worthy of the attention of CSI. Sixty percent of CSI members are students just launching their careers as counselors and the other 40 percent are experienced practitioners and counselor educators.

With these assets in mind, seeking the insight, experience, and collaboration of others in the profession seemed essential. By meeting together, we hoped that all might benefit by a shared vision, a clearer idea of what is being done, what needs to be done, and how best to achieve what we hold as common goals, particularly in the area of professional advocacy for counselors and those they serve. Not only were these hopes realized, but a renewed vigor was uncovered by the participants of all organizations represented. The hope of the participants now is for a sustained, coordinated effort by all those organizations interested in this essential activity.

Six Themes Identified

Representatives at the first conference agreed on a number of vital points. Among the agreements were those about common themes on advocacy, the desirability of collaboration in the definition of those themes, and a commitment to follow through with their implementation. There were six themes identified for further definition: marketplace recognition, inter-professional issues, intra-professional issues, counselor education, research, and client/constituency wellness.

Those present were sensitive to the fact that not all potentially interested groups were represented. Fortunately, a preliminary survey report sponsored by CSI and ACA of a broad representation of counseling groups was presented and the information was included in the deliberations of the focus groups. Data from the completed survey has been distributed widely to others interested in the topic. Among the organizations officially represented in the first conference were ACA, the American College Counseling Association (ACCA), the Association for Counselor Education and Supervision (ACES), the Association for Multicultural

Counseling and Development (AMCD), the American Mental Health Counselors Association (AMHCA), the American Rehabilitation Counseling Association (ARCA), the American School Counselor Association (ASCA), the International Association of Marriage and Family Counseling (IAMFC) the Council for the Accreditation of Counseling and Related Educational Programs (CACREP), Chi Sigma Iota (CSI), ERIC-CASS, the National Board for Certified Counselors (NBCC), and the North Carolina Counseling Association (NCCA) (state branch). A draft report was sent to all participants for their input. Interested organizations were invited to respond to the report as well.

The purpose of the December meeting was to revisit the themes, the goals and objectives for achieving each theme, time lines, and the identification of resources in their implementation and follow through. As with the first conference, there was agreement on a number of important general points.

First, the participants agreed that advocacy is necessarily two pronged in nature. Without advocacy for both counselors and their clients, neither is meaningful. Because "counseling" as an activity is practiced by other service providers, advocacy for clients alone could result in other service providers being the sole source of such counseling services. Likewise, to advocate only for "guild" issues wins neither support nor respect from those whose assistance counselors need. As has been noted by the continuing series of articles in the ACA Counseling Today as well as other publications and the theme for this year's world conference, client issues are central to our efforts as a profession.

Another agreement among the participants was the need to seek broad based, active support for the goals, objectives, and strategies of the overall plan. While much good work is already underway, as evidenced by our several successes of recent months and years, a collaborative, comprehensive approach holds the greatest promise for the best use of our mutual resources. Every counseling association will be invited to adopt resolutions in support of the goals coming out of these conferences. Each will be invited to strengthen our collaboration through some organized forum such as the conferences held in May and December.

Philosophically, the participants agreed that counseling as a profession is unique among service providers because of its historical focus upon facilitating optimum human development across the life span. While no less concerned with the results of human tragedy nor its repair in the process of helping, counselors are members of the one discipline for which prevention and the facilitation of optimum wellness are fundamental goals. Our present health system is dysfunctional in its focus and delivery. Although funding for proactive interventions has been the exception rather than the rule, changes are now evident among insurers, managed care companies, business, and industry. While maintaining an advocacy position for clinical mental health, now is the time to promote our uniqueness as a profession committed to prevention and the enhancement of wellness.

What follows is the outcome of the two conferences. The recommendations of these task forces, each of which dealt with two themes, are presented. Although divided by task force, it should be noted that each report was approved by the conference participants as a whole. It is based upon the insight of experienced, totally dedicated advocates for the profession and our clients. As with all such documents, it can only reflect some of what actually can and should be done to realize our goals. The participants are aware that not all recommendations or activities can or even should be considered a priority for all associations asked to endorse it. The nature of this advocacy initiative has such depth and scope that to endorse it in principle will be sufficient to communicate support for further dialogue.

Likewise, the form of the report cannot do justice to the real work that is and needs to be done. Themes are identified as though they are discrete, but in practice they are not discrete and often cannot be separated. Advocacy, for example, by its very nature must include client as well as counselor concerns and needs. As a consequence, the organizers and participants welcome suggestions and comments in order to help us move forward effectively in this initiative.

*Advocacy Resolution #1*

Whereas, there are national standards for the preparation of professional counselors;

Whereas, there are both nationally accredited and other graduate programs dedicated to the preparation of professional counselors;

Whereas, there are national standards for the certification of professional counselors;

Whereas, there are state legislative requirements for the credentialing of professional counselors;

Whereas, there are state, regional, and national professional associations dedicated to advancing the scientific, educational, and philosophical foundations of the counseling profession and its members;

Whereas, there are individuals, couples, families, and organizations within our society for whom counselors advocate and serve; and

Whereas, there are obstacles to the realization of the full potential of professional counselors in service to those whom they serve, including challenges to the scope of practice, equal opportunity to serve those who need and desire their services, equal payment for services and the right to practice at all;

Therefore, be it resolved that this association supports in principle the goals, objectives, and proposed actions outlined in the Counselor Advocacy Leadership Conferences Report and remains committed to further dialogue on these and other topics related to advocacy.

*Advocacy Resolution #2*

Whereas, there are 125 nationally-accredited counselor education programs;

Whereas, there are over 65,000 state credentialed professional counselors;

Whereas, there are over 45,000 nationally credentialed professional counselors;

Whereas, there are over 110,000 members of state and national counseling associations;

Whereas, there is evidence that counseling services help to alleviate and prevent both acute and transitional human development challenges;

Whereas, there are persistent and substantial challenges to the right of professional counselors to be paid for their services, to be employed in a variety of settings, and to provide services to individuals, couples, families, and organizations who need them; and

Whereas, there is greater resource and potential impact through collaborative, coordinated, cooperative efforts of all professional counselors and their associations;

Therefore, be it resolved that this association supports in principle the need for collaboration on a comprehensive plan of advocacy for clients and the professional counselors who serve them and will be represented in future dialogue about how best to achieve this goal including but not limited to a Consortium for Counselor Advocacy (CCA).

**Optional motions**:

1. This association supports in principle the goals, objectives, and proposed actions outlined in the Counselor Advocacy Leadership Conferences Report and remains committed to further dialogue on these and other topics related to advocacy.

2. This association supports in principle the need for collaboration on a comprehensive plan of advocacy for clients and the professional counselors who serve them and will be represented in future dialogue about how best to achieve this goal including but not limited to a Consortium for Counselor Advocacy (CCA).

Consortium for Counseling Advocacy

The Consortium for Counseling Advocacy (CCA) is a new initiative to insure coordination and collaboration in efforts of the various counseling associations committed to similar goals and objectives for client welfare and counselors' right to practice. All divisions and branches of the American Counseling Association (ACA), the Council for Accreditation of Counseling and Related Educational Programs (CACREP), the National Board of Certified Counselors (NBCC), the Commission for Certified Rehabilitation Counselors, (CRCC), the Council of

Rehabilitation Education (CORE), the American Association of State Counseling Boards (AASCB), and Chi Sigma Iota Counseling Academic and Professional Honor Society International (CSI) are invited to participate in the formation, implementation, and maintenance of the CCA. The need for the Consortium was identified by the participants of two national conferences on counseling advocacy.

The Consortium is designed to provide a forum for the identification of issues, consensus on resolution and action, and mechanisms for cooperation and collaboration at state and national levels of activity. Representatives of the constituent organizations agree to sponsor a representative to come to one meeting per year related to the purposes outlined in the Counselor Advocacy Leadership Conferences report (April, 1999). One goal will be to minimize duplication and maximize the use of existing resources. Among the first priorities will be establishment of means for communication and continuation of the work already underway. Initially, as requested by the conference participants, CSI will continue follow-up activities needed to facilitate the transition from the conference dialogue to actions outlined in the conferences report.

Each association noted above is asked to respond to the invitation for participation through adoption of the resolutions or motions associated with the conferences and appointment of one or more representatives to participate in the work of the Consortium.

### THEME A: COUNSELOR EDUCATION

Goal: To insure that all counselor education students graduate with a clear identity and sense of pride as professional counselors.

Objectives to achieve the goal:

1. All faculty members preparing professional counselors will perceive their primary professional identification as counselor educators and, as a consequence, as members of the counseling associations, especially ACES.

   **Activities:**
   a. CACREP will be encouraged to incorporate into its standards a clear expectation for the faculty to be counselor education graduates (preferably from CACREP accredited programs) and that individuals coordinating the programs will be counselor education graduates.
   b. CACREP will continue to project a clear expectation for all counselor education faculty to attend and be professionally active in state, regional, and national counseling associations.
   c. ACES will be encouraged to work closely with ACA, its divisions, and regions to promote the involvement of counselor educators in their activities as well as its own.

    d.  Universities will be encouraged to employ counselor education graduates through special recognition for doing so by the counseling associations.

2. Students and graduates will identify themselves fundamentally as Professional Counselors and, as a consequence, as members of the ACA and its divisions.

    **Activities:**

    a.  A survey of counselor education students and recent graduates will be conducted to ascertain their current identity preferences, factors influencing those choices, and implications for professional affiliations, credentials, and employment.

    b.  ACA and ACES will be encouraged to establish a task force to identify materials, methods, and techniques for the purpose of promoting a clear professional identity with counseling by professional counselors. These can then be shared with counselor education faculty teaching the professional orientation courses.

    c.  CSI will be encouraged to develop and distribute a protocal for professional counselors to use in identifying themselves to the public upon graduation.

3. Students and graduates will have knowledge of and respect for counseling specialties.

    **Activities:**

    a.  A task force of representatives from ACA, its specialty divisions, NBCC, and ACES will identify materials, methods, and techniques for the purpose of helping to articulate a clear professional identity with counseling by professional counselors and its relationship to the counseling specialties. These will be shared with counselor education faculty teaching the professional orientation courses.

    b.  The ACA web site will include a page with information and explanation of the specialties within counseling.

4. All counselor education faculty will be credentialed as Professional Counselors.

    **Activities:**

    a.  CACREP will be encouraged to continue its standards that provide for all counselor education faculty to maintain a state and/or national credential as a professional counselor.

b. Counselor educators will be encouraged to display their professional counselor certification and/or licenses for students and others to see in their offices.

c. Regional accrediting bodies will be encouraged to incorporate a review of professional credentials especially for counselor education faculty teaching clinical courses and supervising practica and internships.

5. All counselor educators will be active and encourage their students to be active in professional counseling organizations.

**Activities:**

a. CACREP will be encouraged to continue in its standards an expectation for all counselor education faculty to actively participate in local, state, regional, and national professional associations by membership, conference attendance and presentations, and service.

b. Counseling associations will be encouraged to establish methods for recognition of counselor educators, students, and institutional programs that regularly and substantively contribute to the work of the associations.

6. All counselor education programs will be encouraged to work toward achieving CACREP-accreditation.

**Activities:**

a. Counseling associations will be encouraged to establish benefits and recognition for students and programs that are CACREP accredited, e.g., reduced dues, conference registration, and exhibit fees as well as special mention in their publications, programs, etc.

b. Counseling associations will be encouraged to promote national accreditation through their literature, web sites, and other media including, for example, membership applications by inquiring about student and graduate program status with respect to accreditation.

7. All counselor education programs will be encouraged to incorporate into their curriculum the teaching of advocacy for clients and the profession.

**Activities:**

a. Counseling associations will help to develop and distribute advocacy materials for use in the professional orientation courses in counselor education.

   b.  Chi Sigma Iota will be encouraged to compile and distribute advocacy materials designed to inform and educate students and practitioners in all counselor education programs.

   c.  CSI will be encouraged to develop a web page to showcase model advocacy programs for clients and counselors.

8. All counselor education graduates will be eligible for professional counselor credentials upon completion of supervised post-graduate clinical experience.

**Activities:**

   a.  Counseling associations will be asked to provide coverage in their publications on the criteria, benefits, and sources of professional counselor credentials.

   b.  Applicants for membership in counseling associations will be asked to note what professional counseling credentials that they hold.

   c.  Counseling associations will help to educate students and potential counselor education students to both CACREP and credentialing requirements for preparation as a professional counselor.

Responsible Parties

ACA, its branches and divisions, CSI, CACREP, and NBCC.

Assets

The needed structure is in place: counselor education programs (N= 400 possibilities), 125 CACREP nationally accredited programs, state and national credentialing agencies, the professional organizations and their memberships, a web of networks, the individual and organizational skills that will result from these efforts, and opportunities for getting financial support.

Obstacles

Many members of counseling associations including those who work in counselor education are not professional counselors and do not share our passion or efforts for advocacy;

Students/graduates receive mixed messages from faculty and colleagues regarding the adequacy of their preparation, where they should seek advanced preparation, and what they should call what they do and what they are, i.e., counseling and professional counselor vs. therapy and therapist;

Counseling associations send mixed messages to their membership when they highlight disagreements among leaders' points of view between organizations and understate or ignore successes made through collaboration on common goals and objectives.

Too many advocacy efforts are assigned to a small staff or a few volunteer members when many more are needed of both.

### Resources Needed

ACES is the most logical organization within ACA to provide leadership. CSI is next in its potential to provide a positive influence. Naturally, they require the concurrence and involvement of all counseling associations at various times and places.

### Association Actions

1. ACES leaders will incorporate one or more goals and objectives into their strategic plan and annual activities that address the fundamental issues underlying counselor education and advocacy.
2. CSI, in conjunction with other counseling associations, will develop advocacy materials and help distribute them to counselor education programs throughout the country.
3. CACREP will continue its efforts through definitions and standards to make clear that counselor education involves more than a definable body of knowledge and skill. It also includes a philosophy, values, and behaviors associated with the counseling profession that counselor educators trained by CACREP Standards are best able to teach and model.
4. CSI will continue its efforts to promote excellence within the counseling profession through preparation and practice as a matter of advocacy as well. As a consequence, it will incorporate into its leadership training competencies for advocacy.

### Timeline

By the year 2000, counseling associations and agencies will have passed resolutions necessary to establishing a sound basis for the realization of these goals and objectives over a span of five to ten years.

### THEME B: INTRAPROFESSIONAL RELATIONS

Goal: To develop and implement a unified, collaborative advocacy plan for the advancement of counselors and those whom they serve.

Objectives to achieve the goal:

1. Professional counseling associations will agree upon a common identity to articulate publicly.

**Activities:**

a. A task force of counseling association representatives chosen for their scholarship, leadership, and experience in the counseling professionalization movement will be asked to develop an identity, definition, and rationale for a "common identity to articulate publicly."

b. Association governing bodies will be encouraged to reach consensus upon the "common identity" that staff and volunteers can incorporate into all public documents when appropriate.

2. Professional counseling associations will proactively collaborate on advocacy projects, e.g., legislation, research, grants, and related activities.

**Activities:**

a. ACA staff will be encouraged to continue collecting and distributing a compilation of advocacy related activities of all counseling associations on at least a yearly basis. The ACA web site will be a repository for these compilations.

b. Staff and volunteers will be directed to continue seeking opportunities to inform and collaborate with members of other association staff and committees.

3. Professional counseling associations will be unified in seeking counselor-related legislation.

**Activities:**

a. Based upon a common legislative plan developed by the ACA Public Policy and Legislative Committee, all counseling associations will be encouraged to collaborate on common goals and activities.

b. Legislation related to specific clientele and settings will be supported by all counseling association efforts even though one or more specialty associations may be providing leadership for such efforts.

4. Professional counseling associations will be encouraged to consult with each other on matters of advocacy on a regular and systematic basis, including a comprehensive, collaborative advocacy plan for the profession.

**Activities:**

a. Counseling association representatives will be invited to participate in advocacy planning and collaboration conferences at least once and possibly twice a year.

b. A network of advocacy staff and volunteers will be established for purposes of communication, dialogue, and cooperation on matters related to advocacy.

Responsible Parties

ACA, its branches and divisions, CSI, CACREP, and NBCC.

Assets

All counseling associations most interested in advocacy already have an agenda, committees, staff, and ongoing activities.

Our associations already have a history of collaboration and successes, as a consequence.

Our memberships for the counseling associations expect, if not require, that for their continuing support and membership, advocacy for them and their clients must be a high priority of the associations.

Other disciplines expect us to be united in our efforts, otherwise we can be discounted much more readily.

In spite of recent differences among leadership of counseling associations, we have more in common as a profession than the differences suggest.

Obstacles

All counseling associations most interested in advocacy already have an agenda, committees, staff, and ongoing activities. As a consequence, each tends to entertain a proprietary sense of what is most important and how and who is best able to address it.

Existing resources assigned to advocacy efforts are fully committed. There is a very real possibility that a new, comprehensive emphasis upon advocacy could be ambitious beyond what is reasonable for present resources. To over-commit or under-fund the efforts could result in unnecessary frustration, failure, or both.

Resources Needed

There is a need for counseling associations to address these objectives through financial and organizational means. Through strategic plans and specific actions, governing bodies and their officers set the priorities that in turn direct resources and guide staff and volunteers in their efforts.

Association Actions

1. ACA, its divisions and branches, CSI, CACREP, and NBCC will be invited to pass resolutions in support of the goals, objectives, and principles of advocacy outlined by the Counselor Advocacy Leadership Conferences of 1998.

2. ACA, its divisions and branches, CSI, CACREP, and NBCC will be invited to participate in a Consortium for Counseling Advocacy (CCA) through which collaboration, cooperation, and common goals and objectives can be identified and addressed.

Timeline

By the year 2000, counseling associations and agencies will have passed resolutions necessary to establishing a sound basis for the realization of these goals and objectives over a span of five to ten years.

## THEME C: MARKETPLACE RECOGNITION

Goal: To assure that professional counselors in all settings are suitably compensated for their services and free to provide service to the public within all areas of their competence.

Objectives to achieve the goal:

1. Professional counselors will be identified in both state and national legislation as service providers in all areas for which they have competence through preparation and experience.

   **Activities:**
   a. Counseling associations will asked to establish within their strategic plans and annual program of activities both state and federal legislative agendas to insure professional counselors may be service providers in all areas for which they have competence.
   b. A compilation of state and federal classification systems related to counseling service providers will be maintained and made available to all counselors.
   c. A profile of what Licensed Professional Counselors' scope of practice entails will be developed, maintained, and distributed.
   d. A matrix of barriers to full recognition of professional counselors in both state and federal systems will be developed and addressed through association plans of action.
   e. Counseling associations will be asked to establish a plan for joint leadership training in advocacy on a continuing basis for both state and national officers.
   f. All professional counselors will be encouraged to obtain and advocate for their state and/or national credentials through both individual and collegial efforts.
   g. All professional counselors will be encouraged to join and be active members of one or (preferably) more professional associations at state, regional, national, and international levels.
   h. All professional counselors and counselors-in-training will be provided opportunities for developing advocacy skills.

2. Professional counselors will be accepted for employment and/or payment in any setting or for any service to clients for which they have competence and preparation.

**Activities:**

a. Data compiled on the current employment status of professional counselors will be widely distributed in order both to highlight their services and to emphasize the benefits of having more counselors to meet client needs.

b. Opportunities and obstacles to employment will be addressed through advocacy plans of action by counseling associations.

c. Targets of opportunity will be sought to challenge systemic bias against professional counselors and the clients whom they serve through legal or other means.

3. Professional counselors will be broadly recognized in the media and elsewhere as providing needed and valuable service to individuals, couples, families, organizations, and society at large.

**Activities:**

a. A consortium of counseling organizations will be explored to pursue matters of funding, effective organizational collaboration, auditing internal and external resources, and strategic planning.

b. A long-term plan for achieving broad-based, positive recognition in the media and elsewhere will be developed. It will be grounded in client needs and professional counselors' contributions to clients' well being.

c. All counselors and counselors-in-training will be invited to participate in one or more phases of this effort.

Responsible Parties

All counselors, ACA, its branches and divisions, CSI, CACREP, and NBCC.

Assets

Our assets are multiple including:

High public regard for "counseling" and "professional counselors" as a part of normal human development activities versus the negative connotations for "sickness" and dysfunction of "therapy";

Philosophical and scientific grounding in human growth and development with concern both for prevention and optimum wellness across the life span and for assessment of that which is dysfunctional;

National preparation standards that provide both entry level and advanced level educational guidelines for practitioners, educators, supervisors, and researchers;

Nationally accredited preparation programs and a numerically manageable body of other programs through which positive educational change can be implemented in a timely manner;

Credentials for professional counselors by both state and national agencies designed to promote quality assurance for greater public trust and protection;

Approximately 60,000 credentialed professional counselors in a variety of settings located throughout the country, often in areas not served by other mental health service providers;

Evidence that Masters level practitioners are effective within areas of practice for which other professions require doctoral preparation at more cost to the employer and consumer;

Counselor associations at local, state, regional, and national levels represent a powerful coalition for both public and professional good when vision and direction are clear and collaboration is the modus operandi;

Counselor associations provide needed structures for promoting scientific knowledge, leadership on professional issues, visibility to other associations for purposes of collaboration, and a sense of professional identity and unity for members located in every segment of our society and every geographical location in this country and abroad;

There have been notable successes at both state and national levels for legislative and media efforts that are changing the position and posture of professional counselors among legislators, other health providing organizations, and consumer organizations.

Obstacles

Obstacles also are multiple including:

The terms "counseling" and "counselor" are used loosely in every day language;

Even many counselors miss the opportunity for educating others by identifying themselves by other titles gained through "backdoor" methods (e.g., psychologists or therapists);

Many members of counseling associations including those who work in counselor education are not professional counselors and do not share our passion or efforts for advocacy;

Students/graduates receive mixed messages from faculty and colleagues regarding the adequacy of their preparation, where they should seek advanced preparation, and what they should call what they do and what they are, i.e., counseling and professional counselor vs. therapy and therapist;

National accreditation standards permit faculty from other disciplines not only to teach but to coordinate program emphases and chair the entire department of counselor education, thereby influencing who gets hired and promoted among faculty and who gets admitted to the program;

Both state and national credentials are available to other mental health providers and thus can be used by them as evidence that they can do the work of the professional counselor in addition to their primary professional discipline;

There is a movement within psychology to credential Masters level psychologists to do work in areas previously done by other health providers, including counselors;

Graduate degree programs, including "institutions without walls" taught by members of other disciplines, are being designed to meet state and national credential requirements, including course work with CACREP-like counseling curricula designations;

Psychiatric nurses, marriage and family therapists, and especially social workers are politically active at all levels of government and their administrative agencies, designing inroads to settings and clientele counselors might otherwise expect to be working with and serving;

Counseling association leaders have been distracted by organizational and structural issues that both confuse and discourage their memberships from having faith in a common vision and direction for advocacy.

Resources Needed

Among the needs will be those for a clear, articulated plan with a commitment for collaboration by the various counseling associations and agencies toward its implementation, identification of staff and volunteer resources needed to achieve desired outcomes, and financial support for specific activities targeted to specific, desired outcomes.

Association Actions:

1. ACA, its divisions and branches, CSI, CACREP, and NBCC will be invited to pass resolutions in support of the goals, objectives, and principles of advocacy outlined by the Counselor Advocacy Leadership Conferences of 1998.

2. ACA, its divisions and branches, CSI, CACREP, and NBCC will be invited to participate in a Consortium for Counseling Advocacy (CCA) through which collaboration, cooperation, and common goals and objectives can be identified and addressed.

3. A system for soliciting member priorities on legislative and regulatory issues will be established to insure consistency and continuity in our legislative efforts at both state and national levels.
4. A "state of the counseling profession" summary report on advocacy will be updated on a regular basis and will be published on a web site available to all interested professional counselors.
5. A collaborative plan of action will be developed addressing specific activities derived from the priorities of the membership. Various association staff and committees will be assigned to allocate their resources accordingly.
6. Based upon a needs assessment, additional resources required to achieve the goals within a five to ten year span will be identified including staff, consultants, and supporting services. The needs assessment and financial requirements will be placed before the counseling associations for consideration and action.
7. ACA will be asked to establish a program for advocacy grants to address specific issues related to the highest priority goals and objectives of the membership.
8. All of the associations and agencies will educate and encourage members in competencies needed to become advocates for their clients and the services that they provide to them. Association media, workshops, and presentations will regularly address topics and issues related to these competencies in order to reach all members at the state, regional, and national levels.

Timeline

By the year 2000, counseling associations and agencies will have passed resolutions necessary to establishing a sound basis for the realization of these goals and objectives over a span of five to ten years.

THEME D: INTERPROFESSIONAL ISSUES

Goal: To establish collaborative working relationships with other organizations, groups, and disciplines on matters of mutual interest and concern to achieve our advocacy goals for both counselors and their clients.

Objectives to achieve goal:

1. Professional counseling associations will identify associations, groups and disciplines with whom professional counselors at both the state and national levels will desire relationships for dialogue, information sharing, and potential collaboration.

**Activities:**

a.  ACA staff will be asked to identify and compile efforts already under-way by the various counseling association staff and volunteers for distribution and review by all interested parties to ascertain overlap and/or oversight of organizations important to advocacy efforts.

2.  A plan for systematically establishing and maintaining contact with the leadership of significant organizations and individuals that are impor-tant to counselor advocacy will be established and periodically revised to address new or changing concerns, issues, and dynamics.

**Activities:**

a.  A task force of the counseling associations' consortium will develop a plan for reviewing, prioritizing and recommending organizations with which to establish and maintain relationships.

3.  A strategy will be established to address initiatives by other organiza-tions or groups that have the potential for omitting, limiting, or block-ing the employment or practice of professional counselors.

**Activities:**

a.  A task force of the counseling associations' consortium will develop a plan for maintaining vigilance with respect to other disciplines' efforts to negatively affect the employment or scope of practice of professional counselors.

4.  Professional counseling associations will be encouraged to establish and maintain personnel and resources necessary to sustain counselor advo-cacy initiatives.

**Activities:**

a.  Annual plans for advocacy will be prepared by the counseling asso-ciations' consortium including staff and other needs required to ade-quately meet expectations such as those illustrated in this report.

b.  Counseling associations' governing bodies will be asked to review member priorities, progress reports, annual action plans, and requested resources and act accordingly.

Responsible Parties

All counselors, ACA, its branches and divisions, CSI, CACREP, and NBCC.

Assets

All counseling associations at both the state and national levels have on-going opportunities for contact and dialogue with other professional organizations and agencies. In many instances, inter-professional cooperation is already present on some issues. Client needs are held in common in many ways.

Obstacles

Absence of a profession-wide comprehensive plan and vision of what is needed in order to be most effective in inter-professional relations and activities.

Insufficient resources; trained volunteers or staff, or financial support to insure representation at essential functions, coalitions, etc.

Association Actions:

1. ACA, its divisions and branches, CSI, CACREP, and NBCC will pass resolutions endorsing collaboration on the development and implementation of a comprehensive plan for inter-professional relations in order to achieve the objectives identified above.
2. ACA, its divisions and branches, CSI, CACREP, and NBCC will direct its existing staff and committees to participate in this effort to achieve the optimum use of our mutual resources and to identify others still needed to achieve the stated goal and objectives.

Timeline

By the year 2000, counseling associations and agencies will have passed resolutions and taken action necessary to implementing the actions above.

## THEME E: RESEARCH

Goal: To promote professional counselors and the services that they provide based upon scientifically sound research.

Objectives to achieve the goal:

This goal will be addressed by counselor educators, students in counseling, and counseling organizations such as ACA and its divisions, CHDF, CSI, NBCC, CACREP, and ERIC-CASS:

1. To demonstrate the effectiveness of counseling through outcome research by:

   **Activities:**
   a. Promoting research on the effectiveness of counseling with individuals, children, families, groups, and other systems.

    b.  Promoting research on the effectiveness of counseling in new and emerging settings and paradigms.

    c.  Encouraging all practitioners to conduct research.

    d.  Encouraging multiple, broad based approaches to research (e.g., qualitative, quantitative, formative, summative, longitudinal, short term, or case study).

    e.  Encouraging our clients and constituencies (e.g., parents, administrators, under-served populations) to be active participants in the entire research process.

2. To assess the outcomes of counselor preparation by:

**Activities:**

    a.  Evaluating the ability to counsel.

    b.  Evaluating the ability to obtain employment.

    c.  Evaluating the ability to conduct research.

    d.  Evaluating the ability to be effective advocates for the profession and clients.

    e.  Evaluating the ability to manage a business.

3. To determine the state of counselor employability by:

**Activities:**

    a.  Identifying employment opportunities for counselors (e.g., federal/state levels).

    b.  Assessing factors affecting the retention of counselors in the profession (e.g., job satisfaction, salaries, trends).

    c.  Assessing employer perceptions of counselors and counseling services.

    d.  Identifying barriers to practice resulting from legislation and regulations at international, national, state and local levels.

    e.  Identifying comparative data on qualifications and salaries of counselors.

4. To assess public awareness of counseling by:

**Activities:**

    a.  Evaluating knowledge of counseling.

    b.  Determining perceptions of the availability of counseling services.

    c.  Determining patterns of use of counseling services.

    d.  Determining satisfaction with counseling services.

5. To determine sources of funding for research by:

**Activities:**

    a.  Identifying sources of grants/funding relevant to counseling research.

    b.  Investigating additional sources of funding.

6. To encourage the use of research by:

   **Activities:**
   a. Disseminating the results to appropriate and relevant populations (e.g., administrators, clients, professionals, legislators).
   b. Promoting the use of results as a basis for program development and improvement.

Responsible Parties

All counselors, counselors-in-training, counselor educators through ACA, its branches and divisions (particularly ACES), CSI, CACREP, and NBCC.

Assets

Existing publications and conferences, poster sessions,
Recognition of research through awards,
Human resources (e.g., well-trained professionals conducting research),
Commitment of counselor educators to research,
Electronic media (technology and the internet),
New counseling professionals,
AAC research standards,
CSI publication of doctoral dissertation abstracts.

Obstacles

Not enough practitioners contributing to research,
Research not considered a high priority,
Professional headquarters' staff lack of knowledge of counseling,
Lack of research on emerging paradigms (e.g., wellness),
Insufficient time and money allocated to research efforts,
Faculty do not identify with counseling,
Counselor educators are encouraging students in other career tracks,
Expense of attending national/international conferences,
Lack of funding for attending conferences,
Lack of interface with other related professions,
Lack of interface with non-related professions.

Resources Needed

Among the needs will be those for a clear, articulated plan for research with a commitment for collaboration by the various counseling associations and agencies toward its implementation, identification of staff and volunteer resources needed to achieve the desired outcomes, and financial support for specific activities targeted to specific, desired outcomes.

Association Actions

1. ACA, its divisions and branches, CSI, CACREP, and NBCC will pass resolutions endorsing the goals of the Counselor Advocacy Leadership Conferences including those for sound scientific research on counseling.
2. These organizations also will be asked to help identify people to conduct research; provide resources and support for research; disseminate results of research; promote dialogue on research results; and change and endorse policy based on these results.
3. All persons associated with publications in counseling (e.g., editors, publishers, staff) will be identified with and committed primarily to counseling as their profession.
4. ACA will be asked to establish an Office of Research and Development to facilitate and provide leadership for meeting this goal.

Timeline

By the year 2000, counseling associations and agencies will have passed resolutions necessary to establishing a sound basis for the realization of these goals and objectives over a span of five to ten years.

THEME F: PREVENTION/WELLNESS

Goal: To promote optimum human development across the life span through prevention and wellness.

Objectives to achieve the goal:

This goal will be addressed by counselor educators and counseling organizations such as CACREP, ACA, its divisions:

1. To encourage client wellness by:

   **Activities:**
   a. Identifying the needs of clients (e.g., barriers to wellness, factors affecting holistic growth and development).
   b. Identifying and implementing strategies to address the needs of clients.
   c. Identifying and implementing strategies to help clients become self-advocates.
   d. Engaging in social action to address human needs.

2. To encourage all counselors to incorporate wellness into their philosophical orientation, their professional practices, and their advocacy for client welfare by:

   a. Counselor education programs infusing prevention/wellness throughout the curriculum (i.e., awareness, knowledge, and skills).

   b. Association conferences and institutes providing theme sessions, poster sessions, in-service programs on wellness.

   c. Associations bringing attention to wellness for clients and counselors through all sources of media, awards, and funding of committees and task forces addressing the issues associated with wellness.

3. To encourage counselor wellness by:

   **Activities:**

   a. Identifying the needs of counselors (e.g., barriers to wellness, factors affecting holistic growth and development).

   b. Selecting, training, and retaining counseling students who are committed to personal wellness.

## Responsible Parties

ACA and its branches and divisions, CSI, CACREP, NBCC, counselor education programs.

## Assets

Historical central emphasis by the profession upon facilitating human development over the life span;

Publications, conferences, electronic media (technology and the internet) on wellness;

Availability of experts in development, prevention, and wellness;

Public awareness of wellness issues and their importance to life satisfaction;

Existing wellness programs (e.g., business, colleges and universities);

Growing financial support by insurance companies, HMOs, businesses, etc., for wellness-promoting activities and services.

## Obstacles

Lack of reimbursement of wellness/prevention services by managed care (i.e., medical model),

Lack of commitment by counselor educators to prevention/wellness;

Lack of recognition/awards for exemplary wellness programs;

Lack of adequate public awareness of holistic wellness issues;

Dominance of the medical model in health care;

Lack of a clear definition and commitment for advocacy both of the profession and for clients.

Resources Needed

To achieve this goal will require funding for pre-service and in-service training on wellness, effective legislative lobbying with an emphasis upon the right of all citizens to have access to wellness-facilitating life opportunities, and the development of curriculum resources on wellness.

Association Actions

1. ACA, its branches and divisions (particularly AHEAD, AMCD, ARCA, ASERVIC, and AADA), CSI, CACREP, and NBCC will pass resolutions adopting prevention/wellness as a fundamental goal for human development through counseling.
2. All counseling stakeholders will infuse the theme of wellness into research, publications, conventions, and other dissemination modalities (e.g., web).
3. All entities will strive to be broad-based in their focus on prevention/wellness, to include such issues as an emphasis on devalued, underserved, and vulnerable populations.
4. ACA, its branches and divisions, CSI, CACREP, and NBCC will collaborate with all constituencies (e.g., legislators, employers, families, agencies) to enhance prevention/wellness public policy and programs.

Timeline

By the year 2000, counseling associations and agencies will have passed resolutions necessary to establishing a sound basis for the realization of these goals and objectives over a span of five to ten years.

*Source*: From Chi Sigma Iota. (1998, 2011). *Counselors advocacy leadership conferences I and II*. Retrieved from www.csi-net.org/advocacy. Reprinted with permission.

# Appendix D:
# ACA Advocacy Competencies

J. A. LEWIS, M. S. ARNOLD, R. HOUSE,
AND R. L. TOPOREK

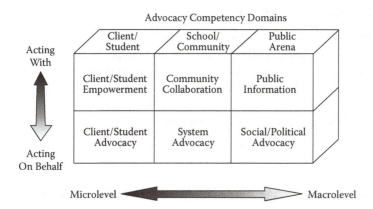

Advocacy Competency Domains

Endorsed by the ACA Governing Council, March 20–22, 2003

## CLIENT/STUDENT EMPOWERMENT

- An advocacy orientation involves not only systems change interventions, but also the implementation of empowerment strategies in direct counseling.
- Advocacy-oriented counselors recognize the impact of social, political, economic, and cultural factors on human development.
- They also help their clients and students understand their own lives in context.
- This lays the groundwork for self-advocacy.

Empowerment Counselor Competencies

In direct interventions, the counselor is able to:

1. Identify strengths and resources of clients and students.
2. Identify the social, political, economic, and cultural factors that affect the client/student.
3. Recognize the signs indicating that an individual's behaviors and concerns reflect responses to systemic or internalized oppression.
4. At an appropriate development level, help the individual identify the external barriers that affect his or her development.
5. Train students and clients in self-advocacy skills.
6. Help students and clients develop self-advocacy action plans.
7. Assist students and clients in carrying out action plans.

## CLIENT/STUDENT ADVOCACY

- When counselors become aware of external factors that act as barriers to an individual's development, they may choose to respond through advocacy.
- The client/student advocate role is especially significant when individuals or vulnerable groups lack access to needed student services.

Client/Student Advocacy Counselor Competencies

In environmental interventions on behalf of clients and students, the counselor is able to:

8. Negotiate relevant services and education systems on behalf of clients and students.
9. Help clients and students gain access to needed resources.
10. Identify barriers to the well-being of individuals and vulnerable groups.
11. Develop an initial plan of action for confronting these barriers.
12. Identify potential allies for confronting the barriers.
13. Carry out the plan of action.

## COMMUNITY COLLABORATION

- Their ongoing work with people gives counselors a unique awareness of recurring themes. Counselors are often among the first to become aware of specific difficulties in the environment.
- Advocacy-oriented counselors often choose to respond to such challenges by alerting existing organizations that are already working for change and that might have an interest in the issues at hand.

- In these situations, the counselor's primary role is as an ally. Counselors can also be helpful to organizations by making available to them our particular skills: interpersonal relations, communications, training, and research.

## Community Collaboration Counselor Competencies

14. Identify environmental factors that impinge upon students' and clients' development.
15. Alert community or school groups with common concerns related to the issue.
16. Develop alliances with groups working for change.
17. Use effective listening skills to gain understanding of the group's goals.
18. Identify the strengths and resources that the group members bring to the process of systemic change.
19. Communicate the recognition of and respect for these strengths and resources.
20. Identify and offer the skills the counselor can bring to the collaboration.
21. Assess the effect of the counselor's interaction with the community.

## SYSTEMS ADVOCACY

- When counselors identify systemic factors that act as barriers to their students' or clients' development, they often wish that they could change the environment and prevent some of the problems that they see every day.
- Regardless of the specific target of change, the processes for altering the status quo have common qualities. Change is a process that requires vision, persistence, leadership, collaboration, systems analysis, and strong data. In many situations, a counselor is the right person to take leadership.

## Systems Advocacy Counselor Competencies

In exerting systems change leadership at the school or community level, the advocacy-oriented counselor is able to:

22. Provide environmental factors impinging on students' or clients' development.
23. Provide and interpret data to show urgency for change.
24. In collaboration with other stakeholders, develop a vision to guide change.
25. Analyze the sources of political power and social influence within the system.
26. Develop a step-by-step plan for implementing the change process.

27. Develop a plan for dealing with probable responses to change.
28. Recognize and deal with resistance.
29. Assess the effect of counselor's advocacy efforts on the system and constituents.

## PUBLIC INFORMATION

- Across settings, specialties, and theoretical perspectives, professional counselors share knowledge of human development and expertise in communication.
- These qualities make it possible for advocacy-oriented counselors to awaken the general public to macro-systemic issues regarding human dignity.

### Public Information Counselor Competencies

In informing the public about the role of environmental factors in human development, the advocacy-oriented counselor is able to:

30. Recognize the impact of oppression and other barriers to healthy development.
31. Identify environmental factors that are protective of healthy development.
32. Prepare written and multimedia materials that provide clear explanations of the role of specific environmental factors in human development.
33. Communicate information in ways that are ethical and appropriate for the target population.
34. Disseminate information through a variety of media.
35. Identify and collaborate with other professionals who are involved in disseminating public information.
36. Assess the influence of public information efforts undertaken by the counselor.

## SOCIAL/POLITICAL ADVOCACY

- Counselors regularly act as change agents in the systems that affect their own students and clients most directly. This experience often leads toward the recognition that some of the concerns they have addressed affected people in a much larger arena.
- When this happens, counselors use their skills to carry out social/political advocacy.

Social/Political Advocacy Counselor Competencies

In influencing public policy in a large, public arena, the advocacy-oriented counselor is able to:

37. Distinguish those problems that can best be resolved through social/ political action.
38. Identify the appropriate mechanisms and avenues for addressing the problems.
39. Seek out and join with potential allies.
40. Support existing alliances for change.
41. With allies, prepare convincing data and rationales for change.
42. With allies, lobby legislators and other policy makers.
43. Maintain an open dialogue with communities and clients to ensure that the social/political advocacy is consistent with the initial goals.

**Note:** The ACA (American Counseling Association) advocacy competencies were endorsed by the ACA Governing Council, March 20–22, 2003. From Lewis, J. A., Arnold, M. S., House, R., and Toporek, R. L. (2002). *ACA advocacy competencies*. Available at http://www.counseling.org/Publications/. Copyright 2002 by the American Counseling Association. Reprinted with permission.

# Appendix E:
# CACREP Standards and
# Corresponding Chapters

## CACREP MASTER'S CORE CURRICULAR AREAS AND CORRESPONDING CHAPTERS WITH ACTIVITIES

| CACREP Master's Entry-Level Core Standard | Chapter(s) |
| --- | --- |
| Reflect current knowledge and projected needs concerning counseling practice in a multicultural and pluralistic society.<br>CACREP Section II.B.1 | 13 |
| History and philosophy of the counseling profession.<br>CACREP Section II.G.1.a | 14 |
| Professional roles, functions, and relationships with other human service providers, including strategies for interagency/interorganization collaboration and communications.<br>CACREP Section II.G.1.b | 6, 14, 15 |
| Counselors' roles and responsibilities as members of an interdisciplinary emergency management response team during a local, regional, or national crisis, disaster, or other trauma-causing event.<br>CACREP Section II.G.1.c | 15 |
| Professional organizations, including membership benefits, activities, services to members, and current issues.<br>CACREP Section II.G.1.f | 6 |
| The role and process of the professional counselor advocating on behalf of the profession.<br>CACREP Section II.G.1.h | 6, 11, 15 |
| Advocacy processes needed to address institutional and social barriers that impede access, equity, and success for clients.<br>CACREP Section II.G.1.i | 7, 8, 11, 15 |
| Multicultural and pluralistic trends, including characteristics and concerns within and among diverse groups nationally and internationally.<br>CACREP Section II.G.2.a | 11 |

*(continued)*

| CACREP Master's Entry-Level Core Standard | Chapter(s) |
|---|---|
| Attitudes, beliefs, understandings, and acculturative experiences, including specific experiential learning activities designed to foster students' understanding of self and culturally diverse clients.<br>CACREP Section II.G.2.b | 11, 14 |
| Theories of multicultural counseling, identity development, and social justice.<br>CACREP Section II.G.2.c | 11 |
| Individual, couple, family, group, and community strategies for working with and advocating for diverse populations, including multicultural competencies.<br>CACREP Section II.G.2.d | 8, 11, 14 |
| Counselors' roles in developing cultural self-awareness, promoting cultural social justice, advocacy, and conflict resolution, and other culturally supported behaviors that promote optimal wellness and growth of the human spirit, mind, or body.<br>CACREP Section II.G.2.e | 6, 8, 11, 14 |
| Counselors' roles in eliminating biases, prejudices, and processes of intentional and unintentional oppression and discrimination.<br>CACREP Section II.G.2.f | 8, 11, 14 |
| Effects of crises, disasters, and other trauma-causing events on persons of all ages.<br>CACREP Section II.G.3.c | 15 |
| Theories and models of individual, cultural, couple, family, and community resilience.<br>CACREP Section II.G.3.d | 11, 15 |
| Human behavior, including an understanding of developmental crises, disability, psychopathology, and situational and environmental factors that affect both normal and abnormal behavior.<br>CACREP Section II.G.3.f | 11, 15 |
| Interrelationships among and between work, family, and other life roles and factors, including the role of multicultural issues in career development.<br>CACREP Section II.G.4.d | 15 |
| Career counseling processes, techniques, and resources, including those applicable to specific populations in a global economy.<br>CACREP Section II.G.4.g | 15 |
| A systems perspective that provides an understanding of family and other systems theories and major models of family and related interventions.<br>CACREP Section II.G.5.e | 11 |
| Group leadership or facilitation styles and approaches, including characteristics of various types of group leaders and leadership styles.<br>CACREP Section II.G.6.b | 14, 15 |
| Social and cultural factors related to the assessment and evaluation of individuals, groups, and specific populations.<br>CACREP Section II.G.7.f | 11 |
| The importance of research in advancing the counseling profession.<br>CACREP Section II.G.8.a | 15 |
| Ethical and culturally relevant strategies for interpreting and reporting the results of research and program evaluation studies.<br>CACREP Section II.G.8.f | 15 |

## CACREP MASTER'S SPECIALTY AREAS AND CORRESPONDING CHAPTERS WITH ACTIVITIES

| CACREP Master's Specialty Standard | Chapter(s) |
|---|---|
| Understands how living in a multicultural society affects clients with addictions. CACREP III.E.1 (Addiction Counseling) | 12 |
| Knows public policies on local, state, and national levels that affect the quality and accessibility of addiction services. CACREP III.E.3 (Addiction Counseling) | 12 |
| Understands effective strategies that support client advocacy and influence public policy and government relations on local, state, and national levels to enhance equity, increase funding, and promote programs that affect the practice of addiction counseling. CACREP III.E.4 (Addiction Counseling) | 12 |
| Advocates for policies, programs, and services that are equitable and responsive to the unique needs of clients with addictions. CACREP III.F.2 (Addiction Counseling) | 14 |
| Identifying alternative approaches to meet clients' career planning needs. CACREP III.F.1.a (Career Counseling) | 14 |
| Designing and delivering career development programs and materials to hard-to-reach populations. CACREP III.F.1.b (Career Counseling) | 14 |
| Demonstrating the ability to advocate for clients' career development and employment. CACREP III.F.1.c (Career Counseling) | 14 |
| Demonstrates the ability to explain, articulate, and advocate for the importance of career counseling, career development, life-work planning, and workforce planning to legislators, other policymakers, and the general public. CACREP III.F.3 (Career Counseling) | 14 |
| Group leadership or facilitation styles and approaches, including characteristics of various types of group leaders and leadership styles. CACREP Section III.G.6.b (Career Counseling) | 14 |
| Understands leadership theories and approaches for evaluation and feedback, organizational change, decision making, and conflict resolution. CACREP III.K.3 (Career Counseling) | 14 |
| Promotes optimal human development, wellness, and mental health through prevention, education, and advocacy activities. CACREP III.D.3 (Clinical Mental Health Counseling) | 12 |
| Knows public policies on the local, state, and national levels that affect the quality and accessibility of mental health services. CACREP III.E.6 (Clinical Mental Health Counseling) | 12 |
| Advocates for policies, programs, and services that are equitable and responsive to the unique needs of clients. CACREP III.F.2 (Clinical Mental Health Counseling) | 14 |

*(continued)*

| CACREP Master's Specialty Standard | Chapter(s) |
|---|---|
| Demonstrates the ability to modify counseling systems, theories, techniques, and interventions to make them culturally appropriate for diverse populations. CACREP III.F.3 (Clinical Mental Health Counseling) | 12, 14 |
| Advocates for policies, programs, and services that are equitable and responsive to the unique needs of couples and families. CACREP III.F.3 (Marriage, Couples, and Family Counseling) | 14 |
| Understands the cultural, ethical, economic, legal, and political issues surrounding diversity, equity, and excellence in terms of student learning. CACREP III.E.1 (School Counseling) | 12, 14 |
| Identifies community, environmental, and institutional opportunities that enhance—as well as barriers that impede—the academic, career, and personal/social development of students. CACREP III.E.2 (School Counseling) | 12,14 |
| Understands multicultural counseling issues, as well as the impact of ability levels, stereotyping, family, socioeconomic status, gender, and sexual identity, and their effects on student achievement. CACREP III.E.4 (School Counseling) | 12, 14 |
| Advocates for the learning and academic experiences necessary to promote the academic, career, and personal/social development of students. CACREP III.F.2 (School Counseling) | 14 |
| Advocates for school policies, programs, and services that enhance a positive school climate and are equitable and responsive to multicultural student populations. CACREP III.F.3 (School Counseling) | 14 |
| Knows the qualities, principles, skills, and styles of effective leadership. CACREP Section III.O.1 (School Counseling) | 2, 14 |
| Knows strategies of leadership designed to enhance the learning environment of schools. CACREP Section III.O.2 (School Counseling) | 12, 14 |
| Knows how to design, implement, manage, and evaluate a comprehensive school counseling program. CACREP Section III.O.3 (School Counseling) | 12, 14 |
| Understands the important role of the school counselor as a system change agent. CACREP Section III.O.4 (School Counseling) | 14 |
| Understands the school counselor's role in student assistance programs, school leadership, curriculum, and advisory meetings. CACREP Section III.O.5 (School Counseling) | 14 |
| Understands organizational, management, and leadership theory and practice. CACREP III.A.8 (Student Affairs and College Counseling) | 14 |
| Understands strategies and leadership required for services encompassed by college student development in postsecondary education, such as admissions, financial aid, academic advising, judicial services, recreational sports, disability services, international student affairs, and health services. CACREP III.A.9 (Student Affairs and College Counseling) | 14 |

| CACREP Master's Specialty Standard | Chapter(s) |
|---|---|
| Demonstrates an understanding of leadership, organization, and management practices that help institutions accomplish their missions.<br>CACREP III.B.5 (Student Affairs and College Counseling) | 14 |
| Advocates for policies, programs, and services that are equitable and responsive to the unique needs of postsecondary students.<br>CACREP III.F.6 (Student Affairs and College Counseling) | 14 |

## CACREP DOCTORAL STANDARDS AND CORRESPONDING CHAPTERS WITH ACTIVITIES

| CACREP Doctoral Standard | Chapter(s) |
|---|---|
| Develop an area of professional counseling expertise as demonstrated through scholarly publications and presentations.<br>CACREP Section II.B.1 | 13 |
| Develop collaborative relationships with program faculty in teaching, supervision, research, professional writing, and service to the profession and the public.<br>CACREP Section II.B.2 | 5, 13 |
| Participate in appropriate professional counseling organizations.<br>CACREP Section II.B.3 | 5 |
| Contribute to and promote scholarly counseling research.<br>CACREP Section II.B.4 | 13 |
| Theories pertaining to the principles and practice of counseling, career development, group work, systems, consultation, and crises, disasters, and other trauma-causing events.<br>CACREP Section II.C.1 | 1, 7 |
| Theories and practices of counselor supervision.<br>CACREP Section II.C.2 | 1, 11 |
| Instructional theory and methods relevant to counselor education.<br>CACREP Section II.C.3 | 1 |
| Pedagogy relevant to multicultural issues and competencies, including social change theory and advocacy action planning.<br>CACREP Section II.C.4 | 1, 6, 7, 11, 12 |
| Design, implementation, and analysis of quantitative and qualitative research.<br>CACREP Section II.C.5 | 13 |
| Models and methods of assessment and use of data.<br>CACREP Section II.C.6 | 14, 15 |
| Ethical and legal considerations in counselor education and supervision (e.g., ACA Code of Ethics, other relevant codes of ethics, standards of practice).<br>CACREP Section II.C.7 | 1, 11 |
| Understands the purposes of clinical supervision.<br>CACREP Section IV.A.1 | 11 |

*(continued)*

| CACREP Doctoral Standard | Chapter(s) |
|---|---|
| Understands theoretical frameworks and models of clinical supervision.<br>CACREP Section IV.A.2 | 11 |
| Understands legal, ethical, and multicultural issues associated with clinical supervision.<br>CACREP Section IV.A.4 | 11 |
| Demonstrates the application of theory and skills of clinical supervision.<br>CACREP Section IV.B.1 | 11 |
| Develops and demonstrates a personal style of supervision.<br>CACREP Section IV.B.2 | 11 |
| Knows the major counseling theories, including their strengths and weaknesses, theoretical bases for efficacy, applicability to multicultural populations, and ethical/ legal considerations.<br>CACREP Section IV.G.1 | 11 |
| Understands various methods for evaluating counseling effectiveness.<br>CACREP Section IV.G.2 | 11 |
| Demonstrates effective application of multiple counseling theories.<br>CACREP Section IV.H.2 | 11 |
| Demonstrates an understanding of case conceptualization and effective interventions across diverse populations and settings.<br>CACREP Section IV.H.3 | 11 |
| Understands theories and skills of leadership.<br>CACREP Section IV.I.1 | 2, 3, 4, 11, 15 |
| Understands advocacy models.<br>CACREP Section IV.I.2 | 3, 5, 6, 11, 12, 15 |
| Identifies current multicultural issues as they relate to social change theories.<br>CACREP Section IV.I.3 | 4, 6, 11, 15 |
| Understands models, leadership roles, and strategies for responding to community, national, and international crises and disasters.<br>CACREP Section IV.I.4 | 3, 4, 6, 9, 11, 13, 15 |
| Understands current topical and political issues in counseling and how those issues affect the daily work of counselors and the counseling profession.<br>CACREP Section IV.I.5 | 3, 4, 6, 11, 13, 15 |
| Demonstrates the ability to provide leadership or contribute to leadership efforts of professional organizations or counseling programs.<br>CACREP Section IV.J.1 | 3, 5, 7, 10, 15 |
| Demonstrates the ability to advocate for the profession and its clientele.<br>CACREP Section IV.J.2 | 4, 6, 9, 12, 13, 15 |

# Appendix F: Sample Rubrics

Rubrics are an assessment tool that counselor educators can use to measure a student's work as well as demonstrate how the student's work meets specific CACREP standards. There are various ways to construct rubrics; however, Pickett and Dodge (n.d.) recommend three common features: (1) measure a stated objective, (2) use a range in order to rate the behavior, and (3) have some way to indicate the degree to which a standard is met.

Below are several sample rubrics for the activities that are presented in Chapter 6. Additionally, there are several web resources where you can find templates for rubrics (see www.rubrics4teachers.com; http://course1.winona.edu/shatfield/air/rubrics.htm).

## Rubric for Professional Organization Fact Sheet Activity

| | |
|---|---|
| Professional Organization Fact Sheet<br>0–3 points<br>Not adequate, adequate, above adequate | |
| Student demonstrates an understanding of professional roles, functions, and relationships with other human service providers.<br>(Entry-level common core, Section II, G.1.b) | |
| Student demonstrates an understanding of professional organizations, including membership benefits, activities, services to members, and current issues.<br>(Entry-level common core, Section II.G.1.f) | |
| Creativity and professional quality of presentation. | |
| Quality of content. | |
| Additional comments: | |

## Rubric for Volunteer Service Activity

| Volunteer Service Experience<br>0–3 points<br>Not adequate, adequate, above adequate | |
|---|---|
| Student demonstrates self-awareness of one's biases. | |
| Student demonstrates an understanding of the role and process of the professional counseling advocating on behalf of the profession.<br>(Entry-level common core, Section II, G1.h) | |
| Student demonstrates an understanding of the advocacy processes needed to address institutional and social barriers that impede access, equality, and success for clients.<br>(Entry-level common core, Section II, G1.i) | |
| Writing style and structure. | |
| Additional comments: | |

## Rubric for Advocacy Project

| Leadership and Advocacy Project<br>0–3 points<br>Does not meet standards, meets standards, exceeds standards | |
|---|---|
| Demonstrates an understanding of advocacy models. (CACREP Doctoral Standards I.2) | |
| Demonstrates an understanding of the current multicultural issues as they relate to social change theories. (CACREP Doctoral Standards I.3) | |
| Demonstrates knowledge of leadership roles and strategies for responding to community, national, and international crises. (CACREP Doctoral Standards I:4) | |
| Demonstrates an understanding of the current topical and political issues in counseling and how those issues affect the daily work of counselors and the counseling profession. (CACREP Doctoral Standards I.5) | |
| Demonstrates the ability to provide leadership and contribute to the leadership efforts of professional organizations and the counseling program. (CACREP Doctoral Standards J:1) | |
| Demonstrates an ability to advocate for the profession and its clientele. (CACREP Doctoral Standards J:2) | |
| Writing style and grammar. | |

## Specific Assignments Within the Leadership and Advocacy Project

| Measure | Available Points | Score |
|---|---|---|
| **Research Paper** | | |
| Students demonstrate a clear connection between research literature and their chosen population/issue. | 5 | |
| Students follow guidelines for formatting the paper and adhere to the page limits. | 5 | |
| Students identify interventions and approaches in working with chosen populations that are directly linked to career counseling theory and are able to articulate how to evaluate appropriateness of the intervention. | 5 | |
| **Take Action** | | |
| Students actively participate in the group planning and executing of all phases of the advocacy project. | 5 | |
| Students demonstrate an understanding of the impact that ecological factors (e.g., crisis, conflict, disaster, trauma, economy, government) have on chosen population. (CACREP—IV, G4) | 5 | |
| Students demonstrate an understanding for the current research base for career (or other specialty chosen), counseling theories, and techniques as related to their chosen population. (CACREP—IV, G3) | 5 | |
| Students demonstrate an understanding for the influence that power, privilege, and oppression exert on chosen population. (CACREP—II, C.4; Section IV, G1.4) | 5 | |
| **Presentation** | | |
| Students are able to clearly report on all aspects of the advocacy project. | 5 | |
| **Totals** | **40** | |

# References

Accordino, M. P., & Guerney, B. G., Jr. (2003). Relationship enhancement couples and family outcome research of the last 20 years. *Family Journal, 11*(2), 162–166.

ACES Committee for Research Mentorship. (2009). *Guidelines for research mentorship in counseling/counselor education.* Retrieved from http://www.acesonline.net/wp-content/uploads/2010/12/ACES-research-mentorship-guidelines.pdf

Alinsky, S. D. (1971). *Rules for radicals: A pragmatic primer for realistic radicals.* New York: Vintage Books.

Amatea, E. S., & West-Olantunji, C. A. (2007). Joining the conversation about educating our poorest children: Emerging leadership roles for school counselors in high poverty schools. *Professional School Counseling, 11,* 81–89.

American Association for Counseling and Development. (1991). *Professionalization directorate strategic plan for professionalization.* Alexandria, VA: Author.

American Counseling Association. (2002). *Advocacy competencies.* Retrieved from http://www.counseling.org/Resources/Competencies/Advocacy_Competencies.pdf

American Counseling Association. (2005). *Code of ethics.* Alexandra, VA: Author.

American Counseling Association. (2009). *Encyclopedia of counseling.* Alexandria, VA: Author.

American Counseling Association. (2010). *20/20: A vision for the future of counseling.* Retrieved from http://www.counseling.org/20-20/index.aspx

American Personnel and Guidance Association. (1974). *Counselor licensure: A position statement.* Falls Church, VA: Author.

American School Counselor Association. (2005). *The American School Counselor Association national model: A framework for school counseling programs.* Alexandria, VA: Author.

American School Counselor Association. (2010a). *ASCA position statements.* Alexandria, VA: Author.

American School Counselor Association. (2010b). *Ethical standards for school counselors.* Retrieved from http://asca2.timberlakepublishing.com//files/EthicalStandards2010.pdf

Ancis, J. R., & Ladany, N. (2001). A multicultural framework for counselor supervision. In L. J. Bradley & N. Ladany (Eds.), *Counselor supervision: Principles, process, and practice* (pp. 63–90). Philadelphia: Brunner-Routledge.

Archer, J., & McCarthy, C. J. (2007). *Theories of counseling and psychotherapy: Contemporary applications.* Upper Saddle River, NJ: Pearson/Merrill Prentice Hall.

Arman, J. F., & Scherer, D. (2002). Service learning in school counselor preparation: A qualitative analysis. *Journal of Humanistic Counseling, Education, and Development, 41,* 69–86.

Arredondo, P., Toporek, R., Brown, S., Jones, J., Locke, D. C., Sanchez, J., & Stadler, H. (1996). Operationalization of the multicultural counseling competencies. *Journal of Multicultural Counseling and Development, 24*, 42–78.

Association for Specialists in Group Work (ASGW). (1998). Best practice guidelines. *Journal for Specialists in Group Work, 23*, 237–244.

Association for Specialists in Group Work (ASGW). (2000). Best practice guidelines. *Journal for Specialists in Group Work, 25*, 327–342.

Astramovich, R. L., & Coker, J. K. (2007). Program evaluation: The accountability bridge model for counselors. *Journal of Counseling and Development, 85*(2), 162–172.

Atkinson, D. R., Thompson, C. E., & Grant, S. K. (1993). A three-dimensional model for counseling racial/ethnic minorities. *The Counseling Psychologist, 21*, 257–277.

Aud, S., Fox, M., & KewalRamani, A. (2010). *Status and trends in the education of racial and ethnic groups* (NCES 2010–015). U.S. Department of Education, National Center for Education Statistics. Washington, DC: U.S. Government Printing Office.

Bain, K. (2004). *What the best college teachers do*. Cambridge, MA: Harvard University Press.

Baldwin, C., & Huggins, D. (1997). Marital and family therapy research: Outcomes and implications for practice. *Family Journal, 6*(3), 212–218.

Ball, A. F. (2000). Empowering pedagogies that enhance the learning of multicultural students. *Teachers College Record, 102*, 1006–1034.

Barbee, P. W., Scherer, D., & Combs, D. C. (2003). Prepracticum service-learning: Examining the relationship with counselor self-efficacy and anxiety. *Counselor Education and Supervision, 43*, 108–119.

Barnett, R. (2004). Women and multiple roles: Myths and reality. *Harvard Review of Psychiatry, 12*(3), 158–164.

Barrio Minton, C. A., Fernanda, D. M., & Ray, D. C. (2008). Ten years of peer reviewed articles in counselor education: Where, what, who? *Counselor Education and Supervision, 48*, 133–143.

Barrio Minton, C. A., Myers, J. E., & Morganfield, M. (2010). *Counselor education in the future: A study of supply, demand, and future trends*. Southern Association of Counselor Education and Supervision Annual Meeting, Williamsburg, VA, September 30, 2010.

Bell, L. A. (1997). Theoretical foundations for social justice education. In M. Adams, L. A. Bell, & P. Griffin (Eds.), *Teaching for diversity and social justice: A sourcebook* (pp. 3–15). New York: Routledge.

Bemak, F., & Chung, R. C. (2005). Advocacy as a critical role for urban school counselors: Working towards equity and social justice. *Professional School Counseling, 8*, 196–202.

Bemak, F., & Chung, R. C.-Y. (2008). New professional roles and advocacy strategies for school counselors: A multicultural/social justice perspective to move beyond the nice counselor syndrome. *Journal of Counseling and Development, 86*, 372–381.

Benishek, L. A., Bieschke, K. J., Park, J., & Slattery, S. M. (2004). A multicultural feminist model of mentoring. *Journal of Multicultural Counseling and Development, 32*, 428–442.

Berdahl, J. L., & Moore, C. (2006). Workplace harassment: Double jeopardy for minority women. *Journal of Applied Psychology, 91*, 426–436.

Bernard, J. M., & Goodyear, R. K. (2009). *Fundamentals of clinical supervision* (4th ed.). Boston: Allyn & Bacon.

Black, L. L., & Magnuson, S. (2005). Women of spirit: Leaders in the counseling profession. *Journal of Counseling and Development, 83*, 337–342.

Black, L. L., Suarez, E. C., & Medina, S. (2004). Helping students help themselves: Strategies for successful mentoring relationships. *Counselor Education and Supervision, 44,* 44–55.

Bloom, B. S., Engelhart, M. D., Furst, E. J., Hill, W. H., & Krathwohl, D. R. (1956). *Taxonomy of educational objectives: The cognitive domain.* New York: Longman.

Bohart, A. C., & Tallman, K. (1999). *How clients make therapy work: The process of active self-healing.* Washington, DC: American Psychological Association.

Bonar, E. E., & Rosenberg, H. (2010). Substance abuse professionals' attitudes regarding harm reduction versus traditional interventions for injecting drug users. *Addiction Research and Theory, 18*(6), 692–707.

Borders, L. D. (1989). Developmental cognitions of first practicum supervisees. *Journal of Counseling and Development, 36,* 163–169. doi: 10.1037/0022-0167.36.2.163

Bradley, L. J., Lewis, J., Hendricks, B., & Crews, C. (2008). Advocacy: Implications for supervision training (ACAPCD-13). Alexandria, VA: American Counseling Association.

Brewer, J. M. (1932). *Education as guidance.* New York: MacMillan.

Briggs, C. A., & Pehrrson, D. E. (2008). Research mentorship in counselor education. *Counselor Education and Supervision, 48,* 101–113.

Briggs, M. K., Slaton, A. R., & Gilligan, T. D. (2009). The girls' leadership experience group: A parallel process of leadership skill development for school counselors-in-training. *Professional School Counseling, 13,* 125–133.

Bronfenbrenner, U. (1979). *The ecology of human development.* Cambridge, MA: Harvard University Press.

Brubaker, M. D., Puig, A., Reese, R. F., & Young, J. (2010). Integrating social justice into counseling theories pedagogy: A case example. *Counselor Education and Supervision, 50,* 88–102.

Bryan, J. (2005). Fostering educational resilience and achievement in urban schools through school-family-community partnerships. *Professional School Counseling, 8,* 219–227.

Bullock, W. A., Sage, J., Hupp, D., Ozbey, T., O'Rourke, M., Smith, M. K., …, Garrity, J. (2009). From illness to wellness: An evaluation of Ohio's Wellness Management and Recovery (WMR) program in community mental health and consumer operated service agencies. *New Research in Mental Health, 18,* 312–321.

Burnett, J. A., Hamel, D., & Long, L. L. (2004). Service learning in graduate counselor education: Developing multicultural competency. *Journal of Multicultural Counseling and Development, 32,* 180–191.

Burns, J. M. (1978). *Leadership.* New York: Harper and Row.

Calley, N. G., & Hawley, L. D. (2008). The professional identiy of counselor educators. *The Clinical Supervisor, 27*(1), 3–16. doi: 10.1080/07325220802221454

Carlson, J., Sperry, L., & Lewis, J. A. (1997). *Family therapy: Ensuring treatment efficacy.* Pacific Grove, CA: Brooks/Cole.

Carter, R. T. (2007). Racism and psychological and emotional injury: Recognizing and assessing race-based traumatic stress. *The Counseling Psychologist, 35,* 13–105. doi: 10.1177/0011000006292033

Casto, C., Caldwell, C., & Salazar, C. F. (2005). Creating mentoring relationships between female faculty and students in counselor education: Guidelines for potential mentees and mentors. *Journal of Counseling and Development, 83,* 331–336.

Chang, C. Y., & Gnilka, P. (2010). Social advocacy: The fifth force in counseling. In D. G. Hays & B. T. Erford (Eds.), *Developing multicultural counseling competency: A systems approach* (pp. 53–71). Columbus, OH: Pearson Merrill Prentice Hall.

Chang, C. Y., Hays, D. G., & Milliken, T. F. (2009). Addressing social justice issues in supervision: A call for client and professional advocacy. *The Clinical Supervisor, 28*(1), 20–35. doi: 10.1080/07325220902855144

Chang, C. Y., Hays, D. G., & Shoffner, M. (2003). Cross-racial supervision: A developmental approach. *The Clinical Supervisor, 22*, 121–138.

Chen, Z., Kirkman, B., Kanfer, R., Allan, D., & Rosen, B. (2007). A multilevel study of leadership, empowerment, and performance in teams. *Journal of Applied Psychology, 92*, 331–346.

Chen, Z., Lam, W., & Zhong, J. (2007). Leader-member exchange and member performance. *Journal of Applied Psychology, 92*, 202–212.

Chi Sigma Iota. (1998, 2011). *Counselors advocacy leadership conferences I and II.* Retrieved from www.csi-net.org/advocacy

Chi Sigma Iota. (2009). *Principles and practices of leadership excellence.* Greensboro, NC: Author. Retrieved from http://www.csi-net.org/leadership

Chi Sigma Iota. (2010a). *20/20 Vision for the Future of Counseling definition.* Greensboro, NC: Author. Retrieved from www.csi-net.org

Chi Sigma Iota. (2010b). *What is a professional counselor?* Greensboro, NC: Author. Retrieved from http://www.csi-net.org/displaycommon.cfm?an=1&subarticlenbr=679

Chi Sigma Iota. (2011). *CSI strategic plan.* Greensboro, NC: Author. Retrieved from http://www.csi-net.org/index.cfm

Chin, J. L. (2010). Introduction to the special issue on diversity and leadership. *Consulting Psychology Journal: Practice and Research, 62*, 150–156.

*City of Cleveland v. Cook*, Municipal Court, Criminal Division, No. 75-CRB 11478, August 12, 1975. (Transcript dated August 19, 1975)

Clark, M. A., & Stone, C. (2007). The developmental school counselor as educational leader. In J. Wittmer (Ed.), *Managing your school counseling program: K–12 developmental strategies* (3rd ed., pp. 75–82). Minneapolis, MN: Educational Media.

Cohen. W. (1998). *The stuff of heroes: The eight universal laws of leadership.* New York: Longstreet Press.

Cohen, W. (2010). *Heroic leadership: Leading with integrity and honor.* San Francisco: Jossey-Bass.

Conger, J. A., & Kanungo, R. N. (1998). *Charismatic leadership in organizations.* Thousand Oaks, CA: Sage.

Constantine, M. G., Hage, S. M., Kindaichi, M. M., & Bryant, R. M. (2007). Social justice and multicultural issues: Implications for the practice and training of counselors and counseling psychologists. *Journal of Counseling and Development, 85*, 24–29.

Conyne, R. K., & Cook, E. P. (2004). *Ecological counseling: An innovative approach to conceptualizing person-environment interaction.* Washington, DC: American Counseling Association.

Council for Accreditation of Counseling and Related Educational Programs. (2001). *The 2001 standards.* Alexandria, VA: Author. Retrieved from http://www.cacrep.org/doc/2001%20Standards.pdf

Council for Accreditation of Counseling and Related Educational Programs. (2007, Fall). CACREP/CORE merger fails. *The CACREP Connection.* Retrieved from http://www.cacrep.org/doc/Connection%20Fall%2007.pdf

Council for Accreditation of Counseling and Related Educational Programs. (2009). *The 2009 standards.* Alexandria, VA: Author. Retrieved from http://www.cacrep.org/doc/2009%20Standards%20with%20cover.pdf

Covey, S. (1990). *The seven habits of highly effective people.* New York: Simon & Shuster.

Crethar, H., Torres Rivera, E., & Nash, S. (2008). In search of common threads: Linking multicultural, feminist, and social justice paradigms. *Journal of Counseling and Development, 86*, 269–278.

Cross, W. E. (1998). Black psychological functioning and the legacy of slavery. In Y. Danieli (Ed.), *International handbook of multigenerational legacies of trauma* (pp. 387–400). New York: Plenum Press.

Dahir, C. A., & Stone, C. B. (2009). School counselor accountability: The path to social justice and systemic change. *Journal of Counseling and Development, 87*, 12–20.

D'Andrea, M. (2000). Postmodernism, constructivism, and multiculturalism: Three forces reshaping and expanding our thoughts about counseling. *Journal of Mental Health Counseling, 22*, 1–16.

D'Andrea, M., & Heckman, E. (2008). A 40-year review of multicultural counseling outcome research: Outlining a future research agenda for the multicultural counseling movement. *Journal of Counseling and Development, 86*(3), 356–363.

Danieli, Y. (1998). Introduction: History and conceptual foundations. In Y. Danieli (Ed.), *International handbook of multigenerational legacies of trauma* (pp. 1–20). New York: Plenum.

DeNavas-Walt, C., Proctor, B. D., & Smith, J. C. (2010). *Income, poverty, and health insurance coverage in the United States: 2009* (Current Population Reports, pp. 60–238). Washington, DC: U.S. Government Printing Office.

Department of Health and Human Services. (2004). *Guide to children's dental care in Medicaid.* Washington, DC: U.S. Government Printing Office.

de Saint-Exupéry, A. (1943). *The little prince.* Orlando, FL: Harcourt.

Dixon, A. L., Tucker, M., & Clark, M. A. (2010). Transforming the preparation of school counselors to promote social justice in schools: Implications for counselor education. *Counselor Education and Supervision, 50*, 103–115.

Dollarhide, C. T., Gibson, D. M., & Saginak, K. A. (2008). New counselors' leadership efforts in school counseling: Themes from a year-long qualitative study. *Professional School Counseling, 11*, 262–271.

Dollarhide, C. T., Smith, A. T., & Lemberger, M. E. (2007). Counseling made transparent: Pedagogy for a counseling theories course. *Counselor Education and Supervision, 46*, 242–253.

Driscoll, A., & Wood, S. (2007). *Developing outcomes-based assessment for learner-centered education: A faculty introduction.* Sterling, VA: Stylus.

Durham, J. C., & Glosoff, H. L. (2010). From passion to action: Integrating the advocacy competencies and social justice into counselor education and supervision. In M. J. Ratts, R. L. Toporek, & J. A. Lewis (Eds.), *ACA advocacy competencies: A social justice framework for counselors* (pp. 139–150). Alexandria, VA: American Counseling Association.

Eder, K. C., & Whiston, S. C. (2006). Does psychotherapy help some students? An overview of psychotherapy outcome research. *Professional School Counseling, 9*(5), 337–343.

Education Trust. (n.d.). *History of TSCI.* Retrieved from http://www.edtrust.org/node/139

Education Trust. (2002). *Challenging the myths: Rethinking the role of school counselors.* Retrieved from http://www.nassgap.org/library/docs/redefining_counseling.pdf

Education Trust. (2003). *The new vision of school counseling.* Retrieved from http://www.edtrust.org/dc/tsc/vision

Education Trust. (2010). *Closing the gaps.* Retrieved from http://www.edtrust.org/issues/pre-k-12/closing-the-gaps

Elkins, D. N. (2009). The medical model in psychotherapy: Its limitations and failures. *Journal of Humanistic Psychology, 49*, 66–84. doi: 10.1177/0022167807307901

Enns, C. Z. (1993). Twenty years of feminist counseling and psychotherapy: From naming biases to implementing multifaceted practice. *The Counseling Psychologist, 21*, 3–87.

Erdogan, B., & Enders, J. (2007). Support from the top: Supervisor's perceived organizational support as a moderator of leader-member exchange to satisfaction and performance relationships. *Journal of Applied Psychology, 92*, 321–350.

Erford, B. T. (2008). *Research and evaluation in counseling.* Boston: Lahaska Press.

Erford, B. T. (2010). Program accountability. In B. T. Erford (Ed.), *Professional school counseling* (2nd ed., pp. 251–259). Austin, TX: Pro-ed.

Erford, B. T., Savin-Murphy, J. A., & Butler, C. (2010). Conducting a meta-analysis of counseling outcome research: Twelve steps and practical procedures. *Counseling Outcome Research and Evaluation, 1*, 19–43. doi: 10.1177/2150137809356682

Eriksen, K. (1997). *Making an impact: A handbook on counselor advocacy.* Washington, DC: Accelerated Development.

Eriksen, K. (1999). Counselor advocacy: A qualitative analysis of leaders' perceptions, organizational activities, and advocacy documents. *Journal of Mental Health Counseling, 21*(1), 33–49.

Estrada, D., Wiggins Frame, M., & Braun-Williams, C. (2004). Cross-cultural supervision: Guiding the conversation toward race and ethnicity. *Journal of Multicultural Counseling and Development, 32*, 307–319.

Etzioni, A. (1991). *A responsive society.* San Francisco: Jossey-Bass.

Fair Access Coalition on Testing. (2007, May 17). Retrieved from www.fairaccess.org/aboutfact/factfaq

Falender, C. A., & Shafranske, E. P. (2004). *Clinical supervision: A competency-based approach.* Washington, DC: American Psychological Association. doi: 10.1037/10806-000

Farquhar, S., & Dobson, N. (2004). Community and university participation in disaster-relief recover: An example from eastern North Carolina. *Journal of Community Practice, 12*, 203–217. doi: 10.1300/J125v12n03_12

Feit, S. S., & Lloyd, A. P. (1990). A profession in search of professionals. *Counselor Education and Supervision, 29*, 216–219.

Fiedler, F. E. (1967). *A theory of leadership effectiveness.* New York: McGraw-Hill.

Field, J. E., & Baker, S. (2004). Defining and examining school counselor advocacy. *Professional School Counseling, 8*, 56–63.

Finifter, D. H., Jensen, C. J., Wilson, C. E., & Koenig, B. L. (2005). A comprehensive, multi-tiered, targeted community needs assessment model. *Family Community Health, 28*, 293–306.

Fong, M. L., Borders, L. D., Ethington, C. A., & Pitts, J. H. (1997). Becoming a counselor: A longitudinal study of student cognitive development. *Counselor Education and Supervision, 37*, 100–115.

Foster, V. A., & McAdams, C. R., III. (2009). A framework for creating a climate of transparency for professional performance assessment: Fostering student investment in gatekeeping. *Counselor Education and Supervision, 48*(4), 271–284.

Freire, P. (2001). *Pedagogy of the oppressed.* New York: Continuum.

Gale, A., & Austin, D. (2003). Professionalism's challenges to professional counselors' collective identity. *Journal of Counseling and Development, 81*(1), 3–10.

Gardner, J. (1990). *On leadership.* New York: Macmillan.

Gaubatz, M. D., & Vera, E. M. (2002). Do formalized gatekeeping procedures increase programs' follow-up with deficient trainees? *Counselor Education and Supervision, 41*, 294–305.

Gelso, C. J. (2006). On the making of a scientist-practitioner: A theory of research training in professional psychology. *Training and Education in Professional Psychology, S*(1), 3–16.

George, J. M. (2000). Emotions and leadership: The role of emotional intelligence. *Human Relations, 53*, 1027–1055.

Georgia State University. (2011). CPS 7900: Consultation, advocacy, and leadership in mental health counseling syllabus. Unpublished document.

Gibson, D. M., Dollarhide, C. T., & McCallum, L. J. (2010). Nontenured assistant professors as American Counseling Association division presidents: The new look of leadership in counseling. *Journal of Counseling and Development, 88*, 285–292.

Girl Scouts of America. (2008, March). *Change it up: What girls say about redefining leadership.* New York: Author.

Gladding, S. (2008). *Counseling: A comprehensive profession.* Upper Saddle River, NJ: Pearson Prentice Hall.

Glosoff, H. L., & Durham, J. C. (2010). Using supervision to prepare social justice counseling advocates. *Counselor Education and Supervision, 50*, 116–129.

Glover, J., Lee, S., Nevins, S., Pollard, S. D., & Robinson, B. (Producers). (2006). *When the levees broke: A requiem in four acts* [Television series]. New Orleans, LA: Home Box Office, Inc.

Goodman, L. A., Liang, B., Helms, J. E., Latta, R. E., Sparks, E., & Weintraub, S. R. (2004). Training counseling psychologists as social justice agents: Feminist and multicultural principles in action. *The Counseling Psychologist, 6*, 793–837.

Goodman, R. D., & West-Olatunji, C. A. (2009). Applying critical consciousness: Culturally competent disaster response outcomes. *Journal of Counseling and Development, 87*, 458–465.

Graen, G. B., & Uhl-Bien, M. (1995). Relationship-based approach to leadership: Development of leader-member exchange (LMX) theory of leadership over 25 years: Applying a multi-level multi-domain perspective. *Leadership Quarterly, 6*, 219–247. doi: 10.1016/1048-9843(95)90036-5

Granello, D. H. (2000). Encouraging the cognitive development of supervisees: Using Bloom's Taxonomy in supervision. *Counselor Education and Supervision, 40*, 31–46.

Green, E. J., McCollum, V. C., & Hays, D. G. (2008). Teaching advocacy counseling within a social justice framework: Implications for school counselors and educators. *Journal for Social Action in Counseling and Psychology, 1*, 14–30.

Green, M., & Piel, J. A. (2002). *Theories of human development: A comparative approach.* Boston: Allyn and Bacon.

Greenleaf, R. K. (1970a). *The servant as leader.* Retrieved from www.greenleaf.org

Greenleaf, R. K. (1970b). *What is servant leadership?* Retrieved from http://www.greenleaf.org/whatisis/

Greenleaf, R. K. (1998). *The power of servant-leadership.* San Francisco: Berrett-Koehler.

Greenleaf, R. K. (2003). In H. Beazley, C. L. Spears, & J. Beggs (Eds.), *The servant-leader within: A transformative path* (pp. 39–40). Mahwah, NJ: Paulist Press.

Greenleaf, R. K. (2004). *A life of servant leadership.* San Francisco: Berrett-Koehler.

Guiffrida, D. A. (2005). The emergence model: An alternative pedagogy for facilitating self-reflection and theoretical fit in counseling students. *Counselor Education and Supervision, 44*, 201–213.

Hage, S. M., Hopson, A., Siegel, M., Payton, G., Defanti, E. (2006). Multicultural training in spirituality: An interdisciplinary review. *Counseling and Values, 50*(3), 217–234.

Hale, J. E. (2001). *Learning while Black: Creating educational excellence for African American children.* Baltimore: Johns Hopkins University Press.

Hall, T., & Janman, K. (2010). *The leadership illusion.* New York: Macmillan.

Hamrin, S. A., & Erickson, C. E. (1939). *Guidance in the secondary schools.* New York: Appleton-Century-Crofts.

Hanna, F. J., & Bemak, F. (1997). The quest for identity in the counseling profession. *Counselor Education and Supervision, 36*(3), 194–206.

Harley, D. A., Jolivette, K., McCormick, K., & Tice, K. (2002). Race, class, and gender: A constellation of positionalities with implications for counseling. *Journal of Multicultural Counseling and Development, 30,* 216–239.

Harrell, J. P., Hall, S., & Taliaferro, J. (2003). Physiological responses to racism and discrimination: An assessment of the evidence. *American Journal of Public Health, 93,* 243–248.

Harry, B., & Klingner, J. K. (2006). *Why are so many minority students in special education?* New York: Columbia University, Teachers College Press.

Haycock, K., Jerald, C., & Huang, S. (2001). Closing the gap: Done in a decade. In *Thinking K-12* (pp. 3–22). Washington, DC: The Education Trust.

Hays, D. G. (2010). Introduction to counseling outcome research and evaluation. *Counseling Outcome Research and Evaluation, 1,* 1–7. doi: 10.1177/2150137809360006

Hays, D. G., & Chang, C. Y. (2003). White privilege, oppression, and racial identity development: Implications for supervision. *Counselor Education and Supervision, 43,* 134–145.

Hendricks, C. B. (2008). Introduction: Who are we? The role of ethics in shaping counselor identity. *The Family Journal: Counseling and Therapy for Couples and Families, 16*(3), 258–260.

Hennessy, K. D., & Chambers, D. A. (2009). Delivery of excellent mental health care and acceleration of research: Federal activities since the president's commission report. *Psychiatric Services, 60*(4), 433–438.

Heppner, P. P., Wampold, B. E., & Kivlighan, D. M. (2008). *Research design in counseling.* Belmont, CA: Thomson/Brooks/Cole.

Herr, E. L. (2004). *ACA fifty years plus and moving forward.* Retrieved from http://counselingoutfitters.com/vistas/vistas04/3.pdf

Herr, E. L. (2010). *Leadership: A position paper.* Retrieved from http://www.csi-net.org/leadership

Herr, E. L., Heitzman, D. E., & Rayman, J. R. (2006). *The professional counselor as administrator: Perspectives on leadership and management in counseling services.* Mahwah, NJ: Lawrence Erlbaum.

Hiebert, B. (1997). Integrating evaluation into counseling practice: Accountability and evaluation intertwined. *Canadian Journal of Counselling, 31*(2), 112–126.

Hill, N. R. (2003). Promoting and celebrating multicultural competence in counselor trainees. *Counselor Education and Supervision, 43*(1), 39–51.

Hill, T., & Westbrook, R. (1997). SWOT analysis: It's time for a product recall. *Long Range Planning, 30,* 46–52. doi: 10.1016/S0024–6301(96)00095–7

Hof, D. D., Dinsmore, J. D., Barber, S., Suhr, R., & Scofield, T. R. (2009). Advocacy: The T.R.A.I.N.E.R. model. *Journal of Social Action in Counseling and Psychology, 2*(1), 15–28.

Hof, D. D., Scofield, T. R., & Dinsmore, J. A. (2006). Social advocacy: Assessing the impact of training on the development and implementation of advocacy plans. In G. R. Walz, J. C. Bleuer, & K. Yep (Eds.), *VISTA: Compelling perspectives on counseling 2006* (pp. 211–213). Alexandria, VA: American Counseling Association.

Holcomb-McCoy, C., & Bryan, J. (2010). Advocacy and empowerment in parent consultation: Implication for theory and practice. *Journal of Counseling and Development, 88,* 259–268.

Holland, J. L. (1985). *Making vocational choices: A theory of personality and work environments* (2nd ed.). Englewood Cliffs, NJ: Prentice-Hall.

Holland, J. L., & Gottfredson, G. D. (1976). Using a typology of persons and environments to explain careers: Some extensions and clarifications. *The Counseling Psychologist, 6*(3), 20–29.

Holloway, E. L., & Wampold, B. E. (1986). Relation between conceptual level and counseling related tasks: A meta-analysis. *Journal of Counseling Psychology, 33,* 310–319. doi: 10.1037/0022–0167.33.3.310

Hooijberg, R., & Quinn, R. E. (1992). Behavioral complexity and the development of effective managerial leaders. In R. L. Phillips & J. G. Hunt (Eds.), *Strategic management: A multiorganizational-level perspective* (pp. 161–176). New York: Quorum.

House, R. J. (1971). A path-goal theory of leader effectiveness. *Administrative Science Quarterly, 16,* 321–339.

House, R. J. (1996). A path-goal theory of leadership: Lessons, legacy, and reformulated theory. *The Leadership Quarterly, 7,* 323–352.

House, R. M., & Sears, S. J. (2002). Preparing school counselors to be leaders and advocates: A critical need in the new millennium. *Theory into Practice, 41,* 154–162.

Hoyt, K. B. (1974). In E. L. Herr (Ed.), *Vocational guidance and human development* (pp. 502–527). Boston: Houghton Mifflin.

Human Rights Watch. (2010). *World report 2010: Events of 2009.* New York: Author.

Ilies, R., Nahrgang, J., & Morgeson, F. (2007). Leader-member exchange and citizenship behaviors. *Journal of Applied Psychology, 92,* 269–277.

Ingersoll, R. E., Bauer, A., & Burns, L. (2004). Children and psychotropic medication: What role should advocacy counseling play? *Journal of Counseling and Development, 82,* 337–343.

Institute of Medicine. (2001). *Crossing the quality chasm: A new health system for the 21st century.* Washington, DC: National Academies Press.

Jacoby, B. (Ed.). (1996). *Service learning in higher education.* San Francisco: Jossey-Bass.

Janson, C., Stone, C., & Clark, M. A. (2009). Stretching leadership: A distributed perspective for school counselor leaders. *Professional School Counseling, 13,* 98–106.

Jennings, L., & Skovholt, T. M. (1999). The cognitive, emotional, and relational characteristics of master therapists. *Journal of Counseling Psychology, 36,* 3–11.

Jett, S. T., & Delgado-Romero, E. A. (2009). Prepracticum service-learning in counselor education: A qualitative case study. *Counselor Education and Supervision, 49,* 106–121.

Jones, A. J. (1934). *Principles of guidance* (2nd ed.). New York: McGraw-Hill.

Judge, T. A., Bono, J. E., Ilies, R., & Gerhardt, M. W. (2002). Personality and leadership: A qualitative and quantitative review. *Journal of Applied Psychology, 87,* 765–780.

Judge, T. A., Piccolo, R., & Ilies, R. (2004). The forgotten ones? The validity of consideration and initiating structure in leadership research. *Journal of Applied Psychology, 89,* 36–51.

Kacmar, K., Witt, L., Ziunuska, S., & Gully, S. (2003). The interactive effect of leader-member exchange and communications frequency on performance ratings. *Journal of Applied Psychology, 88,* 764–772.

Kaiser, R. B., and Overfield, D. V. (2010). Assessing flexible leadership as a mastery of opposites. *Consulting Psychology Journal: Practice and Research, 62*(2), 105–118. doi: 10.1037/a0019987

Kazdin, A. E., & Weisz, J. R. (Eds.). (2003). *Evidence-based psychotherapies for children and adolescents.* New York: Guilford Press.

Kelly, E. W. (1995). Counselor values: A national survey. *Journal of Counseling and Development, 73,* 648–653.

Kelly, K. R. (1996). Review of clinical mental health counseling process and outcome research. *Journal of Mental Health Counseling, 18*(4), 358–376.

Kenagy, G. P. (2005). Transgender health: Findings from two needs assessments studies in Philadelphia. *Health and Social Work, 30*(1), 19–26.

Kenagy, G. P., & Hsieh, C. (2005). Gender differences in social service needs of transgender people. *Journal of Social Service Research, 31*(3), 1–21.

King, M. L. (1964). *Why we can't wait.* New York: Mentor.

Kirkpatrick, S. A., & Locke, E. A. (1991). Leadership: Do traits matter? *Academy of Management Executive, 5,* 48–60.

Kirkpatrick, S. A., & Locke, E. A. (1996). Direct and indirect effects of three core charismatic leadership components on performance and attitudes. *Journal of Applied Psychology, 81,* 36–51.

Kiselica, M. S., & Robinson, M. (2001). Bringing advocacy counseling to life: The history, issues, and human dramas of social justice work in counseling. *Journal of Counseling and Development, 79,* 387–397.

Korsgaard, M., Brodt, S., & Whitener, E. (2002). Trust in the face of conflict: The role of managerial trustworthy behavior and organizational context. *Journal of Applied Psychology, 87,* 312–319.

Kouzes, J. M., & Posner, B. Z. (2007). *Leadership Practices Inventory (LPI): Deluxe facilitator's guide package* (3rd ed.). San Francisco: Jossey-Bass.

Kozol, J. (1991). *Savage inequalities: Children in America's schools.* New York: Crown.

Kress, V. E., & Protivnak, J. J. (2009). Professional development plans to remedy problematic counseling student behaviors. *Counselor Education and Supervision, 48,* 154–166.

Krumboltz, J. D. (1998). Serendipity is not serendipitous. *Journal of Counseling Psychology, 45,* 390–392.

Labouvie-Vief, G., & Diehl, M. (2000). Cognitive complexity and cognitive-affective integration: Related or separate domains of adult development? *Psychology and Aging, 15,* 490–504. doi: 10.1037/0882-7974.15.3.490

Ladany, N., Marotta, S., & Muse-Burke, J. (2001) Counselor experience related to complexity to case conceptualization and supervision preference. *Counselor Education and Supervision, 40,* 203–219.

LaFountain, R. M., & Bartos, R. B. (2002). *Research and statistics made meaningful in counseling and student affairs.* Pacific Grove, CA: Brooks/Cole.

Lambert, M. J., & Ogles, B. M. (2004). The efficacy and effectiveness of psychotherapy. In M. J. Lambert (Ed.), *Bergin and Garfield's handbook of psychotherapy and behavior change* (5th ed, pp. 139–193). New York: Wiley.

Lee, C. C. (1998). Counselors as agents of social change. In C. C. Lee & G. R. Walz (Eds.), *Social action: A mandate for counselors* (pp. 3–14). Alexandria, VA: American Counseling Association.

Lee, C. C. (Ed.). (2007a). *Counseling for social justice.* Alexandria, VA: American Counseling Association.

Lee, C. C. (2007b). A counselor's call to action. In C. C. Lee (Ed.), *Counseling for social justice* (pp. 259–263). Alexandria, VA: American Counseling Association.

Lee, C. C. (In press a). A conceptual framework for counseling across cultures. In C. C. Lee (Ed.), *Multicultural issues in counseling: New approaches to diversity* (4th ed.). Alexandria, VA: American Counseling Association.

Lee, C. C. (In press b). Global literacy: The foundation of culturally competent counseling. In C. C. Lee (Ed.), *Multicultural issues in counseling: New approaches to diversity* (4th ed.). Alexandria, VA: American Counseling Association.

Lee, C. C., & Diaz, J. M. (2009). The cross-cultural zone in counseling. In C. C. Lee, D. A. Burnhill, A. L. Butler, C. Hipolito-Delgado, M. Humphrey, O. Muñoz, & H. Shin (Eds.), *Element of culture in counseling* (pp. 95–104). Columbus, OH: Pearson.

Lee, C. C., & Hipolito-Delgado, C. (2007). Counselors as agents of social justice. In C. C. Lee (Ed.), *Counseling for social justice* (pp. xiii–xxviii). Alexandria, VA: American Counseling Association.

Lee, C. C., & Walz, G, R. (Eds.). (1998a). *Social action: A mandate for counselors.* Alexandria, VA: American Counseling Association.

Lee, C. C., & Walz, G. R. (1998b). A summing up and call to action. In C. Lee & G. R. Walz (Eds.), *Social action: A mandate for counselors* (pp. 307–312). Alexandria, VA: American Counseling Association.

Lee, C. C., & Walz, G. R. (1998, 2004, 2010). *Social action: A mandate for counselors.* Greensboro, NC: ERIC/CASS.

Lee, M. W. (Producer & Director). (1995). *The color of fear* [Motion picture]. Berkeley, CA: Stir-Fry.

Lewin, K. (1936). *Principles of topological psychology.* New York: McGraw-Hill.

Lewis, J. A., & Arnold, M. S. (1998). From multiculturalism to social action. In C. Lee & G. R. Walz (Eds.), *Social action: A mandate for counselors* (pp. 51–65). Alexandra, VA: American Counseling Association.

Lewis, J. A., Arnold, M. S., House, R., & Toporek, R. L. (2002). *ACA advocacy competencies.* Retrieved from http://www.counseling.org/Publications

Lewis, J. A., & Bradley, L. (Eds.). (2000). *Advocacy in counseling: Counselors, clients, and community.* Greensboro, NC: ERIC Counseling and Student Services Clearinghouse.

Lewis, J., Toporek, R., & Ratts, M. J. (2010). Advocacy and social justice: Entering the mainstream of the counseling profession. In J. Ratts, R. Toporek, and J. Lewis (Eds.), *ACA advocacy competencies: A social justice framework for counselors* (pp. 239–244). Alexandria, VA: American Counseling Association.

Lewis, T. F., & Wester, K. L. (2004). *Leadership styles and characteristics among counseling professionals: Implications for training programs.* Paper presented at the American Counseling Association, Kansas City, MO.

Liles R. G., & Wagner, M. (2010). The CACREP 2009 standards: Developing a counselor education program assessment. Retrieved from http://counselingoutfitters.com/vistas/vistas10/Article_23.pdf

Ling, Y., Simsek, Z., Lubatkin, M. H., & Veiga, J. F. (2008). The impact of transformational CEOs on the performance of small to medium sized firms: Does organizational context matter? *Journal of Applied Psychology, 93,* 923–934.

Liu, W. M. (2001). Expanding our understanding of multiculturalism: Developing a social class worldview model. In D. B. Pope-Davis & H. L. Coleman (Eds.), *The intersection of race, class, and gender in counseling psychology* (pp. 127–170). Thousand Oaks, CA: Sage.

Liu, W. M., & Ali, S. R. (2008). Social class and classism: Understanding the psychological impact of poverty and inequality. In S. Brown & R. Lent (Eds.), *Handbook of counseling psychology* (pp. 159–175). Hoboken, NJ: John Wiley & Sons.

Liu, W. M., Pickett, T., Jr., & Ivey, A. E. (2007). White middle-class privilege: Social class bias and implications for training and practice. *Journal of Multicultural Counseling and Development, 35,* 194–207.

Loesch, L. C., & Ritchie, M. H. (2009). *The accountable school counselor* (2nd ed.). Austin, TX: Pro-ed.

Luke, M., & Goodrich, K. M. (2010). Chi Sigma Iota chapter leadership and professional identity development in early career counselors. *Counselor Education and Supervision, 50,* 56–78.

Magnuson, S., Wilcoxon, S. A., & Norem, K. (2003). Career paths of professional leaders in counseling: Plans, opportunities, and happenstance. *Journal of Humanistic Counseling, Education and Development, 42*, 42–52.

Maki, D., & Tarvydas, V. (2011). *The professional practice of rehabilitation counseling* (2nd ed.). New York: Springer.

Marsella, A. J. (2006). Justice in a global age: Becoming counselors to the world. *Counseling Psychology Quarterly, 19*, 121–132. doi: 10.1080/09515070600808861

Martin, P. J. (2002). Transforming school counseling: A national initiative. *Theory into Practice, 41*(3), 148–153.

Martín-Baró, I. (1994). The role of the psychologist. In A. Aron (Ed. & Trans.) & S. Corne (Ed.), *Writings for a liberation psychology* (pp. 33–46). Cambridge, MA: Harvard University Press.

Mason, E. C. M., & McMahon, H. G. (2009). Leadership practices of school counselors. *Professional School Counseling, 13*, 107–115.

Mazade, N. A., & Glover, R. W. (2007). Critical priorities confronting state mental health agencies. *Psychiatric Services, 58*, 1148–1150.

McAdams, C. R., Foster, V., & Ward, T. J. (2007). Remediation and dismissal policies in counselor education: Lessons learned from a challenge in federal court. *Counselor Education and Supervision, 46*, 212–229.

McCann, E. (2010). Building a community-academic partnership to improve health outcomes in an underserved community. *Public Health Nursing, 27*, 32–40.

McMahon, H. G., Mason, E. C. M., & Paisley, P. O. (2009). School counselor educators as educational leaders promoting systemic change. *Professional School Counseling, 13*, 116–124.

McMahon, M., & Simons, R. (2004). Supervision training for professional counselors: An exploratory study. *Counselor Education and Supervision, 43*, 301–309.

McManus, T. (2010, August 20). Judge rejects Keeton lawsuit. *The Augusta Chronicle.*

Meany-Walen, K., Barrio Minton, C. A., Pronchenko, Y., & Purswell, K. (2010, March). *Leading the way: Factors prompting counselors to assume leadership positions in professional counseling organizations.* Session presented at the American Counseling Association annual convention, Pittsburgh, PA.

Mellin, E. (2009). Responding to the crisis in children's mental health: Potential roles for the counseling profession. *Journal of Counseling and Development, 87*, 501–506.

Messer, S. B. (2004). Evidence-based practice: Beyond empirically supported treatments. *Professional Psychology: Research and Practice, 35*, 580–588.

McIntosh, P. (1989). White privilege: Unpacking the invisible knapsack. *Peace and Freedom, 2*, 10–12.

McWhirter, E. H. (1994). *Counseling for empowerment.* Alexandria, VA: American Counseling Association.

Miller, D. (1999). *Principles of social justice.* Cambridge, MA: Harvard University Press.

Milsom, A. (2009). Advocacy for the counseling profession. In B. T. Erford (Ed.), *Orientation to the counseling profession* (pp. 321–338). Boston: Pearson Education.

Moody, J. (2001). Race, school integration, and friendship segregation in America. *The American Journal of Sociology, 107*(3), 679–716.

Moore, J. (2005). Is higher education ready for transformative learning? A question explored in the study of sustainability. *Journal of Transformative Education, 3*, 76–91.

Murray, C. E., Lampinen, A., & Kelley-Soderholm, E. L. (2006). Teaching family systems theory through service-learning. *Counselor Education and Supervision, 46*, 44–58.

Myers, I. B. (1987). *Introduction to type* (3rd ed.). Palo Alto, CA: Consulting Psychologist.

Myers, J. E. (1995). Specialties in counseling: Rich heritage or force for fragmentation? *Journal of Counseling and Development, 74*(2), 115–116.

Myers, J. E., & Harper, M. C. (2004). Evidence-based effective practices with older adults. *Journal of Counseling and Development, 82*(2), 207–218.

Myers, J. E., & Sweeney, T. J. (2001). Specialties in counseling. In D. C. Locke, E. L. Herr, & J. E. Myers (Eds.), *The handbook of counseling* (pp. 43–54). Riverside, CA: Sage Publications.

Myers, J. E., & Sweeney, T. J. (2004). Advocacy for the counseling profession: Results of a national survey. *Journal of Counseling and Development, 82*, 466–471.

Myers, J. E., & Sweeney, T. J. (Eds.). (2005). *Wellness in counseling: Theory, research, and practice.* Alexandria, VA: American Counseling Association.

Myers, J. E., & Sweeney, T. J. (2008). Wellness counseling: The evidence basis for practice. *Journal of Counseling and Development, 86*, 482–493.

Myers, J. E., Sweeney, T. J., & White, V. E. (2002). Advocacy for counseling and counselors: A professional imperative. *Journal of Counseling and Development, 80*, 394–402.

Myers, J. E., Sweeney, T. J., & Witmer, J. M. (2000). The wheel of wellness counseling for wellness: A holistic model for treatment planning. *Journal of Counseling and Development, 78*, 251–266.

Myers, J. E., Willse, J. A., & Villalba, J. A. (2011). Promoting self-esteem in adolescents: The influence of wellness factors. *Journal of Counseling and Development, 89*, 28–36.

National Board for Certified Counselors. (1998). *National Board for Certified Counselors Code of Ethics.* Greensboro, NC: Author. Retrieved from http://www.counselingexam.com/nce/resource/code.html

National Career Development Association. (2009). *Minimum competencies for multicultural career counseling and development.* Retrieved from www.ncda.org

National Center for Education Statistics. (2010). *Special analysis 2010: High poverty schools.* Retrieved from http://nces.ed.gov/programs/coe/2010/analysis/section1a.asp

National Child Traumatic Stress Network and National Center for PTSD. (2005). *Psychological first aid: Field operations guide.* Los Angeles: Author.

Nelson, J., Zaccaro, S. J., & Herman, J. L. (2010). Strategic information provision and experiential variety as tools for developing adaptive leadership skills. *Consulting Psychology Journal: Practice and Research, 62*(2), 131–142. doi: 10.1037/a0019989

Nelson, M. L., & Neufeldt, S. A. (1998). The pedagogy of counseling: A critical examination. *Counselor Education and Supervision, 38*(2), 70–89.

Nevill, D. D., & Super, D. E. (1986). *Manual for salience inventory: Theory application, and research.* Palo Alto, CA: Consulting Psychologist.

Newcomb, M. E., & Mustanski. B. (2010). Internalized homophobia and internalizing mental health problems: A meta-analysis. *Clinical Psychology, 30*(8), 1019–1029.

Niles, S., Engels, D., & Lenz, J. (2009). Training career practitioners. *Career Development Quarterly, 57*, 358–365.

Northouse, P. G. (2004). *Leadership: Theory and practice.* Thousand Oaks, CA: Sage.

Ober, A. M., Granello, D. H., & Henfield, M. S. (2009). A synergistic model to enhance multicultural competence in supervision. *Counselor Education and Supervision, 48*, 204–221.

Office of Veterans Affairs. (2010, September 28). *Licensed professional mental health counselor qualification standard* (Publication GS-101). Washington, DC: Veterans Health Administration.

Orr, J. J. (2010). CPS 8370: Advanced career counseling course syllabus. Unpublished document.

Owen, J., & Lindley, L. D. (2010). Therapists' cognitive complexity: Review of theoretical models and development of an integrated approach for training. *Training and Education in Professional Psychology, 4,* 128–137. doi: 10.1037/a0017697

Paradise, L. V., Ceballos, P. T., & Hall, S. (2010). Leadership and leader behavior in counseling: Neglected skills. *International Journal of Advanced Counselling, 32,* 46–55.

Parker, M., & Myers, J. E. (1991). The impact of the ANWC/AMCD name change. *AMCD Journal, 19*(1), 52–64.

Parr, G. D., Jones, E. G., & Bradley, L. J. (2005). Facilitating effective committees. *Journal of Professional Counseling: Practice, Theory and Research, 2,* 99–109.

Parsons, F. (1909). *Choosing a vocation.* Boston: Houghton Mifflin.

Penney, S. H., & Neilson, P. A. (2010). *Next generation leadership.* New York: Macmillan.

Peter, L. J. (1977). *Peter's quotations: Ideas for our time.* New York: Bantam.

Pickett, N., & Dodge, B. (n.d.). *Rubrics for web lessons.* Retrieved from http://webquest.sdsu.edu/rubrics/weblessons.htm

Ponton, R. F., & Duba, J. D. (2009). The ACA Code of Ethics: Articulating counseling's professional covenant. *Journal of Counseling and Development, 87*(1), 117–121.

Portman, T. A. A., & Garrett, M. T. (2005). Beloved women: Nurturing the sacred fire of leadership from an American Indian perspective. *Journal of Counseling and Development, 83,* 284–291.

Prilleltensky, I. (1994). *The morals and politics of psychology: Psychological discourse and the status quo.* Albany: State University of New York Press.

Prilleltensky, I. (1997). Values, assumptions, and practices: Assessing the moral implications of psychological discourse action. *American Psychologist, 52,* 517–535.

Provan, K. G. (1997). Services integration for vulnerable populations: Lessons from community mental health. *Family and Community Health, 19*(4), 19–30.

Ratts, M., D'Andrea, M., & Arredondo, P. (2004, September 13). Social justice counseling: "Fifth force" in field. *Counseling Today, 47,* 28–30.

Ratts, M. J., Lewis, J. A., & Toporek, R. L. (2010a). Advocacy and social justice: A helping paradigm for the 21st century. In M. J. Ratts, J. A. Lewis, & R. L. Toporek (Eds.), *ACA advocacy competencies: A social justice framework for counseling* (pp. 3–10). Alexandria, VA: American Counseling Association.

Ratts, M. J., Toporek, R. L., & Lewis, J. A. (Eds.). (2010b). *ACA advocacy competencies: A social justice framework for counselors.* Alexandria, VA: American Counseling Association.

Rawls, J. A. (1971). *A theory of justice.* Cambridge, MA: Harvard University Press.

Reflection. (n.d.). In American Heritage online dictionary. Retrieved from http://www.answers.com/topic/reflection

Remley, T. P., Jr., & Herlihy, B. (2007). *Ethical, legal, and professional issues in counseling* (2nd ed.). Upper Saddle River, NJ: Pearson Merrill Prentice Hall.

Rhode, B. (2010). *ALBTIC history.* Retrieved from http://www.algbtic.org/about/history.htm

Ritchie, M. H. (1990). Counseling is not a profession—Yet. *Counselor Education and Supervision, 29*(4), 220–227.

Robbins, S. P., & Judge, T. A. (2010). *Organizational behavior* (14th ed.). Upper Saddle River, NJ: Prentice Hall.

Robinson, T. L., & Ginter, E. J. (Eds.). (1999). Racism healing its effects [Special issue]. *Journal of Counseling and Development, 77*(1).

Rogers, E. S., Anthony, W. A., Lyass, A., & Penk, W. E. (2006). A randomized clinical trial of vocational rehabilitation for people with psychiatric disabilities. *Rehabilitation Counseling Bulletin, 49*(3), 143–156.

Ropers-Huilman, B. (2001). Feminist post-structuralism in higher education: Opportunities for transforming teaching and learning. *Organization, 8,* 388–395.

Rose, S. J., Brondino, M. J., & Barnack, J. L. (2009). Screening for problem substance use in community-based agencies. *Journal of Social Work Practice in the Addictions, 9,* 41–54.

Roysircar, G., Arredondo, P., Fuertes, J. N., Ponterotto, J. G., & Toporek, R. L. (2003). *Multicultural counseling competencies 2003: Association for Multicultural Counseling and Development.* Alexandria, VA: Association for Multicultural Counseling and Development.

Saad, L. (2010, May 25). American's acceptance of gay relations crosses 50% threshold. *Gallup.* Retrieved from http://www.gallup.com/poll/135764/americans-acceptance-gay-relations-crosses-threshold.aspx

Sangganjanavanich, V., & Cavazos, J. (2010). Workplace aggressions: Toward social justice and advocacy in counseling for transgender individuals. *Journal of LGBT Issues in Counseling, 4*(3–4), 187–201.

SB 1070. (2010). State of Arizona Senate, Forty-ninth Legislature, Second Regular Session. Retrieved December 9, 2010, from www.azleg.gov/legtext/49leg/2r/bills/sb1070s.pdf

Schein, E. H. (2004). *Organizational culture and leadership* (3rd ed.). San Francisco: Jossey-Bass.

Schultz, D., & Schultz, S. E. (2010). *Psychology and work today* (10th ed.). Upper Saddle River, NJ: Prentice-Hall.

Seiler, G., & Messina, J. J. (1979). Toward professional identity: Dimensions of mental health counseling in perspective. *AMHCA Journal, 1,* 3–8.

Self-reflection. (n.d.). In Merriam-Webster's online dictionary. Retrieved from http://www.merriam-webster.com/dictionary/self%20reflection

Sexton, T. L. (1996). The relevance of counseling outcomes research: Current trends and practical implications. *Journal of Counseling and Development, 74,* 590–600.

Sexton, T. L., & Griffin, B. L. (Eds). (1997). *Constructivist thinking in counseling practice, research, and training.* New York: Teachers College Press.

Shadish, W. R., Montgomery, L. M., Wilson, P., Wilson, M. R., Bright, I., & Okwumabua, T. M. (1993). Effects of family and marital psychotherapies: A meta-analysis. *Journal of Consulting and Clinical Psychology, 61*(6), 992–1003.

Shamir, B., House, R. J., & Arthur, M. B. (1993). The motivational effects of charismatic leadership. *Organizational Science, 4,* 577–594.

Shapiro, J. P. (2009). Integrating outcome research and clinical reasoning in psychotherapy planning. *Professional Psychology: Research and Practice, 40,* 46–53.

Shaw, S. K. (2005). *The intentional leader.* New York: Syracuse University Press.

Shechtman, Z. (2002). Child group psychotherapy in the school at the threshold of a new millennium. *Journal of Counseling and Development, 80*(3), 293–300.

Sheperis, C. J., Young, J. S., & Daniels, M. H. (2010). *Counseling research: qualitative, quantitative and mixed methods.* Upper Saddle River, NJ: Pearson.

Shor, I., & Freire, P. (1987). What is the "dialogical method" of teaching? *Journal of Education, 3,* 11–31.

Siebold, T. (2010). *Stand by your quote.* Retrieved from www.workshopexercises.com

Simmons, R., Ungemack, J., Sussman, J., Anderson, R., Adorno, S., Aguayo, J., et al. (2008). Bringing adolescents into substance abuse treatment through community outreach and engagement: The Hartford youth project. *Journal of Psychoactive Drugs, 40*(1), 41–54.

Singh, A. A., Urbano, A., & Haston, M. (2010). School counselors' strategies for social justice change: A grounded theory of what works in the real world. *Professional School Counseling, 13,* 135–145.

Solmonson, L. (2010). *Developing advocacy skills: A program model.* Retrieved from http://counselingoutfitters.com/vistas/vistas10/Article_27.pdf

Solomon, J. (2007). *Metaphors at work: Identity and meaning in professional life.*

Smith H. B. (2001). Professional identity for counselors. In D. C. Locke, J. E. Myers, & E. L. Herr (Eds.), *Handbook of counseling* (pp. 569–580). Thousand Oaks, CA: Sage Publications.

Smith, M. L., & Glass, G. V. (1977). Meta-analysis of psychotherapy outcome studies. *American Psychologist, 32,* 752–760.

Smith, S. D., Reynolds, C. A., & Rovnak, A. (2009). A critical analysis of the social advocacy movement in counseling. *Journal of Counseling and Development, 87,* 483–491.

Snowman, J., McCown, R., & Biehler, R. (2009). *Psychology applied to teaching* (12th ed.). New York: Houghton Mifflin Company.

Sprengler, P. M., & Strohmer, D. C. (1994). Clinical judgmental biases: The moderating roles of counselor cognitive complexity and counselor client preferences. *Journal of Counseling Psychology, 41,* 8–17. doi: 10.1037/0022-0167.41.1.8

Steele, J. M. (2008). Preparing counselors to advocate for social justice: A liberation model. *Counselor Education and Supervision, 48,* 74–85.

Stewart, R. (1979). The nature of needs assessment in community mental health. *Community Mental Health Journal, 15,* 287–295.

Stiehl, R., & Lewchuk, L. (2008). *The outcomes primer: Reconstructing the college curriculum* (3rd ed.). Corvallis, OR: The Learning Organization.

Stoltenberg, C. (1981). Approaching supervision from developmental perspective: The counselor complexity model. *Journal of Counseling Psychology, 28,* 59–65. doi: 10.1037/0022-0167.28.1.59

Stone, C., & Clark, M. A. (2001). School counselors and principals: Partners in support of academic achievement. *NASSP Bulletin, 85*(624), 46–53. doi: 10.1177/019263650108562407

Studer, J. R. (2005). Supervising school counselors-in-training: A guide for field supervisors. *Professional School Counseling, 8,* 353–359.

Sue, D. W. (2008). Multicultural organizational consulting: A social justice perspective. *Consulting Psychology Journal: Practice and Research, 60,* 157–169. doi: 10.1037/0736-9735.60.2.157

Sue, D. W., Arredondo, P., & McDavis, R. J. (1992). Multicultural counseling competencies and standards: A call to the profession. *Journal of Counseling and Development, 70,* 477–486.

Sue, D. W., Carter, R., Casas, J. M., Fouad, N., Ivey, A., Jensen, M., …, Vazquez-Nuttall, E. (1998). *Multicultural counseling competencies: Individual and organizational development.* Thousand Oaks, CA: Sage.

Sue, D. W., Ivey, A. E., & Pedersen, P. B. (1996). *A theory of multicultural counseling and therapy.* Pacific Grove, CA: Brooks/Cole.

Super, D. E. (1980). A life-span, life-space approach to career development. *Journal of Vocational Behavior, 16,* 282–298.

Super, D. E. (1990). A life-span, life-space approach to career development. In D. Brown, L. Brooks, & Associates (Ed.), *Career choice and development: Applying contemporary theories to practice* (2nd ed., pp. 197–261). San Francisco: Jossey-Bass.

Sweeney, T. J. (2001). Counseling: Historical origins and philosophical roots. In D. C. Locke, J. E. Myers, & E. L. Herr (Eds.). *The handbook of counseling* (pp. 3–26). Riverside, CA: Sage Publications.

Sweeney, T. J. (2003). Milestones and history makers. In J. D. West, C. J., Osborn, & D. L. Bubenzer (Eds.), *Leaders and legacies: Contributions to the profession of counseling* (pp. 23–50). New York: Brunner-Routledge.

Sweeney, T. J., & Sturdevant, A. D. (1974). Licensure in the helping professions: Anatomy of an issue. *Personnel and Guidance Journal, 52*, 575–580.

Sweeney, T. J., & Witmer, J. M. (1991). Beyond social interest: Striving toward optimum health and wellness. *Individual Psychology, 47*, 527–540.

Taylor, E. W. (2009). Fostering transformative learning. In J. Mezirow, E. Taylor, and Associates (Eds.), *Transformative learning in practice: Insights from community, workplace, and higher education* (pp. 3–17). San Francisco: Jossey-Bass.

Theriot, M. T., & Segal, S. P. (2005). Involvement with the criminal justice system among new clients at outpatient mental health agencies. *Psychiatric Services, 56*, 179–185.

Thomas, P. L. (2010). The Payne of addressing race and poverty in public education: Utopian accountability and deficit assumptions of middle-class America. *Souls, 12* (3), 262–283.

Thomas, R. V., & Pender, D. A. (2008). Association for Specialists in Group Work: Best practice guidelines 2007 revisions. *Journal for Specialists in Group Work, 33*, 111–117.

Tjaden, P., & Thoennes, N. (2006). *Full report of the prevalence, incidence, and consequences of violence against women: Findings from the national violence against women survey.* Washington, DC: National Institute of Justice.

Toporek, R. L. (2000). Creating a common language and framework for understanding advocacy in counseling. In J. Lewis & L. Bradley (Eds.), *Advocacy in counseling: Counselors, clients, and community* (pp. 5–14). Greensboro, NC: Caps Publications.

Toporek, R., Lewis, J. A., & Ratts, M. J. (2010). The ACA advocacy competencies: An overview. In M. J. Ratts, R. L. Toporek, & J. A. Lewis (Eds.), *ACA advocacy competencies: A social justice framework for counselors* (pp. 11–20). Alexandria, VA: American Counseling Association.

Townsend, P. L., & Gebhardt, J. E. (1997). *Five-star leadership: The art and strategy of creating leaders at every level.* New York: Wiley & Sons.

Trusty, J., & Brown, D. (2005). Advocacy competencies for professional school counselors. *Professional School Counseling, 8*, 259–265.

United Nations. (1948). *Universal declaration of human rights.* San Francisco: Author.

U.S. Department of Education. (2002). *Profile of undergraduates in U.S. postsecondary institutions: 1999-2000* (NCES 2002-168). Washington, DC: National Center for Education Statistics.

U.S. Department of Health and Human Services. (2010). *Healthy People 2020.* Retrieved from http://www.healthypeople.gov/2020/about/default.aspx

U.S. Department of Homeland Security, Federal Emergency Management Agency (FEMA). (2010). *National incident management system (NIMS) training.* Retrieved from http://www.fema.gov/emergency/nims/NIMSTrainingCourses.shtm#item3

Vera, E. M., & Speight, S. L. (2003). Multicultural competence, social justice, and counseling psychology: Expanding our roles. *The Counseling Psychologist, 31*, 253–272. doi: 10.1177/0011000003031003001

Vereen, L. G., Hill, N. R., & McNeal, D. T. (2008). Perceptions of multicultural counseling competency: Integration of the curricular and the practical. *Journal of Mental Health Counseling, 30*, 226–236.

Vygotsky, L. (1978). *Mind in society.* London: Harvard University Press.

Walker, J. A. (2006). A reconceptualization of mentoring in counselor education: Using a relational model to promote mutuality and embrace differences. *Journal of Humanistic Counseling, Education and Development, 45*, 60–69.

Wall, J. E. (2004). *Why counselors should let testing leave them behind*. Retrieved January 9, 2011, from http://counselingoutfitters.com/vistas/vistas04/6.pdf

Wampold, B. E. (2001). *The great psychotherapy debate: Models, methods, and findings*. Mahway, NJ: Lawrence Erlbaum Associates.

*Ward v. Wilbanks et al.*, No. 09-CV-11237 (E.D. Mich 2010).

Warren, E. S. (2005). Future colleague or convenient friend: The ethics of mentorship. *Counseling and Values, 49*, 141–146.

Welfare, L. E., & Borders, D. (2010). Counselor cognitions: General and domain-specific complexity. *Counselor Education and Supervision, 49*, 162–178.

Wellness Management and Recovery. (2010). Information video. Retrieved from http://www.wmrohio.org/video.html

West, J. D., Bubenzer, D. L., Osborn, C. J., Paez, S. B., & Desmond, K. J. (2006). Leadership and the profession of counseling: Beliefs and practices. *Counselor Education and Supervision, 46*, 2–16.

West, J. D., Hosie, T. W., & Mackey, J. A. (1987). Employment and roles of counselors in mental health agencies. *Journal of Counseling and Development, 66*, 135–138.

West, J. D., Osborn, C. J., & Bubenzer, D. L. (2003a). Dimensions of leadership in the counseling profession. In J. D. West, C. J. Osborn, & D. L. Bubenzer, *Leaders and legacies: Contributions to the profession of counseling* (pp. 3–21). New York: Brunner/Routledge.

West, J. D, Osborn, C. J., & Bubenzer, D. L. (Eds.). (2003b). *Leaders and legacies: Contributions to the profession of counseling*. New York: Brunner-Routledge.

West, P. L., & Warchal, J. (2009). The role of evidence-based therapy programs in the determination of treatment effectiveness. In G. R. Walz, J. C. Bluer, & R. K. Yep (Eds.), *Compelling counseling interventions: VISTAS 2009* (pp. 291–301). Alexandria, VA: American Counseling Association.

Wester, K. L. (2007). Teaching research integrity in the field of counseling. *Counselor Education and Supervision, 46*, 199–211.

Wester, K., & Lewis, T. F. (2005). Chi Sigma Iota, it's not just another line on your resume . . . Retrieved from www.csi-net.org/advocacy

Whiston, S., & Campbell, W. (2010). Randomized clinical trials in counseling: An introduction. *Counseling Outcome Research and Evaluation, 1*, 8–18. doi: 10.1177/2150137809356681

Whiston, S. C., & Sexton, T. L. (1998). A review of school counseling outcome research: Implications for practice. *Journal of Counseling and Development, 76*, 412–426.

White, R. P., & Shullman, S. L. (2010). Acceptance of uncertainty as an indicator of effective leadership. *Consulting Psychology Journal: Practice and Research, 62*, 94–104. doi: 10.1037/a0019991

Wilcox, D. A., Wesp, K., Rich, S., & Watson, A. (2009). Multicultural competency evidence-based practice (MCC-EBP): Building community across differences through Ohio's Wellness Management and Recovery (WMR) program. Concept paper.

Wilson, F. R., & Newmeyer, M. D. (2008). A standards based inventory for assessing perceived importance of and confidence in using ASGW's Core Group Work Skills. *Journal for Specialists in Group Work, 33*, 270–289.

Wood, C., & D'Agostino, J. V. (2010). Assessment in counseling: A tool for social justice work. In M. J. Ratts, R. L. Toporek, & J. A. Lewis (Eds.), *ACA advocacy competencies: A social justice framework for counselors*. Alexandria, VA: American Counseling Association.

Wrigley, B. J. (2002). Glass ceiling? What glass ceiling? A qualitative study of how women view the glass ceiling in public relations and communications management. *Journal of Public Relations Research, 14*(1), 27–55.

Yammarino, F. J., & Bass, B. M. (1990). Long-term forecasting of transformational leadership and its effects among naval officers: Some preliminary findings. In K. E. Clark & M. B. Clark (Eds.), *Measures of leadership.* West Orange, NJ: Leadership Library of America.

Yukl, G. A., & Mahsud, R. (2010). Why flexible and adaptive leadership is essential. *Consulting Psychology Journal: Practice and Research, 62,* 81–93. doi: 10.1037/a0019835

Zaccaro, S. J., Foti, R. J., & Kenny, D. A. (1991). Self-monitoring and trait-based variance in leadership: An investigation of leader flexibility across multiple group situations. *Journal of Applied Psychology, 76,* 308–315.

Zeidner, M., Matthews, G., & Roberts, R. D. (2004). Emotional intelligence in the workplace: A critical review. *Applied Psychology: An International Review, 53,* 371–399.

# Index